YALE HISTORICAL PUBLICATIONS, MISCELLANY, 107

Within the engraving, the following inscriptions appear:

M.ʳ Babilone va prêcher la foi aux Nations Infidelles

M.ʳ de Babilone donne plusieurs Evêques à l'Eglise d'Utreck.

NOUVELLES ECCLESIASTIQUES

M.ʳ Bossuet forcé de se démettre de son Evêché.

Dominique-Marie Varlet Evêque de Babilone meurt dans une terre étrangère.

O Dieu *les Nations sont entrés dans votre héritage.* Pseaume 78.

Lorsque le Seigneur ramenera Sion de captivité, notre délivrance nous paroitra comme un songe Ps. 125.

Alors on dira parmi les Nations le Seig.ʳ a fait pour eux de grandes choses. Pseaume 125.

M.ʳ Poncet de la Rivière ravage le Diocèse de Troye.

Exil des Religieuses du Calvaire.

Années. 1750 — 1753

Il n'aboit point, mais Il éclaire

"Oh God, the Heathen have come into your inheritance." —Psalm 78:1

"When the Lord brings Zion's captives home, our deliverance will seem like a dream." —Psalm 125:1

"And then they will say among the Nations, the Lord has done great things for them." —Psalm 125:2

The scriptural passages quoted on this Nouvelles Ecclésiastiques *frontispiece are taken from the Jansenist abbé Nicolas Le Gros's French translation of the Bible, anonymously published at Cologne in 1739. Though confessedly based on Lemaistre de Saci's earlier translation, Le Gros's translation differs from De Saci's in many particulars, among them its rendering of Psalm 125:1–2 (126:1–2 in modern versions) in the future tense, rather than the standard past. Perhaps the fact that by 1739 the Jansenists had come to regard themselves as "Zion's inhabitants" and their Jesuit and episcopal oppressors as the "Heathen" is not unrelated to Le Gros's preference for the future tense, for it was to the future that the Jansenists looked for the Lord's deliverance. But to interpret the psalms thus "figuratively"—at least before the Jesuits' expulsion—they indeed needed the aid of the lamb that "bleats not, but rather enlightens."*

The Jansenists and the Expulsion of the Jesuits from France 1757-1765

DALE VAN KLEY

New Haven and London
Yale University Press
1975

Library of Congress catalog card number: 74-26390
International standard book number: 0-300-01748-0

Designed by Sally Sullivan
and set in Monotype Bembo type.
Printed in the United States of America by
The Murray Printing Co., Forge Village, Mass.

Published in Great Britain, Europe, and Africa by
Yale University Press, Ltd., London.
Distributed in Latin America by Kaiman & Polon,
Inc., New York City; in India by UBS Publishers'
Distributors Pvt.,Ltd., Delhi; in Japan by John
Weatherhill, Inc., Tokyo.

To Sandy

Contents

Preface

MY INITIAL RESEARCH FOR THIS STUDY WAS BASED ON THE hypothesis that Jansenists had had something to do with the suppression of the Jesuit Order in the eighteenth century. The connection between the Jansenists and the suppression of the Jesuits had sometimes been assumed by nineteenth-century historians, more often ignored by twentieth-century historians, but never convincingly proven or disproven by anyone. Largely through the help of the Le Paige papers in the Bibliothèque de Port Royal (the relevant portions of which I stumbled upon quite by accident), my research confirmed the hypothesis. Hence the central thesis of this book: that it was the Jansenists who principally engineered the suppression of the Jesuits in France, and that they did so at least partly because of their Jansenism.

Moreover, I began my work entirely sharing the widespread assumption that Jansenism and religious disputes were peripheral to the central importance of the Enlightenment in eighteenth-century France. Whether because of a growing areal solipsism familiar to many historians, or because the evidence itself really forced me to a different opinion, I gradually came to question this assumption. Indeed, by the end of my research I had come to regard the disputes between Jansenists and Jesuits (together with the related quarrels between the monarchy, the parlements, and the episcopacy) as being just as essential to an understanding of the French eighteenth century—even its "intellectual" history—as the Enlightenment narrowly defined. Thus the temptation to relate eighteenth-century Jansenism and its victory over the Jesuits to the larger eighteenth century, and to the French Enlightenment specifically, proved irresistible. My success in this endeavor is for my readers to judge.

In the course of my researches in France and my writing here, I have accumulated an overwhelming indebtedness to individuals and institutions on both sides of the Atlantic, and I can only hope to acknowledge the most outstanding of them here. In France the père François de Dainville, who has since died, first sent me in the direction of the Bibliothèque de Port Royal, where M. André Gazier, its *bibliothécaire gratuit*, not only opened its doors to me but gave me the freest access to the Le Paige collection. This book—and my knowledge of the Old Regime's religious history in general—benefited in more ways than I can know from frequent conversations with Frère Clément of the order of the Frères des Ecoles Chrétiennes, who also helped me decipher particularly hieroglyphic handwritings. At the Archives Nationales, M. Michel Antoine helped me through the labyrinth of catalogues, while M. Gourmelon obtained for me the marquis de Rosanbo's permission to consult his Lamoignon papers, conserved in microfilm at the Archives. Both helped me immensely in my search for private archives. I am particularly grateful to M. Michel Vinot-Prèfontaine, who graciously invited me into his home to read his copy of Robert de Saint-Vincent's memoirs and eventually gave me a photocopy of these; to the *bibliothécaires* of the Bibliothèque Municipale de Rouen, who permitted me to work there for several days during the month of August, when the library was officially closed; and to Mlle Hélène Walbaum, who sometimes functioned as my landlady, more often looked after me, and invariably put up with me.

Among American specialists in French history, I owe much to Professor Stanley S. Mellon for having suggested the topic in the first place; to Professor David D. Bien and Mr. Steven Kaplan for crucial archival and organizational suggestions as I was undertaking my research; to Professors Franklin Le Van Baumer and Orest Ranum for helpful criticisms of the manuscript; and in particular to Professor Robert R. Palmer, who went far beyond any call of duty in his careful reading and criticism of the manuscript and the kind interest he took in its fate. A very special word of thanks should go to my good friends Mr. Philip Bertocci and Mr. Raymond F. Kierstead—indeed, to the entire Kierstead family—upon whom I mercilessly inflicted my interest in this project while both in France and in this country, and without whose constant encouragement and help I might never have completed it. To Mrs. June Guicharnaud should go the credit for a skillful job of editing which considerably improved the final product. It goes without saying that to all of these is due the credit for numerous improvements; to myself alone the blame for the defects that remain.

A Woodrow Wilson Dissertation Fellowship supported me in Paris in 1966–67, when I did most of my research. Subsequent short-term grants from the Calvin College Faculty Enrichment Fund, the Calvin Foundation, the Grand Rapids Foundation, and the National Endowment for the Humanities, as well as a semester's leave from Calvin College, together enabled me to undertake additional research in France and to transform what was originally a dissertation into a book. To all of these institutions, my profoundest thanks. Without their financial support this book could obviously not have been written.

DALE VAN KLEY

Calvin College
August 1974

Abbreviations

A.D.P.O.	Archives Départmentales des Pyrénées Orientales
A.D.S.I.	Archives Départmentales de la Seine Inférieure
A.N.	Archives Nationales
A.P.	Archives Privées of the Archives Nationales
B.M.R.	Bibliothèque Municipale de Rouen
B.N.	Bibliothèque Nationale
B.P.R.	Bibliothèque de Port-Royal
L.P.	Collection Le Paige

Introduction

ON OCTOBER 29, 1709, LOUIS XIV SENT HIS LIEUTENANT OF police, Voyer d'Argenson, with two hundred archers to disperse the remaining sisters of the abbey of Port-Royal des Champs because they had refused to sign a formulary declaring certain of the doctrines of one Jansenius, a bishop of Ypres who had died in 1638, to be heretical. Having put his hand to the plow and uninclined to turn either to the right or to the left, the aging "Sun King," this time with the blessings of his Jesuit confessor, the père Le Tellier, two years later completed the work. He razed the abbey, exhumed the bones of all who had been buried there, including those of Racine and the entire Arnauld family, and literally turned its grounds into farmland. With this act, the Catholic counterpart of the revocation of the Edict of Nantes, the heresy of "Jansenism," was presumed to be extirpated.[1] Yet only a half century later, on August 6, 1762, the parlement of Paris, reputedly a stronghold of Jansenism, definitively dissolved the Jesuit Order in France as "perverse, destructive of all principles of religion, and even of honesty," and "injurious to Christian morality," and shortly thereafter gave all French Jesuits the unattractive choice of either signing an oath which in effect declared their order to be impious or of leaving the realm.[2]

"What a revolution among the centuries!" cried one anonymous author who was sympathetic to the Jesuits in 1762.[3] But whether a "revolution" or not, whether, in fact, the wheel had really come full circle or no, few contemporaries of the destruction of the Jesuits doubted that the two events were somehow related, that the fall of the Jesuits in 1762 constituted in some sense the revenge of the destruction of the abbey of Port-Royal in 1711. The philosophe Jean Le Rond d'Alembert reported that many Jesuits looked upon the "spectacle of their destruction" as the "stones of Port-Royal which were falling on their heads to crush them"; D'Alembert himself said that Jansenism had been the "so-

---

1. Augustin Gazier, *Histoire générale du mouvement janséniste depuis ses origines jusqu'à nos jours* (2 vols. Paris, 1923), Vol. 1, pp. 228–33. A more recent account, Louis Cognet's *Le Jansénisme* (Paris, 1964), p. 97, denies any responsibility on the part of Louis XIV's previous confessor, the père La Chaise, in the dispersion of 1709.

2. Quoted in Paul Hazard, *European Thought in the Eighteenth Century from Montesquieu to Lessing*, trans. J. Lewis May (Cleveland and New York, 1963), p. 167.

3. *Mes Doutes sur l'affaire présente des Jésuites* (1762), p. 39.

I

licitor" in the condemnation of the Jesuits; and Voltaire—even Voltaire—proclaimed from his fortress at Ferney that it was "neither Sanchez, nor Lessius, nor Escobar, nor the absurdities of the casuists which have destroyed the Jesuits," but rather "Le Tellier . . . who has exterminated them in nearly all of France," that "the plow which the Jesuit Le Tellier had made pass over the ruins of Port-Royal has produced, at the end of sixty years, the fruits which they are reaping today."[4]

But the names of D'Alembert and Voltaire—we could add those of Diderot, Montesquieu, Rousseau, Helvétius, and others—remind us that the eighteenth century is habitually represented, not as the century of the Jesuits and much less that of the Jansenists, but as the age of Reason, the age of Enlightenment, or as contemporaries themselves called it, the "century of lights." It was the century which witnessed the publication of the baron de Montesquieu's *Esprit des lois*, Voltaire's *Lettres philosophiques, Candide,* and *Histoire du siècle de Louis XIV*, Rousseau's *Le Contrat social* and *Emile*, Helvétius's *De l'Esprit*, and, beginning in 1751, volume after volume of Denis Diderot's famous *Encyclopédie*. It is well known that in these writings and countless others the philosophes, as they were called, dislodged the idea of divine grace and put "nature" in its place, opposed faith in things unknown in the name of knowledge based upon empirical observation, substituted a concern for secular civilization for loyalty to an ineffable "Christendom," held forth the prospect of progress in this world instead of hope for salvation in another, fought priestly dogmatism and persecution in the name of humanity and tolerance—in short, laid successful siege to the Catholic Church as the exclusive depository of "Truth" under the banner of what they called "reason," by which they meant scientific knowledge founded upon the empirical investigation of both human and physical nature.[5]

The philosophes believed, however, they had not only to storm the Church itself but to slay two *bêtes noires* that protected it—monastic orders and theological disputes—against which they aimed some of their sharpest arrows. These two beasts, they maintained, together bred religious fanaticism, which in turn produced more monks and theological quarrels, thereby establishing the vicious reproductive circle which had tragically stunted the progress of the human mind and—especially during the Middle Ages and the "barbaric" sixteenth

4. Jean Le Rond d'Alembert, *Sur la Destruction des Jésuites en France* (1765), pp. 96–97, 192–93; Voltaire, *Précis du siècle de Louis XV*, in *Œuvres complètes de Voltaire* (Kehl edition, 92 vols., 1785–89), Vol. 25, p. 437. All succeeding quotations from Voltaire refer to the Kehl edition.

5. The body of secondary literature on the Enlightenment is of course far too immense to refer to in any detail here. Suffice it to say that my characterization of "enlightened" thought in terms of antitheses owes most to Carl Becker's classic, *The Heavenly City of the Eighteenth-Century Philosophers* (New Haven and London, 1932), esp. pp. 30–31; and Robert Palmer, *Catholics and Unbelievers in Eighteenth-Century France* (Princeton, 1939), passim.

century—had wrought infinite havoc in Europe as a whole. Was it possible, then, that in 1762, beneath the intense glare of the Enlightenment's high noon and in the face of all Europe, the Society of Jesus, the most formidable of all monastic orders, which sat at the right hand of the papacy itself, was laid low in France, not by the philosophes, but by a fanatical religious sect within the Catholic Church by reason of a theological dispute which had its origins in the "barbaric" sixteenth century?

Many historians have not thought so. Following the lead of D'Alembert, who in 1765 boasted that "it was properly philosophy . . . which by the mouths of the magistrates issued the decree against the Jesuits," they have variously represented the destruction of the Jesuit Order in France, sometimes as the work of disciples of the philosophes, who had somehow infiltrated the parlements of France, sometimes as the result of lesser and more accidental causes, but just the same, if only in terms of its consequences, as the most signal "triumph of the philosophes, the philosophy of the Enlightenment over Catholic traditionalism" before the French Revolution.[6] Still others have seen in the destruction of the Jesuits, if not the triumph of the Enlightenment, at least the victory of enlightened Gallicanism, which, from its stronghold in the parlement of Paris, had always vigorously opposed the Jesuits as agents of foreign papal interference in France's internal affairs and for precisely this reason had expelled the Jesuits from France nearly two centuries earlier, in 1594, before either Jansenism or the Enlightenment had raised its head.[7]

Yet there is reason to believe that the "century of lights" was not altogether above the works of darkness. For one thing, the eighteenth century in France heard at least as much talk about shadows as it did of lights. In an age of censorship vast numbers of polemical pamphlets and books were published anony-

6. R. W. Harris, *Absolutism and Enlightenment, 1660–1789* (New York, 1966), p. 337. The quotation from D'Alembert is to be found in his *Sur la Destruction des Jésuites*, p. 109, whose interpretation of the expulsion of the Jesuits as a philosophic victory is also accepted by Hazard, in *European Thought*, p. 109, and, to a lesser extent, by Christopher Hollis, in *A History of the Jesuits* (Liverpool, London, and Prescot, 1968), p. 156. Among 19th-century historians it was somewhat more common to say that the expulsion of the Jesuits was the triumph of a league quite consciously formed between Jansenists and philosophes. See, for example, J. Crétineau-Joly, *Clément XIV et les Jésuites* (3d ed. Paris, 1848), p. 181; and F. Z. Collombert, *Histoire critique et générale de la suppression des Jésuites au XVIIIᵉ siècle* (Lyons, 1846), pp. 64–65.

7. Among recent historians the purely Gallican interpretation of the event has been propounded by David Bien in *The Calas Affair, Persecution, Toleration, and Heresy in Eighteenth-Century Toulouse* (Princeton, 1960), pp. 61–62; and M. S. Anderson, in *Europe in the Eighteenth Century, 1713–1783* (Norwich, Great Britain, 1961), pp. 326–27. Among 19th-century historians see, for example, Jules Flammermont, *Les Jésuites et les parlements au XVIIIᵉ-siècle* (Paris, 1885), p. 5; and Ernest Glasson, *Le Parlement de Paris: Son Rôle politique depuis le règne de Charles VII jusqu'à la révolution* (2 vols. Paris, 1901), Vol. 2, pp. 266–79.

mously, and it was common to describe their authors as tenebrous and their content as "having been born among shadows from which it never should have
emerged." Even a weekly journal, the Jansenists' *Nouvelles Ecclésiastiques*, was
published in an anonymity that no one seemed able to penetrate, and it was
therefore regularly described as a "work of shadows." For an "Age of Reason,"
moreover, there was a good deal of talk about fanaticism and enthusiasm. The
philosophes described both Jansenists and Jesuits as religious fanatics and enthusiasts; the Jansenists reproached the Jesuits for their fanatical loyalty to their
general and to the papacy; the Jesuits accused the Jansenists of doctrinal fanaticism; and both Jansenists and Jesuits charged the philosophes with a fanaticism
of their own. Jansenists and Jesuits likewise shared doubts that the eighteenth
century was enlightened at all. To the Jesuit Joseph Antoine Cerutti it was "a
century in which too often virtue is sacrificed to its shadow"; the Jesuit Henri
Griffet found it "difficult to believe that a century which prided itself in being
the century of lights" could condemn his order on charges so "evidently
absurd"; and an anonymous Jansenist thought his "amiable and jocular" and
"enlightened" century to be, in reality, "frivolous" and "corrupt."[8] Relatively
impartial memoirists such as D'Argenson and Barbier spent far more time
describing the quarrels between Jansenists and Jesuits than in discussing the
works of the philosophes, and even the undisputed chief of the philosophes
himself, Voltaire, found it necessary to devote considerably more pages of his
Précis du siècle de Louis XV to ridiculing the droning of "insects"—so he described the Jansenists and Jesuits—"risen from the cadaver of Molinism and
Jansenism," than to celebrating the "progress of the human spirit."[9]

"Do not have the vanity of flattering yourself with this honor," a Jansenist
responded to D'Alembert when in 1765 the latter interpreted the fall of the
Jesuits as the triumph of "reason." "When you attribute this great catastrophe
to yourself," the Jansenist added, "you are nothing other than the fly of the
Fable who, seated on a carriage which is carrying the mail, cries 'look at the dust
I am raising!' "[10] Somewhat overstated perhaps, but what this study will argue
is that this Jansenist was essentially correct, that Voltaire too was correct when
he interpreted the destruction of the Jesuits as the revenge of Port-Royal, that it
was real Jansenists who in 1761 engineered the destruction of the Jesuit Order in
France, and that if the event was in any sense a victory for the Enlightenment, it

---

8. Joseph-Antoine-J. Cerutti, *Apologie de l'institut des Jésuites* (1763), Vol. 1, p. 10; Henri
Griffet, *Remarques sur un écrit intitulé: 'Compte rendu des constitutions des Jésuites,'* par M.
Louis-René de Caradeuc de la Chalotais (n.d.), p. 72; and anon., *Le Philosophe redressé, ou
Critique impartiale du livre intitulé: 'Sur la Destruction des Jésuites en France* (1765), p. 164.

9. Voltaire, *Précis*, in his *Œuvres complètes*, Vol. 25, p. 399.

10. Louis-Adrien Le Paige, *Le Philosophe redressé, ou Réfutation de l'écrit intitulé: Sur la
Destruction des Jésuites en France, par un curé de village* (1765), pp. 27–28.

was so in a way different from that imagined by D'Alembert. The study will also show that if the Jansenists sometimes had recourse to the language of Gallicanism, that if in fact without the arguments of Gallicanism the Jansenists could never have persuaded the parlements of France to dissolve the Jesuit Order, they nonetheless did what they did in part because they were Jansenists, because like their spiritual ancestors at Port-Royal, they opposed the Jesuits for theological and religious as well as political reasons.

But by nearly everyone's admission, the Jansenism of the mid-eighteenth century was a mere shadow of its former self and its representatives hardly worthy of the glory of their illustrious predecessors. How were they able, then, to destroy the most formidable monastic order in France and thereby accomplish what Pascal with all his wit and Arnauld with all his learning had been powerless to do in the seventeenth century? The answer to this question will take us principally to the parlement of Paris, but often to the secret apartments of its magistrates, sometimes to Versailles, occasionally to the provinces, several times to Rome, and once even to Lisbon. But who, first of all, were the Jansenists, who were the Jesuits, what originally was their quarrel, and what did it become?

1. Jansenism, Molinism, and Gallicanism

IN 1759 AN ANONYMOUS PAMPHLETEER ASSERTED THAT THERE
were "many people who call themselves Jansenists uniquely out of party spirit,
and who in truth understand not a single word of what Jansenism means but
who merely, because of hatred for the Jesuits . . . do not respectfully bow
before the bull *Unigenitus*."[1] The equally anonymous editor of the *Nouvelles
Ecclésiastiques*, a Jansenist weekly journal, replied that he knew of "many people
who call themselves Molinists and constitutionaries uniquely out of party spirit"
and "attachment to the Jesuits," but that he knew "no people who call themselves Jansenists" who were motivated by comparably trivial considerations.[2]

Far from canceling each other out, these conflicting judgments tended rather
to confirm each other in the minds of many contemporaries. Only a few years
previous to the exchange between the anonymous pamphleteer and the *Nouvelles Ecclésiastiques*, the marquis d'Argenson observed in his journal that "it is
no longer a question of calling the ones Jansenists and the others Molinists: in
place of these names," he suggested, "substitute those of nationals and sacerdotals: Frenchmen or partisans of the inquisition and superstition and royal
authority perverted by intrigue."[3]

What the acrimonious exchange between the anonymous pamphleteer and
the *Nouvelles Ecclésiastiques* seemed to indicate was that by the mid-eighteenth
century the high-minded theological debate between Jansenists and Molinists of
the previous century had degenerated into a less than edifying quarrel between
members and partisans of a religious order, the Company of Jesus, and all those
who, for whatever reasons, opposed it; what D'Argenson in turn suggested was
that it was primarily political motives which sustained this quarrel, that the
terms "Jansenism" and "Molinism," though they originally referred to opposing sides in a theological controversy, now only thinly concealed an essentially political division in France, uniting all good "Frenchmen," "nationals,"
or "Jansenists"—to D'Argenson's mind these terms were more or less inter-

1. *Réflexions d'un Portuguais sur le mémorial présenté par ces pères à N.S.P. le pape Clément
XIII heureusement régnant: Exposées dans une lettre écrite à un ami à Rome* (1759), p. 379.

2. *Nouvelles Ecclésiastiques, ou Mémoires pour servir à l'histoire de la bulle Unigénitus* (May 1,
1759), p. 75. Hereafter cited as *Nouvelles Ecclésiastiques*.

3. René-Louis d'Argenson, *Journal et mémoires*, ed. E.-J.-B. Rathery (8 vols. Paris, 1859–
67), Vol. 8, p. 313.

changeable—against all papal interference in France's internal affairs, all acts of ecclesiastical or royal despotism, and all individuals or groups—"Molinists," or "sacerdotals," and particularly Jesuits—who favored either.

Originally, both Molinism and Jansenism were contradictory Catholic reactions to the equally contradictory intellectual and spiritual forces set loose by the Renaissance and the Reformation of the fifteenth and sixteenth centuries. This was most obviously true of the Molinism propounded by the Jesuit Order. Assigned as it was to the task of combatting the Protestant menace in Europe, this order, from its very founding in 1540, took especial alarm at the apparent similarity between Saint Augustine's doctrines of gratuitous predestination and efficacious grace—the related notions that God, out of his eternal and all-powerful decrees, dispenses to some an efficacious grace whereby he effects their salvation, while leaving others to their damnation for lack of this grace—to the Protestant doctrine of justification or salvation by faith alone. In reaction to these doctrines and in conformity to emphases already apparent in Renaissance humanism, the Jesuits therefore tended to minimize man's corruption and the effects of Adam's "fall" and to stress man's residual goodness and, above all, his freedom of will in the matter of salvation. Well under way from the mid-sixteenth century, the Jesuits' efforts to find a theology "better accommodated to the needs of the times"—as their general, Lainez, put it in 1558—attained systematic expression when the Spanish Jesuit Luis Molina published his treatise *Concordia liberi arbitrii cum gratiae donis* at Lisbon in 1588.[4]

Without contesting the Christian doctrine of Adam's fall, Molina nonetheless minimized its consequences. Mankind did not as a result become totally corrupt and incapable of any good, but was simply deprived of God's supernatural gifts such as eternal life. His "nature"—above all, his freedom of will to choose to do either good or evil—remained essentially intact. And in order to supplement man's free will and compensate for the loss of the supernatural gifts, God moreover dispensed to each man on every particular occasion a "sufficient" grace which, given the individual's free choice to use it, enabled him to overcome each particular temptation, to keep all God's commandments, and eventually to merit eternal life. Instead of Augustine's efficacious grace and gratuitous predestination, Molina, then, held to a sufficient grace and a kind of divine prescience: God simply foresaw the merits and demerits that men would freely choose to earn and rewarded them accordingly. The practical effect of Molinism was therefore to exalt, like Renaissance humanism, man's nature in its

---

4. Lainez's instruction to the Jesuit Order is quoted in Gazier, *Histoire générale du mouvement janséniste*, Vol. 1, p. 12. On the origins of the Jesuits in general, see René Fülop-Miller, *The Jesuits, a History of the Society of Jesus*, trans. F. S. Flint and P. R. Tait (New York, 1963), pp. 1–100; James Brodrick, *The Origin of the Jesuits* (New York, 1960); and Hollis, *A History of the Jesuits*, pp. 1–34.

present state, partly by somewhat debasing it in the state of innocence before Adam's fall. It also tended to scale down the moral demands of the Gospel. Since human nature was not radically corrupt, there was no need for a radical regeneration or conversion. Though they adhered to a high moral standard themselves, the Jesuits generally demanded of their penitents little more than a rather exterior conformity to the decalogue and the precepts of the Church.[5]

But that by the mid-eighteenth century the originally theological term *Molinism* could have become synonymous with a certain political attitude should hardly have surprised D'Argenson. Inasmuch as Molinism was humanistic, to the extent, in other words, that it exalted human nature in its present state, safeguarded its freedom of will and its ability to improve, and assigned a certain value to terrestrial existence in general, it was also free to be optimistic about society as a whole and develop justifications and goals for political thought and activity. Moreover, Molinism was from the very outset most ardently championed by the Jesuits, who also, as it happened, swore a special vow of obedience to the papacy, most outspokenly defended the papacy's most extreme claims to temporal authority over the crowned heads of Europe, and at the same time contrived to become the personal confessors of most of these heads. So from a very early date—certainly by the beginning of the seventeenth century—Molinism was associated with the Jesuit Order, and these two, in turn—at least in France—were associated with the arts of political intrigue and the pro-papal, anti-"national" political stance which D'Argenson described in 1754.

If Molinism was originally a humanistic reaction to the Augustinian theology of the Reformation, pristine Jansenism was in turn an Augustinian revolt within the Catholic Church against the "devout humanism" of the Jesuits. The Catholic reaction to Molinist theology was apparent as early as the close of the sixteenth century, when the Dominicans, jealous of the authority of Saint Thomas Aquinas, unsuccessfully attempted to persuade the papacy to condemn certain propositions from Molina's book. But it was not until the posthumous publication in 1640 of the treatise *Augustinus* by one Corneille Jansen or Jansenius—a professor of theology at the University of Louvain and Bishop of Ypres from 1636 to 1638—that Catholic hostility toward Molinism reached its strongest and most systematic expression. Thereafter "Jansenism" became an influential spiritual force in Jansenius's native Hapsburg Netherlands and most particularly

5. Summaries of Molinism are to be found in practically all histories of the Jesuit Order or Jansenism, but perhaps its clearest exposition in English is in Palmer, *Catholics and Unbelievers in Eighteenth-Century France*, pp. 23–52. For more theologically specialized treatments, see F. Stegmüller, *Geschichte des Molinismus* (Münster, 1935); and Nigel Abercrombie, *Origins of Jansenism* (Oxford, 1936), which, despite its title, is more enlightening on Molinism than on Jansensim, toward which the author is systematically unsympathetic.

in France, where Jansenius's nearly lifelong friend, Duvergier de Hauranne, the abbé of Saint-Cyran, won numerous adherents to the movement among important Parisian families and within the reformed abbey of Port-Royal des Champs, where he was the spiritual director.[6]

In sharp contrast to Molina and in conformity with the most rigid interpretation of Saint Augustine, Jansenius insisted upon the full gravity of Adam's fall and the consequent total corruption of human nature. Far from being free, man's will was thereafter invincibly prone toward all manner of evil and incapable of loving God or keeping his Commandments. In order to render men once again capable of good, God chose to dispense to some men an "efficacious" grace which miraculously transformed the human will in such a way that henceforth it preferred the Creator and his Commandments to finite creatures and sin. But God did not dispense efficacious grace to all men; some, rather—and according to eternal and impenetrable decrees fully understood only by himself— he permitted to remain within the throes of concupiscence and, ultimately, damnation. Hence all men were animated by one of two all-powerful spiritual forces or "delectations": love for God the Creator—also called charity—or concupiscence. Against, then, Molinism's rather optimistic and complacent vision of human nature and somewhat terrestrial interpretation of Christianity as a whole, Jansenius pitted the most tragic and pessimistic vision of man and an interpretation of both human nature and Christianity full of the sharpest, almost lunar contrasts: contrasts between man's pristine innocence before Adam's fall and his total corruption thereafter, between man's helplessness in the state of sin and his regained power in the state of grace, and more generally, between the rugged heights of Christian truth and the flat, concupiscent plain of any humanistic alternative.[7]

As such, however, Jansenism might appear to be very similar to Protestantism, more particularly to Calvinism, and in fact has often been interpreted as a kind of crypto-Calvinism. Both Calvinism and Jansenism were, after all, revolts

6. On the history and character of Jansenism in general nothing will ever entirely supplant Charles Augustin Sainte-Beuve's *Port-Royal,* ed. Maxime Leroy (Paris, 1952). Also indispensable, however, are Gazier, *Histoire générale;* Bernhard Groethuysen, *Die Entstehung der Bürgerlichen Welt-und Lebensanschaung in Frankreich* (Halle/Salle, 1927); Jean Orcibal, *Jean Duvergier de Hauranne, abbé de Saint-Cyran et son temps* (Louvain and Paris, 1947); Paul Bénichou, *Morales du grand siècle* (Paris, 1948); Cognet, *Le Jansénisme;* Jean Mesnard, *Pascal* (Paris, 1962); and, most recently, Antoine Adam, *Du Mysticisme à la révolte: Les jansénistes du XVIIIe siècle* (Paris, 1968).

7. On the theology of Jansenius and early Jansenism in general, see Jean La Porte, *La Doctrine de Port-Royal,* 2 vols.: *Les Vérités de la grâce* (Paris, 1923) and *La Morale d'après Arnauld* (Paris, 1951); Jean Orcibal, *Correspondance de Jansénius* (Louvain and Paris, 1947), and *La Spiritualité de Saint-Cyran, avec ses écrits de piété inédits* (Paris, 1962). Jean Orcibal's projected volumes on the life and work of Jansenius and the "birth of Jansenism" have not yet appeared.

against humanism, and both stressed man's total depravity and helplessness in his present state, the unqualified sovereignty of God, and man's complete dependence upon God for salvation. Yet in fact Jansenism was quite Catholic and considerably more otherworldly than Calvinism. Calvinists, like Lutherans, believed in justification by faith alone quite independently of good works; Jansenists believed in salvation by the good works which only "charity" as bestowed by efficacious grace could enable them to perform. Again, Calvinists believed in what the Synod of Dordtrecht in 1619 defined as the perseverance of the saints—the notion that, once a recipient of divinely bestowed faith, a man need no longer fear for his salvation, however short he might subsequently fall from the glory of God—whereas the Jansenists believed that there were other kinds of grace, that one could never be entirely certain that he possessed the right kind, and that if one possessed any other he might easily fall from the state of grace at any moment. Deprived, then, of the assurance that the doctrines of justification by faith alone and the perseverance of the saints afforded the Calvinists, the Jansenists were consequently condemned forever to hover—in this life, at least—somewhere between the certainty of salvation and the terror of damnation. Consequently, too, the Jansenists could develop no counterpart to Calvinism's ennoblement of secular callings or vocations. For the good Jansenist the "world" offered too many distractions and diversions capable of turning his mind from God and thereby removing him from the state of grace. Jansenist "conversions" therefore typically resulted in the cessation of all secular activity and an ascetic retreat from the world: Blaise Pascal sacrificed science—or at least tried to; Antoine Lemaistre gave up a brilliant career in the Parisian bar; Thomas du Fossé sold his charge in the parlement of Rouen; and all, finally, took up an ascetic life of study and contemplation as "solitaries" around the abbey of Port-Royal. In their shoes any good Calvinist, far from giving up these vocations, would have redoubled his efforts, therein the better to honor and glorify God by his frenetic activity.[8]

Seventeenth-century Jansenism, then, was at once more pessimistic, ascetic, and otherworldly than either Calvinism or Molinism. That a bit more than a century later the term *Jansenist* should have come to mean simple opposition to the Jesuits synonymous with a category so blatantly political as "nationals," indiscriminately including anyone opposed to the papacy's claims to temporal authority, sacerdotal authority in general, and all acts of royal despotism, is quite puzzling. For the political Jansenism which D'Argenson described in the mid-eighteenth century stood in a fairly direct line of succession from a seven-

8. The important doctrinal and ethical differences between Jansenism and Calvinism are nowhere made clear except in La Porte, *La Doctrine de Port-Royal,* esp. Vol. 2, pp. 1–23; and Jean Orcibal, "Le Premier Port-Royal, Réforme ou Contre-Réforme," *Nouvelle Clio* (Brussels, May-June 1950), pp. 238–80.

teenth-century religious movement which, far from having filled its ranks with camel-like plodders, attracted rather only those rare spiritual athletes capable of maneuvering their way through the eye of the biblical needle and whose original adherents, far from being political types, were so otherworldly in outlook that the cardinal de Retz once described them as "the most inept persons in the world in the matter of intrigues and affairs of state."[9]

How, then, is one to explain the fact that the Jansenism which arose as a devoutly Augustinian protest against semi-Pelagian or "Molinistic" theological tendencies within the Catholic Church in general became synonymous by the mid-eighteenth century with almost any kind of opposition to a particular institution, the Company of Jesus? How is one further to account for the fact that the character of this anti-Jesuitical opposition became in large measure political, especially since its spiritual ancestor, the Jansenism of Pascal and Arnauld, was so exclusively theological and otherworldly in character?

The answer to the first question, how Jansenism came to be almost completely consumed with hostility toward the Jesuit Order, is not quite as obvious as at first it might appear. To be certain, Jansenism was profoundly opposed to Molinism, and Molinism was from the very outset intimately associated with the Jesuit Order. But not all Jesuits adhered to Molinist theology, and Molinism could claim many converts outside the Jesuit Order, including, in a general way, the papacy itself. For it was not, of course, the Jesuit Order but rather the papacy which, with the cooperation of a majority of the French bishops and the active solicitation of the French government, condemned and persecuted Jansenism in France. The part which the Jesuits played in the matter was mostly clandestine or indirect.

The hostility of the French government toward Jansenism had its origin in Jansenius's and Saint-Cyran's opposition to Cardinal Richelieu's anti-Hapsburg, pro-Swedish foreign policy during the Thirty Years' War. Like the other leaders of the French Counter-Reformation—collectively referred to as the *parti dévôt*—from which the original "Jansenists" were quite indistinguishable, Jansenius and Saint-Cyran opposed a foreign policy which sacrificed the interests of the Catholic reconquest of Europe to those of the Bourbon dynasty. Saint-Cyran, moreover, insisted particularly upon the necessity of true contrition or love for God rather than merely attrition or fear of eternal punishment in the sacrament of penance, a moral doctrine which not only contradicted the view expressed in Richelieu's own catechism but, had it been applied in the confessional to Louis XIII himself—as, ironically, had briefly been done in 1634 by the King's confessor, the père Caussin, a Jesuit—would have entailed a veritable

9. Quoted in René Tavenaux, *Jansénisme et politique* (Paris, 1965), p. 30.

diplomatic revolution: the abandonment of Richelieu's "sinful" alliance with
the Swedish, Dutch, and German Protestants in favor of an alignment with
France's mortal enemies, the Catholic Hapsburgs. It was for this reason primarily that Richelieu arrested and imprisoned Saint-Cyran in 1638.[10]

Richelieu had also ordered Saint-Cyran's theological manuscripts combed in
an unsuccessful attempt to buttress his purely political motives with an indictment of heresy. But the posthumous publication of Jansenius's *Augustinus* in
1640 considerably facilitated and enlarged the matter. Shortly after Richelieu's
death in 1642, the theologian of Notre-Dame, Isaac Habert—to whom Richelieu had left instructions to this effect—attacked Jansenius in his sermons. And
though temporarily quieted by the Archbishop of Paris, the campaign against
what was already called "Jansenism" began to acquire a theological momentum
of its own when the Jesuit Jacques Sirmond accused the Jansenists of adhering,
like the Calvinists, to a "predestinarian" heresy and yet others attacked the
abbey of Port-Royal's practice, introduced by Saint-Cyran, of abstaining from
the Eucharist until an interior "renewal" had been effected.[11] After increasingly
sharper polemics from both sides, the debate finally reached the Sorbonne. On
July 1, 1649, the Syndic of the Sorbonne, Nicolas Cornet, requested the examination of seven propositions which, he said, had been conspicuous among
recent baccalaureat theses but which in fact everyone knew to be an attempted
summary of Jansenius's *Augustinus*. Unable, however, to gain a decisive majority
in the still very Augustinian Sorbonne, the "Molinist party," led by Cornet and
Habert, took its case to Rome, where it presented the first five of Cornet's
seven propositions together with a request for their condemnation by no less
than seventy-eight bishops. With the support of both the overwhelming
majority of the French episcopacy and Cardinal-Minister Mazarin, who faithfully adhered to the ecclesiastical policy of his predecessor Richelieu, the cause
of the Molinists could not long remain in doubt. On May 31, 1653, Pope
Innocent X signed the bull *Cum occasione*, which condemned the first four
propositions as heretical and the fifth as false.[12]

---

10. C. V. Wedgewood, *Richelieu and the French Monarchy* (New York, 1962), pp. 86–87;
Orcibal, *Jean Duvergier de Hauranne*, pp. 477–594.
11. On the theory and practice of Saint-Cyran's "renouvellement," see Orcibal, *Jean
Duvergier de Hauranne*, pp. 405–73; Sainte-Beuve, *Port-Royal*, Vol. 1, pp. 361–407.
12. The five propositions in question are:
(1) "Some commandments of God are impossible for the just by reason of their
present forces no matter what intentions they have or what efforts they make, for they
lack the grace by which these commandments are made possible for them."
(2) "In the state of fallen nature one can never resist interior grace."
(3) "To merit or sin in the state of fallen nature it is unnecessary for man to possess
a liberty opposed to (psychological) necessity, but it suffices that he possess a liberty
opposed to [physical] constraint."

By 1653 Innocent X's condemnation affected a yet small but nonetheless significant group of Jansenists in France. Besides the sisters of the abbey of Port-Royal, whom Saint-Cyran, as their spiritual director, had almost completely won over before his death in 1643, Jansenism had made serious inroads into the French episcopacy and Parisian high bourgeois and aristocratic society: twelve or thirteen bishops, even more numerous sympathizers in the parlement of Paris, and several protectors such as the duchesse de Longueville at Versailles. A single influential parliamentary family, the numerous progeny of the celebrated lawyer Antoine Arnauld, constituted an octopus-like center for Jansenism's various tentacles. Robert Arnauld d'Andilly, the eldest and a convert of Saint-Cyran himself, represented the cause of Jansenism at the court; six of his younger sisters, headed by the famous abbesse Angélique, dominated the life of the abbey of Port-Royal; another brother, Henry Arnauld, defended Jansenism within the episcopacy as Bishop of Angers, while the youngest brother, Antoine or "the great" Arnauld, not only did the same as a doctor of theology in the Sorbonne but, as Saint-Cyran's most gifted student, became Jansenism's chief strategist and spokesman until his death at the end of the century. Add to this number such converts and "solitaries" as the scientist Blaise Pascal, the lawyer Antoine Lemaistre, and the theologian Pierre Nicole, and the Jansenists, if not numerous, could utilize a disproportionate array of talent and look for some protection in high places.[13]

In the face of the bull *Cum occasione* the Jansenists' first tactic was purely defensive. As it happened, the bull failed to specify clearly either whether the five condemned propositions were to be found word for word in Jansenius's *Augustinus* or, assuming they were there, whether the context in which they occurred revealed them to have been asserted with heretical intentions or otherwise. Antoine Arnauld immediately seized the opportunity thus afforded him to assert that the propositions lent themselves to both an orthodox and an heretical interpretation, that the "Jansenists"—he and Nicole already maintained that "Jansenism" was a purely imaginary heresy—condemned with all their

---

(4) "The semi-Pelagians conceded the necessity of an interior prevenient grace for all actions, even for the beginning of faith, but they were heretics to the extent that they wished this grace to be such that the will of man could resist or obey it."

(5) "It is a semi-Pelagian error to maintain that Jesus Christ died and shed his blood for all men generally." (Sainte-Beuve, *Port-Royal*, Vol. 1, pp. 580–84). The most economical survey of the events preceding the condemnation of the five propositions is in Cognet, *Le Jansénisme*, pp. 38–61. See also Gazier, *Histoire générale*, Vol. 1, pp. 38–53, 79–92. For a more detailed account, see Albert de Meyer, *Les Premières Controverses jansénistes en France, 1640–1649* (Louvain, 1917).

13. For the interior development and exterior relations of Port-Royal before 1653, see Sainte-Beuve, *Port-Royal*, Vol. 1, pp. 361–558, 734–62, and Gazier, *Histoire générale*, Vol. 1, pp. 54–78.

hearts any heretical interpretations the propositions might have, and that as a matter of fact neither the condemned propositions nor their heretical interpretations were to be found in Jansenius's treatise at all. And when, in response to this somewhat Fabian evasion, Pope Alexander VII promulgated the bull *Ad sacram* in 1656, declaring that the five propositions were in fact in Jansenius's *Augustinus* and that they had been condemned in the sense in which Jansenius himself had understood them, Arnauld and Nicole countered by maintaining that the pope was quite simply mistaken and that the papacy, though infallible in matters of eternal truth, could not possibly be infallible in matters of contingent facts.[14] Hence arose the famous Arnauldian distinction, destined to play an important role in the history of Jansenism, between *droit*, or right, and *fait*, or fact. Arnauld declared the Jansenists ready to condemn the five propositions *de droit* but to reserve a "respectful silence" on the question of whether *de fait* they were to be found in Jansenius's treatise or whether in asserting anything similar to these propositions, he had meant to propound something heretical.[15]

But the Arnauldian strategy of evasion ultimately resulted in defeat. On one front the assembly of the French clergy and the council of state successfully trapped the elusive Jansenists by requiring of all secular and regular clergy the signature of a formulary condemning the doctrine of Jansenius. When in 1661 the formulary was first brought to Port-Royal, the sisters managed to sign it with the reservation of "respectful silence" on the question of "fact." But the new king, Louis XIV, the Molinist clergy, and Rome all united in insisting upon more. Finally, in 1664, the new Archbishop of Paris, Hardouin de Péréfixe, cajoled twelve of the sisters into signing the formulary "purely and simply," exiled twelve others to disparate monastic communities, deprived the remainder of the sacraments, placed them under police surveillance at Port-Royal des Champs, and thereby initiated a tragic progression of persecution which ended only in the complete destruction of the abbey in 1711.[16] Meanwhile, on another front, Arnauld lost the battle of the Sorbonne. In 1655 Arnauld had gone to

---

14. However trivial the distinction might seem, it constitutes evidence of the influence of Cartesian rationalism on the Jansenist movement. Descartes drew a radical distinction between the certainty of mathematical or geometrical propositions and the doubtful quality of statements concerning empirical matters of fact, whereas the opposing position of Leibnitz, who regarded the latter as mathematical identities in the mind of God, would have considerably buttressed the position of the papacy, regarded as God's representative on earth. The Jansenist distinction between *droit* and *fait*, moreover, become a serious embarrassment to Catholic apologetic efforts in the face of the 18th-century Enlightenment inasmuch as the predominant Catholic approach was to argue the truth of Christianity on the basis of the empirically verifiable "fact" of revelation. (See Palmer, *Catholics and Unbelievers*, pp. 77–102.)

15. Cognet, *Le Jansénisme*, pp. 62–75; Gazier, *Histoire générale*, Vol. 1, pp. 113–36.

16. Cognet, *Le Jansénisme*, pp. 76–84; Gazier, *Histoire générale*, Vol. 1, pp. 159–87.

print in the defense of the duc de Liancourt, a close friend of Port-Royal, whose Molinist parish curé had threatened him with refusal of the sacraments—the first recorded such incident—unless he broke all the ties which united him to the abbey. Arnauld's Molinist enemies in the Sorbonne immediately seized upon this occasion to uncover two "heretical" propositions in his polemic, and on these grounds—and also by packing the assemblies with forty mendicant monks instead of the legal eight—expelled Arnauld from the Sorbonne on February 15, 1656.[17]

With the papacy, the ministry, the larger part of the episcopacy, and now the Sorbonne against them, and the probability of persecution looming ominously on the horizon, the outlook for the Jansenists was bleak indeed in 1656. There remained only a single court of appeals from which they could hope to gain a favorable verdict: the public. And to plead their case effectively before this notoriously fickle tribunal the Jansenists desperately needed at once a case more accusatory than the purely defensive distinctions of Arnauld and an advocate who could present it in language more eloquent than the all but impenetrable jargon of the professional theologians. It was at this critical juncture that the Jansenists received unhoped-for succor in the person of Blaise Pascal, until then renowned only for his scientific works but, since his second and definitive "conversion" in 1654, a penitent under the spiritual direction of Antoine Lemaistre de Sacy and a devoted friend of Port-Royal. By chance present at a meeting with Arnauld and Pierre Nicole at Port-Royal des Champs on January 25, 1656, Pascal, at the suggestion of Arnauld, began work on what became *Les Provinciales*.[18]

It was immediately evident from the first "provincial" letter, which appeared on January 23, 1656, that Pascal had found the proper tone to reach the public. This letter, as well as the seventeen which followed, enjoyed immediate and enormous public success, and the controversy, as one historian has put it, "passed from the Sorbonne to the *salons*."[19] But the first three letters were yet an attempt to influence the course of events at the Sorbonne. They attempted, though without success, to convince the Dominican doctors at the Sorbonne that their own theology of grace was closer to that of the Jansenists than that of the Molinists, with whom the Dominicans were nonetheless allied for political reasons. But when despite Pascal's best literary efforts Arnauld was excluded from the Sorbonne and eventual persecution appeared certain, Pascal and his friends calculated that they had to counterattack, and to counterattack in such a way as to focus public indignation upon someone other than themselves. The

---

17. Cognet, *Le Jansénisme*, pp. 67–69; Gazier, *Histoire générale*, Vol. 1, pp. 93–102.
18. Sainte-Beuve, *Port-Royal*, Vol. 2, pp. 65–70; Mesnard, *Pascal*, pp. 59–75.
19. Cognet, *Le Jansénisme*, p. 70.

group they singled out for flagellation was the Jesuits; the principal accusation: that the society's casuist authors had undermined the Gospel by their lax interpretations of the Gospel's ethical imperatives.[20]

The Jansenists could hardly have made a happier tactical decision. The Jesuits were an easily identified and vulnerably conspicuous group of people who had already stepped on many toes both ecclesiastical and temporal and had thereby rendered themselves unpopular enough for other than theological reasons. And everyone knew the Jesuits to be particularly vulnerable at the point of their lax casuistry. Casuistry itself was nothing more than the indispensable art of applying general moral principles to specific and diverse situations, but the Jesuits were above all a missionary order, and in their missionary zeal to make Christianity as palatable to as many people as possible, many—too many perhaps—of the society's ethicists had undoubtedly rendered the "yoke of the Savior" considerably lighter than the Savior had meant it to be. Was it not notorious fact that under certain circumstances Jesuit authors had condoned theft, fornication, adultery, murder, and even regicide, and that as missionaries in China they were already so accommodating Christianity to pagan "Chinese rites" as to render it all but unrecognizable? [21]

Not that the Jansenists had totally ignored the Jesuits' lax casuistry before. As early as 1626 Saint-Cyran had leveled the accusation against the Jesuit Garasse, and in 1643 Arnauld published his *Théologie morale des Jésuites*, which in about ten turgid pages enumerated most of the Jesuitical sins later dwelt upon by Pascal.[22] But at first with mordant irony, then with increasingly eloquent indignation, Pascal now ridiculed the key methodological concepts by which the Jesuits justified their less than evangelical ethical decisions: the principle, later called "invincible ignorance," that no act could be considered a sin unless he who performed it was fully conscious that it was a sin, which had as its absurd consequence that more men were "justified by this ignorance and this forgetfullness of God than by grace or the sacraments"; or the doctrine of "probability" (later called "probabilism"), which consisted in condoning an action on the sole condition that at least one "grave author," preferably a Jesuit, had judged it sinless, even if his opinion was less probable than that of other casuists who had asserted the contrary; or the method, finally, of "directing the intention," which amounted to justifying a whole host of sins—slander, theft, simony,

20. On the evolution of *Les Lettres provinciales,* see Henri Lefebvre, *Pascal* (Paris, 1954), Vol. 2, pp. 57–86; Mesnard, *Pascal,* pp. 75–87; but, above all, Sainte-Beuve, *Port-Royal,* Vol. 2, pp. 67–179.

21. For a recent treatment of the Chinese Rites controversy, see Arnold H. Rowbothan, *Missionary and Mandarin: The Jesuits at the Court of China* (New York, 1966), pp. 119–75.

22. For Saint-Cyran's polemic with Garasse, see Orcibal, *Jean Duvergier de Hauranne,* pp. 249–82. Arnauld's *Théologie morale des Jésuites* is in his *Œuvres complètes* (42 vols. Lausanne, 1775–83), Vol. 29, pp. 74–94.

and murder among them—by the simple device of directing the intention of the "penitent," not to the sin itself, but to some professedly irreprehensible end to which the sin was a means.[23] And though not always obviously related to these ethical questions, the more fundamental theological opposition between Jansenism and Molinism was never far in the background. For the Molinist Jesuits whom Pascal described, man was not totally corrupt or sinful, and his sins, therefore, they regarded as individual acts capable of being isolated and dealt with individually and systematically. For Pascal and the Jansenists, on the other hand, man was totally and fundamentally sinful, and his most indifferent acts, even if performed with no conscious intent to sin, were as "filthy rags" before the sight of God.

Despite the importance of the issues raised by Pascal, *Les Provinciales* did much to trivialize and debase the controversy between Jansenists and Molinists. Pascal indeed achieved his goals brilliantly—in fact far too brilliantly for the integrity of Jansenism. For by gaining the support of a certain public, by creating what Sainte-Beuve has called a "party of favorable indifferents," Jansenism in turn acquired obligations to this same public which before long led it into lands strangely political in nature.[24] Already in 1656 the Jansenists were talking about their *amis du dehors*, or "friends on the outside"; yet the lengths to which Jansenists in the following century would go to please their ever-expanding gallery of "friends on the outside" would have shamed the least austere of their predecessors.

As for the Jesuits, Sainte-Beuve may have been right in maintaining that Pascal had delivered them the mortal blow in 1656, that any signs of life they displayed thereafter were merely the death rattles of a genius having sustained an attack of apoplexy fortissimo.[25] But if so, the Jansenists failed to perceive it. After *Les Provinciales* came *La Morale des Jésuites extraite fidèlement de leurs livres* (1667), then Arnauld's multivolume *Morale pratique des Jésuites* (1669–1694), and finally a veritable avalanche of anti-Jesuitical libels until, by the mid-eighteenth century, anti-Jesuitism had become for the Jansenists a true fixation, almost completely obscuring all other issues. From a debate between Jansenists and Molinists, it had become a battle of Jansenists against Jesuits.

The story, then, of Jansenism's growth, condemnation, and persecution and the Jansenists' first attempts to defend themselves explains in large measure the

23. Blaise Pascal, *Les Provinciales*, in his *Œuvres complètes*, ed. Louis Lafuma (Paris, 1963). For invincible ignorance see the "quatrième lettre," p. 383; for probabilism, the "sixième lettre," p. 393; for direction of intention, the "septième lettre," p. 397. All subsequent quotations from Pascal are taken from the Lafuma edition.
24. Sainte-Beuve, *Port-Royal*, Vol. 2, p. 91. On the subject of the effect of *Les Provinciales* on the character of Jansenism, see ibid., esp. pp. 65–66, 90–93, 199–222.
25. Ibid., p. 214.

fact that by the eighteenth century Jansenism had become a movement including the most diverse persons united primarily by their common opposition to the Company of Jesus. But that this opposition also became partly political in nature, that Jansenists came to hate the Jesuits not only on account of their Molinist theology and lax ethical teachings but also as representatives of papal, episcopal, and even royal authority "perverted," as D'Argenson expressed it, "by intrigue"—this development certainly is a somewhat more perplexing matter which suggests at least one prior question: How did a religious movement so otherworldly in character as Jansenism develop a set of political attitudes at all?

That Jansenists sometimes went to extremes in their rejection of the world there can be no doubt. No one was more extreme in this respect than Pascal himself, for whom, as for Saint-Cyran and his nephew Barcos, there existed no temporal approximation of equity, justice, or natural law because Adam's fall had rendered them totally inaccessible to human reason and had left men with nothing to govern themselves except force and habit. "And thus being unable to make what is just strong," he concluded, "we have made what is strong just."[26] Pascal's profound pessimism toward the temporal order naturally led him to an attitude of complete abnegation in the face of all temporal powers and principalities, which excluded, it goes without saying, the possibility of any political opposition or resistance.[27] Yet the extreme otherworldliness that characterized Pascal and to a lesser extent Barcos, Singlin, and Angélique Arnauld was by no means true of all Jansenists. Even Pascal was willing to play the leading role in the highly political maneuver of attacking the Jesuits in 1656, and his companions in arms in this affair, Pierre Nicole and Antoine Arnauld, refused to share their more illustrious colleague's totally pessimistic and docile attitude toward the temporal order. Considerably influenced in this respect by Thomistic thought, and for this reason recently classified by some historians as "centrists," Arnauld and Nicole were able to envision the possibility of Christian princes guided by upright counselors implementing "Christian" governmental policies.[28] Hence their rejection of the world was hardly as systematic as Pascal's. Hence, too, they were considerably more upset than Pascal by the prospect of blatantly tyrannical rulers issuing orders directly contrary to what

26. Pascal, *Pensées,* in *Œuvres complètes,* p. 512.
27. On Pascal's political thought, see Etiennette Demahis, *La Pensée politique de Pascal* (Saint-Amand, 1931); Lefebvre, *Pascal,* Vol. 2, pp. 129–46; Lucien Goldmann, *Le Dieu caché, étude sur la vision tragique dans les Pensées de Pascal et dans le théâtre de Racine* (Paris, 1955), passim, but esp. pp. 304–14; Taveneaux, *Jansénisme et politique,* pp. 23–25.
28. The classification of Jansenists into "extremists" and "centrists" has been developed by Goldmann in *Le Dieu caché,* passim, but esp. pp. 157–82; see also the *Correspondance entre Martin de Barcos, abbé de Saint-Cyran, avec les abbesses de Port-Royal et les principaux personnages du groupe janséniste* (Paris, 1956), pp. 10 ff.; and G. Namer, *L'Abbé Le Roy et ses amis: Essai sur le Jansénisme extrémiste intramondain* (Paris, 1964), passim, but esp. pp. 9–17.

they considered justice or the law of God, such as an order to sign the formulary without distinction between *droit* and *fait*. Not that either countenanced armed resistance under such a circumstance, but Arnauld, at least, recommended both passive resistance to such orders and the attempt to enlighten the offending prince by means of "respectful remonstrances."[29]

Respectful remonstrances—these two words in combination bring to mind an institution conspicuous in French history whose "respectful remonstrances" often led it to anything but respectful recalcitrance in the face of royal edicts and declarations: the parlement of Paris. This institution was originally a primarily judicial body, an offspring of the medieval kings' *curia regis*, whose inner core (peers and princes also had the right to attend its sessions) consisted of trained legists responsible for administering the king's justice in the royal domains. But at a time when judicial and legislative functions were hardly distinguishable, the parlement also had the task of proclaiming and recording all new royal edicts and declarations in its registers (called "registration"), to which King Philip the Fair added the right of "remonstrating" against new royal acts of legislation if these were found to conflict with previous edicts, declarations, or the "fundamental laws of the realm." Through the fourteenth century king and parlement tended to work in close cooperation, and the parlement's limited participation in affairs of state or what contemporaries called "public affairs" caused only minimal tension between itself and the throne. But under the strain, in succeeding centuries, of the rising power of the "new monarchy" and the divisive religious wars of the sixteenth century, the interests of the kings and their parlements began to diverge, particularly in matters of ecclesiastical and financial policy. And with the gradual demise, in the sixteenth century, of such representative institutions as the estates-general and the provincial estates, the parlement of Paris grew accustomed to regarding itself and its right of "remonstrance" as the last remaining obstacle between the monarchy and despotism, the sole surviving guardian of the monarchy's true interests against the often arbitrary, capricious, and contradictory whims of the individual monarchs themselves, and as the last available voice of a population weighed down by superfluous taxes and browbeaten by extraparliamentary arrests. In 1648, finally, the long latent tension between the royal government and the parlement of Paris erupted into the civil war known as the Fronde when the population of Paris and some of the princes supported the parlement's refusal to register certain financial edicts sent to it by the regency government of Anne d'Autriche and Cardinal Mazarin.[30]

Now the period of the Fronde more or less coincides with the first bloom of

29. Quoted in Taveneaux, *Jansénisme et politique*, p. 27.
30. J. H. Shennan, *The Parlement of Paris* (Ithaca, 1968), pp. 151–284. On the Fronde itself the most recent works are E. H. Kossman, *La Fronde* (Leyden, 1954); and Lloyd Moote, *The Revolt of The Judges: The Parlement of Paris and The Fronde* (Princeton, 1972).

Jansenism in France, and historians of Jansenism ever since Sainte-Beuve have noted not only that Jansenism found particular favor among the magistrates of the parlement of Paris, but that some of the most illustrious Jansenist families—the Arnaulds and Pascals, for example—either came from or were closely associated with parliamentary or "robe" society. Starting from these well-grounded observations,[31] several Marxist—or neo-Marxist—historians have recently propounded some far-reaching and provocative theses concerning the relationship between Jansenism and the parliamentary milieu.[32] The parliamentary high bourgeoisie or the "nobility of the robe," they maintain, was in the mid-seventeenth century suffering from a severe social and economic crisis resulting from the changing nature of the French monarchy itself. During the later Middle Ages the monarchy had found it necessary to rely on the urban bourgeoisie in its long battle to gain supremacy over the feudal aristocracy, and the parlement of Paris, composed primarily of professional legists of bourgeois extraction, was one of the most important administrative instruments in this policy. But by the seventeenth century the monarchy found itself strong enough to adopt a new policy of "equilibrium" which, rather than leaning exclusively on one class in order to oppose another, played one class off against another with the administrative help of a new "bureaucracy of commissioners"—members of the royal council and the provincial intendants—dependent exclusively and immediately upon itself. Feeling themselves increasingly cut off from the monarchy and seeing their functions progressively usurped by the novel bureaucracy, holders of the older parliamentary offices naturally opposed this development in diverse ways, among them the open opposition of the Fronde. Yet no more than the parliamentary Fronde itself could this opposition be total, because the *parlementaires* paradoxically held their offices directly from the king and to destroy the monarchy was therefore to destroy the foundation of their economic and social existence. More typically, the paradoxical dilemma of the magistrates found expression in at least a certain reserve toward their social life and public functions and at most in the systematic ideological rejection of the "world" of extreme Jansenism. Hence Jansenism was an ideological—or rather theological—expression of the social and economic malaise of the mid-seventeenth-century nobility of the robe.

However attractive as an explanation of the appearance of Jansenism in mid-seventeenth-century France, this thesis suffers from some serious deficiencies. Besides relying upon an oversimplified view of the growth of the French monarchy, the thesis simultaneously explains far too much and far too little. It explains too much, on the one hand, because it seems to account not only for

31. Sainte-Beuve, *Port-Royal*, Vol. 1, pp. 98–102.
32. Particularly Lefebvre, in *Pascal*, Vol. 1, pp. 11–80; Vol. 2, pp. 7–51; and Goldmann, in *Le Dieu caché*, pp. 115–56.

the seventeenth-century Jansenist-Molinist controversy in France but for the
Calvinist-Arminian controversy in Holland and England during the same
general period and the appearance of Augustinian Christianity at diverse times
everywhere. The hypothesis also explains too much because it apparently
explains why all or most French *parlementaires* became Jansenists, whereas this
in fact did not occur. Jansenism could claim only a small minority of converts
within the parlement of Paris, while the same body contained many partisans
of the Jesuits as well. On the other hand, the thesis fails to account for the presence of significant numbers of Jansenist converts within the clergy, the religious
orders, and around the court who came from social groups other than—and
even opposed to—the nobility of the robe; nor does it explain why the period
of the parlement's most obvious Jansenist coloring and most active opposition
to the crown occurred not during the mid-seventeenth century crisis but much
later, during the first half of the eighteenth century.[33] To lump the eighteenth-
century parlements in with the rising opposition of the third estate is to fly in
the face of what now seems a well-documented thesis, that the parliamentary
personnel became not less but more aristocratic in orientation.[34]

It remains nonetheless true that both Richelieu and Louis XIV himself dis-
cerned a collusion between the parlement of Paris and the Jansenists, and that
Louis XIV in particular saw the Jansenists as both dangerously "republican"
and as potential, if not actual, *frondeurs*. To be sure, the Sun King probably
meant no more by the description of "republican" than that the Jansenist community around Port-Royal was a relatively free association of individuals without any clear lines of authority, or that the Jansenists' refusal to sign the formulary gave evidence that they attached too much importance to the rights of
the individual conscience, or—still another possibility—that the Jansenists'
austere morals smacked of republican Rome. Probably he tried to eliminate
Jansenism for the same general reason that he tried to eradicate Protestantism
and that he interpreted all religious dissent as a veiled political threat to his
conception of the unitary monarchy. But without attaching undue significance
to the opinions of someone as theologically benighted and politically prejudiced
as Louis XIV, there is no contesting the accuracy of what he simply observed:
that the parlement of Paris had recently led the Fronde, that the Jansenists'
loyalty to himself stopped short of the individual conscience, and that some
close ties existed between Jansenism and the parliamentary milieu.[35]

33. A similar though briefer criticism is given in Taveneaux, *Jansénisme et politique*, pp.
20–21.
34. Franklin L. Ford, *Robe and Sword: The Regrouping of the French Aristocracy after Louis
XIV* (Cambridge, Mass., 1962); François Bluche, *Les Magistrats du parlement de Paris au
XVIIIᵉ siècle, 1715–1771* (Paris, 1960).
35. Taveneaux, *Jansénisme et politique*, pp. 30–33. See also Lionel Rothkrug, *Opposition to
Louis XIV: The Political and Social Origins of the French Enlightenment* (Princeton, 1965),

One hesitates to invoke the law of parsimony in history, but it is nonetheless certain that both Jansenism's increased political activity and its collusion with the parlement of Paris can at least be explained more economically than it has been by the Marxist historians. That Jansenism won a disproportionate number of converts among *parlementaires* should surprise us no more than Calvinism's success within the cultivated urban bourgeoisie: a religious movement as spiritually intense and theologically sophisticated as Jansenism quite naturally most attracted a social group as leisured, intellectually cultivated, and morally austere as the parliamentary "robins." That Jansenists, for their part, began to draw distinctions between *fait* and *droit*, to intrigue at the papal court, to lay down limits to monarchical authority, and to talk of respectful remonstrances can be most simply interpreted as the kind of inevitable defensive political opposition to which Louis XIV's oppressive policies could drive even the most otherworldly of men. And that they early found a protector in the parlement of Paris is best explained not only by individual conversions from among its ranks but by a parliamentary tradition which antedated Jansenism by about four centuries: Gallicanism.

The origins of French Gallicanism go back to the quarrels between King Philip the Fair and Pope Boniface VIII during the first years of the fourteenth century—a tradition first fully stated in the Pragmatic Sanction of Bourges in 1438. But it was not until the occasion of Louis XIV's quarrel with Pope Innocent XI in 1682 over royal rights to the revenues of vacant bishoprics (*régale*) that the doctrine acquired definitive articulation. As defined by Bishop Bossuet at that time, Gallicanism adhered to the claim of the Council of Constance of 1415 that Church councils were superior to the pope in matters pertaining to faith; asserted the right of the French Church to govern itself solely by the usages and practices accepted in that realm, and to receive no papal briefs or bulls without the free and unanimous consent of the French episcopacy; and defended the King of France's claim to be subject to none but God in matters temporal. Together, these assertions were known as the Gallican liberties of the French Church, and although they most directly concerned the Church, the parlement of Paris had always been their most zealous defender. It was in the interest of these Gallican liberties, for instance, that the parlement of Paris had often made common cause with the French throne against the claims of the papacy, as in the affair of the *régale* in 1682, or had often seen fit to oppose the king himself, as it did by refusing to register the Concordat of 1516 negotiated by Francis I and Pope Leo X. In fact, the parlement's attachment to the Gallican liberties rendered it instinctively hostile to almost everything that came from Rome, including papal bulls which condemned French Jansenists.[36]

---

pp. 45–85. On Louis XIV's policy toward the Protestants, see Jean Orcibal, *Louis XIV et les Protestants* (Paris, 1951).

36. It is common among French historians to distinguish between an episcopal Galli-

Effectively muzzled after the Fronde by Louis XIV, the parlement of Paris showed only slight reluctance to register the bull *Cum occasione* in 1653. For that matter, the bull directly offended none of the tenets of Gallicanism. But it was quite otherwise in the case of Clement XI's bull *Unigenitus* in 1713, which, solicited by the aging Louis XIV as the ultimate weapon against the "republican" Jansenists, condemned 101 propositions from the book *Réflexions morales* by Arnauld's friend Pasquier Quesnel. For besides condemning a number of propositions which even the parlement's attorney general, Daguesseau, judged to be pure Augustinian doctrine, the bull's ninety-first article, which condemned the statement: "the fear of an unjust excommunication ought never to impede us from doing our duty," raised an old Gallican nightmare by seemingly defending the papacy's right to excommunicate kings and release their subjects from obedience. Worse yet, Louis XIV failed to obtain the unanimous adhesion of the French episcopacy. In an assembly of the clergy hastily called for the occasion, nine bishops, the Archbishop of Paris Antoine de Noailles at their head, refused to accept *Unigenitus* without important clarifications from the papacy. Now according to the Gallican articles of 1682, the parlement could legitimately argue—and it did so argue—that this bull had not received the free and unanimous consent of the Gallican clergy, that in consequence the bull had not become a law of the Church, and that the parlement for its part could not possibly register it as a law of the State. Under severe pressure the parlement nonetheless registered the bull with significant modifications, but it was clear when the "Sun King" died in 1715 that it persisted in regarding the registration as forced, contrary to the "fundamental laws of the realm," and therefore invalid.[37]

---

canism, which emphasized the independence of the Gallican clergy from Rome and the superiority of Church councils over the papacy: a royal Gallicanism, which stressed the monarchy's absolute independence and undivided authority in all temporal affairs; and a parliamentary Gallicanism, which tended to assert the State's control over all aspects of ecclesiastical affairs except those which were purely and indisputably doctrinal. See Edmond Préclin, *Les Jansénistes du XVIIIe siècle et la constitution civile du clérgé: Le Développement du richérisme, sa propagation dans le bas clergé, 1713–1791* (Paris, 1929), pp. 8–11; and Philippe Godard, *La Querelle des refus de sacrements, 1730–1765* (Paris, 1937), pp. 1–18. In practice, however, the various Gallicanisms usually overlapped and are only theoretically distinguishable. On the origins of parliamentary Gallicanism, see Shennan, *The Parlement of Paris,* pp. 166–87. On the circumstances surrounding the declaration of the Gallican liberties in 1685, see Jean Orcibal, *Louis XIV contre Innocent XI: Les Appels au futur concile de 1688 et l'opinion française* (Paris, 1949).

37. Augustin Gazier, *Fragment inédit des mémoires du Chancelier Daguesseau* (Paris, 1920). See also Jacques Parguez, *La Bulle Unigénitus et le Jansénisme politique* (Paris, 1936), pp. 29–50. Parguez's work, together with Léon Séché, *Les Derniers Jansénistes depuis la ruine de Port-Royal jusqu'à nos jours* (Paris, 1891); Léon Cahen, *Les Querelles religieuses et parlementaires sous Louis XV* (Paris, 1913); Gazier, *Histoire générale;* Georges Hardy, *Le Cardinal de Fleury et le mouvement janséniste* (Paris, 1925); Préclin, *Les Jansénistes du XVIIIe siècle;* Jean Carreyre, *Le Jansénisme durant la Régence* (3 vols. Louvain, 1929–33); Godard, *La Querelle des*

Subsequent attempts in 1720 and 1730 to gain the parlement's free registration of the bull ultimately foundered, like the first, upon the rock of unalterable parliamentary hostility and its impeccable legal position. On the other hand, the parlement acquired means to protest the enforcement of the bull when in 1715 it regained the right to remonstrate in return for authorizing a change in Louis XIV's will in favor of the regency of the duc d'Orléans. Eloquently encouraged, moreover, by such sincere Jansenists as the abbé Pucelle within its ranks, the parlement of Paris became from 1715 onward a persistent if not altogether effective protector of Jansenists within its jurisdiction. In 1718, for example, it refused to accept the papal letters *Pastoralis officii*, which excommunicated all French ecclesiastics, some three thousand "appellants," as they were called, who during the previous year had appealed the bull *Unigenitus* to a future ecumenical council. In 1727, again, it did what little it could for one of these appellants, the Bishop of Senez, when the irregular provincial council of Embrun deprived him of his episcopal see.[38] And when in 1749 the zealously Molinist Archbishop of Paris Christophe de Beaumont adopted the "ultimate solution" of depriving all dying persons suspected of Jansenism of the last sacraments unless they could produce a *billet de confession* proving that they had been confessed by an orthodox priest, the parlement of Paris discussed, remonstrated, refused to administer justice, sustained exile at Bourges, dragooned Jansenist priests from diverse parishes to administer the sacraments in others, fined and imprisoned priests who cooperated with the Archbishop of Paris—in short, did everything within its power to protect the disconsolate and expiring appellants. All this, moreover, the parlement did on the official grounds that the bull *Unigenitus* had not become a law of either Church or State and that no one could therefore be prosecuted on its account.[39]

But in return for such important services, these indispensable parliamentary "friends on the outside" exacted a political price from the Jansenists: loyalty to parliamentary Gallicanism. The original Jansenists were so far from being Gallican that Saint-Cyran and Jansenius himself opposed Richelieu's dynastic policies during the Thirty Years' War beneath the standard of the militant Hapsburg and ultramontane Counter-Reformation, and as late as 1682 Arnauld, Quesnel, and others sided with the papacy against Louis XIV in the very controversy which occasioned the French Church's declaration of the liberties of the Gallican clergy. Yet by 1717 hundreds of Jansenist ecclesiastics were appealing the "badly informed pope" Clement XI's condemnation of Quesnel's book to a general Church council whose authority they held to be superior to

refus de sacrements; and Taveneaux, *Jansénisme et politique*—all constitute the best general, as opposed to regional, studies on 18th-century "political" Jansenism.

38. On these conflicts see Parguez, *La Bulle Unigénitus*, pp. 51–88.

39. Godard, *La Querelle des refus de sacrements*, pp. 61–134.

that of the papacy;[40] by 1728 the Jansenist Bishop of Montpellier, Joachim Colbert, was telling the king that since the bull *Unigenitus*, "Gallican is the same thing as that which is called Jansenist";[41] by 1731 the Jesuit Dominique Colonia was asserting that refusal to recognize the Church's infallibility except in a general council was an infallible mark of a Jansenist;[42] and by 1753 Jansenists were zealously justifying the parlement of Paris's interference in the administration of the sacraments on the basis, again, of the Gallican liberties of 1682.[43]

Not, of course, that the Jansenists' progressive conversion to Gallicanism is solely attributable to their gratitude to the parlement of Paris. However mistaken Louis XIV might have been about the Jansenists' actual complicity in the Fronde, his more general suspicions of "republicanism" on their part were valid to the extent that, from the very outset, Jansenists preferred the relatively loose association of individuals at Port-Royal to the more monarchical structure of most monastic orders and insisted upon the inviolate rights of the individual conscience in the face of royal decrees to the contrary. Moreover, from the closing decades of the seventeenth century—and in proportion, it might be added, as Jansenism found refuge among the lower ranks of the clergy—these Jansenist "republican" proclivities found ecclesiastical expression in the adoption of the theses of Edmond Richer, elected Syndic of the Sorbonne in 1608, who maintained not only that the entire Church assembled in council was superior to the papacy but that the spiritual authority of the simple parish priests, direct successors, he thought, of the seventy-two disciples commissioned by Christ to preach the Gospel, was equal in substance to that of the bishops. Referred to by contemporaries as *Richérisme*, or Richerism, and considerably expanded toward the middle of the eighteenth century by the Nantese Jansenist curé Nicolas Travers, these doctrines not only became as inseparable from Jansenism as Gallicanism, but went considerably beyond Gallicanism in audacity. For unlike Gallicanism, which favored a papal monarchy severely restrained by a kind of episcopal aristocracy, Richerism envisioned the Church as something of a clerical democracy, with bishops distinguished from simple priests only for purposes of administrative convenience.[44]

The collusion between Jansenists and the parlement of Paris, the force of "republican" tendencies within Jansenism—in short, reasons of both external

40. Carreyre, *Le Jansénisme durant la Régence*, Vol, 1. pp. 141–68.

41. Valentin Durand, *Le Jansénisme au XVIIIᵉ siècle et Joachim Colbert, évêque de Montpellier, 1696–1738* (Toulouse, 1907), pp. 225–26.

42. Dominique de Colonia, *Bibliothèque janséniste, ou Catalogue alphabétique des principaux livres jansénistes, ou suspects de Jansénisme, qui ont paru depuis la naissance de cette hérésie* (2d ed. 1731), p. 12.

43. See Gabriel-Nicolas Maultrot and Claude Mey, *Apologie de tous les jugements rendus par les tribunaux séculiers en France contre le schisme* (1752), passim.

44. Préclin, *Les Jansénistes du XVIIIᵉ siècle*, passim, but esp. pp. 151–62.

circumstance and internal proclivity—soon drove the Jansenists to extend their conception of ecclesiastical government to the State and to defend the parlement of Paris's most extravagant claims concerning its place in the French "constitution." These claims were of course invented neither by Jansenism nor by the eighteenth century. They had been first put forward during the Fronde of the seventeenth century, when certain partisans of the parlement of Paris asserted that the parlement, as the direct successor of the Merovingian assemblies held every March between the king and his Frankish subjects, was as essential to the State as the monarchy itself, and whose unforced registration of royal edicts and declarations was indispensable to the legislative process.[45] What was new to the eighteenth century was that numerous Jansenists took up these parliamentary claims, in some instances expanded them, and altogether made them so much a part of Jansenism's general political outlook that in July 1752 the lawyer Barbier could remark that "all those of the Jansenist party are a little republican" because they "concede . . . full power to the Parlement."[46]

Though long implicit in the Jansenists' refusal to recognize the bull *Unigenitus* as a law of State, the parliamentary conception of the French monarchy first clearly surfaced in Jansenist political thought during the mid-century holocaust occasioned by the refusal of the sacraments to Jansenists. In 1754 the Jansenist abbé Pierre Barral, in a pamphlet entitled *Manuel des souverains*, equated the English Parliament with the French parlement, severely censured King James I for having attempted to tax the English people without the consent of the Parliament, and insisted that the registration of edicts and declarations by the parlement of Paris, far from being a "vain ceremony," was a "part of the forms of the State, inseparable from the legitimate usage of legislation."[47] The previous year, in 1753, the Jansenist legists Gabriel-Nicolas Maultrot and Claude Mey asserted in their *Apologie de tous les jugements rendus par les tribunaux séculiers en France contre le schisme* that the parlement was the legitimate voice of the wishes of the people,[48] and in the same year the Jansenist lawyer Louis-Adrien Le Paige published the first volume of his *Lettres historiques sur les fonctions essentielles du parlement; sur le droit des pairs, et sur les loix fondamentales du royaume,* in which he reunited in a single work all that the parliamentary pamphleteers of the Fronde had said on the subject, together with some improvements of his own. To believe Le Paige, the parlement of Paris was the "successor" and

45. On parliamentary constitutional theory during the Fronde, see Paul Rice Doolin, *The Fronde* (Cambridge, Mass., 1935). For 18th-century parliamentary pretensions, see Roger Bickart, *Les Parlements et la notion de souveraineté nationale au XVIIIe siècle* (Paris, 1932).
46. E.-J.-F. Barbier, *Chronique de la Régence et du règne de Louis XV, ou Journal de Barbier, 1718–1763,* ed. Charpentier (8 vols. Paris, 1866), Vol. 5, p. 253. Henceforth cited as *Journal.*
47. Pierre Barral, *Manuel des souverains* (1754), p. 171.
48. Maultrot and Mey, *Apologie,* passim.

"representative" of the Merovingian assemblies at the Champ de Mars; the king's obligation to consult with the parlement at every turn was one of the "fundamental laws" of the realm; the proposition that "no edict has the force of law unless . . . examined and registered at the Parlement" was another such law; and the parlement's essential function was to constitute "the reciprocal tie between the Sovereign and the Subjects," which, if broken, brought "the most horrible confusion" and "despotism" in its train.[49]

This Jansenist campaign in favor of the parlement came in the midst of a general brawl between the royal council and a parlement of Paris increasingly in league with diverse provincial parlements, a brawl which lasted with varying degrees of intensity from the controller-general Machault's attempt to levy a twentieth-tax, or *vingtième*, on the entire population in 1749 until the chancellor Maupeou's suppression of the parlements in 1771.[50] The issues in this contest were diverse—royal taxation, the boundaries of episcopal jurisdiction, the administration of the sacraments, supposed or real threats to the Gallican liberties, the parlements' right to proceed against peers and crown officers— but on all of them an increasingly articulate public opinion sided quite passionately with the parlement of Paris. And both because some of these issues directly concerned Jansenism and because most Jansenists publicly supported the parlement in all its quarrels with the king—even on matters of taxation—it was to be expected that Jansenism would share the popularity of the parlement of Paris.[51] Testimony to this effect certainly abounds. "But it must be avowed, all Paris is Jansenist," exclaimed Barbier in his journal in May 1752, and he never tired of repeating that "the whole public" was "in general . . . Jansenist."[52] The marquis d'Argenson, who devoted much of his leisure to observing the public scene after his dismissal as secretary of foreign affairs in 1745, was equally insistent that Jansenism was becoming the "universal religion of the realm," and even Voltaire, hardly a friend of Jansenism, conceded in his *Histoire du*

49. Louis-Adrien Le Paige, *Lettres historiques sur les fonctions essentielles du parlement, sur les droits des pairs, et sur les loix fondamentales du royaume* (2 vols. Amsterdam, 1753–54). On the parlement as successor and representative of Merovingian assemblies, see Vol. 1, p. 12; for the king's obligation to consult with the parlement, Vol. 1, pp. 11–12; on the necessity of registration, Vol. 1, pp. 85–86; on the parlement as link between king and subjects, Vol. 2, p. 132; on confusion and despotism, Vol. 1, pp. 224, 252; Vol. 2, p. 133.

50. On these quarrels in Paris, see Félix Rocquain, *L'Esprit révolutionnaire avant la Révolution, 1715–1789* (Paris, 1878); Jules Flammermont, *Le Chancellier Maupeou et ses parlements* (Paris, 1883); Cahen, *Les Querelles religieuses et parlementaires*; and Légier Desgranges, *Madame de Moysan et l'extravagante affaire de l'hôpital générale, 1749–1758* (Paris, 1954).

51. Jansenism as a popular party of political dissent has so far received scant scholarly attention, but it is recognized as such by Ford, in *Robe and Sword*, pp. 89–104; by Tavenaux, in *Jansénisme et politique*, pp. 41–42; and by Rocquain, in a much older study, *L'Esprit révolutionnaire avant la Révolution*, passim.

52. Barbier, *Journal*, Vol. 5, p. 221; Vol. 6, p. 145.

parlement de Paris that "France was entirely Jansenist, except for the Jesuits and the bishops of the Roman party."[53]

Now obviously none of these witnesses meant to assert that all of France or Paris was morally austere and held to the doctrines of efficacious grace and the predestination of the elect. What in effect they were saying was not unlike what D'Argenson observed in 1754, that it was no longer a battle of Jansenists against Molinists, but one of "nationals" against "sacerdotals," of "Frenchmen" against the "partisans of the inquisition and superstition and royal authority perverted by intrigue." With the progressive accretions of Gallicanism, Richerism, and parliamentary constitutional pretensions, Jansenism had come to represent to most Frenchmen, not an Augustinian theology or an austere moral attitude, but any kind of opposition to papal or "Italian" intrusion into France's internal affairs represented by the bull *Unigenitus*; to all bishops who, like Christophe de Beaumont, took the side of the papacy and attempted to enforce the bull *Unigenitus* by means of *billets de confession* and rigged provincial synods like that at Embrun; in some measure to episcopal authority and ecclesiastical opulence as such; and to royal authority itself inasmuch as it seconded the efforts of ultramontane bishops, attempted, like them, to enforce *Unigenitus* as a law of Church and State, and not only refused to heed the parlement's "respectful remonstrances" on the subject but periodically exiled and imprisoned its magistrates with judicially irregular *lettres de cachet*. The word *Jansenist* therefore came increasingly to refer to a kind of vague political front (the phrase *parti janséniste* was commonly employed by contemporaries) uniting all good Frenchmen (the phrase "every good Frenchman" was forever on the lips of the editor of the *Nouvelles Ecclésiastiques*) against the foreign, sacerdotal influences which were corrupting both court and episcopacy, and whose adherents, as one Jesuit put it, spoke the "jargon of patriotism mixed with the language of rebellion."[54]

This state of affairs was reflected in the confusion that contemporaries increasingly experienced when they employed the words *Jansenist* and *Jansenism*. Those at least who thought about the matter no longer felt at all certain about what they meant by these words. After writing with confident ambiguity about Jansenists for years, the marquis d'Argenson began in 1752 to put order in his vocabulary by distinguishing between "Jansenists by profession" and "what

53. D'Argenson, *Journal et mémoires*, Vol. 7, p. 270; Voltaire, *Histoire du parlement de Paris*, in *Œuvres complètes*, Vol. 30, p. 372.

54. Cerutti, *Apologie de l'institut des Jésuites*, Vol. 1, p. 10. The above characterization of mid-18th-century Jansenism does not of course hold equally true for all parts of France. René Taveneaux, for example, has recently demonstrated, in his exhaustive thesis *Le Jansénisme en Lorraine, 1640–1789* (Paris, 1960), that in Lorraine the Jansenist movement was little affected by the Parisian parliamentary quarrels and retained much of the spirit of Port-Royal and 17th-century Jansenism.

they call Jansenists these days." By the former he meant real, believing Jansenists who "are intolerant with a vengeance," who "hate . . . suspect," and "judge with temerity everyone who they imagine believes less than they"; by the latter, he meant those who opposed "the counsels of clemency and reason" to the Jesuitical and ultramontane persecution of the parlement and the poeple.[55] Barbier, for his part, decided after much reflection that Robert François Damiens, who attempted to assassinate Louis XV in 1757, was a "parliamentary fanatic rather than a Jansenist, for this appellation," he reasoned, "arose to distinguish a sect."[56] The distinction could indeed be drawn, but the fact that Barbier felt obliged to make it indicates to what extent the terms *Jansenist* and *parlementaire* had become confounded.

Now early Jansenists had quite frankly distinguished between themselves and their somewhat less than saintly "friends on the outside." But in sharp contrast to the spiritual integrity of seventeenth-century Jansenists, the quasi-official voice of their eighteenth-century descendants, the *Nouvelles Ecclésiastiques*, welcomed all such attempts at clarification with the proverbial douse of cold water. When in 1760 the anonymous author of a pamphlet entitled *Projet pour les assemblées provinciales* suggested that besides "believing Jansenists" (*Jansénistes de croyance*), who were "far fewer in number than people imagine," there was an infinity of "Jansenists in name, libertines in spirit and heart," who strove to "relieve themselves of the sacred weight of episcopal and royal authority which hampers them," the editor of the *Nouvelles Ecclésiastiques* could find only the words *calumnious, temerarious, inexcusable*, and *insane* sufficiently appropriate to describe the idea.[57] But perhaps he could hardly have responded otherwise. The *parti janséniste* needed whatever allies it could muster, certainly including "Jansenists in name" only, for the approaching and final reckoning with the Jesuits.

"For more than a century and a half," announced the *Nouvelles Ecclésiastiques* on May 1, 1759, "there has been an open and uninterrupted war between the Jesuits on the one side, and on the other the *messieurs* of Port-Royal, the appellants, and all those who are called Jansenists."[58] It was also further clear that the *Nouvelles Ecclésiastiques* deemed the decisive battle to be close at hand. For beginning in 1757 the Jansenist press launched an anti-Jesuitical campaign at least as intense and far more sustained than even Pascal's attacks of exactly a

---

55. D'Argenson, *Journal et mémoires*, Vol. 8. For comment on "les Jansénistes de profession," see pp. 110–11; on "ce qu'on appelle aujourd'hui Jansénistes," p. 204; also pp. 181, 202.

56. Barbier, *Journal*, Vol. 6, pp. 508–09.

57. *Nouvelles Ecclésiastiques* (April 9, 1760), pp. 74–75.

58. Ibid. (May 1, 1759), p. 75.

century before. During this period the *Nouvelles Ecclésiastiques* alone accused the Jesuits of Pelagianism, Nestorianism, Arianism, and Socinianism, of swindling unsuspecting citizens, carrying on commerce, amassing enormous riches, and assassinating princes, while the journal's omnipresent correspondents uncovered instances of Jesuitical misbehavior ranging from a Jesuit seminary superior's appearance in a cabaret in Alby to a Jesuit ticket-taker's fist fight with a notary in Clermont-Ferrand.[59]

So single-minded was this campaign that it tended to obscure whatever sense the conflict yet possessed, with the result that the term *Jansenism* came increasingly to mean any kind of opposition to the Jesuits. D'Argenson used the word in this sense in 1755 when, referring to a person "reputed a Jansenist," he explained that this meant only that "he is opposed to the Jesuitical persecution."[60] It was precisely this, too, that the anonymous author of *Réflexions d'un Portuguais* asserted in 1759 when he spoke of the "many people who call themselves Jansenists uniquely out of party spirit and . . . hatred for the Jesuits." But the use of the word *Jansenism* to designate simple opposition to the Jesuits was far from unrelated to the Gallican, Richerist, and parliamentary connotations which the term had acquired by the same period. For besides the theological and ethical weapons bequeathed to them by their seventeenth-century predecessors, the Jansenists of the mid-eighteenth century were employing the arms of antipapal Gallicanism, antihierarchical Richerism, and antiroyal parliamentary constitutionalism in their continuing warfare against the Jesuits.

Of the elements new to the Jansenists' hostility toward the Jesuits, that of Gallicanism was by far the oldest and in fact antedated the appearance of Jansenism itself. It was to be expected that Gallican sentiment, which favored conciliar ecclesiastical government to papal supremacy, the temporal independence of kings to papal pretensions of universal authority, and French usages and customs in general to anything which came from "over the mountains," would take particular umbrage at a religious order which swore a special fourth vow of obedience to the papacy, faithfully supported all papal pretensions both spiritual and temporal, and came armed with papal privileges exempting it from all ordinary ecclesiastical and temporal jurisdictions. In fact, no sooner had the Jesuits set foot on French soil after 1540 than the parlement of Paris, the University of Paris, and much of the Gallican clergy raised a cry of protest so loud that it was not until 1563 that the parlement of Paris registered the decision of an assembly of the Gallican clergy at Poissy to receive the Jesuits, and then only as a "society or college" rather than as a "religious order newly established," and on condition that the Jesuits assume some title other than the pretentious "Society of Jesus," remain in subjection to the ordinary ecclesiastical and temporal

59. On the latter two incidents, *ibid.* (July 30, 1760), p. 137; (October 9, 1759), p. 168.
60. D'Argenson, *Journal et mémoires*, Vol. 10, p. 2.

authorities, and renounce the usage of both past and future papal privileges to the contrary.[61]

The Jesuits' subsequent behavior was hardly of a sort to allay Gallican qualms and often seemed to confirm the University of Paris's eloquent lawyer Etienne Pasquier's prediction of 1564 that "no Prince or Potentate" would be able to "assure his state against their assaults."[62] Particularly decisive in this regard were the divisive religious civil wars in France of the late sixteenth century, in which the Jesuits, true to their ultramontane principles, quite consistently supported the Guises' ultra-Catholic League against the monarchy, opposed the accession of the "heretical" Henry IV until the papacy had absolved him, quite generally defended papal claims to temporal authority over kings, and in some instances theoretically justified regicide in the case of heretical princes. Worse yet, certain Jesuits' espousal of the doctrine of regicide lent such plausibility to suspicions that the Jesuits had actually masterminded Jacques Clément's assassination of Henry III that, when on December 4, 1594, a certain Jean Chastel unsuccessfully attempted to assassinate Henry IV, the parlement of Paris immediately seized the occasion to expel the Jesuits from its territorial jurisdiction. Yet despite this setback, the Jesuits obtained Henry IV's permission to return to France in 1603, somehow weathered suspicions that they had assassinated this monarch in 1610, after years of litigation finally gained royal permission to give public instruction in their hôtel de Clermont in Paris in 1618, and, with continued royal support, reached the pinnacle of their prestige and influence under Louis XIV.[63]

When the Jansenist controversy broke over France in the 1640s, it did little immediately to rekindle the flames of an apparently dying anti-Jesuitical Gallicanism. To be sure, the father of the many Jansenist Arnaulds was none other than the lawyer Antoine Arnauld, who gave classic utterance to the Gallican case against the Jesuits in a famous *plaidoyer* on the eve of the Jesuits' expulsion in 1594; indeed, Jansenists later referred to Antoine Arnauld's performance as the "original sin of the Arnauld family," a sin which in Jesuit eyes carried with it Jansenist rather than Molinist consequences. But by the mid-seventeenth century the Jesuits had won the confidence of most of the Gallican clergy; the parlement of Paris, Gallicanism's last and most redoubtable stronghold, could do little under the strict tutelage of Richelieu and Louis XIV; and the Jansenists,

---

61. For the terms of the Jesuits' reception in France, see A.N.; G[8], 589[P]; or E. Piaget, *Histoire de l'établissement des Jésuites en France, 1540–1640* (Leiden, 1893), pp. 26–27.

62. Louis-Adrien Le Paige and Christophe Coudrette, *Histoire générale de la naissance et des progrès de la Compagnie de Jésus en France, et analyse de ses constitutions et privilèges* (Paris, 1761), Vol. 1, p. 127. Henceforth cited as *Histoire générale de la Compagnie de Jésus en France*.

63. The best accounts of the history of the Jesuits in France during the 16th and 17th centuries are Piaget, *Histoire de l'établissement,* and Henri Fouqueray, *Histoire de la compagnie de Jésus en France des origines à la suppression* (Paris, 1910–25).

for their part, took on the Jesuits with exclusively theological weaponry. If not inevitable, however, it was yet to be expected that in proportion as Jansenism progressively allied itself with the Gallican parlements and itself became more generally Gallican, it would sooner or later employ the arms of Gallicanism in its continuing warfare against the Jesuits. "Before there were any Jansenists," one of their polemicists could admit by 1759, "many good Frenchmen sounded the alarm against the Jesuits and predicted that . . . the ultramontane prejudices to which they were endeared would produce some horrible upheaval in the realm." The "Jansenists," he added, "have seized upon the presumptions of the nation; they have not invented them."[64]

No need here to trace this development in any detail; suffice it to say that by 1760 it was already an accomplished fact. In the course of that year alone the *Nouvelles Ecclésiastiques* repeatedly accused the Jesuit Order of aspiring toward a "universal monarchy in the political order" and of having "already assured itself and employed the privilege of escaping from the authority of all the powers established by God, in order to make of its own interest its supreme law and in order to depend upon no one except the will of a single master, himself obliged to subordinate himself to this first supreme interest";[65] another Jansenist pamphleteer reproached the Jesuits for having "a foreigner as founder," for including in their order "more foreigners than Frenchmen," and for being "submissive by the vow of a blind obedience to a General who always resided outside the Realm" and "obliged to defend . . . the chimerical pretensions of the Popes over the temporal of the Kings";[66] and yet another anonymous Jansenist polemicist declared "the doctrine which places the authority of the popes over that of the general council and the princes of the world, which concentrates in the hands of the Sovereign Pontiff all authority both civil and ecclesiastical," and "which makes Kings into the vassals of the Popes" to be "the veritable patrimony of the Jesuits."[67] Short of the expulsion of the order, yet a fourth Jansenist pamphleteer could think of no other solution to the problem than for French Jesuits to isolate themselves from other Jesuits to form a "body called the Gallican Company of Jesus" so that they might "tear themselves away from the slavery which renders them totally dependent upon a man [their general] who is by principle an enemy of our maxims, of our liberties;

64. *Avis d'un militaire à son fils, Jésuite, ou Lettres dans lesquelles on développe les vices de la constitution de la Compagnie de Jésus, qui la rendent également pernicieuse à l'église et à l'état, et fournissent les motifs et les moyens de la détruire* (1760), p. 36.
65. *Nouvelles Ecclésiastiques* (January 9, 1760), p. 3.
66. *Les Jésuites criminels de lèse-majesté, dans la théorie et dans la pratique* (The Hague, 1758), pp. 4–5.
67. *Abrégé chronologique de l'histoire de la société de Jésus . . . pour servir à l'instruction au procès que le public fait aux Jésuites et à la justification des édits du roi de Portugal contre ces pères* (1760), p. 59.

enemy by national prejudice of the independence of our Kings, the sacred right of the Episcopacy and the corporation of our magistracy."[68]

Nor did the Jansenists limit themselves to such general declamations against the Jesuits' ultramontanism. Unsuccessful attempts to assassinate Louis XV on January 5, 1757, and Joseph I, King of Portugal, on September 3, 1758, enabled the Jansenist press to revive the memory of the "furors of the League" and assassinations of Henry III and Henry IV, to recall that the Jesuits "have long been only too legitimately suspected of divers assassinations of sovereign princes," and to transform their Gallican press campaign against the Jesuits into something like a witch hunt.[69] In 1757 the *Nouvelles Ecclésiastiques* made the most of the reprinting in Toulouse of the seventeenth-century German Jesuit Hermann Bausembaum's *Theologia moralis*, which maintained both the papacy's claims to temporal sovereignty over kings and the rights of subjects to assassinate heretical rulers.[70] In the same year the appearance of a condensed version of the seventeenth-century Jesuit Turselin's *Historiae sacrae et profanae*, written, in the words of one polemicist, "during the time of the furor of the League, probably for the League, and infested with the most extravagant ultramontane principles," provided the *Nouvelles Ecclésiastiques* with additional Gallican ammunition.[71] In 1759 the *Nouvelles Ecclésiastiques* devoted numerous issues to villifying a certain père de Dessus-Le-Pont, who at the Jesuit mission at Rennes both used and lauded Busembaum's *Theologia moralis*, and a certain père Mamachi, prefect of the Jesuit college at Rouen, who indiscreetly dictated to his students the words: "It is sometimes fortunate crimes which make heroes." "The reader," commented the *Nouvelles Ecclésiastiques*, "easily senses the full horror of parallel maxims, and particularly amid present circumstances."[72] Early in 1760 the journal even saw sinister significance in the denied request of some Jesuits to preach to and confess a regiment of the French guards stationed at Saint-Omer. "One senses"— or at least the Jansenist editor sensed—"how much Messrs. the Almoner and Officers of the French Guards were well advised not to abandon to the confreres of Busembaum . . . a corps of troops destined by estate to the protection of our Kings."[73]

---

68. *Conversation intéressante dénoncée par un espion de la ladrérie prétendue des Jésuites français, où l'on trouve des faits graves, des reproches fondés, des avis salutaires pour et contre les bons pères Jésuites* (1759), p. 70.

69. *Nouvelles Ecclésiastiques* (October 22, 1760), p. 186.

70. The *Nouvelles Ecclésiastiques* regarded the reprinting of Busembaum's *Theologia moralis* as "proof" that the Jesuits had in fact attempted to assassinate the King of Portugal in 1759 (ibid.).

71. Ibid. (May 7, 1760), p. 89.

72. On le père de Dessus-Le-Pont, ibid. (August 28, 1759), p. 141; on le père Mamachi, ibid. (April 17, 1759), p. 67.

73. Ibid. (January 16, 1760), p. 14.

Examples of this sort could be multiplied indefinitely. What they all add up to is that the Jansenist campaign against the Jesuits in the mid-eighteenth century, like the Jansenist movement in general, possessed a pronounced Gallican character. This is not of course to say that Jansenism altogether ceased to have a theological or religious character, or even that theological considerations ceased to form the basis of Jansenist hostility toward the Jesuits. On the contrary, the same years, 1757 to 1760, during which the Jansenist press intensified its Gallican campaign against the Jesuits, also witnessed a full-scale Jansenist theological offensive against the Jesuit Isaac Berruyer's *Histoire du peuple de Dieu*, in which all the authentic Jansenist themes—the necessity of efficacious grace, the obligation to love God and relate every action to him, the unworthiness of all acts not performed in this spirit—were repeated and reemphasized.[74] And, as before, the bulk of the *Nouvelles Ecclésiastiques'* pages continued to be concerned basically with theological and ecclesiastical issues. Yet if one is to believe the journal itself, the political portion of its quarrel with the Jesuits was just as, if not more, important than the theological. "Just as they [the Jesuits] have a universal political design," explained the editor, "so also they have a universal religious design; but the latter," he significantly added, "has received its form from the former, and has been exactly tailored to it."[75]

This "universal political design," this aspiration toward a "universal monarchy" with which the Jansenists increasingly reproached the Jesuits, what was it exactly? If the accusation amounted to nothing more than that the Jesuits professed ultramontane principles, were therefore against the Gallican articles of 1682, and had sometimes taught and perhaps even practiced the doctrine of regicide, there was at least nothing original about the Jansenists' latter day polemics against the Jesuits. This much the Jansenists not only conceded but, placing small stock in originality anyway, were not above boasting about the hoary ancestry of some of their anti-Jesuitical observations. But no, their disclaimers notwithstanding, the Jansenists, who in the 1760s finally destroyed the Jesuits in France, reached beyond the armory of Gallicanism and employed the more recently acquired ammunition of Richerism and parliamentary political theory to make a new—perhaps the only new—charge against the Jesuits, the charge of despotism.

Exactly where and when the charge of despotism was first leveled against the Jesuits in France is extremely difficult, if not impossible, to determine with certainty. It first seems to have appeared in France in 1758 when an anonymous-

---

74. See esp. ibid. (March 19, 1760), which was an expanded, 16-page issue devoted to the Bishop of Soisson's *Mandement et instruction pastorale* . . . (Paris, 1759) against Berruyer's book. It was common knowledge that the Jansenist abbé Gourlin, the bishop's theological consultant, had written the pastoral instruction.

75. *Nouvelles Ecclésiastiques* (January 1, 1759), p. 2.

ly written polemic entitled *Les Jésuites criminels de lèse-majesté, dans la théorie et dans la pratique* complained about the "despotism of the General of the Jesuits over those of his Order."[76] But it was not until the intrepid Jansenist polemicists Christophe Coudrette and Louis Adrien Le Paige published their four-volume *Histoire général de la naissance et des progrès de la compagnie de Jésus en France* in 1761 that the accusation of despotism assumed coherent form and acquired great significance. Quite accurately described by the *Nouvelles Ecclésiastiques* in 1764, after the expulsion of the Jesuits from France, as "the germ of everything which has been accomplished during the last four years against the famous society," this book based its case against the Jesuits not only upon their behavior and doctrines but upon the "despotic" structure of their society itself.[77] Unlike most other monastic orders—so ran the argument—the individual Jesuit establishments or houses administered or decided upon nothing democratically or "capitularly"; on the contrary, the Jesuit Order's constitutions vested "the totality of authority" in the "sole hand" of their general, who, resident at Rome, possessed unregulated power over the disposition of the order's property and the personal fate and even the opinions of its members.[78] For his part, the individual Jesuit vowed a "blind obedience" in all things to his general and was hence "really a slave in respect to the General; a blind instrument of all his wishes, servilely sworn to everything which it pleases him to command."[79] Thus structured, the Jesuit Order, Le Paige and Coudrette concluded, "exclusively inclines to arrogate itself into a monarchy or rather a universal despotism; to concentrate everything within itself, to overturn everything capable of obstructing it, to render itself the sovereign and despotic arbiter of all the dignities and riches of the Christian world; to produce, finally, all the evils in the Catholic Universe which we have actually seen arise during the past two centuries."[80]

In other words, Coudrette and Le Paige accused the Jesuit Order not only of being despotically structured but of aspiring to govern despotically, if indirectly, all of Christendom—indeed, the entire world. Without doubt an extravagant accusation! Yet it convinced many *parlementaires* who, during precisely the same period, were rather loudly accusing the government of Louis XV of despotism because it sometimes exiled the parlement's magistrates, refused to hear their remonstrances, and seemed to prefer the advice of the Archbishop of Paris and the Jesuit confessors and preachers at court, who in

76. *Les Jésuites criminels de lèse-majesté*, p. 63.
77. *Nouvelles Ecclésiastiques* (August 20, 1764), p. 135.
78. Le Paige and Coudrette, *Histoire générale de la Compagnie de Jésus en France*, Vol. 3, p. 294; Vol. 4, pp. 28–29, 48.
79. Ibid., Vol. 4, pp. 58, 73.
80. Ibid., Vol. 3, p. 225.

turn were hostile to the parlement because of its protection of Jansenists and opposition to the bull *Unigenitus*. To an extent, therefore, Jansenism's accusation of despotism against the Jesuits represented a transferal of parliamentary charges against the government of Louis XV to the Jesuits, who were increasingly considered responsible for its actions. But at the same time the Jansenists' charge of despotism represented an application of their Richerist conception of ecclesiastical government to the structure of monastic orders, just as their parliamentary conception of the French constitution represented a transferal of Richerism to the secular State. "Jesus Christ, in establishing his Church," argued Coudrette and Le Paige, "expressly excluded all domination from within it. He declared that this type of government belonged only to the kings of the world. Far from establishing a monarchy, he wished that all should be decided by assemblies and lay councils, so that by reciprocally communicating the light, the authority remained common. All the religious orders, in formulating their rules—and here the authors explicitly applied their Richerism to the monastic order—"have fought to approximate the spirit of government established by Jesus Christ for his Church," except, of course, the Jesuits, whose constitutions were "dictated by an immoderate ambition, not only to establish within the society an absolute monarchy, but to elevate the society into a monarchy over all the universe, by enslaving to itself all other authority."[81]

In order, however, to savor the full significance of the Jansenists' accusation of despotism against the Jesuits in 1760, one must recall that back in the days of Louis XIV the Jesuits had accused the Jansenists of being "republican" and had been instrumental in convincing the Sun King of the same. Indeed, in a secret memoir delivered to Louis XIV his Jesuit confessor, Le Tellier, argued that the Oratory, at that time a notoriously Jansenist order, ought to be dissolved because they "are always in favor of the judgments of assembled people, everything which has the air of a republic enchants them; everything which emanates from the authority of single person displeases them." The Jesuits, he further explained, "are perfectly acquainted with the politics of kings, they relate everything to royal authority," and are "very necessary in a monarchical state, but are bad republicans," whereas the Oratorians are "very knowledgeable concerning the politics of the people, they relate everything to the people," and are "excellent personages in a republic, but are bad subjects of kings."[82] Though no document clearly attests to it, it is difficult to believe that the Jansenists, who generally remembered so much, were not explicitly conscious of this background when they decided, around 1760, to call the Jesuits "despotic." In any case the wheel had come full circle; the day of reckoning had dawned.

81. Ibid., Vol. 1, pp. 17–18.
82. Gazier, *Histoire générale*, Vol. 1, pp. 325–26.

2. The Parti Janséniste *within the* Parlement *of Paris*

WORDS ALONE WERE POWERLESS AGAINST THE JESUITS. HAD it been otherwise, the *bons mots* of Pascal would surely have dislodged them a hundred years earlier. Firmly entrenched behind the dikes of royal and ecclesiastical protection, the Jesuits could regard with relative sanguinity the verbal escalation of the Jansenist war against them. "The suppression and total destruction of the Society of Jesus," a Jesuit sarcastically observed in 1759, "is one of the most useful projects the human mind has ever conceived in the interest of civil society." But the accomplishment of this project, he said, would demand not "fabulous histories, crude invectives and burlesque pieces," but "solid and reasoned factums, authentic and reliable documents and judicious memorials beyond dispute." Since, among the enemies of the Jesuits, "the most eager for their prosecution are the Jansenists . . . it is therefore to them," he added, "that I address these remarks which I have permitted myself to make about their brochures, so that by correcting the enormous mistakes which disfigure them they can give them the perfection essentially required by the importance of the affair, the sagacity of their party and the inflexible equity of their magistrates."[1]

We must go a step farther than this anonymous Jesuit. Far more necessary to the Jansenist cause than "solid and reasoned factums" or "authentic and reliable documents" was the sympathy, if not the "inflexible equity," of the magistrates and lawyers of the parlement of Paris. Without their active cooperation, the Jansenists could never have destroyed the Jesuits. But the fact of cooperation between the Jansenists and the parlement of Paris in the affair of the Jesuits—the fact, in short, that the parlement of Paris, not some officially Jansenist organization, promulgated the definitive decree dissolving the Company of Jesus—raises the question of the nature of the connection between Jansenism and the parlement of Paris, a problem which Professor Franklin Ford has described as "one of the most difficult . . . in any analysis of this period."[2] Whether difficult or not, however, the problem is unavoidable, and it is hence best to face it squarely.

1. *Additions aux Motifs pressants et déterminants d'anéantir la société des Jésuites* (1759), pp. iii–vi.
2. Ford, *Robe and Sword*, p. 87.

For the period between 1715 and 1771—the period, that is, which covers the expulsion of the Jesuits—the question of Jansenism's relation to the parlement of Paris has been approached in two apparently opposed ways. One of these approaches proceeds somewhat as follows. For the most part, the magistrates of the parlement of Paris were Jansenists or at least sympathetic to Jansenism. But what motivated their attacks on the bull *Unigenitus* and its episcopal defenders were not religious or even theological considerations. The bull *Unigenitus* offended the magistrates, not because it condemned the doctrine of efficacious grace, but rather because it seemed to them a violation of the Gallican principles of 1682. In the bull's ninety-first article, for example, which condemned Quesnel's assertion that an unjust excommunication ought not to prevent one from doing one's duty, the magistrates saw a restatement of the papacy's pre-tended right to dissolve the tie of obedience on the part of subjects to their king. As such, the article violated the Gallican principle that kings were subject to none but God in matters temporal. Similarly, the magistrates contended that the bull *Unigenitus* could not be regarded as a law of either the Church or the State because the French bishops had failed, in 1713, to accept the bull unanimously, and the parlement of Paris had registered it only with significant modifications. To enforce the bull as a law of Church and State was therefore, in the opinion of the magistrates, a violation of another Gallican principle, that which required that all papal documents be both accepted by the French bishops and registered purely and simply by the parlement of Paris before they became binding in France. The magistrates' Gallican objections to the bull also explain their op-position to the episcopacy's attempt, in the 1750s, to refuse the last sacraments to all dying Jansenists; for this episcopal campaign based itself on the premise that *Unigenitus* was a law of Church and State, a premise the magistrates were un-willing to accept. Parliamentary Gallicanism, moreover, similarly accounts for the magistrates' hostility toward the Jesuits, because the Jesuits, champions of the papacy's most extravagant claims to temporal authority, were the self-declared enemies of the Gallican articles of 1682. The motive, then, which drove the magistrates into opposition to the bull *Unigenitus*, the episcopacy, and the Jesuits was entirely Gallican or political in nature, and the so-called Jansenism of the eighteenth century, a mere shadow of its former Port-Royalist self, was therefore a purely political phenomenon.[3]

Based on much the same evidence, the other estimate of Jansenism's relation to the parlement of Paris can be stated more briefly. This approach proceeds along the following general lines. Jansenism, it holds, whether of the seventeenth or eighteenth century, was a purely religious and theological movement. Against the rights of nature Jansenism consistently pitted the sovereign power of

3. See, for example, Parguez, *La Bulle Unigénitus et le Jansénisme politique*, p. 28.

grace; to the notion of man's free will it opposed his absolute dependence on God; and against the idea of man's partial innocence it asserted his absolute corruption. In contrast, the force which dictated the magistrates' stance in the religious quarrels of the eighteenth century was entirely political in character. It was in defense of the Gallican principles of 1682, not the doctrine of efficacious grace, that the magistrates opposed the bull *Unigenitus*, the refusal of sacraments to Jansenists, and the Company of Jesus. Though the magistrates, for example, often came to the defense of dying Jansenists deprived of the last sacraments, they did not themselves suffer refusal of sacraments, the litmus test of Jansenism. In reality, therefore, Jansenism and the parlement of Paris had little to do with each other. The magistrates were not Jansenists, and the Jansenists, though not unhappy to see the Jesuits smitten, had themselves no hand in their destruction.[4]

On the surface these two approaches seem diametrically opposed. The first begins with the assumption that the magistrates were in some sense Jansenists, and then concludes from the basically political nature of parliamentary proceedings that eighteenth-century Jansenism was primarily a political phenomenon. The second approach begins by defining eighteenth-century Jansenism as a purely religious and theological movement, and then concludes, again from the primarily political activity of the parlements, that Jansenists and the parlements had nothing to do with each other. Now without subjecting either argument to logical scrutiny, it may be simply observed that the conflict between them is more apparent than real. Both approaches, for example, assume that Jansenism, either properly or originally defined, was a purely religious and theological movement. Again, both approaches agree that the eighteenth-century phenomenon in question, whether called Jansenism, belligerent Gallicanism, or whatever, was primarily political in nature. Finally, both approaches agree that no magistrates were sincere Jansenists in a religious or theological sense, or that if some of them were, they exercised no appreciable influence on parliamentary behavior. A successful challenge to these three assumptions would reveal Jansenism, on the one hand, as both a political and a religious movement, and the magistrates, on the other, as not only good Gallicans but in some instances sincere Jansenists as well. If tenable, such a conclusion would have at least the value of transferring some of the existing confusion from the historiographical scene to the historical scene itself, where, if it must exist at all, it more properly belongs.

The first assumption common to the two approaches—that Jansenism properly speaking was a purely religious and theological movement—is of a type which immediately excites a certain skepticism. For only a nodding acquain-

---

4. See Bien, *The Calas Affair*, p. 61; and Gazier, *Histoire générale*, Vol. 1, pp. 100–06.

tance with the history of religious reform movements within Christendom would seem to indicate that it is easier for the biblical camel to go through the eye of a needle than for a religious movement, however oriented toward the kingdom of heaven at the outset, to remain forever aloof from the affairs of this world. Jansenism, as we have already seen, was no exception to this general rule. Even Jansenism's founders were by no means unanimous in their condemnation of mundane engagement. In opposition to those who, like Martin de Barcos and Pascal himself, anathemized all political engagement on the part of the Christian, the Jansenist "centrists" Antoine Arnauld and Pierre Nicole envisioned the possibility of Christian kings guided by Christian counselors following Christian policies. Arnauld and Nicole, it is true, were unwilling to countenance the further possibility of active political resistance to royal policies which, by their own standards, were manifestly un-Christian. But their spiritual descendants were not so unbending as they. By the middle of the eighteenth century the Jansenist lawyers Nicolas Maultrot, Claude Mey, and Adrien Le Paige, sorely pushed, on the one side, by royal and episcopal persecution of Jansenists, and violently pulled, on the other, by parliamentary opposition to the bull *Unigenitus*, emerged as advocates of the parlement of Paris's most extravagant claims about its role as bulwark against royal despotism. The highly political charge of "despotism," moreover, simultaneously and conspicuously protruded its head above the jaded theological, ethical, and even Gallican mass of Jansenist accusations against the Jesuit Order.[5]

That which defines a movement and that which characterizes it during any given period of its existence are two quite distinct considerations. It is only by their confusion that one can maintain that eighteenth-century Jansenism, or for that matter seventeenth-century Jansenism, remained a purely religious and theological movement. What defined Jansenism was certainly, in theological terms, its vindication of the rights of grace and degradation of those of nature. It is moreover important to insist upon this definition in the face of loose talk about the "political Jansenism" of the eighteenth century, as if Jansenism could ever be meaningfully discussed without reference to the doctrinal stance and religious sensibility by which the movement originally articulated itself. This consideration, however, should not obscure the fact that eighteenth-century Jansenism was in part characterized by a sharp increase in the political thought and activity of its adherents. Conversely, the fact that they engaged in political thought and activity does not mean that they ceased thereby to be Jansenists.

Now the political thought and activity in question can perhaps best be characterized as Gallican. It is moreover upon Gallicanism as a sufficient explanation of the activity of the parlement of Paris during the eighteenth century that the second assumption common to our two approaches—which maintains

5. See above, pp. 25–27, 34–36.

that what has sometimes been called eighteenth-century Jansenism was in reality purely political in nature—ultimately rests its case. Let us, then, test the hypothesis of Gallicanism as a sufficient explanation of parliamentary activity against the period from 1750 and 1758, the period which witnessed the ferocious opposition of the parlement of Paris to the episcopal campaign to exact *billets de confession* from dying Jansenists who demanded the last sacraments.

According to the assumption in question, the magistrates opposed this episcopal project because it was founded on the assumption that the bull *Unigenitus* was a law of both Church and State. This assumption, in turn, the magistrates opposed because the condition of the parlement's preliminary registration of the bull in 1714, that it be freely and unanimously accepted by the French bishops, had never been fulfilled. By resisting, therefore, the Archbishop of Paris Christophe de Beaumont's attempt to deny the last sacraments to all those opposed to the bull *Unigenitus*, the parlement, though incidentally protecting some Jansenists, was essentially defending one of the fundamental liberties of the Gallican Church, that of independently judging papal decisions in matters of faith. That the parlement was defending this Gallican liberty against part of the French episcopacy itself indicates only that the episcopacy, not the parlement of Paris, had become heterodox. The parlement, for its part, was acting within a Gallican tradition which long antedated the appearance of Jansenism and which itself suffices to explain the parlement's hostility toward the exaction of *billets de confession*.

However attractive at first glance, the hypothesis of Gallicanism as an adequate explanation of the parlement's behavior during those eight years encounters difficulty once its behavior is examined more closely. On March 23, 1752, for example, the parlement presented to Louis XV remonstrances protesting his council's annullment of a parliamentary sentence against the already notorious Brother Bouettin, curé of Saint-Etienne-du-Mont, who had refused to administer the last sacraments to an old Jansenist priest named LeMerre. Simply to have drafted remonstrances was, in this instance, entirely consonant with the exigencies of Gallicanism. But was it really necessary, in these same remonstrances, to have described the Jansenist opponents of the bull *Unigenitus* as "saintly priests, who had passed their lives in the laborious functions of the ministry to which they had dedicated themselves, enlightened doctors, yet more commendable for their piety than for their knowledge," and "pious daughters who, exclusively occupied with God and their salvation in the depth of their retreats, live in the most rigorous works of penitence"?[6] To consider another example, it was entirely natural, given the premises of Gallicanism, that

6. "Remontrances du 15 avril 1752," *Remontrances du parlement de Paris au XIIIe siècle*, ed. Jules Flammermont (3 vols. Paris, 1888), Vol. 1, pp. 489–90. For a concise account of the affair which occasioned these remonstrances, see ibid., pp. 482–88.

the parlement should have proceeded in 1756 against the chapter of Orléans for having withheld the sacraments from one of its Jansenist members, a canon named Cougniou, both during his lifetime and at his death. But was it really necessary to have sentenced this chapter to pay twelve hundred livres to Cougniou's parish so that it could hold a "perpetual and annual" service for the "repose of his soul" and erect a conspicuous marble monument bearing his name, rank, date of his death, and an extract from the parlement's sentence?[7] In both these instances—and there are many more—the parlement of Paris seems to have gone considerably above and beyond the call of Gallican duty. In both these instances, too, one detects a certain "enthusiasm," possibly Jansenist in origin, lurking behind the Gallican exterior of the parlement's official pronouncements.

That such Jansenist "enthusiasm," if it existed, would have voluntarily dampened itself beneath the Gallican exterior of the parlement of Paris should not be surprising. It was simply not the business of the parlement of Paris to make theological pronouncements, and Jansenism, of course, could unmistakably articulate itself only in theological terms. As things were, the parlement was precariously sustaining a constant barrage of episcopal accusations of encroaching upon its exclusive rights to spiritual jurisdiction. On the other hand, it was undoubtedly the business of the parlement to protect the Gallican principles of 1682 which denied the papacy indirect authority over the king in matters temporal and direct authority over the episcopacy in decisions of faith. Assuming, then, the existence of real Jansenists among the magistrates of the parlement of Paris, they would quite naturally have sought to protect the interests of Jansenism by means of the only lawful weapons immediately at their disposal: the Gallican principles of 1682. To seek, therefore, among the official pronouncements and acts of the parlement of Paris for unambiguous evidence of Jansenism is to comb, say, the Fourteen Points for unmistakable evidence of Woodrow Wilson's Presbyterianism. And to demonstrate that the magistrates argued in Gallican terms their case against the refusal of sacraments to Jansenists is to say precisely nothing about their personal religious commitments.

Any attempt, obviously, to determine the religious convictions of individual magistrates and thereby examine our third assumption—that during the eighteenth century the parlement of Paris contained either no sincere Jansenists at all or at least none who could noticeably alter the course of parliamentary behavior—requires not only more space but sources far more confidential than the remonstrances and decrees of the parlement of Paris. Unfortunately, this kind of evidence is notoriously sparse. Very few magistrates wrote personal memoirs during the eighteenth century, and of those who witnessed the de-

7. Barbier, *Journal*, Vol. 6, p. 194.

struction of the Jesuits, only Rolland d'Erceville, Durey de Mesnières, Guillaume Lambert, and Robert de Saint-Vincent have left anything of note. Confidential letters and memoranda are sparser still, or in any case very difficult to locate.

One obvious and valuable source, however, is the *Nouvelles Ecclésiastiques,* which was published through most of the eighteenth century. From its inception in 1727 until the Jesuits were definitively suppressed in 1764, the journal often devoted entire issues to the proceedings of the parlement of Paris and lavished its unction or vitriol upon individual magistrates according to its peculiarly Jansenist criteria. From the *Nouvelles Ecclésiastiques* we learn, for example, that the counselor, Rolland de Challerange, owed his "bent for the sciences and affection for the truth" to his former tutor Jean Drouet, a Jansenist priest, and that Guillaume Lambert of the second chamber of inquests was a "young counselor of great promise."[8] Of the *doyen* Jean-Jacques Severt, on the other hand, we learn that he belonged to a Jesuit congregation, and of Chancellor Lamoignon de Malesherbes that he distinguished himself by his "devotion to the Jesuits."[9]

Relying primarily on this type of evidence and confining himself to the period from 1715 to 1771, M. François Bluche has recently attempted to classify the magistrates of the parlement of Paris according to their religious complexions.[10] Among the "active members" of the parlement's *parti janséniste,* Bluche first distinguishes a number of real saints. At the top of this list, of course, is the deacon Paris de Branscourt who sold his charge in the parlement of Paris to dedicate himself to works of mercy and penitence, and whose death in 1727 occasioned a notorious epidemic of Jansenist miracles around his tomb in the cemetery of Saint-Médard. Hard on his heels are the counselors Nicholas Jérome Paris de Branscourt, who was converted by his brother's posthumous miracles, and Carré de Montgeron, whose zeal knew so few bounds that in 1737 he penetrated the king's apartments at Versailles and presented his recently published defense of the miracles of Saint-Médard to Louis XV in person. Rounding out the list of saints, finally, is the celebrated abbé Pucelle, whose eloquent tirades against the bull *Unigenitus* provoked the admiration of his friends and enemies alike.

Bluche next delineates a second group of about twenty-five magistrates within the parlement's *parti janséniste.* Less zealous, perhaps, than the saints, but church-going, tithe-paying members of the *parti janséniste* nonetheless, this

---

8. On Rolland de Challerange, see the *Nouvelles Ecclésiastiques* (June 19, 1745), p. 98. On Lambert, ibid. (April 10, 1751), p. 59.

9. On Severt, ibid. (October 16, 1761), p. 167. On Lamoignon de Malesherbes, ibid. (November 13, 1761), p. 183.

10. Bluche, *Les Magistrats du parlement de Paris au XVIIIe siècle, 1715–1771,* pp. 242–69.

group includes such judges as the counselor-clerk Guillebauld, who was nearly refused the last sacraments at his death in 1732 because of his "sentiments against the Bull"; the counselor Nicolas de Vrévin, one of the "most intrepid defenders" of the "Truth" and "greatest Adversaries" of the bull *Unigenitus*; the president Nicolas Le Clerc de Lesseville, "humble, sweet, of a tender piety and above all very devoted to prayer"; and the counselor Langlois de Resy, who in 1756 died deprived of the last sacraments.[11] Others in this category, according to Bluche, are Louis Alexandre Angran, R. F. Boutin, Ambroise Julien Clément de Feuillet, Le Febvre de Saint-Hilaire, and Rolland de Challerange, who together led the attack on the execution of *billets de confession,* and the abbé Chauvelin, Laverdy de Nizeret, and Robert de Saint-Vincent, who distinguished themselves during the trial of the Jesuits. Lastly, Bluche distinguishes a group which, known among Jansenists as the "friends on the outside" and best represented by magistrates like the attorney general, Guillaume François Joly de Fleury, and President de Murard, occupied the narrow ground between pure Jansenism and pure Gallicanism. Including these Jansenist Gallicans or Gallican Jansenists, the *parti janséniste,* according to Bluche, could muster a force representing nearly a fourth of the parlement's total numerical strength of 250 magistrates. "Nothing more precise," he concludes, than the lawyer Barbier's estimate in 1732 that about 60 magistrates were "infatuated with Jansenism."[12]

However accurate Barbier's estimate in 1732, one is inclined to suspect the method by which Bluche not only substantiates this estimate but applies it to the entire period from 1715 to 1771. Indeed, the method has all the rigor of a rubber band. In the first place, more than half a century's resources in the way of parliamentary Jansenists, both living and dead, are contracted in such a way as to substantiate Barbier's estimate in the year 1732. This estimate, thus substantiated, is in turn expanded so as to apply to any given year within the half-century period from which the resources were originally drawn. Now of the nearly thirty magistrates whom Bluche classifies as pure Jansenists, eight had not yet entered the parlement by the year 1732. And during the period which most interests us, that between 1757 and 1765, when the Jesuits were expelled, only nine of Bluche's Jansenist magistrates remained at their posts. The rest had either died, retired, or left the parlement for royal services of another kind.[13]

11. On Guillebauld, see René Cerveau, *Nécrologe des plus célèbres défenseurs et confesseurs de la vérité du dix-huitième siècle* (2 vols. 1760), Vol. 1, (March 1732), p. 202. On Nicolas de Vrévin, ibid., p. 203; on President de Lesseville, *Nouvelles Ecclésiastiques* (April 6, 1737), p. 53; and on Langlois de Resy, D'Argenson, *Journal et mémoires,* Vol. 9, p. 330. The appelatives I have quoted are different from and, I think, more relevant than those cited by Bluche.

12. Bluche, *Les Magistrats du parlement de Paris,* p. 250; Barbier, *Journal,* Vol. 2, p. 297.

13. These calculations, and others like them, are based on François Bluche, *L'Origine des*

The nine magistrates in question are the presidents Louis Angran and R. F. Boutin, and the counselors Clément de Feuillet, Jean Baptiste Titon, Laverdy, the abbé Chauvelin, Le Febvre de Saint-Hilaire, Rolland de Challerange, and Robert de Saint-Vincent. Can it be said with certainty that all nine were Jansenists? Given Bluche's supporting evidence from the *Nouvelles Ecclésiastiques,* the answer must unfortunately be an emphatic "No!" For what Bluche has done is simply to interpret any complimentary reference to a magistrate in the *Nouvelles Ecclésiastiques* as conclusive evidence of his Jansenism. "Respectable in every sense," "often distinguished by his zeal for the public good" —appositives such as these signify nothing more about the magistrates to whom they were appended than that these magistrates happened to say or do something favorably regarded by the journal. If it were otherwise, the notoriously uncompromising Jansenists would find themselves in the company of strangely compromising bedfellows indeed. To consider a single example, the *Nouvelles Ecclésiastiques* showered much the same kind of praise upon La Chalotais, the attorney general of the parlement of Brittany, when in 1762 he delivered his famous *Compte rendu* against the Jesuit Order.[14] But the Jansenists were no more ignorant than others of the rumor that La Chalotais was a disciple of the encyclopedists and dangerously infected with philosophical ideas.

Did the *Nouvelles Ecclésiastiques* thereby compromise itself? Hardly. For a close examination of its editorial policy reveals that it distributed its praise to individual magistrates according to a precisely defined and rigorously graduated set of criteria. Least zealous, to begin with, were those magistrates who, though not themselves Jansenists, often did or said things favorable to the Jansenist cause. The most they could expect of the *Nouvelles Ecclésiastiques* was to be described on certain occasions as "wise," "judicious," or "zealous," or at least to have some of the opinions they expressed in parlement quoted with obvious approval. And it is to this category of "friends on the outside" that magistrates such as La Chalotais belong. To be next in order of zeal—to be recognized, in other words, as a member in good and regular standing of the *parti janséniste* —the *Nouvelles Ecclésiastiques* demanded the attributes of personal piety and conscientious opposition to the bull *Unigenitus.* The very least the Jansenist magistrate could expect in return was to be noted, like the counselor-clerk Guillebauld, for his "sentiments against the Bull," or be lauded, like President de Lesseville, for his "humble, sweet," and "tender" piety. At the very most, he could expect the *Nouvelles Ecclésiastiques* to commemorate his death with a substantial and unctuous obituary and subsequently to find a place in René Cerveau's *Nécrologe des plus célèbres défenseurs et confesseurs de la vérité du dixhuitième siècle,* eighteenth-century Jansenism's book of martyrs. To qualify as a

---

*magistrats du parlement de Paris au XVIII*e *siècle* (Paris, 1956).

14. *Nouvelles Ecclésiastiques* (May 29, 1762), p. 85.

Jansenist saint, finally, the *Nouvelles Ecclésiastiques* expected a magistrate either to oppose the bull *Unigenitus* with a zeal unknown to others, as did the abbé Pucelle, or to suffer in some personal way for his devotion and convictions, as did Carré de Montgeron by spending much of his life in one royal prison after another. And the saint, too, had his reward. Not only could he be certain of a place in René Cerveau's *Nécrologe,* but he could confidently hope to be an object of veneration from one generation of readers of the *Nouvelles Ecclésiastiques* to another.

If we apply, now, the journal's litmus test for Jansenism to our nine allegedly Jansenist magistrates, we obtain the most discouraging results. For they seem to reveal themselves, not as acid Jansenists, but merely as base Gallicans. Most of them were at one time quoted with obvious approval, and most were on some occasion described as wise, judicious, or zealous. But the *Nouvelles Ecclésiastiques* explicitly recognized none of them for his personal piety and conscientious opposition to the bull *Unigenitus*, and rewarded none of them with an obituary after his death. More discouraging still, the same applies to all of the nearly 250 magistrates in office during the trial of the Jesuits. Those who satisfactorily fulfill the *Nouvelles Ecclésiastiques'* qualifications for Jansenism, such as Guillebauld and Lesseville, belong to the heyday of eighteenth-century Jansenism, when bishops and curés alike were appealing the bull *Unigenitus,* when the abbé Pucelle was overwhelming all of France with his anti-Molinist eloquence, and when the deacon Paris was producing his posthumous miracles in the cemetery of Saint-Médard. But they had all left the scene by 1757.

Must we then conclude that there were no Jansenists in the parlement of Paris during the trial of the Jesuits? The answer must again be in the negative. For the *Nouvelles Ecclésiastiques* itself is fraught with far too many variables for its test of Jansenism to be taken as conclusive in any particular case. However precise and rigorous, the criteria by which the Jansenist journal praised magistrates and others could not have been applied systematically. Assuming that the Jansenists were only half as fallible as they asserted all men to be, we may further assume that their journal either overlooked a number of the faithful or insufficiently appreciated their talents. Moreover, several of the nine suspected Jansenist magistrates could not possibly have received obituaries in the *Nouvelles Ecclésiastiques.* Robert de Saint-Vincent and possibly Louis Alexandre Angran died after the journal had ceased publication, and Laverdy, guillotined by Robespierre in 1793, died at a time and under circumstances that were hardly appropriate for laudatory obituaries.[15] And all nine magistrates, finally, died after the *Nouvelles Ecclésiastiques* had ceased to take an active interest in the affairs of the parlement of Paris, and hence in its personnel.

15. Robert de Saint-Vincent died in 1802. I have been unable to determine the date of Louis Alexandre Angran's death.

Just the same, the admittedly scanty evidence of the *Nouvelles Ecclésiastiques* would seem to indicate that at least two of the nine suspiciously Jansenist magistrates are suspicious indeed. We have already noticed that the journal ascribed Counselor Rolland de Challerange's "bent for the sciences and love for the truth" to the influence of his former tutor, a Jansenist curé named Jean Drouet.[16] That Rolland de Challerange had early been subjected to Jansenist influence, that the word "truth" was generally understood among Jansenists to mean the doctrine of efficacious grace—both considerations point to something more than simple Gallicanism on the part of this magistrate. No comparable reference, on the other hand, exists to honor the memory of Counselor Clément de Feuillet. But the Jansenist journal indicates that his father, the counselor Alexandre Julien Clément, was so zealous in defense of the miracles at the cemetery of Saint-Médard that he distributed portraits of the deacon Paris, counseled all his handicapped friends to seek his intercession, and on May 1, 1735, sustained several blows to the stomach for having attended a service in his memory at Saint-Médard.[17] Add to this the consideration that, like most sectarian movements, Jansenism tended to perpetuate itself within individual families, and Clément de Feuillet, too, becomes suspect. For the same reason, finally, we may legitimately suspect a third counselor unmentioned by Bluche, one Claude Guillaume II Lambert. He himself was once described by the *Nouvelles Ecclésiastiques* as a "young counselor of great promise."[18] But the reason that it attached such exalted hopes to the young Lambert becomes clear only when it is known that the same journal honored his father, the *doyen* of the *grand conseil*, with an obituary which rendered "homage to the virtues of this respectable magistrate, to the great Sentiments of Religion with which he always lived, to his love for the truth."[19]

Beyond these three magistrates, however, the guidance of the *Nouvelles Ecclésiastiques* is impossibly murky. Even with respect to the three, its evidence is inconclusive. To progress any further in our search for magisterial Jansenists in office during the trial of the Jesuits we must therefore turn for help to the memoirs of the counselor, Robert de Saint-Vincent.[20]

Pierre-Augustin-Robert de Saint-Vincent was born in 1725, the son of a

16. *Nouvelles Ecclésiastiques* (June 19, 1745), p. 980.
17. Ibid. (1732), p. 228; (1735), p. 125.
18. Ibid. (April 10, 1751), p. 59.
19. Ibid. (April 3, 1780), p. 56.
20. "Mémoires de Pierre-Augustin-Robert de Saint-Vincent, 1725–1799," in the archives de M. Michel Vinot Préfortaine. A 625-page typewritten copy of these important unpublished recollections was shown me by M. Michel Vinot Préfontaine, to whom I wish here, as well as in the Preface, to express my sincerest gratitude. Those recollections will henceforth be cited as Saint-Vincent, "Mémoires."

counselor in the parlement of Paris. At the age of twenty-three Pierre-Augustin himself entered the parlement of Paris as a counselor in the fifth chamber of inquests. No sooner had he set foot within the Palais de Justice than he became one of the more active members of the parlement's *parti janséniste*. He not only contributed significantly to the composition of the Great Remonstrances of April 9, 1753, against the refusal of sacraments to Jansenists, but helped President Durey de Mesnières to write the Bourges memoirs while in exile in that town from May 1753 to September 1754.[21] Feverishly active, as we shall see, during the trial of the Jesuits in France, Robert de Saint-Vincent was given the honor of drafting, unassisted, the parlement's last significant decree concerning the Company of Jesus, that which in 1766 required its former members either to take an oath condemning the constitutions of their sometime order or to leave France forever.[22] And some five years later, on January 12, 1771, Robert de Saint-Vincent, according to his own estimate, hastened by eight days Chancellor Maupeou's suppression of the parlement of Paris by proposing to the company a resolution which in general condemned Maupeou and more particularly singled him out as an agent of the defunct but vindictive Order of Jesus.[23] Returning to Louis XVI's reconstituted parlement of Paris after four years of exile, he distinguished himself as late as 1787 as a parliamentary champion of Louis XVI's Edict of Toleration for Protestants.[24] Like many of his colleagues, finally, he fled during the French Revolution of 1789 and died an émigré in the German town of Brunswick in 1802.

There can be no doubt that Robert de Saint-Vincent was a Jansenist. Indeed, his memoirs provide us with a unique and precious insight into the religious sensibilities and political instincts which animated eighteenth-century parliamentary Jansenism. Like his colleague and distant relative Rolland de Challerange, Robert de Saint-Vincent was early exposed to Jansenist influence in the person of a Jansenist tutor, in this case his uncle the abbé Nivelle. It was the abbé Nivelle, according to Robert de Saint-Vincent, "who at the baptismal font named me Pierre-Augustin, as if to dedicate me by a special engagement to the efficacious grace of which he was all his life the zealous defender."[25] It was also the abbé Nivelle who not only made certain that the young Pierre-Augustin was sheltered from all the "temptations and seductions of the world,"[26] but later placed his education under the direction of another Jansenist, the "pious

21. Ibid., p. 528. I refer to the *Journal anecdotique sur la vie du Parlement à Bourges* (A.N.: kk, 821).
22. Saint-Vincent, "Mémoires," pp. 378–79.
23. Ibid., pp. 502–03.
24. Ibid., p. 27.
25. Ibid., p. 103. For evidence of Nivelle's Jansenism, see René Cerveau, *Suite du nécrologe des plus célèbres défenseurs et amis de la vérité du XVIIIᵉ siècle* (1767), pp. 64–72.
26. Saint-Vincent, "Mémoires," p. 112.

and virtuous" M. Bon, who guided youths in the "path of piety" in a small pension in the village of Picpus outside Paris.[27] Both men, the abbé Nivelle and Bon, continued to take a special interest in the career of Robert de Saint-Vincent. Bon, for example, arranged Robert de Saint-Vincent's marriage, and the abbé Nivelle persuaded him to enter the magistracy despite his "mediocre fortune." And toward both men Robert de Saint-Vincent maintained a lifelong veneration. As if specifically to repay the abbé Nivelle for having specially dedicated him at the baptismal font to the cause of efficacious grace, Robert de Saint-Vincent wrote of his former tutor in his memoirs that "nothing more surely proves efficacious grace and gratuitous predestination than to see a venerable saint emerge from a family so divided as that of Nivelle, but God when he wishes makes Peters even of the sons of Abraham." With Bon, too, Robert de Saint-Vincent remained on the best of terms, even though his parents somewhat resented the "varnish of Jansenist devotion," always prejudicial to one's "establishment in the world," which the tutor had imputed to their son.[28]

The efforts of Nivelle and Bon were not in vain. His "varnish of Jansenist devotion" and "mediocre fortune" notwithstanding, Robert de Saint-Vincent successfully established himself in the parlement of Paris, where he unashamedly held high the banner of Port-Royal until the end of his parliamentary career. The memory of Port-Royal, of course, he revered. It was "with regret," he confessed in his memoirs, that he was unable to uncover any connections between his grandfather, a lawyer in the parlement of Paris from 1660 to 1727, and the celebrated writers of Port-Royal. His only consolation, he said, was the thought that he detected a "trait of resemblance" between his grandfather's style and that of Pascal. But Robert de Saint-Vincent more than compensated for his poverty in ancestral ties with Port-Royal by rigorously modeling himself after the ideals for which the abbey stood. As his interpretation of the career of the abbé Nivelle shows, he was not ashamed of the gospel of efficacious grace and gratuitous predestination. On the contrary, the most disparate kinds of events reconfirmed these doctrines in his mind. In the parlement's decree of April 18, 1752, for example, which forbade priests to refuse the sacraments to opponents of the bull *Unigenitus*, Robert de Saint-Vincent recognized "the finger of God who makes use of men like machines in order to execute his designs." Again, the "bizarre circumstance" that a magistrate so detestable as the abbé Chauvelin should have had the honor of first denouncing the Company of Jesus before the parlement of Paris caused him once more to admire "the finger of God which uses an agent when such is useful to the order of Providence and then casts down the human vanity which it did not raise up

27. Ibid., p. 63. For biographical information on Bon, see Cerveau, *Nécrologe*, Vol. 2, pp. 410–11.
28. Ibid., pp. 410–11, 48, 110.

except for a sole and unique object." And like any good eighteenth-century Jansenist, Robert de Saint-Vincent upheld the parlement's most extravagant estimates of its place in the French "constitution," scorned the pretensions of the Jesuit-infected episcopacy, and at the feet of the Jesuits themselves laid the responsibility for most of the misfortunes which during his century had befallen France. Damiens's attempted assassination of Louis XV in 1757, Chancellor Maupeou's suppression of the parlements in 1771, the French Revolution of 1789—all these events he ascribed at least in part to their pernicious intrigues. The French Revolution itself was unable to dislodge the Jesuits from the dominant position they occupied in his mind. One of the very last things he did was to warn the Spanish minister Alcudia against reestablishing the Jesuits in Spain, lest that country, too, fall victim to the revolutionary contagion.[29]

But the memoirs of Robert de Saint-Vincent are valuable not only as a mirror of an individual Jansenist's soul but for what they reveal about the composition of the *parti janséniste* of the parlement of Paris. And among the more obvious conclusions which these memoirs dictate is that despite his brilliant performance on April 17, 1761, as denunciator of the Jesuit Order, the name of the abbé Chauvelin must ultimately be stricken from Jansenism's book of the living. It is true that the abbé Chauvelin was held in rather high regard by his Jansenist colleagues from around 1752 until after the affair of the Jesuits. "It had been some time," reported Robert de Saint-Vincent when writing about the performance of April 17, 1761, "since the abbé Chauvelin had abandoned dissolute society in order to dedicate himself to what was then known as the *parti janséniste* in the world and to acquire a certain esteem among the most zealous magistrates." Indeed, like Robert de Saint-Vincent himself, Chauvelin had been highly vocal in denouncing instances of refusals of sacraments to Jansenists before the parlement of Paris, had played an active if not decisive role in the composition of the Great Remonstrances of April 9, 1753, and had zealously tried to demonstrate that the Jesuits, not his parliamentary colleagues, lurked behind Damiens's attempt on the life of Louis XV in 1757. But his famous denunciation of the Jesuit Order on April 17, 1761, proved to be the occasion of his backsliding. "The seventeenth of April," Robert de Saint-Vincent wrote, "was the stumbling block of his vanity and God permitted that after having served the Parlement in combatting and destroying Jesuitism he so inflated himself with pride . . . that he assumed an air of haughtiness toward all of his colleagues." This pride, he added, "led him once again to ruin himself . . . amidst the society of the fashionable world and beautiful women which in turn made him abdicate entirely, at the end of his life, the parliamentary society in

29. Ibid., pp. 4,5, 130, 229, 377–78. On Damiens's attempted assassination of Louis XV, see ibid., pp. 195–96.

which he had lived most intimately for more than ten years."[30] Although for a while, then, a member of the *parti janséniste*, the abbé Chauvelin cannot be conidered a Jansenist in the fullest sense of the term. He was at most an unfortunate ase of withdrawn grace.

So much for the negative side of the ledger. On the positive side, the memoirs of Robert de Saint-Vincent confirm what we had already suspected about Counselor Guillaume Lambert on the basis of his ancestry and the comments in the *Nouvelles Ecclésiastiques*. Lambert was both a Jansenist and Robert de Saint-Vincent's most trusted friend in the parlement of Paris. Having both ntered the parlement in 1748, the two magistrates first collaborated four years ater when together they composed the Great Remonstrances of April 9, 1753. The consequent exile at Bourges in 1753, the exile of 1757, the trial of the esuits—these events served only to fortify the cooperation they had begun in 752. Robert de Saint-Vincent quite frankly confessed in his memoirs that he nd Lambert "were particularly designated as chiefs" of the *parti janséniste*. And far from denying the designation, he rather confirmed it by complacently epeating it in several other instances and regretting only that the designation was regarded at Versailles as "an irremissible crime."[31]

That the reputation of Jansenism was indeed an "irremissible crime" at Versailles is most clearly shown by Robert de Saint-Vincent's remarks about nother of his colleagues, Laverdy de Nizeret. Laverdy, to be sure, was at the very least an associate of the parlement's *parti janséniste*, and his contribution to he destruction of the Jesuits was if anything more important than those of Robert de Saint-Vincent and Lambert. And when in 1763 the duc de Choiseul prought him news of his appointment as controller general of finance, his eaction, according to Robert de Saint-Vincent, was that of a good parliamenary Jansenist: ". . . and they do not even believe in God at Versailles!" he tammered. "I would find myself entirely alone and uprooted in soil where eligion is so little known." Once established at Versailles, however, his attitude oward Jansenism and his former colleagues began rapidly to change. "From the moment of his entry into the ministry of finance," Robert de Saint-Vincent eported, "he was inculcated with the notion that in order to succeed at the Court e would have to protect himself against his reputation as a Jansenist. . . . Rarely did he see me," he sadly added, "without making some declaration gainst Jansenism . . . and while maintaining with me all the exterior liaisons of politeness and friendship he augmented from day to day his prejudices and pite against me."[32] Though less exaggerated, then, than that of Chauvelin, the

30. Ibid., pp. 228–29.
31. Ibid., pp. 303, 287.
32. Ibid., pp. 292, 304.

case of Laverdy is also one of religious backsliding. But that he was once a Jansenist or at least regarded as such by his closest friends in the parlement of Paris can hardly be doubted.

About the other magistrates more or less suspected of Jansenism, Robert de Saint-Vincent had little to say. The counselor, Le Febvre de Saint-Hilaire, classified by Bluche as a Jansenist, Robert de Saint-Vincent indeed described as one "very pious, very religious, and very commendable by reason of the sanctity of his life," a description which surely places this magistrate in the category of those particularly suspicious.[33] But the two others who yet remain in this category, Rolland de Challerange and Clément de Feuillet, Robert de Saint-Vincent passed by in near silence. I must therefore take leave of the memoirs of Robert de Saint-Vincent, which established Guillaume Lambert and Robert de Saint-Vincent himself as indubitable Jansenists; put Rolland de Challerange, Clément de Feuillet, and Le Febvre de Saint-Hilaire in the category of probable Jansenists; and left the abbé Chauvelin and Laverdy defying categorization as backsliding Jansenists.

Fortunately, a curious but highly informative footnote in a manuscript history of the Great Remonstrances of April 9, 1753, at least partially breaks the impasse at which the memoirs of Robert de Saint-Vincent have left us.[34] The author of this manuscript history is yet another of Robert de Saint-Vincent's colleagues, President Rolland d'Erceville, celebrated for his role in reforming the schools which the expulsion of the Jesuits had left vacant.

What occasioned this curious footnote in Rolland d'Erceville's manuscript history was a remark made by President Gilbert de Voisins during one of the sessions of the assembled chambers of parlement in which the Great Remonstrances of April 9, 1753, then still in the process of composition, were being discussed. Gilbert de Voisins had simply observed that were the remonstrances to insist too vehemently upon the intrinsic evils of the bull *Unigenitus*, the parlement would only lend credence to those who habitually accused the parlement of Jansenism.[35] Now having duly recorded Gilbert's remark, D'Erceville suddenly launched into a long and involved footnote which attempted to refute the charge of Jansenism against the parlement of Paris. Precisely because he attempted to refute this charge, and because, moreover, he was himself beyond suspicion of Jansenism, Rolland d'Erceville's remarks possess a special value.

D'Erceville began the footnote with the admission that the very history he

33. Ibid., p. 289.
34. B.N.: Ms. fr., nouv. acq. 8496 (518), *Histoire des remontrances du 9 avril 1753 par Rolland d'Erceville*. The footnote in question begins on p. 124 and extends to p. 128. The work will henceforth be cited as D'Erceville, *Histoire des remontrances*.
35. Ibid., pp. 123–24.

was writing seemed to substantiate the charge of Jansenism because it showed that only five or six magistrates effectively led the whole parlement, and most of these "passed as Jansenists." But he immediately expressed reservations about the term *Jansenist*, a term, he said, he would nonetheless "consent to apply to the opponents of the bull *Unigenitus*, not because they defend the errors contained in the propositions attributed to Jansenius, but because (thanks be given to the Jesuits) this epithet has become synonymous with opposition to the bull and it is best to conform to the actual way of speaking in the world." But even assuming that Jansenists directed the parlement of Paris, what harm is done, he rhetorically asked, "if the Jansenists direct it well?" Admitting, however, that he was only thereby begging the question, D'Erceville then proposed to silence forever the enemies of the parlement with "two simple reflexions." First, some of the magistrates, he confessed, "who have a large fund of credit in the parlement are effectively what are called Jansenists." This appellation he judged appropriate to Clément de Feuillet, Guillaume Lambert, and Robert de Saint-Vincent. "But should this title be given," he asked, "to the abbé Chauvelin or President Gilbert, to Durey de Mesnières, Gaultier de Bézigny, Frémont du Mazy or to M. Chavaunes, Davy de la Fautrière and Bèze de la Blouze?" Second, even the magistrates properly designated as Jansenists and who "are," he admitted, "the sinews of nearly everything that happens" direct the parlement not, he insisted, because they are Jansenists but because "more laborious than the others in the parlement, they are better informed, and joining a sureness of judgment with much learning they ordinarily seize upon the course of action best to adopt, suggest it with humility, amend themselves voluntarily . . . and try to compromise neither the authority of the King unwisely exposed by his ministers, nor the fundamental Maxims of the Realm which are the force and support of this Empire."[36]

As an attempt to acquit the parlement of the charge of Jansenism, Rolland d'Erceville's curious footnote was an unqualified fiasco. Indeed, it far more successfully creates the impression that the counsels of Jansenism directed the parlement of Paris than does his entire history of the remonstrances of April 9, 1753. To attribute, for example, the concept of Jansenism to a perverted Jesuitical inventiveness was only to profess his faith in a proposition which by the mid-eighteenth century had become a fundamental article in the Jansenist creed: that Jansenism was an imaginary heresy. If indeed the Jesuits invented Jansenism, it was nonetheless the Jansenists Nicole and Arnauld who first observed that the Jesuits had done this. And to the argument that the Jansenists directed the parlement of Paris only because they worked hard, one could justly reply that they worked hard precisely because they were Jansenists.

36. Ibid., pp. 124–26.

Hence, the Jansenists directed the parlement because they were what they were —namely, Jansenists.

As indices to the strength of Jansenism within the parlement of Paris, however, both the *Histoire des remontrances du 9 avril, 1753* and its curious footnote are of considerable interest. The footnote, for its part, confirms and further clarifies our picture of the parlement's *parti janséniste* tentatively sketched from the *Nouvelles Ecclésiastiques* and the memoirs of Robert de Saint-Vincent. The abbé Chauvelin, as we had suspected, can only with reservations be labeled a Jansenist, but Rolland d'Erceville classified Clément de Feuillet as well as Guillaume Lambert and Robert de Saint-Vincent among those "effectively . . . called Jansenists." What D'Erceville meant by this was probably that all three magistrates objected to the bull *Unigenitus* for religious or theological reasons, since he himself, an opponent of the bull on Gallican grounds, would by no means have welcomed the label of Jansenism. But in any case, his observations about his colleagues entitle us to elevate Clément de Feuillet from the rank of a merely probable Jansenist to that of an indubitable Jansenist.

Indubitable Jansenists Clément de Feuillet, Guillaume Lambert, and Robert de Saint-Vincent, probable Jansenists Rolland de Challerange and Le Febvre de Saint-Hilaire, the ultimately fickle Laverdy and the future apostate abbé Chauvelin—together these magistrates, as Rolland d'Erceville himself observed, constituted an effective *parti janséniste* of only about five or six persons. Now five or six persons might seem inconsiderable indeed given a total of nearly 250 magistrates in the parlement of Paris, but what this small group of men could accomplish both by their indefatigable activity and by the manipulation of the Gallican sentiments of the vast majority of their colleagues is amply illustrated by the story of the composition of the famous remonstrances of April 9, 1753.

On June 8, 1750, an important procedural change took place within the parlement of Paris. About a month before this date the parlement had commissioned its first president, at that time René Charles Maupeou, to write remonstrances against several of Louis XV's recent edicts and declarations concerning taxation. Having completed his task, Maupeou announced on June 6 that he would read his final draft of the remonstrances before the assembled chambers of parlement the following morning, just before going to Versailles to present them to the king. There was nothing unusual about this announcement. Ever since the accession of Louis XIV, it had been the generally recognized prerogative of the first president both to write the remonstrances unaided and to read them before the parlement on whatever day he chose, usually the morning before their presentation to the king. On this particular occasion, however, the practice of reading the remonstrances immediately before their presentation at Versailles was vigorously challenged by several magistrates. The abbé de Vougny, for one, argued that it was unreasonable that the assembled chambers of parlement should have no time in which to make whatever changes in the remonstrances they deemed desirable, whereas the erudite Durey de Mesnières observed that for his part he knew of instances as late as 1732 in which the procedure in question had not been observed, and that if the parlement allowed him only one hour to return to his home, he would be able to prove his contention in writing. Durey de Mesnières, of course, was not given the hour, and the opinion of Maupeou carried the day by a vote of 150 against 145. But the adverse vote did not deter the intrepid Durey de Mesnières from submitting his promised memoir to Maupeou, who on June 8 announced to everyone's surprise that Durey de Mesnières, and not himself, had had the matter right. The parlement consequently decreed that the procedure followed on June 7 could not be regarded as binding.[37]

Personally appointed by the king himself, the first president of the parlement of Paris was directly dependent upon the throne for his office and could usually be trusted to do the king's bidding. The king could at least expect him to do everything in his power to persuade the parlement to register promptly the royal edicts and declarations sent before it and in general to keep the conflicts between parliamentary obstinacy and the royal good pleasure at a minimum. So long, therefore, as the first president continued to compose the remonstrances unaided, the king was assured in advance of their moderate and relatively inoffensive tone. This assurance, however, was destroyed by the procedural resolution of June 8. For by requiring that the first president read at any time his finished remonstrances before them, the assembled chambers of parlement acquired the right to scrutinize these remonstrances and subject them to certain revisions. And the trend thereby established was only augmented the following year when, during the composition of the remonstrances of March 4, 1751, President Durey de Mesnières, with the help of the counselors Phillipe Thomé, Davy de la Fautrière, and the abbé Chauvelin, persuaded First President Maupeou to make some revisions which rendered the remonstrances more bellicose than they would otherwise have been.[38]

The trend in favor of increased participation of simple counselors in the composition of the remonstrances culminated on January 25, 1753. For reasons which remain unclear, First President Maupeou announced on that day that he had no intention of writing the remonstrances which the parlement had pre-

---

37. For two somewhat different accounts of this event, see Saint-Vincent, "Mémoires," pp. 121–22; and the Bibliothèque du Sénat, Fonds Boissy d'Anglas, 800, fol. I, *Journal du Parlement par Durey de Mesnières*, pp. 13–17, henceforth cited as Mesnières, *Journal du Parlement*. Robert de Saint-Vincent stressed the novelty of this procedural change more than did Durey de Mesnières, who insisted on its historical precedents. Jules Flammermont, in his *Remontrances du Parlement de Paris au XVIIIᵉ siècle*, Vol. 1, pp. 404–05, reports the event, but without interpretive comment.

38. Mesnières, *Journal du Parlement*, pp. 45–54.

viously decided to draft against continued instances of refusal of sacraments, and in his place appointed the counselors, Du Trousset d'Héricourt, René François Boutin, Henri de Revol, and Rolland de Challerange. These four magistrates therefore immediately busied themselves with separate drafts which they hoped eventually to combine in the form of finished remonstrances. To those well-informed, however, it soon became apparent that the four would never be able to collaborate successfully, and it was further rumored about that all four were both hopelessly incompetent and unrepentant lackeys of the court at Versailles. Now into the vacuum of collegial confidence thereby created stepped the *parti janséniste*. With a view toward writing remonstrances of its own and having them somehow accepted by the parlement as the work of the appointed four magistrates, the *parti janséniste* organized itself into an ad hoc committee consisting of Clément de Feuillet, Guillaume Lambert, Robert de Saint-Vincent, Laverdy, the abbé Chauvelin, and Durey de Mesnières. This committee, in turn, was not without the help of either the Jansenist lawyers Adrien Le Paige and the abbé Mey or the Jansenist curé Fontaine de la Roche, also chief editor of the *Nouvelles Ecclésiastiques*, and the abbé Christophe Coudrette. Although Guillaume Lambert, according to Rolland d'Erceville, "ought to be regarded . . . as the veritable author of the remonstrances," all the others nonetheless made their particular contributions.[39] Durey de Mesnières furnished learned memoranda, the abbé Chauvelin contributed "the section concerning the constitution," Robert de Saint-Vincent claimed authorship of the last few pages, Fontaine de la Roche made stylistic corrections, and it was probably Adrien Le Paige who persuaded Henri de Revol, R. F. Boutin, and Rolland de Challerange (the latter's rather dishonorable role in this affair explains why, though probably a Jansenist, he was not really a part of the parlement's *parti janséniste*) to present the remonstrances to the parlement as the work of the legally appointed commissioners. The abbé Mey's contribution was particularly unique. Not only did his recently published book *Apologie de tous les jugements rendus par les tribunaux séculiers en France contre le schisme* serve the committee as a guide and a model for the remonstrances, but he himself both contributed several articles to the remonstrances and functioned as something like the committee's double agent. While in reality working closely with Lambert, Robert de Saint-Vincent, and the abbé Chauvelin, the abbé Mey pretended at the same time to be serving the four officially appointed magistrates, to whom he sent some unrevised fragments at a rate sufficiently slow to guarantee his true employers ample time in which to complete their own remonstrances.[40]

The rest of this story is well known. Successful in its attempt to make its own

39. D'Erceville, *Histoire des remontrances*, p. 155.
40. For two accounts of this story, see, of course, ibid., and Saint-Vincent, "Mémoires," pp. 145–50.

remonstrances those of the parlement of Paris, the *parti janséniste* was without success in persuading Louis XV of their justice. Louis XV's only response to them was to send his parlement into exile from May 1753 to September 1754. The story is significant, however, because it demonstrates that by taking advantage of the diminishing authority of the first president, by carefully translating its religiously motivated opposition to the bull *Unigenitus* into the language of Gallicanism, and by its tireless activity, the *parti janséniste*, however small, was able to outmaneuver the more moderate elements in the parlement of Paris and, with the leverage gained thereby, move parliamentary mountains in the direction of its goals.

The story of the composition of the remonstrances of April 9, 1753, has revealed something of the influence exerted by simple lawyers upon the formulation of public policy within the parlement of Paris. In view of the conspicuous role played by the lawyers in the affair of the Jesuits I cannot take leave of the parlement of Paris without saying a word more about those representatives of the third estate within its walls.

The Parisian bourgeoisie of the robe made its debut in the quarrels of Jansenism when, in 1727, fifty lawyers of the parlement of Paris signed and published a legal consultation composed by the Jansenist lawyer Aubri of "superior talents which he so frequently employed in behalf of the Truth,"[41] in favor of the Jansenist Bishop of Senez, who had just been deprived of his episcopal functions by a provincial synod held at Embrun. Once the precedent had been established, similar consultations followed hard and fast: consultations in favor of Jansenist curés maligned by their Molinist superiors, consultations in favor of Jansenist bishops maligned by the Jesuits, consultations in favor of the lawyers' right to compose such consultations. Only three years later, in 1730, forty Parisian lawyers published a legal consultation which attempted to prove the parlement's right to protect priests persecuted by their episcopal superiors. And in the ensuing verbal war between the corporation of lawyers and the king's council, understandably shocked by the consultation's assertion that the royal power was in no way superior to that of the parlements, the lawyers succeeded not only in negotiating directly with the king's ministry without the mediation of the parlement or its solicitors general, but in justifying their conduct in what was supposed to be a retraction of their consultation.[42] By 1751 the marquis d'Argenson could write in his memoirs that "every lawyer is a Jansenist."[43] Doubtless he exaggerated, but it is no exaggeration to say that by this date the Parisian bar sheltered a considerable nest of the most unrepentant

41. *Nouvelles Ecclésiastiques* (December 19, 1737), p. 197.
42. Parguez, *La Bulle Unigénitus*, pp. 65–87.
43. D'Argenson, *Journal et mémoires*, Vol. 6, p. 468.

Jansenists. Indeed, by the middle of the eighteenth century the bar was beginning to replace the Parisian magistracy itself as the lay stronghold of Jansenism. Indications of this trend on a more general level are to be found in René Cerveau's *Nécrologe*. Between 1700 and 1741, for example, seven magistrates were thought sufficiently zealous to merit a place in the *Nécrologe*, while during the same period only five lawyers were honored with this distinction. Between 1742 and 1760, however, the number of lawyers who appeared in Cerveau's *Nécrologe* rose to eleven, while the number of magistrates to have done as well sank to four.

How account for this development? Some historians have regarded this trend as an instance of a profound change in the character of Jansenism as a whole—the change, that is, which saw Jansenism assume a distinctively political hue which in turn rendered the movement increasingly comprehensible and thus popular among the bourgeoisie of the robe and the second order of the clergy. The "republican" tendencies in the Jansenism of the lawyers, who were politically thwarted by the second estate, they therefore see as parallel to the Presbyterianism or *Richérisme* of the parish priests, who were often persecuted by their episcopal superiors.[44] However accurate as a broad description of the development of Jansenism during the eighteenth century, such an hypothesis nonetheless suffers from being far too general to explain anything in particular. While writing his memoirs during the Revolution, Robert de Saint-Vincent gave a far simpler and more concrete explanation for the growth of Jansenism among the lawyers. "Ever since it was decided," he observed, "that the clergy of France would require of those desiring to enter the service of the altars that they swear by the door of paradise that some ambiguous propositions which everyone interprets according to his whim are to be found in a Latin book written 150 years ago which no one reads nor wishes to read . . . a great number of those from respectable families, motivated by neither poverty nor ambition, discarded their plans for entering the ecclesiastical state." And these respectable unfortunates who refused either to sign the Formulary of Alexander VII or retract their acts of appeal against the bull *Unigenitus*—to what shelter could they repair? "The bar of Paris," reported Robert de Saint-Vincent, "was as it were the refuge of a very great number of these subjects who found themselves frustrated in their desire to enter the Church." And why, finally, did they choose the bar? Because unlike the faculty of theology, which required adherence to the Formulary of Alexander VII and the bull *Unigenitus*, the faculty of law protected its subjects of delicate conscience, and unlike the faculty of medicine, which did the same, the faculty of law charged relatively little for the degrees it bestowed.[45]

44. See esp. Taveneaux, *Jansénisme et politique*, pp. 41–45.
45. Saint-Vincent, "Mémoires," pp. 9–10.

It is difficult, of course, to substantiate Robert de Saint-Vincent's explanation. In most instances it is simply impossible to determine whether an individual lawyer at one time intended to become a priest or a monk and then changed his mind because of his opposition to the Formulary of Alexander VII and the bull *Unigenitus*. Some positive evidence, however, is to be found in Cerveau's *Nécrologe* and the *Nouvelles Ecclésiastiques*. The lawyer François Denis Simon, for example, who served in the parlement of Paris from the 1730s until 1745, decided to quit his ecclesiastical habit and study law only after the Bishop of Beauvais had deprived him of the chair of philosophy in the College of Beauvais because of his adherence to the appeal against the bull *Unigenitus* in 1731.[46] Again, the lawyer M. Fuet, one of the fifty who signed the famous consultation of 1727, was "at first destined for the ecclesiastical state from which the signature of the formulary alone diverted him,"[47] and the abbé Mey manifestly found himself in a similar boat. A case less clear is that of the abbé Christophe Coudrette. Born a Parisian in 1701, Coudrette's family maintained particularly cordial relations with the Jesuits at the College of Louis-Le-Grand, where Coudrette himself was educated. But the young Coudrette, whose life, according to the *Nouvelles Ecclésiastiques*, "presents very singular marks of divine protection," was early "shocked and scandalized" by the Jesuits' lax confessional ethics, and instead of Louis-Le-Grand he therefore chose to pursue his courses in philosophy at the Collège du Plessis, which "he knew to be most opposed to the doctrine of the Jesuits."[48] The Jansenist influence to which he was there subjected was soon reinforced by the abbé Boursier, who both enlightened him on the subject of the bull *Unigenitus* and persuaded him to become an ecclesiastic. Soon a priest, Coudrette exercised his sacerdotal functions first in the parish of Sainte-Barbe, then, in 1730, at the parish of Saint-André-des-Arts. He had hardly installed himself at Saint-André, however, when the new Archbishop of Paris, Charles Gaspard de Vintimille, revoked his sacerdotal powers because he had refused to sign the Formulary of Alexander VII. Ecclesiastically defunct, he earned his licentiate in law, cultivated his relations with the lawyers and magistrates of the parlement of Paris, and, though never himself entering the bar, employed both his knowledge of law and his acquaintances in robe society to advance the cause of those persecuted for Jansenius's sake.[49] It was this same Coudrette, described by Rolland d'Erceville as an "ecclesiastic formerly residing at Saint-André-des-Arts and who . . . possessed a remarkably wide knowledge of our registers," who contributed so importantly to the remonstrances of 1753, against the exaction of *billets de confession*.[50] It was again the

46. Cerveau, *Nécrologe*, Vol. 2, pp. 100–01.
47. *Nouvelles Ecclésiastiques* (December 19, 1739), p. 200.
48. Ibid. (December 22, 1774), p. 197.
49. Ibid., pp. 197–98.
50. D'Erceville, *Histoire des remontrances*, p. 91.

abbé Coudrette who, with the lawyer Adrien Le Paige, published in 1761 the vitriolic *Histoire générale de la compagnie de Jésus en France*, which in large measure instructed the parlement's case against the Jesuits in 1761 and 1762.

The importance of the abbé Mey's *Apologie de tous les jugements rendus par les tribunaux séculiers en France contre le schisme* in the conception of the remonstrances of April 9, 1753, and the role of Coudrette's and Le Paige's *Histoire générale de la compagnie de Jésus en France* in the trial of the Jesuits—both of which had considerable influence upon the course of events—suggests more generally the magnitude of the influence exerted by the bar's own *parti janséniste* upon the formulation of public policy in the parlement of Paris. In trying to account for what he called the "revolt of the bar" in 1789, Robert de Saint-Vincent placed particular emphasis on the contrast between the general incompetence of the magistrates, holders of prestigious offices by virtue of social standing and family fortune, and the relatively high competence of the lawyers, who occupied their comparatively lowly positions because of their proficiency in the study of law. This contrast, he reasoned, quite naturally excited both the indignation and the jealousy of the lawyers, who therefore felt justified in revolting against their erstwhile superiors in 1789.[51] Neither the affair of the refusal of the sacraments nor the trial of the Jesuits produced, of course, anything like the "revolt of the bar" in 1789. But Robert de Saint-Vincent's observation about the remarkable competence of the lawyers in comparison to that of the magistrates is otherwise applicable to the Jansenist lawyers of the parlement of Paris during the 1750s and 1760s. For it was they who, to a much larger extent than the magistrates, laid the legal foundations upon which the parlement's positions on the religious and ecclesiastical controversies of this period were erected.

None of the careers we have so far mentioned better illustrates this generalization than that of the lawyer Louis Adrien Le Paige. Le Paige was born in 1712, the son of a lawyer in the parlement of Paris. His two uncles, Jacques Le Paige and P. Le Paige, were both doctors of theology at the Sorbonne and appellants of the bull *Unigenitus*. The latter, who was also a canon at the Saint-Sépulcre in Paris, found his way into René Cerveau's *Nécrologe* of those who had most zealously confessed and defended the truth.[52] M. Hideux, his great uncle and curé at Saints-Innocents in Paris, was likewise a doctor of the Sorbonne and an appellant of the bull *Unigenitus*. It was his father's profession, however, that Adrien Le Paige chose to follow, whether because he refused to sign the Formulary of Alexander VII we do not know. In any case, he soon became a lawyer in the parlement of Paris, established a reputation as the bar's most learned specialist in canon law, and nurtured his relationships not only with

51. Saint-Vincent, "Mémoires," pp. 12–13.
52. Cerveau, *Nécrologe*, Vol. 1, pp. 267–68.

lawyers and magistrates but also with the prince de Conty, the grand-prior of Malta, who made Le Paige his personal librarian and bailiff of the Temple. Endowed, therefore, with a sterling reputation, valuable aristocratic connections, and an entrenched position which effectively protected him from persecution for his religious opinions, Le Paige succeeded in exercising an influence which simply staggers the imagination. Few important affairs, whether parliamentary, ecclesiastical, or both, were foreign to his prodigious activity. Besides numerous pamphlets and many of the articles about parliamentary proceedings in the *Nouvelles Ecclésiastiques,* Le Paige composed episcopal mandements, remonstrances for both the parlement of Paris and provincial parlements, several royal edicts, and possibly some papal briefs. It was he and the prince de Conty, for example, who more than anyone else negotiated the return of the exiled magistracy in 1754, and it was at his desk that Louis XV's famous Law of Silence, by which the king hoped to stifle the religious disputes in France, originated.[53] A curious note concerning a projected episcopal mandamus which Le Paige wrote to a bishop in 1765 reveals something of his character. "No one," he wrote, "speaks less than myself about what occupies me the most. I have accustomed myself to this for more than thirty-four years. Concerning these kinds of matters I live in the most singular solitude, almost always reduced to conversing with myself alone: always surrounded, that is, by men who, having no kind of connection with these affairs, are for myself and for my friends an absolutely foreign world: who would not even understand my language or would certainly contradict it if they did. This is my cross and torment," he added, "but God wishes it so."[54]

But who were these "friends" to whom his note referred and with whom, presumably, Le Paige could sometimes converse about what occupied him the most? The prince de Conty, undoubtedly, but also the counselors Robert de Saint-Vincent, Guillaume Lambert, Clément de Feuillet, Laverdy, and Le Febvre de Saint-Hilaire, as well as the abbé Coudrette, the abbé Mey, and still others whom we have not yet met, such as the lawyer Charlemagne Lalourcé. What together they were able to accomplish in the affair of the Jesuits we shall soon see.

53. Cécile Gazier, "Notice sur Adrien Le Paige et sa bibliothèque" (unpublished article conserved at the Bibliothèque de Port-Royal), and her *Histoire de la société et de la bibliothèque de Port-Royal* (Paris, 1966), pp. 25–26.

54. B.P.R.: L.P. 541, ms. 130.

3. Conspiracies Real and Imagined: The Decision to Destroy the Jesuits

ON JANUARY 27, 1753, CHARLES DE CAYLUS, THE JANSENIST Bishop of Auxerre, received a package containing a detailed indictment of the Company of Jesus and a long letter explaining how the indictment was to be used. The anonymous author of this letter offered to reveal his identity if Caylus, for his part, would promise to contribute to the project against the Jesuits. But the upright Bishop of Auxerre refused to cooperate, and his pious biographer, the abbé Dettey, observed that the Jesuits themselves engineered their destruction when, only a few years later, the "Almighty delivered the Society to a spirit of intoxication and infatuation which led it to judgment . . . at the Tribunal of the Parlement, where it cited and produced its constitutions in order to avoid paying debts contracted in its name."[1]

Though without immediate consequence, the incident nonetheless reveals that the idea of expelling the Jesuits from France was in the air as early as 1753. A year earlier, in fact, Rolland d'Erceville publicly recalled during one of the sessions of the parlement that according to the provisions of their acceptance in 1561 the Jesuits were not to call themselves "Jesuits" in France, but only "priests of the College of Clermont."[2] His observation was subversive in the extreme, for it questioned the legality of the Jesuits' very existence in France. And though it fell among the thorns in 1752, the charge of illegal existence against the Jesuit Order was to bring forth fruit a hundredfold only nine years later. Nor is it improbable that the members of the parlement's *parti janséniste* seriously entertained the idea of banishing the Jesuits during their exile in the town of Bourges from May 1753 to September 1754. Behind the parlement's rude treatment at the hand of Louis XV for its opposition to the refusal of the sacraments, these magistrates perceived the hand of the zealous Archbishop of Paris, and behind the Archbishop of Paris, finally, they detected the sinister and omnipresent hand of the Jesuits.[3]

1. Gazier, *Histoire générale*, Vol. 2, p. 82.
2. D'Erceville, *Histoire des Remontrances*, pp. 126–29.
3. "Destruction des Jésuites en France, anecdote politique et intéressante trouvée dans les papiers d'un homme bien instruit des intrigues du temps; publiée a Londres en 1766," in *Documents historique, critiques, apologétiques concernant la compagnie de Jésus* (2 vols. Paris, 1827), Vol. 1, p. 9.

Historical reason

If the idea that the Jesuits were existing illegally in France took root in 1752, another important charge against the order, that it possessed the pernicious habit of assassinating kings, suddenly appeared in full blossom in 1757. Not that the accusation was new. Its roots lay no less deep than the French wars of religion of the sixteenth and early seventeenth centuries, when the Catholic League did battle with the Protestant nobility and the newly established Jesuits, whether justly or no, were suspected of having engineered the assassinations of both Henry III and Henry IV. But an unhoped-for event early in 1757 injected the charge of regicide with pristine vigor. At six o'clock on the evening of January 5, 1757, Louis XV was stabbed as he was walking toward his waiting carriage in the court of Versailles.

The would-be assassin, a certain Robert François Damiens from Arras, was arrested on the spot. Louis XV, for his part, was little more than scratched, and his first surgeon, La Martinière, was of the opinion that had it been anyone but the King of France, he would have considered himself out of danger by the following day.[4] In any case, he was back on his feet within a week. Nor can it be said that the attempted assassination significantly influenced the course of events to follow. But like a bolt of lightning in a black night, this event suddenly and brilliantly illuminated the political landscape in France. All the different but interrelated political and ecclesiastical disputes in France—the fiercely Gallican parlements against the somewhat ultramontane episcopacy, the pacifically inclined king against the excesses of both, the young and ardent magistrates in the parlement's chambers of inquests and requests against their older and politically more docile colleagues in the *grand' chambre*, the Jansenists both within and without the parlement against the Jesuits and their protectors in the episcopacy —were brought by this event into a clear though momentary focus.

The assassination shattered an atmosphere already reverberating to the thunder of a fresh clash between Louis XV and the parlement of Paris. Not long before, on December 10, 1756, Louis XV, in a *lit de justice*, had forced the parlement of Paris to register an edict which, while conceding that the bull *Unigenitus* was not a "rule of faith," denied the parlement jurisdiction over cases of sacraments refused in its name, suppressed the last two chambers of inquests and the office of president in them all, and restricted the right to assemble the chambers for the purpose of discussing public affairs to the first president, the solicitor general, and the *grand' chambre* alone. To the edict's admission that *Unigenitus* was not a rule of faith, the parlement of Paris, of course, could only rejoice. To this proposition the parlement had dedicated itself since 1713. But the effect of the edict's remaining clauses was to render the parlement forever powerless to resist either episcopal or royal good pleasure, and in protest against

4. L. Dussieux and E. Soulié, eds., *Mémoires du duc de Luynes sur la cour de Louis XV, 1735–1758* (Paris, 1860–65), Vols. 15–16, p. 351.

these measures, nearly all the magistrates in the chambers of inquests and requests and a significant number of those in the *grand' chambre* tendered their resignations to Louis XV on December 12, 1756. The lawyers, for their part, locked their cabinet doors and refused to plead any cases before those magistrates who remained.[5]

Equally disgruntled when the assassination attempt occurred were the Archbishop of Paris, Christophe de Beaumont, and all those in the clergy of like mind. Beaumont had never reconciled himself to Louis XV's Law of Silence of September 2, 1754, which forbade ecclesiastics to speak of *Unigenitus* and related doctrinal controversies, and for this, as well as for his unabated zeal in depriving Jansenists of the sacraments within his diocese, Louis XV had exiled him to his château at Conflans in 1755. This mark of royal displeasure, however, had not deterred Beaumont from ordering the Parisian curés to persist in refusing the sacraments to Jansenists. Nor had it prevented him, on September 19, 1756, from violating the Law of Silence by publishing an episcopal mandamus which threatened with excommunication not only all ecclesiastics who obeyed parliamentary orders to administer the sacraments but every person who solicited such orders.[6] The article in Louis XV's edict of December 10, 1756, which declared that *Unigenitus* was not a "rule of faith," left him no happier, and rumor had it that he was about to publish another mandamus to that effect.[7]

It was therefore a rump *grand' chambre*—the Jansenists derisively called it *le carcasse du parlement*—consisting of magistrates trusted by neither their colleagues nor the episcopacy, which, together with the princes and peers of the realm, tried the unsuccessful assassin of Louis XV. To the protestations of loyalty on the part of the magistrates who had resigned their posts, as well as to their offer to resume them under the critical circumstances precipitated by the assassination, Louis XV turned a deaf ear. His sole response was to exile sixteen of these magistrates—among them the leaders of the *parti janséniste*—to various towns in France on January 27, 1757. And, as if in a purposeful effort further to burden an atmosphere already too heavy with suspicion and hostility, Louis XV accorded the right to interrogate Damiens to only four magistrates: First President Maupeou, President Mathieu François Molé, and the counselors Severt and Denis Louis Pasquier. The most the peers, princes, and remaining magistrates could do was to hear, criticize, and rule upon the reports of the interrogators during plenary judicial sessions.[8]

5. Roquain, *L'Esprit révolutionnaire avant la Révolution, 1715–1789*, pp. 200–01.

6. *Mandement et instruction pastorale de monseigneur l'archévêque de Paris, touchant l'autorité de l'église, l'enseignement de la foi, l'administration des sacrements, la soumission due à la constitution Unigénitus, portant défense de lire plusieurs écrits* (Paris, 1756). See also Roquain, *L'Esprit révolutionnaire*, pp. 185–99.

7. Barbier, *Journal*, Vol. 6, p. 441.

8. B.P.R.: L.P. 547; Saint-Vincent, "Mémoires," pp. 195–205.

The interrogators' official conclusion, published to vindicate themselves under the title of *Pièces originales et procédures fait à Robert-François Damiens*, constituted no exception among the annals of political assassinations: Damiens was of course guilty, but he was an isolated fanatic who had acted without accomplices.[9] Nor was it long before their verdict sustained heavy fire from quarters both Jansenist and Jesuitical. "Each of the two, parties, Molinist and Jansenist," noted the marquis d'Argenson, "wants to prove that Damiens acted at the instigation of its adversary."[10] But the Jansenists were especially bellicose in their denunciations of the court's procedure and findings. Robert de Saint-Vincent, for one, entertained no doubt that the Jesuits had commissioned Damiens to perform the bloody deed. Had not Louis XV's edict of December 10, 1756, denied the bull *Unigenitus* the qualification of "rule of faith"? Had not this edict thereby deprived the Jesuits of a cudgel with which they had bludgeoned their enemies since 1713? And was it not palpable that the Jesuits had all to gain and nothing to lose if the dauphin, whose pro-Jesuitical and antiparliamentary sentiments he had manifested on numerous occasions, were to inherit the crown?[11] These suspicions were dark enough, but Saint-Vincent suspected more. He suspected that the only reason for the exile of himself and fifteen other magistrates on January 27, 1757, was Maupeou's and Pasquier's determination to interrogate the assassin in the absence of all those whose zeal for the truth might lead them to uncover the Jesuits' complicity in his deed. "It is impossible," he wrote, "to explain otherwise the exile of the sixteen magistrates at that time. There was no plausible and apparent motive for this fresh disgrace."[12] And he was far from alone in his thoughts. Even the dispassionate and erudite Durey de Mesnières, who was by no means a Jansenist, suspected as much.[13]

Robert de Saint-Vincent designated the abbé Chauvelin, who was "very convinced that the Jesuits had a larger share than all others in the assassination of the King Louis XV," as the magistrate who expended the most energy in marshaling "all the traces and indications" of their complicity in the affair. The abbé Chauvelin, in turn, communicated all that he could find to the prince de Conty, who as a prince of the realm attended the judicial sessions, and both men, Chauvelin and Conty, were "marvelously seconded by M. Le Paige . . . the prince de Conty's ordinary advisor to whom all threads converged when one wanted to deal with the prince."[14] Of Chauvelin's activities there remain only a

9. *Pièces originales et procédures du procès fait à Robert-François Damiens, tant en la prévôté de l'hôtel qu'en la cour du Parlement* (Paris, 1757).
10. D'Argenson, *Journal et Mémoires*, Vol. 6, p. 385.
11. Saint-Vincent, "Mémoires," p. 186.
12. Ibid., p. 196.
13. B.N.: ms. fr. 7573, p. 5.
14. Saint-Vincent, "Mémoires," pp. 195–96. Letters from the abbé Chauvelin to Le Paige on this subject are to be found in B.P.R.: L.P. 547, ms. 120–21.

few "traces and indications," but Saint-Vincent was by no means mistaken about the role of Adrien Le Paige. More than two volumes of manuscripts in his minuscule hand attest to his frenetic and sustained efforts to pin the guilt upon the Jesuits.[15]

Whether real or imagined, conspiracies animating the hands of political assassins are notoriously difficult to unveil. The Damiens affair was no exception. Not, of course, that it was hard for Le Paige to assemble considerable evidence suggesting that Damiens had acted with the help of accomplices. On the same evening, for instance, that Damiens attempted the assassination, two men were found killed on the road from Versailles to Trianon, which Louis XV was to have traveled—seemingly the work of accomplices bent upon assuring the assassination's secrecy and success. Again, a woman of Versailles claimed that a moment after the attempted assassination occurred, she had observed two men on horseback passing before the gate of the château who, as soon as one had informed the other that the "blow" had just failed, sped off in opposite directions. This much was perhaps hearsay, but in any case, two fully bridled horses were found tied to the gate of the chateau of Versailles and were not subsequently claimed by anyone. A small girl in Paris was said to have announced the news of the assassination before it actually took place; others in the provinces seemed to have known about the event long in advance of ordinary communications. And on the morrow of the unsuccessful assassination some insidious placards appeared on the walls of Paris: one of them threatened that "the next time we will not fail," and all of them, thought Le Paige, bore the mark of "men animated by the same spirit as the murderer, and without doubt his accomplices." The would-be assassin himself said on one occasion that "his accomplices" were "very far away," and on another that if the king condemned him to perpetual imprisonment instead of to death, he would reveal his accomplices. "There are some then," concluded Le Paige in his notebook. Of this he had no doubt.[16]

But to identify Damiens or his supposed accomplices as either Jesuits or their creatures could not be accomplished without the grossest misapplication of the Jesuitical doctrine of probabilism to matters of fact. The Jesuits, to be sure, had both educated Damiens and employed him in the kitchen of their college at Arras until 1749. But these facts proved nothing. For that matter, some of the most zealous Jansenists, such as the abbé Coudrette, as well as scores of militantly Gallican magistrates, had likewise attended the Jesuits' colleges. Nor was Damiens's avowal that he had confessed to a Jesuit father in Arras shortly before committing the assassination in any way decisive, for he subsequently retracted

15. B.P.R.: L.P. 548–49.
16. Ibid.; L.P. 548—two unnumbered and uncatalogued manuscripts, one titled "Faits qui peuvent estre important à aprofondir [*sic*]" and the other "Indiculus."

this statement and said he had rather confessed to a priest of the Oratory, a notoriously anti-Jesuitical order. Yet Le Paige and his friends could assemble no stronger scraps of evidence than these. The other "traces and indications" fell uselessly into the judicial trashcan of hearsay and unsubstantiated rumor—the warning, for example, supposedly given by several Jesuits to their penitents shortly before the assassination, that in the event of some serious trouble they should declare themselves on the side of religion, or a conversation supposedly overheard in the Luxembourg Gardens between two Jesuits about a "blow" which would soon "finish everything," or the "fact," to which Le Paige attached "great consequence," that an officer of dragoons had told both a merchant draper and a squire of the Academy of Jouan that a Jesuit had tried to force yet a fourth person to join a "holy league of all good Christians" to defend the true religion, considered in "imminent danger."[17]

Nor did the evidence, such as it was, point in solely Jesuitical directions. While still in the jail at Versailles and at the prodding of an officer named Bélot, Damiens had written a letter to the king in which he named seven magistrates of the parlement of Paris, among them Lambert, Clément de Feuillet, and Rolland de Challerange, as having indirectly determined him to perform the assassination. At the height of the controversy over the refusal of sacraments in 1753, Damiens, it seems, had been working as a valet in the home of the counselor Bèze de Lys, where he had overheard animated remarks on the part of these seven against the despotism of the king and the ministry's disregard for the fundamental laws of the realm.[18] During his interrogation, moreover, the unsuccessful assassin cursed the bishops and priests in general and the Archbishop of Paris in particular, and said that he detested the Jesuits and their doctrine. Had five or six bishops been beheaded, he added, he would have never decided to assassinate the king, a deed he resolved to do only because of the treatment which the parlement had recently suffered at the hands of Louis XV.[19]

It was not until the judicial session of February 12 that Pasquier, forced by the prince de Conty to read the entire procès-verbal of the interrogation to the *grand' chambre*, made public the information about the seven magistrates and Damiens's pro-parliamentary leanings. But the Jansenists' reaction was no less violent for that. Robert de Saint-Vincent initially viewed the evidence as a sword of Damocles forged by Maupeou in order to thwart the zealous activities of magistrates like his friend Lambert, whose head, he sometimes believed, "would not sustain the impetus of this shock."[20] Le Paige, who at least believed

17. Ibid.
18. *Pièces originales et procédures du procès fait à Robert-François Damiens*, pp. 45, 66, 68–69, 79, 163–64. See also Barbier, *Journal*, Vol. 6, pp. 480–81.
19. *Pièces originales*, pp. 50–51, 69, 79, 103, 142, 144–45; B.P.R.: L.P. 548, unnumbered ms.
20. Saint-Vincent, "Mémoires," p. 203.

that Damiens made the remarks ascribed to him, nonetheless refused to see in them anything more than a new facet of a carefully planned Jesuit conspiracy. "This man poses as the *parlementaire* and almost the Jansenist," he wrathfully noted in a small journal he kept during the trial. "This is the diabolical turn he gives to his whole affair! Such is the mask with which he covers himself!"[21] But whether a mask or not, the evidence impressed many as conclusive against the parlement of Paris and the *parti janséniste*. The lawyer Barbier, no Jansenist but no more inclined to take the side of the Jesuits, wrote that "there is every appearance that the trial will do no honor to the parlement, and that the troubles and evils which we have witnessed will rebound upon the *parti janséniste*."[22] And the partisans of the Jesuits and the ultramontane episcopacy of course went further. The anonymous author of *L'Histoire de Robert François Damiens* baldly asserted that Damiens had been inspired to commit his crime by the example of insubordination given by the parlement of Paris, and the Archbishop of Paris, in a mandamus published shortly after the assassination, more subtly suggested the same.[23]

Caught unprotected in the crossfire between Jansenists and Jesuits were the assassin's four interrogators—Maupeou, Pasquier, Molé, and Severt. First President Maupeou and the interrogators' spokesman Pasquier were in particular the object not only of sporadic crossfire but of point-blank volleys from the Jansenist lines. Robert de Saint-Vincent, as we have already seen, suspected Maupeou of both engineering the exile of the sixteen magistrates and fabricating the evidence against the seven magistrates supposedly named by Damiens. Le Paige, for his part, suspected Pasquier as the executor of secret instructions from someone in the government to cover the traces of the Jesuits, rather loudly complained that Severt was a member of a Jesuit congregation, and through the prince de Conty, his spokesman in the judicial sessions, openly accused the interrogators of procedural negligence. Why, Conty persistently asked Pasquier, was there no monitor posted in Arras, where Damiens lived? Why no special investigation in Flanders, where the assassin had spent some time on his journey to Paris? Why no attempt, as Le Paige expressed it, "to unmask him by following him in the details of his life, by ascertaining his liaisons and natural discourses, and by interviewing the masters with whom he lived and the servants with whom he worked . . . ?" The prince de Conty culminated his attacks upon the assassin's examiners during the judicial sessions of February 25. In an eloquent speech he argued that the court should content itself with nothing short of the "last elucidations." Whether Damiens had accomplices or not, he

21. B.P.R.: L.P. 548, unnumbered ms.
22. Barbier, *Journal*, Vol. 6, p. 479.
23. *L'Histoire de Robert François Damiens* (Paris, 1757). The book was reviewed unfavorably by the *Nouvelles Ecclésiastiques* (August 7, 1757), p. 129.

said, the court should leave no stone unturned in its effort to find them, in order to place the king and the State forever in safety and tranquillity. But should a single doubt be left, he added, he himself would inherit a "most bitter life in the constant terror of witnessing another offshoot of a conspiracy which could be real."[24]

De Conty's opinion that the "safety and tranquillity" of both King and State depended on discovering the assassin's accomplices diametrically opposed a remark which Le Paige, in his journal, attributed to the reporter Pasquier. Pasquier, to believe Le Paige, admitted to a certain Mlle. Ferrier that Damiens's interrogators had acted not as judges but as good physicians. As judges, he supposedly explained, they would have had to prove the existence of accomplices, ascertain their identity, and thereby "destroy everything" by "plunging the King into the most terrible alarms"; as "good physicians," however, they were able to "heal the wounds and calm the inquietudes of the King" and by so saving the royal person save the entire State as well.[25] That Pasquier actually made this statement is most improbable. But it is quite probable that someone said something very much like it. For the two conflicting opinions—Conty's and that attributed to Pasquier—about the proper role of the judge investigating a political assassination represent perfectly the conspiratorial and "official" attitudes which have arisen in response to most such assassinations, particularly when they occurred in countries as politically and religiously divided as France in 1757. Yet another remark which Le Paige ascribed to Pasquier—one, incidentally, he more probably made—points rather to the nature of the quarrels dividing France at this time. On March 13, according to Le Paige, Pasquier complained to a friend that the prince de Conty tended to "spread trouble all around" in the Damiens affair, that it was less Conty's fault than that of the lawyers who "stoked the fire in his loins," that these lawyers were "full of Jansenism," and that "the Jansenists were trying to blame the entire affair on the Jesuits, as the Jesuits, for that matter, were trying to blame it on the Jansenists."[26] And between these Jansenist lawyers and magistrates and their Jesuit opponents nothing, certainly not Pasquier's publication of the trial's minutes, could prevent the impending Armageddon.

The Jansenist suspicions against the Jesuits in the Damiens affair did not confine themselves to private correspondence and personal memoirs. These suspicions flooded the pages of both polemical pamphlets and the *Nouvelles Ecclésiastiques*. Three pamphlets of Jansenist inspiration—*Lettre d'un patriote, Déclaration de guerre contre les auteurs du parricide,* and *Réflexions sur l'attentat commis le 5 janvier contre la vie du Roi*—raged so violently against the Jesuits and

24. B.P.R.: L.P. 548, unnumbered mss.
25. Ibid., L.P. 549, unnumbered mss.
26. Ibid., L.P. 548, unnumbered ms.

the magistrates unwilling to see them as Louis XV's true assassins that the *grand' chambre,* unaccustomed to suppressing Jansenist publications, condemned all three to be burned on March 30, 1757.[27] And despite the paucity of evidence, the *Nouvelles Ecclésiastiques* never tired of letting it be heard that the Jesuits were the veritable authors of the unsuccessful assassination. "We do not say," the gazeteer conceded on January 1, 1759, "that the Jesuits are the authors of the attempted assassination. . . . But we fear that they are," he proceeded to say, "because they have the principles and interests which render them suspect."[28] The Jansenists, moreover, wrote these things for a public described by Barbier as "very disposed to believe them."[29] No sooner had the news of the attempted assassination reached Paris, for example, than Parisians withdrew two hundred children from Jesuit boarding-schools.[30] One man successfully convinced a whole crowd that a sign on the door of the church of the Jesuits' College of Louis-Le-Grand which read: "Prayers for M. the King," really meant "Prayers to massacre the King." The "M" on the sign last used during the illness of M. *le Dauphin* had simply not been well effaced for the occasion of the assassination of *le Roi.*[31] Nor was the Jesuits' cause advanced by the appearance in Toulouse of a new edition of the seventeenth-century Jesuit Hermann Busembaum's *Theologia moralis.* For this ethical treatise, first published in 1645, insisted upon the absolute independence of the clergy within the State, the sovereignty of the pope over the temporal authority of kings, and, in the case of a king refusing to recognize this sovereignty, the right of his subjects to revolt and even to assassinate him.[32] Worse yet, this new edition appeared in 1757, not long after Damiens's crime of January 5 of the same year. "How remarkable the choice of time! How suspicious! Could it not be said," suggested the *Nouvelles Ecclésiastiques,* "that the crime had been anticipated, and that this new edition was being held ready to appear under such a circumstance?"[33] It was in vain that the Jesuits of Toulouse affirmed their innocence of Busembaum's publication and protested

27. *Lettre d'un patriote, où l'on rapporte les faits qui prouvent que l'auteur de l'attentat commis sur la vie du Roi a des complices, et la manière dont on instruit son procès (11 mars)*; *Déclaration de guerre contre les auteurs du parricide tenté sur la personne du Roi (le 22 mars)*; and *Réflexions sur l'attentat commis le 5 janvier contre la vie du Roi (le 5 mars).* There is much evidence that Le Paige himself is the author of *Lettre d'un patriote.* Not only does this pamphlet call attention to precisely the same bits of evidence as does Le Paige in his manuscripts "Indiculus" and "Faits qui peuvent estre important à aprofondir [*sic*]," but it often does so in exactly the same language. See also Barbier, *Journal,* Vol. 6, p. 512.

28. *Nouvelles Ecclésiastiques* (January 1, 1759), p. 4.

29. Barbier, *Journal,* Vol. 6, p. 497.

30. Ibid., p. 435.

31. Ibid., pp. 441–42.

32. Rocquain, *L'Esprit révolutionnaire,* p. 207.

33. *Nouvelles Ecclésiastiques* (January 1, 1759), p. 4.

their loyalty to the Gallican articles of 1682 before the parlement of Toulouse on September 10, and that the Jesuits of Paris, on their own accord, did the same before the first parlement of the realm several months later.[34] It was in vain, too, that the Jesuit Balbani painstakingly proved four years later that the edition of Busembaum in 1757 was no new edition at all, but rather an old edition published in Cologne covered with a new frontispiece, and that the Jesuits of Toulouse had had nothing to do with its appearance.[35] The Jansenists countered with pamphlets and articles showing that by virtue of the doctrine of probability, no Jesuit's disavowal could be taken seriously. And the Jansenists, not the Jesuits, were believed.

The Jansenists, then, emerged from the storm of the Damiens affair sparkling clean, the Bourbon-white defenders of the crown against the dark and Jesuitically inspired conspiracy aimed in its direction. But their ardor, dampened perhaps by the compromising evidence in Damiens's letter to the king, was not yet strong enough to press immediately home their advantage over the Jesuits, who were themselves no less than thunderstruck by the Jansenists' publicity campaign against them. For the Damiens affair occasioned neither a definite plan nor a firm decision to expel the Jesuits from France. True, the *Nouvelles Ecclésiastiques* of January 2, 1758, launched a ferocious attack upon the Jesuits in which the editor declared himself "astounded" that "such men were still tolerated in France and allowed to enjoy an impunity which emboldened them to ever new crimes."[36] But this bold challenge points not to a project but to a mood, incapable by its nature of execution. The first indications of a firm resolve to destroy the Jesuits take us temporarily out of the parlement of Paris and onto the traditional pilgrimage to Rome, out of the shadows of an imaginary conspiracy and into the webs of a real one.

In 1758 the long pontificate of Prospero Lambertini was approaching its end. Ever since his election as Benedict XIV in 1740, the Jansenists in France had tended to regard him as at least an *ami du dehors* and at most one of their own. An objective glance at Benedict XIV's pontificate, however, reveals the French Jansenists' estimates of Benedict XIV's sentiments to have been in large measure mistaken. To be sure, Benedict XIV, like Benedict XIII before him, often expressed his personal preference for Saint Thomas's and even Saint Augustine's formulations of the delicate balance between divine grace and human responsibility. He also anathemized the Jesuits' accommodation to the Chinese rites in

34. Barbier, *Journal*, Vol. 6, pp. 582–84, 606–08.

35. André Christophe Balbani, *Appel à la raison des écrits et libelles publiés par la passion contre les Jésuites de France* (Brussels, 1762), pp. 43–47.

36. *Nouvelles Ecclésiastiques* (January 2, 1758), p. 5; and Barbier, *Journal*, Vol. 7, p. 8.

the bull *Ex quo singulari* in 1742, while in 1749 he condemned unequivocally the doctrine of probabilism in a circular letter to the episcopacy. But none of this prevented him from regarding the Jansenists as both schismatics and heretics. A close friend and a regular correspondant of the cardinal de Tencin, Benedict XIV lauded the cardinal's behavior in the provincial council of Embrun, which in 1727 divested the Jansenist Bishop of Senez of his episcopal functions. He consistently excluded appellants of the bull *Unigenitus* from the celebration of his promulgated jubilees, and turned a deaf ear to repeated and conciliatory overtures on the part of the schismatic Jansenist diocese of Utrecht. There can be no doubt, however, that the pope sincerely desired to heal the religious quarrels dividing the Church of France. For Benedict XIV was both temperamentally and theologically a moderate, desirous himself of avoiding the extremes of either Molinism or Jansenism and at the same time of protecting the more moderate representatives of both. He was, in short, a perfect representative of what M. Emile Appolis has recently defined as the Catholic "third party," a group of pacifically spirited churchmen who, during the eighteenth century, stood equally distant from the zealous partisans of the bull *Unigenitus* and their comparably zealous adversaries.[37]

Louis XV had already turned to his profit the pacific dispositions of Benedict XIV when, in 1755, the quinquennial assembly of the French episcopacy found itself sharply divided over the question of the refusal of sacraments to opponents of the bull *Unigenitus*. Sixteen bishops, Christophe de Beaumont at their head, held that refusal to submit to the bull "in mind and spirit" constituted a mortal sin which, when its commission was "so certain in the public that it could not be concealed by any tergiversation," should be punished by the deprivation of both the last sacrament and the Eucharist. These sixteen bishops were opposed by seventeen others who, led by the cardinal de la Rochefoucauld and enjoying the tacit support of Louis XV, adhered to the more conciliatory position that opponents of the bull *Unigenitus* committed only a "sin in a grave matter" which should not be punished by refusal of the sacraments except in cases of "notoriety of fact." Unable to resolve their differences, the French bishops obtained Louis XV's permission to request the pope to decide the question himself. Simultaneously, Louis XV instructed the duc de Choiseul, at that time ambassador to Rome, to persuade Benedict XIV to resolve the issues in favor of the moderate stand taken by the cardinal de la Rochefoucauld. For nearly a year Choiseul tactfully advised the pope and his theologians, patiently counteracted the inflammatory pastoral instructions and letters written by the Archbishop of Paris and his partisans, and, by October 1756, finally brought the negotiations to a successful conclusion. The encyclical letter *Ex omnibus,* which

37. Emile Appolis, *Le 'Tiers Parti' catholique au XVIIIe siècle* (Paris, 1960), pp. 155–76.

formed the theological basis of Louis XV's edict of December 10, 1756, carefully neglected to describe the bull *Unigenitus* as a "rule of faith" and so limited the number of cases under which one could legitimately be denied the sacraments for opposition to the bull that only a handful of people were affected.[38]

Unfortunately, neither the encyclical letter *Ex omnibus* nor Louis XV's edict of December 10, 1756, produced the pacific effect that their authors had intended. Christophe de Beaumont's stubborn insistence upon refusing the sacraments to Jansenists, the parlement of Paris's equally stubborn refusal to acknowledge episcopal authority over the administration of the sacraments, Damiens's unsuccessful attempt to assassinate Louis XV in 1757—all these factors further envenomed the strife between the partisans and adversaries of the Jesuits and the bull *Unigenitus*. But by trying to curb the excesses of the enthusiasts of the bull, Benedict XIV had at least demonstrated his willingness to further the cause of religious peace in France. In Rome, moreover, the rumor got around that he was willing to do considerably more, that he wanted to publish a bull which would forever efface the memories of *Unigenitus* and the controversies it had occasioned.[39]

Well-founded or not, these glad tidings began to reach the parlement of Paris during the closing months of 1757. So optimistic, in fact, were the letters which Adrien Le Paige received from his correspondents in Rome that by the middle of February 1758 he and President Alexandre François de Murard were seriously thinking of attempting to persuade Louis XV to initiate fresh negotiations with Benedict XIV in view of a papal bull which would forever protect French Jansenists from the Archbishop of Paris and his kind. For the advice of Le Paige's Roman correspondents was unanimous: though by himself Benedict XIV would do nothing, he would do something if the impulse for negotiations came from Versailles. Without himself appearing to meddle in the affair, Le Paige therefore began quietly to make straight the tortuous roads which led to Rome. One of these roads led from Le Paige to his good friend the abbé Gourlin; from the abbé Gourlin to the Jansenist Bishop of Soissons, Fitz-James, who employed Gourlin as his theological consultant; and from the Bishop of Soissons, finally, to the first president of the parlement of Paris, Mathieu François Molé. Two supplementary routes, moreover, one which led from Le Paige to the Archbishop of Lyons, Melvin de Montazet, and the other from Le Paige to Murard, likewise converged upon First President Molé. There-

---

38. Maurice Bouty, ed., *Choiseul à Rome, 1754–1757: Lettres et mémoires inédits* (Paris, 1895). The correspondence between Choiseul, Louis XV, and the secretary of foreign affairs, Antoine Louis Rouillé, concerning these negotiations may be found on pp. 4–218, but for the division of the French clergy on *Unigénitus*, see specifically pp. 56–57, and for the text of the encyclical *Ex omnibus*, pp. 320–27.

39. B.P.R.: L.P. 547, ms. 312.

by pressured from three separate directions, Molé finally agreed to employ his good relations with the abbé de Bernis, who was then the secretary of foreign affairs.[40]

By April 1758 Le Paige was working in close contact with Molé and Murard. Not the simple desire to procure religious peace in France, however, but fear of the coming wrath of the Jesuits was his foremost motive in soliciting a new bull from Benedict XIV. In order fully to understand Le Paige's reasoning, we must remember that in 1758 the Jesuits were experiencing reversals of fortune with few precedents in their history. In France the Damiens affair and the publication of Busembaum had effectively cast suspicions upon the Jesuits' loyalty to their king. In Rome repeated royal condemnations of the Jesuit Berruyer's *Histoire du peuple de Dieu* had seriously compromised the order's theological reputation. And in Portugal, King Joseph I's all-powerful minister, the marquis de Pombal, was accusing the order of engaging in commerce in South America and had just obtained from Benedict XIV a papal brief which empowered the Portuguese cardinal Saldanha to reform the Jesuits in that country. All these developments Le Paige stressed in repeated conferences with Molé and Murard. He especially emphasized a conversation of which he had recently been informed between the Jesuit Berthier, editor of the Jesuits' *Journal de Trévoux* and a member of the Academy of Sciences, a conversation in which Berthier supposedly predicted that the Jesuits were "on the eve of a most violent storm" and opined that his order should "profit from the moment to retire in order not to be enveloped by this tempest." But far from concluding from this conversation that the parlement should take advantage of the Jesuits' crisis to expel them, "this remark," Le Paige reasoned, "shows us that the Jesuits are alarmed by the present crisis, and consequently of what importance it is to conclude [our negotiations] definitively. For if," he added, "these men begin once again to become the masters they will utilize this crisis to conclude that they should put themselves in a position never to have to sustain another and that to do this they will have to lay violent hands upon all those who oppose them."[41]

Le Paige's certainty that the Jansenists would have no difficulty in accepting the projected bull was hardly a reflection of his confidence in the independent judgment of Benedict XIV. For what Le Paige had in mind was a draft of a bull which the Jansenist theologian Boursier had prepared in 1724 on the occasion of a similar, though unsuccessful, attempt to negotiate with Rome under the pontificate of Benedict XIII. To prepare the materials for negotiation, Le Paige and his friend Gourlin had only to make a few changes in Boursier's draft, write an alternative preamble and conclusion, and add a list of doctrinal errors

40. Ibid., mss. 314, 319.
41. Ibid., mss. 326, 321.

to be condemned which the cardinal de Noailles, the Jansenist Archbishop of Paris during the Regency, had drawn up in 1720. Progress was therefore rapid. On April 13 Molé and Murard corrected and approved Le Paige's memoranda for Louis XV and the ministry, and on April 30 Molé brought them to the cardinal de Bernis, who, though frightened by the difficulties of the project, promised to do what he could. By April 22 Le Paige and Gourlin were already retouching Boursier's draft bull; by May 11 their work was completed. On the following day Murard finally took Le Paige's carefully prepared manuscripts to Molé. "But what," exclaimed Le Paige, "was our surprise when we learned from this magistrate that a special courier had just brought to the King the news that the pope had died on May 3 from an inflammation of the lungs."[42]

The death of Benedict XIV, of course, rendered the entire project stillborn. The news, according to Le Paige, left First President Molé "penetrated with sorrow," and Le Paige declared himself unable to express his own, although he did not, he said, have "big hopes for the success of an affair which had become so difficult because of the multiplicity and antiquity of the engagements binding the two courts." But they did not lose all hope. As they had originally planned, Le Paige, Murard, and Molé met at the home of Clément de Feuillet on May 13. To believe Le Paige, the meeting had no other purpose than "to deplore this death." But they nonetheless decided that the abbé Augustin Clément, the Jansenist treasurer of the cathedral of Auxerre and Clément de Feuillet's brother, should make a journey to Rome for the sake of his health but also to "form liaisons at Rome which could be useful in the future" and to send back "the portraits and characters" of the cardinals who would be papal candidates at the coming conclave. All agreed that an alliance between the courts of Versailles, Vienna, Lisbon, and Madrid would empower the French cardinals to elect a "good pope."[43]

The abbé Clément left Paris three days later and arrived in Rome on May 30, 1758. His position there was strange indeed. He was in effect an unofficial ambassador charged with carrying out the equally unofficial foreign policy of the *parti janséniste* of the parlement of Paris. As such, of course, he was unable to exercise any considerable influence over the election of the new pope. The most he could do was to send his personal recommendations to his confidants in the episcopacy and the parlement of Paris in the hope that they, in turn, could influence the preferences of the ministry at Versailles. By the end of his stay in Rome, moreover, whatever influence he might have been able to exert was at least partly negated by the suspicions which his presence excited in the Bishop of Laon, Louis XV's ambassador to Rome since 1757, whose Molinist influence Clément himself was originally supposed to have neutralized. Far more impor-

42. Ibid., mss. 319, 321.
43. Ibid., ms. 321.

tant, on the other hand, was the second of Clément's commissions: to form liaisons at Rome among the Italian "friends of the Truth," whom the relatively benevolent pontificate of Benedict XIV had permitted to flourish in some numbers. Chief among these liaisons was Gaetano Giovanni Bottari, the "principal confidant" of Cardinal Corsini, with whom he lived, secret chaplain to Benedict XIV, first guardian of the Vatican Library, and, by 1758, an outspoken critic of the Jesuits and strong partisan of the appellants of the bull *Unigenitus* in France.[44] It was Bottari who by his letters had in part persuaded the abbé Clément to undertake the trip to Rome, and it was Bottari, too, who welcomed Clément when he arrived there on May 30.[45] Through Bottari, moreover, Clément soon became acquainted with two other ecclesiastics who, if not Jansenists, were certainly no friends of the Jesuits. The first of these was Bottari's friend the abbé de Gross, a Sardinian count who had "neglected his rights of birth to retire from the world" and who, "distinguished by his virtue" and "full of religion and zeal for the Church, possessed a sufficiently firm knowledge of her doctrine to serve her usefully."[46] The second was Giuseppi Simioli, theological counselor to Cardinal Giuseppi Spinelli and a "priest who is very learned and very attached to the doctrine of Saint Augustine and a cruel enemy of the maxims of all the Jesuits."[47] Through Bottari, Simioli, and De Gross, Clément enjoyed at least an indirect access to Cardinals Corsini and Spinelli, whom, among others, the French Jansenists deemed their protectors and the best possible candidates for the papacy.[48]

But none of these men became the new pope. On July 6, 1758, the conclave instead elected the Venetian cardinal Carlo Rezzonico, who assumed the name of Clement XIII. The Jansenists' reaction to his election was at first one of extreme dismay. "He has Jesuit brothers and Jesuit nephews, a young prelate, one of his nephews, is more than a Jesuit by inclination, and he himself is full of veneration for this society," exclaimed Clément upon first hearing the name of Rezzonico.[49] And his Italian friends, he reported, "had difficulty explaining the worth of this event and feared the saddest consequences." But a guarded optimism soon replaced Clément's initial despair. From his friends De Gross and Simioli he learned that Rezzonico had "no other dependence upon the society

44. M. Clément, *Journal de correspondances et voyages d'Italie et d'Espagne pour la paix de l'église en 1758, 1768, et 1769* (Paris, 1802), p. 15. See also Appolis, *Le 'Tiers Parti' catholique*, pp. 180–81.

45. Clément, *Journal de correspondances*, pp. 15–16, 57.

46. Ibid., p. 68; and Maurice Vaussard, "Les Jansénistes italiens et la Constitution civile du clergé," *Revue Historique*, 205 (April–June 1951), 257. De Gross is here described as "un fervent propagateur de la littérature janséniste d'Utrecht et de Paris."

47. B.P.R.: L.P. 547, ms. 342. See also Clément, *Journal de correspondances*, p. 116.

48. B.P.R.: L.P. 547, ms. 321.

49. Clément, *Journal de correspondances*, pp. 107–08.

of Jesuits than that inspired by his esteem for the regularity of their conduct and their zeal for the functions of the ministry," that he had indicated on more than one occasion that he was acquainted with "their disorders, their ambition, and their interest," and that "however little enlightened in this respect," he had never witnessed "any inclination for their doctrine." As time went on, Clément himself noted with satisfaction that Clement XIII retained Cardinal Archinto—he had helped negotiate the encyclical *Ex omnibus* of October 16, 1756, under Benedict XIV—as his secretary of state, that he chose a secular priest rather than a Jesuit as his personal confessor, and that he seemed inclined, like Benedict XIV before him, to proceed with the condemnation of the second part of the Jesuit Berruyer's *Histoire du peuple de Dieu*. Nor was it long before Clément was urging his correspondents in the parlement of Paris to resume their attempt to obtain a new bull which the death of Benedict XIV had so rudely interrupted.[50]

Such, at least in Clément's mind, was the state of affairs when Clement XIII's secretary of state, Cardinal Archinto, died suddenly on September 30, 1758. Now Archinto was in no sense a Jansenist, but as Benedict XIV's secretary of state he had nonetheless cooperated with Choiseul when in 1756 he negotiated the brief *Ex omnibus*, and his continued good offices were absolutely essential to the negotiation of any new bull under Clement XIII. His death could therefore only dash the hopes of the French Jansenists. Worse yet, Clement XIII promptly named Cardinal Torrigiani, a "penitent of the general of the Jesuits," as Archinto's successor. The abbé Clément was taking a short vacation in Naples when, on October 5, he received the news of Archinto's death. He immediately suspected the Jesuits of having poisoned Archinto in an effort to save their society in Portugal, where Cardinal Saldanha, with Archinto's cooperation, had been proceeding against the Jesuits' supposed commercial activities. And when Clément returned to Rome on October 17, his friend Bottari confirmed his most pessimistic premonitions. Archinto's death, Bottari told Clément, "could hardly be of greater consequence." Rome, he said, was no longer the same city that Clément had inhabited before his trip to Naples, there "was no longer anything which the Jesuits could not do with impunity," and the pontificate no longer left "anything to hope for the peace of the Church."[51]

That there was no longer any hope for the peace of the Church under Clement XIII of course meant that Le Paige's plans for obtaining a bull protecting opponents of *Unigenitus* in France would have to be shelved at least until the next pontificate. Could the Jansenists wait that long? Not in Le Paige's opinion. It was precisely because he reckoned that time was on the side of the Jesuits, not the Jansenists, that he had decided in April to press energetically for a new bull.

50. Ibid., pp. 114–15, 122, 135, 220, 134.
51. Ibid., pp. 231, 226, 228.

For he fully expected, as we have seen, that the Jesuits would successfully sustain their current reverses and then carry the war with unprecedented ferocity into the camp of their adversaries in France. With no prospect, then, of a protective bull in sight, the Jansenists—at least according to Le Paige's reasoning—were left with only one alternative: to take the offensive as they had never done before.

If Le Paige himself did not immediately draw this conclusion, the abbé Clément's Roman friends soon did. Clément had left Rome on October 2, 1758, because, all hopes for a new bull dashed, there remained no useful function for him to perform there. Once back at his home in Auxerre, however, he did not neglect to remain in correspondence with his friends Bottari, De Gross, and Simioli in Rome. And in December 1758 they sent him letters whose advice was unanimous. "It is necessary . . . ," wrote Bottari to Clément on December 12 (1758), "that good writers . . . attack the Jesuits in any area except that which concerns the Bull *Unigenitus* or any other which is common to themselves and the court of Rome because in that case they pose as the defenders of Rome and force her to make the strongest demarches, apparently in her own defense but in reality exclusively in favor of the Jesuits." Again, in a letter he wrote on December 20, Bottari advised Clément to urge the French Jansenists to "separate entirely the cause of the Jesuits from that of Rome. In this way," he explained, "the Jesuits will become an abomination to Rome herself, and when they will have lost their reputation—a development already rather advanced—we can retrace our steps and rectify the mistakes of the past." The abbé de Gross, for his part, sent similar advice to Clément on the same day.[52]

On January 23 the abbé Clément sent the letters from his Roman friends to the person who could "more usefully" employ them than anyone else: Adrien Le Paige. In a covering letter Clément told Le Paige that he detected a "palpable difference" between the advice of Bottari and that of the other Italians. "Everyone in Rome," he explained, "is agreed upon the utility and necessity to say no more about the Bull *Unigenitus*." But the others advocated silence because they assumed that Rome would never disavow the bull, and concluded from this that they should "unite against the Jesuits," who make of the bull "a powerful weapon for Molinism," whereas Bottari, though also an advocate of silence on the subject of *Unigenitus* and an attack upon the Jesuits, rejected the premise that Rome would "never retreat from this Bull" and hoped that Rome, once free from the influence of the Jesuits, would judge the bull "with more discernment." In other words, Bottari's compatriots urged an attack upon the Jesuits in order to eliminate their pernicious use of the bull, whereas Bottari advocated the same attack in order eventually to eliminate the bull itself. The abbé Clément, an appellant of the bull *Unigenitus*, naturally found himself on the side of

52. B.P.R.: L.P. 551, ms. 30.

Bottari. But he detected enough "truth" in the views of the others to recommend that the French Jansenists say less about the bull than before, that they carefully "detach the sentiments of the Holy See, entirely . . . in favor of Saint Augustine and Saint Thomas, from that of the Jesuits, so notoriously opposed," and that they speak of the bull, finally, only as an "obscure oracle" and "a characteristic product" of the "personal intrigues of the Jesuits."[53]

To rephrase Clément's analysis, everyone agreed upon the major premise that at least for the immediate future it was futile to attempt to negotiate any kind of papal disavowal of the bull *Unigenitus*. And whether from Clément's and Bottari's minor premise that the Jesuits constituted the sole remaining obstacle in the way of such a disavowal, or from the "other Italians'" minor premise that the Jesuits would in any case continue to wield *Unigenitus* as a "powerful weapon for Molinism," or from Le Paige's minor premise, finally, that the Jesuits were soon to attack the Jansenists in France with unprecedented ferocity, they all arrived at precisely the same conclusion: the need to divide the cause of Rome and the bull *Unigenitus* from that of the Jesuits and to conquer the latter. Nor was the new order of divide and conquer long in manifesting itself. On January 2, 1759—eighteen days before the abbé Clément even sent the letters from his Roman friends to Le Paige—the *Nouvelles Ecclésiastiques,* in its New Year's editorial, opened fire on the Jesuits in a manner that made Pascal's provincial letters seem polite in comparison. All mention of the bull *Unigenitus* was carefully omitted; the sins of even such zealous Jesuit partisans as the Archbishop of Paris were excused on the strangely Jesuitical grounds of invincible ignorance. They served the Jesuits' most secret designs "without knowing it."[54] Against the Jesuits themselves the *Nouvelles Ecclésiastiques* lofted the first clear cry for their destruction. Among "the things most necessary to the Church and the salvation of her children," asserted the Gazeteer, is "the grace to be delivered from a Society so injurious to both."[55]

The Jansenists' failure to obtain a protective bull from Rome accounts, then, for their firm resolve to observe a cease-fire toward Rome and the bull *Unigenitus* and to assault with undivided force the phalanxes of the Jesuits. But the *Nouvelles Ecclésiastiques'* cry on January 2, 1759, for the deliverance of the children of Pascal and Arnauld from the hand of the Jesuits was not yet tantamount to a fixed plan with which to implement this deliverance. Before the Jansenists could formulate such a plan, they had to ask themselves one very important question: Was it really possible to destroy the powerful Society of Jesus, for so long the advance guard of the papacy, the conscience of kings, and the educator of the European aristocracies? The answer to this question came

53. Ibid., mss. 30–31.
54. *Nouvelles Ecclésiastiques* (January 2, 1759), p. 1.
55. Ibid., p. 7.

from the most unexpected corner of Europe, from the Jesuits' very "cradle" in Portugal.

In 1759 the real ruler of Portugal was not King Joseph I, but his all-powerful first minister, Sebastian Carvalho e Melho, known in France as the marquis de Pombal. Pombal fancied himself the Portuguese incarnation of Richelieu. In reality he was considerably more than that, for he directed the weak-minded Joseph I in a way that Richelieu had never controlled the sometimes stubborn Louis XIII. Like Richelieu before him and the "enlightened despots" of his time, Pombal set out to streamline the Portuguese administration, mercantilize the Portuguese economy, increase the royal revenues, and in general to revive the moribund monarchical authority at the expense of aristocratic and ecclesiastical prerogatives. In his path stood two powerful obstacles: the Portuguese aristocrats and their allies the Jesuits, who as confessors to the royal family exercised a remarkable influence over state policy.[56]

Pombal's quarrel with the Jesuits dated at least to 1750, when Spain and Portugal signed a treaty whereby seven reductions of the Spanish but Jesuit-administered colony of Paraguay were to be transferred to Portuguese rule. The exchange of territory meant, of course, that the Jesuits would cease to exercise the kind of authority in the seven reductions they had so long enjoyed. Not such relatively minor matters, however, but rather the Jesuits' familial connections among the high aristocracy and their entrenched position at the royal court are what really irritated Pombal. It was not hard for him to dislodge the Jesuits from the court. He had only to convince the malleable Joseph I that the Jesuit court confessors were seconding his brother Don Pedro's political aspirations in order to exile these confessors from the royal entourage on September 19, 1757. But to destroy the roots of aristocratic and Jesuitical opposition to his policies was a more difficult matter. Nonetheless Pombal had already succeeded in obtaining from Benedict XIV a papal brief which empowered the Portuguese cardinal Saldanha to reform the Jesuits in Portugal for their alleged commercial activities in South America when a fortuitous event played into his hands. On the night of September 3, 1758, someone unsuccessfully attempted to assassinate Joseph I with a pistol.

It was not long before Pombal pointed his finger at the Marquis of Tavora, who had been understandably irritated by the king's nocturnal visits to his wife. The case against Tavora can no longer be taken seriously, but Pombal's suspicions provided him with an excellent opportunity to purge the high court aristocracy. Moreover, the Jesuits' international reputation as regicides, which

56. Comte J. Du Hamel de Breuil, "Un Ministre philosophe, Carvalho, Marquis de Pombal," *Revue Historique*, 59 (1895), 17–18. On Pombal, see also F. L. Gomes, *Le Marquis de Pombal* (Lisbon, 1869).

the Damiens affair in France had only recently reinforced, rendered it all but impossible for Pombal to resist the temptation to slay the proverbial two birds with a single stone. More than three months of political lull followed the unsuccessful attempt on Joseph I's life, but the long awaited storm broke with compressed fury when on December 12 Pombal arrested the Duke of Aveiro, the Marquis of Tavora, his mother the Dona Elenora, as well as the family's Jesuit friends and confessors Gabriel de Malagrida, Juan de Mattos, and Jean Alexandre. At the same time, Pombal stationed troops around all the Jesuit houses in Portugal. On January 12, 1759, an "exceptional commission" presided over by Pombal himself declared the entire Jesuit Order in Portugal the accomplice of the Marquis of Tavora's crime and pronounced the death sentence against all those arrested, a sentence executed against the Duke of Areiro and the Tavora family on the very next day. For the Jesuits Pombal reserved a more imaginative fate. Having failed to obtain a papal brief dissolving the Company of Jesus in Portugal, Pombal fabricated one of his own, and on September 1, 1759, crowded the Portuguese Jesuits in ships bound for the coast of Italy. Only a single order of business remained to be dispatched: the three Jesuits arrested but not yet punished for their supposed complicity in the attempted assassination. Unable to persuade them to confess their crime, Pombal reactivated the Inquisition, which conveniently found one of these Jesuits, the eighty-year-old Malagrida, guilty of heretical writings composed in prison. Malagrida was therefore burned in a solemn auto-da-fé on September 2, 1761.[57]

A month had hardly passed before a French translation of the judgment of the Sovereign Court of Lisbon of January 12 appeared on every bookstand in Paris. "The affair of the Jesuits of Lisbon," wrote Barbier, immediately became "the conversation of all of Paris. . . . The most moderate," he reported, "think it necessary to destroy this society here and secularize all the Jesuits who are priests . . . so that they become simple ecclesiastics who would not be members of a religious order."[58] The Jansenist press, for its part, lost no time in seconding such projects with a veritable deluge of pamphlets which unanimously accepted without question Pombal's version of events in Lisbon. And when in October 1759 the Jansenists learned that Pombal had definitively expelled the Jesuits from the Portuguese dominions, their elation no longer knew any bounds. "When at the beginning of last year we insisted upon the necessity of exterminating the Institute of the Jesuits . . . we were still ignorant of the fact that these monks were guilty, and guilty in the first degree, of the

---

57. Fülop-Miller, *The Jesuits, A History of the Society of Jesus*, pp. 124–40, 375–79; J. Crétineau-Joly, *Histoire religieuse, politique et littéraire de la compagnie de Jésus* (Paris, 1859), Vol. 5, pp. 118–77; Magnus Mörner, ed., *The Expulsion of the Jesuits from Latin America* (New York, 1965), pp. 117–33.
58. Barbier, *Journal*, Vol. 7, p. 133.

attempt committed on September 3, 1758, against the life of the King of Portugal," triumphantly confessed the *Nouvelles Ecclésiastiques* in its New Year's editorial of January 2, 1760.[59] But now that the Jesuits' complicity in the assassination had been established beyond all question by a "trial conducted with such maturity by the Sovereign Council of a Nation, . . . can there yet be someone," rhetorically asked the gazeteer, "who . . . is not obliged to confess that there is a God in Heaven who is the sovereign justice and avenger of crimes . . .?" What struck the gazeteer as singularly providential was that "the judgment of God" had chosen to "humiliate this Society in the very place which had been as it were its cradle and had most contributed to its initial elevation," and where "since 1588 with the book by Molina the Jesuits had been laying the foundations of their Pelagian system which deprives God of his empire over souls in order to give it to man."[60]

The events in Portugal, then, proved beyond all doubt that the Jesuits were vulnerable to the attack of their enemies. Should not the French, long in the forefront of the war against the Jesuits, be able to accomplish as much as had their comparatively benighted Portuguese neighbors in the Jesuits' most redoubtable stronghold? Such was undoubtedly the opinion of Le Paige and his friends in the parlement of Paris. But where was the parlement's *parti janséniste* to find a man who, if not a Pombal, could at least counteract the influence of the Jesuits' powerful friends at the court of Versailles? Fortunately for the Jansenists, they found such a man in the duc de Choiseul, who by 1758 had returned from his post in Rome and was now secretary of the departments of both war and foreign affairs. The evidence concerning Choiseul's complicity in the affair of the Jesuits is both fragmentary and controversial and merits, therefore, the closest examination.

Sometime in June 1760 the dauphin handed Louis XV a memoir which he claimed to have received from Lefebvre d'Amécourt, a counselor in the parlement of Paris. The memoir accused the duc de Choiseul of plotting the destruction of the Jesuits with certain members of the parlement of Paris. As early as December 1759, according to the memoir, the duc de Choiseul invited Lefebvre d'Amécourt to Versailles, and, in the conversation that followed, depicted the Jesuits as the principal enemies of religious peace in France, suggested that the parlement go to the "source of the evil" by eliminating the Society of Jesus, assured him that such a project would meet no serious opposition from the government, and urged D'Amécourt to confer on the subject with trustworthy and influential members of the parlement of Paris. No sooner, however, had D'Amécourt returned to Paris and had spoken with some of his colleagues

59. *Nouvelles Ecclésiastiques* (January 2, 1760), p. 1.
60. Ibid., p. 2.

1an he perceived that Choiseul had already confided in others than himself.
These magistrates, D'Amécourt, and Choiseul, therefore began to hold secret
onferences among themselves and their colleagues for the purpose of deciding
pon a definite plan. Some wanted to deprive the Jesuits of their colleges, while
thers thought this idea too limited. Finally, Choiseul "settled their doubts and
imself dictated the plan." He proposed that the parlement "attack the Jesuits
y way of their doctrine and the abuses which reigned in their education," and
present . . . their society as dangerous by its constitution and intolerable to
n enlightened government." The parlement should then implore the King "to
ive the necessary orders for the total destruction of such a pernicious society"
nd, at the same time, "provisionally prohibit the Jesuits from receiving any
ovices in the future" and "order them to close their colleges and attribute to
he universities the property which had been put at their disposition." This
lan the magistrates liked and adopted. They directed the abbé Chauvelin to
enounce the Jesuit congregations and thereby begin the attack to be consum-
nated on April 16, after which they would try to restore the Peace of Clement
X. Choiseul had postponed this date several times, but had now irrevocably
ecided upon July 1. He had also ordered a history of the Jesuits to be composed
or the purpose, and this history was already printed and awaited only his signal
o appear in public. Its author was the abbé Boucher, "a known Jansenist;" and
he lawyer Pinot, "who was no less one," had been charged with the translation
f the *Lettres de Portugal,* concerning the troubles of the Jesuits in that country.
The lawyer Le Paige, "long initiated into the mysteries of the Parlement and
he confidant of the Prince de Conti," was reviewing the work of his colleague
Pinot and establishing the necessary relations with the parlement of Rouen.[61]

Surprisingly enough, Choiseul published both the memoir and his personal
xplanation of it eighteen years later on his private printing press at Chanteloup,
he place to which Louis XV had exiled him in 1771.[62] According to Choiseul's
ccount, the memoir represented nothing more than an attempt on the part of
he duc de la Vauguyon, then governor of the Children of France, to discredit
Choiseul in the eyes of Louis XV. At the beginning of 1760, to believe Choiseul,
Madame de Pompadour asked for his judgment on an anonymous memoir
oncerning the political affairs of Europe. Choiseul found the memoir "ab-
olutely destitute of common sense and political knowledge of the most trivial
cind" and told Madame de Pompadour as much. Madame de Pompadour, in

61. Etienne François, duc de Choiseul, "Anecdote particulière à la cour de Louis XV,"
n *Mémoires du duc de Choiseul,* ed. F. Calmettes (Paris, 1904), pp. 180–85; henceforth refer-
ed to as *Mémoires du duc de Choiseul.* Choiseul's own explanation of this memoir, together
with the text of D'Amécourt's interview in the presence of Choiseul, Saint-Florentin, Chau-
elin, Bertin, and Berruyer are to be found on pp. 172–93.

62. Ibid., pp. 11–12.

turn, indiscreetly transmitted Choiseul's opinion to the memoir's true author, the duc de la Vauguyon, who, deeply offended, resolved to avenge himself in whatever way he could. To this purpose he persuaded his son's Jesuit superior, the père Quillebeuf, to write the memoir accusing Choiseul of plotting the expulsion of the Jesuits, and under the name of Lefebvre d'Amécourt promptly sent it to the dauphin. When finally confronted with the memoir, Choiseul offered his resignation, protested his innocence, and arranged to prove it by questioning Lefebvre d'Amécourt in the presence of Saint-Florentin, the controller general, Bertin, the lieutenant of police, Berruyer, and the abbé Chauvelin. In this interview both Lefebvre d'Amécourt and the abbé Chauvelin denied knowing anything about either the memoir or the anti-Jesuitical intrigues of Choiseul, and that, according to Choiseul, was the end of the affair.

The interrogation of D'Amécourt might have ended Choiseul's affair, but it by no means ended the Jesuits'. For if the memoir attested to no real plot against the Jesuits, its author most certainly possessed the gift of prophecy. To be sure, the parlement of Paris had already proceeded against unauthorized religious congregations by June 1760, and to interpret this demarche as a covert attack upon the Jesuits, the author of the memoir needed to do no more than to stay abreast of the gossip in Paris. But how could he have known in 1760 that the parlement would choose the Jesuits' constitutions and their incompatibility with the State as the order's Achilles' heel, or that it would attempt to force the hand of Louis XV by provisionally ordering the Jesuits to close their colleges and cease receiving novices? How could he have known that the abbé Chauvelin would be the principal actor in the trial of the Jesuits, and that the environs of April 16—April 17, 1761, as it turned out—would be decisive? How could he have known, finally, that some important polemics against the Jesuits were about to appear, and that Adrien Le Paige was both correcting these works and negotiating with the parlement of Rouen? It was of course not, as the memoir asserted, the abbé Boucher, but rather the abbé Coudrette and Le Paige himself who were the principal authors of the *Histoire générale de la naissance et des progrès de la compagnie de Jésus en France,* which later appeared in 1761. But this small mistake serves only to confirm the memoir's overall accuracy.

That the same memoir should be so remarkably accurate about the details of the Jesuits' imminent expulsion and totally mistaken about the activities of Choiseul would seem unlikely. Certainly Lefebvre d'Amécourt's negative testimony in no way establishes Choiseul's innocence. For Choiseul chose his witnesses carefully. Of all those present at D'Amécourt's interrogation, only Saint-Florentin and Bertin could have been very sympathetic to the Jesuits, and the abbé Chauvelin, who was a part of the plot if there was one, could have forever discredited D'Amécourt in the eyes of his parliamentary colleagues in the case of a single false response on his part. Nor does this mysterious memoir constitute the only evidence against Choiseul. Robert de Saint-Vincent, who was in a position to know something of the matter, wrote that Choiseul "wanted to topple and destroy the Jesuits" without exposing either himself or the king to their "profound vengeance" and for this purpose chose the counselors Lambert, Lavardy, and above all Chauvelin, whom he thought "the most fit to execute his plan with the necessary secrecy."[63] Moreover, on January 4, 1762—the trial of the Jesuits was of course well under way by this date—Alexandre François de Murard, president of the third chamber of inquests, wrote Adrien Le Paige a letter containing a piece of information potentially damaging to the Jesuits which Le Paige was to "have reach the Duc de Choiseul" by means of a "way" capable of exercising "great weight over the mind" of Choiseul. "I pray you to burn my letter," Murard finally instructed Le Paige. Le Paige neglected to do so in this instance, but Murard's request suggests a mass of additional evidence compromising for Choiseul which was carefully destroyed.[64]

What then should be made of Choiseul's story? The simplest and most probable explanation is that both in 1760 and in 1778, when Choiseul published the memoir, he told truly breathtaking lies. A clue pointing in this direction is to be found in the first real edition of Choiseul's memoirs, which Soulavie, Choiseul's personal secretary, published in 1790, five years after his master's death. In a note with which Soulavie introduced the fragment about Choiseul and the Jesuits, he speculated that Choiseul, while casually conversing with D'Amécourt, manifested in a general way his indifference toward the fate of the Jesuits and that "d'Amécourt perhaps reported the remarks of Choiseul to M. de la Vauguyon, who listened to them and gave them coherence." Such, at least, is what Choiseul probably told Soulavie. To complete the story one need only add that what D'Amécourt told La Vauguyon—and what Choiseul, for that matter, told D'Amécourt—did not in all likelihood consist in some general remarks about Choiseul's indifference toward the Jesuits but was precisely the contents of the memoir which La Vauguyon gave to the dauphin and the dauphin, finally, to Louis XV. The duc de Choiseul, then, had simply misplaced his confidence in Lefebvre d'Amécourt, who then leaked the information to the duc de la Vauguyon, one of the pillars of the pro-Jesuitical party at Versailles, who in turn attempted to save the Jesuits and topple Choiseul by sending the memoir to Louis XV. When confronted with the evidence against him, Choiseul covered his tracks as best he could by arranging the interrogation of D'Amécourt in the presence of others privy to the plot, and then, in 1778,

---

63. Saint-Vincent, "Mémoires," pp. 210–11; 227–28.
64. B.P.R.: L.P. 582, ms. 6. The entire letter reads as follows:
"Voicy monsieur une nouvelle que vous ne serez pas fache d'apprendre.
"Le general des jesuites a esté invité par la Cour de France de faire cesser l'equivoque

published the memoir with his own version of the incident in an effort to discredit Lefebvre d'Amécourt, then one of the *parti dévôt*'s candidates for the post of controller general of finance.[65]

The detail of Choiseul's involvement in a plot against the Jesuits is of course

resultante du decret d'aquaviva sur le Tyrannicide en ecrivant au Roy une lettre à Sa Majeste dans la quelle il condamneroit nettement la doctrine Parricide des Rois. Le general a repondu au ministere de France qu'il avoit ecrit au Roy une lettre dans la quelle il luy avoit fait part des sentiments de Respect et d'attachement inviolable de la Societé pour la personne du Roy qu'il ne lui estoit possible de l'exliquer autrement.

"Voicy presentement qui est sous le secret et dont il ne faut faire usage que pour le faire parvenir a Mr. le Duc de Choiseul s'il est possible et le plus promptement par la voye dont nous avons parlé et avec laquelle vous avez correspondance. Cette voye a du poids sur l'espirit de Mr. de Choiseul. j'en suis instruit.

"Mr. de Quebec a dressé son avis tout prest dans le quel il y a des choses fort interessantes et surtout des faits importants. Mais on est Comme assuré qu'il n'en donnera son avis qu'autant qu'il y sera invité de la part du Roy.ne pouroit-on pas et cela auroit moins d'affectation inviter egalement Mr. l'arch.D'embrun et Mr. leveque dagde a envoyer aussi leurs avis au Roy. Ce seroit une espece de reparation de la malhonneste que l'on a eu a leur egard. Au surplus dans la mesme Conversation qu'il seroit necessaire que vous eussiez le plutost possible avec celui qui peut parler a Mr. de Choiseul vous pouviez insinuer ce que nous disions il y a quelques jours par rapport aux Puissances etrangeres.

"Je vous observe que la voye que vous avez fera surement beaucoup plus deffet que celle que je pourois avoir. Je vous en dirai les Raisons.

A Paris le 4 janvier 1762

Je vous prie de Bruler ma lettre."

"Celui qui peut parler a Mr. de Choiseul" probably refers to the Prince de Conty, for whom Le Paige acted as counselor and librarian.

65. One of the few discernable continuities in court history during the late 18th century is the seesaw battle between the pro-philosophical and parliamentary party represented by Choiseul, Berruyer, and Madame de Pompadour (there were rumors that the latter two had conspired with Choiseul against the Jesuits, although I have uncovered no conclusive evidence to this effect) and the more ultramontane, pro-Jesuitical *parti dévôt* represented by the dauphin, the duc de la Vauguyon, and Controller General Bertin. Generally out of power since 1754, the *parti dévôt* scored a great victory in 1771 when Louis XV disgraced Choiseul and permitted Chancellor Maupeou to suppress the parlements. But Choiseul's exile by no means ended his political influence. From his estate at Chanteloup he continued to intrigue against his enemies at Versailles, and after Louis XV's death in 1774 there was frequently question of his recall. Now the appointment of the "philosophical" Necker as controller general in 1776 was very much to Choiseul's liking, but beginning around 1778, Necker's position was threatened by Choiseul's old enemy Bertin (*Mémoires du duc de Choiseul*, p. 413), then director of agriculture and manufactures, and the minister of the navy, Gabriel de Sartine, who allied himself with the *parti dévôt* and intrigued to have Necker replaced by Lefebvre d'Amécourt. It was in an attempt to influence the outcome of this contest, I believe, that Choiseul published his "Anecdote particulière," which was compromising for both Bertin and D'Amécourt. It is of course difficult to measure the influence of Choiseul's maneuver, but in 1780 Louis XVI in any case disgraced both Bertin and Sartine, the latter in favor of the duc de Castries, a friend of Choiseul. See le marquis de Ségur, *Au Couchant de la monarchie: Louis XVI et Necker, 1776–1781* (Paris, 1913), pp. 287–92.

largely a conjectural matter. But if the mysterious memoir is accurate about the time that Choiseul first spoke to members of the parlement of Paris—and we have every reason to assume that it is—then we may date the birth of a definite plan to destroy the Jesuits in France at December 1759. Corroborative evidence tends to confirm this date. It was on January 11, 1760, for instance, that the parlement of Paris first ordered the *gens du roi* to proceed against religious congregations and associations for laymen which were unauthorized by royal letters-patent. This parliamentary order was couched in the most general terms, but as the memoir of June 1760 itself attests, it was an open secret in Paris that the parlement was interested in Jesuit-directed congregations alone.[66]

At about the same time, the Jansenist press began to wax suspiciously prophetic about the Jesuits' imminent demise. On February 27, 1760, for example, the *Nouvelles Ecclésiastiques* assured its readers that after the events in Portugal, whatever evidence of "force, intrepidity and confidence" the Jesuits might yet manifest were only "convulsive movements, unmistakable signs of an approaching death."[67] Two months and eight issues later, the editors confessed themselves guilty of a misprint and instructed their readers to substitute the word *certaine* (certain) for *prochaine* (approaching).[68] The difference in meaning between these two words is so suggestive that one might legitimately wonder whether the editors really made a mistake at all. For the word *certaine* implied only that the editors confessed confidence in divine providence; *prochaine,* on the other hand, seemed to indicate that the editors were in some way privy to the otherwise inscrutable plans of God and that they were acting according to the more Jesuitical assumption that God helps those who help themselves. Not long thereafter, on May 7, 1760, the *Nouvelles Ecclésiastiques* reviewed an anonymous book entitled *Avis paternels d'un militaire à son fils, Jésuite,* which sketched a hypothetical trial before the *grand conseil* between the Jesuit Order and an old soldier whom the order had charged with calumny in private letters to his Jesuit son. Beginning with the particular charge of calumny, the trial soon developed into a general denunciation of the Jesuit Order in a way suspiciously resembling the manner in which, only a year later, the La Valette affair would develop into a general denunciation of the Jesuits' constitutions and doctrines.[69]

66. A.N.: G⁸ 692, "Procès-verbal de l'assemblée générale du clergé de 1760." See also the correspondence between Molé and Omer Joly de Fleury on this subject in B.N.: Collection Joly de Fleury, fol. 369, esp. mss. 10, 36–37. It is clear from Molé's remarks here that, in his opinion at least, the magistrates who sponsored the measure were aiming at the Jesuits alone.

67. *Nouvelles Ecclésiastiques* (February 27, 1760), p. 40.

68. *Nouvelles Ecclésiastiques* (April 30, 1760), p. 88.

69. *Avis paternels d'un militaire à son fils, Jésuite, ou Lettres dans lesquelles on développe les vices de la constitution de la compagnie de Jésus, qui la rendent également pernicieues à l'église et à l'état, et fournissent les motifs et les moyens de la détruire* (1760). According to P. Lelong, the author is Joseph-Adrien Le Large de Lignac.

More important, perhaps, was the book's "natural and sensible reflection" that because the Jesuit Order legally possessed not "a single inch of terrain" in France, "the King could, without violating the right of property, give to others all these large estates to which the Society lays claim and often uses to the prejudice of the State."[70] It was the first time, according to the *Nouvelles Ecclésiastiques,* that this reflection had been made; and it would soon compensate for lost time by serving as an important element in the parlement's case against the Jesuits.

But the portents of the Jesuits' impending doom were by no means restricted to the printed page. Beginning in the month of February 1760 the Jesuits sustained such an impressive series of juridical reverses that one may legitimately suspect a common source of inspiration. The first in this series was the case of the solicitor general of the *cour des aides* in the province of Auvergne, who in 1759 observed that the Jesuit college in the town of Billom was not paying taxes proportionate to the value of the estate. The solicitor general promptly brought the affair to the attention of the *cour des aides,* which in February 1760 judged the case in favor of the town of Billom.[71]

On April 30 and again on September 3 a special bureau of the *grand conseil,* which had been established in 1721 to hear litigation concerning the union of benefices to Jesuit colleges but had never judged a single case, suddenly decided two such cases to the prejudice of the Jesuits. In the judgment of April 30 the *grand conseil* ordered the Jesuits to restore to the Benedictines all the revenues they had ever appropriated from the Dominican priory of Avron, which, some years before, the Jesuits had succeeded in financially uniting to their College of Louis-Le-Grand for the purpose of supporting Jesuit missionaries in the Levant. It was found that these revenues, far from supporting missionaries in the Near East, were actually being used to maintain an expensive château near Versailles, where the père La Tour, rector of the College of Louis-Le-Grand, was entertaining distinguished guests. In the case judged on September 3 the *grand conseil*'s special bureau declared as abusive a recent union between the Benedictine priory of Bousic and the Jesuit college at Sarlat in Périgord, and ordered the Jesuits to pay the costs of litigation. Only a day earlier, the Châtelet of Paris finally sentenced the Jesuits to pay a thousand livres in damages and interests to the Paris corporation of apothecaries because the Jesuit house on the rue Saint-Antoine had been illegally selling theriac, hyacinth, and other medicines to particulars. The Jesuit house at Saint-Antoine had long been selling these medicines, but for some reason it was not until 1760 that the Parisian apothecaries and druggists found the courage to bring their "long-robed" competitors to trial.[72]

70. *Nouvelles Ecclésiastiques* (May 7, 1760), p. 90.
71. Ibid. (August 7, 1761), p. 128.
72. Ibid. (May 28, 1760), pp. 103–04; (November 12, 1760), pp. 197–99; (August 6, 1760),

"The Priory of Avron returned to the Benedictines . . . that of Bousic restored to its rightful owner, the sentence of the Consuls concerning the letters of exchange, that of the Châtelet in favor of the Apothecaries—these," triumphantly proclaimed the *Nouvelles Ecclésiastiques* on November 12, 1760, "are events which instruct the entire Realm that whoever today has claims authorized by the Laws against the Jesuits ought to have no fear of succumbing in asserting his rights in the courts."[73] The Jesuits seemed to be of the same opinion, for they appealed none of these judgments except the one we have not yet mentioned, that of the "Consuls concerning the letters of exchange." And in this they acted foolishly, for thereby they swallowed the bait which their enemies had been otherwise vainly dangling before them.

pp. 141–42; (October 29, 1760), pp. 189–90.

73. Ibid. (November 12, 1760), p. 197.

4. The La Valette Affair: From the Island of Martinique to the Parlement of Paris

WHILE IN FRANCE THE JANSENISTS WERE BUSILY PLOTTING the strategy for their final campaign against the Jesuits, France herself was locked in mortal combat against both Prussia and England. These two wars—the one fought between France and her enemies and the other within France herself; the one fought with soldiers, ships, and guns, and the other with words, pamphlets, and subterranean parliamentary maneuvers—followed courses which for the most part were mutually independent. It is perhaps symptomatic of the intensity of the political and religious divisions in French society that the events of the Seven Years' War only rarely impinged upon the consciousness of the antagonists in the closing battles of the more than hundred years' war between the Jansenist and Jesuitical parties in France. At one crucial point, however, the two wars crossed paths. In 1755, just as the Seven Years' War was beginning, the English captured several French vessels bearing merchandise sent by the Jesuits' West Indian mission on the island of Martinique in payment of a debt to their commercial correspondents in Marseilles.[1]

Contemporaries reacted to the news of this event in vast unison. Few indeed were those who shed any tears over the commercial loss to France of fifteen vessels, but nearly all marveled at the evidently temporal character of the Jesuits' missionary zeal on the island of Martinique. The marquis d'Argenson's reaction was typical: "There is reason at least to wonder about the affairs of these monks," he wrote.[2] But the Jesuits had many times before successfully sustained popular indignation at their allegedly extra-ecclesiastical activities, and rumors had long circulated in Europe about the immense riches which the order had supposedly accumulated in the New World, especially in Paraguay. What made the scandal of 1755 qualitatively more serious than others of its kind is that in this instance the seizure of the Jesuits' merchandise on the high seas plunged their commercial correspondents in Marseilles, Lioncy and Gouffre, into a spectacular bankruptcy which ruined not only themselves but their creditors in France. These creditors eventually proceeded against Lioncy and Gouffre, and Lioncy and Gouffre, in turn, accusingly pointed their fingers at

1. *Nouvelles Ecclésiastiques* (July 17, 1761), p. 113.
2. D'Argenson, *Journal et mémoires*, Vol. 10, p. 225.

the Jesuit mission on the island of Martinique. Someone had to pay, and the Jesuits of Martinique seemed the responsible party.[3]

But to speak of the "Jesuits" and their "commercial correspondents" is already to prejudice the issue on at least two counts. Was the Jesuit mission of Martinique really engaging in commerce? If so, was the entire Jesuit Order to be held responsible for the unpaid debts of this one mission? On the first count even contemporary Jesuits were willing to admit that the missionary zeal of their visitor general and apostolic prefect on the island of Martinique, the père de la Valette, had been at least in some respects misdirected.[4] Originally sent to Martinique in 1743 as the priest of a small parish near Saint-Pierre, La Valette's "talents manifested themselves so rapidly," according to the *Nouvelles Ecclésiastiques,* that in 1747 he was named superior general of the mission of Saint-Pierre on Martinique, then attorney general of missions in the West Indies, in 1753 superior of missions in the West Indies, and in 1755 visitor general and apostolic prefect of the same.[5] The apostolic labors by which La Valette effected his meteoric rise consisted partly in acquiring considerable lands in both Martinique and on the neighboring island of Saint Dominique, upon which he cultivated manioc, sugar, and cocoa, and constructed a sugar and a huge vinegar factory. To people the newly acquired lands with cheap labor, La Valette was even rumored to have sailed disguised as a pirate to the English island of Barbados and to have purchased five hundred Negroes at very low cost. The sugar, coffee, cocoa, and vinegar La Valette of course sold in Europe through the intermediary of companies such as Lioncy and Gouffre on whom he periodically drew bills of exchange. It was the inability of Lioncy and Gouffre to acquit several such bills that resulted in their bankruptcy in 1755.[6]

However offensive to pious ears, this much of La Valette's activities was not strictly speaking commercial. According to both civil and canon law, one did not legally engage in commerce unless one bought products with the intention of reselling them at a profit. If, then, La Valette had restricted himself to selling products grown or manufactured on lands owned or administered by the Jesuit Order, he would have done nothing essentially different from what monastic orders had in fact done since the early Middle Ages. Unfortunately for the Jesuit Order, however, La Valette did considerably more. The island of Martinique was full of natural born Frenchmen who wanted to return to France and there obtain full value for the goods they had acquired at Martinique. The difficulty was that the money of Martinique lost a third of its value when converted into French money, so that six thousand livres in Martinique money,

3. *Nouvelles Ecclésiastiques* (July 17, 1761), pp. 113–14.
4. Cerutti, *Apologie de l'institut des Jésuites,* Vol. 1, pp. 121–23.
5. *Nouvelles Ecclésiastiques* (July 10, 1761), p. 110.
6. Ibid. See also P. C. Rochmontaix, *Le Père Lavalette à la Martinique* (Paris, 1908).

for example, was worth only four thousand livres in French money. Into thi:
monetary breach stepped the père de la Valette, who assured the inhabitants o:
Martinique that if they would entrust their possessions to him, he would obtair
their full value in French money within the space of two or three years. Disinterested on the surface, La Valette's services were not so disinterested in fact
For what he did with the money entrusted to him was first to convert it inte
sugar and coffee in Martinique, next sell the sugar and coffee in France at a loss
of only one-fifth instead of one-third of its original value, then convert the
French livres thereby acquired into Portuguese gold pieces, and finally sell the
Portuguese gold pieces in Martinique,where they netted him sixty-six Frencl
livres apiece. Now by repeating this fruitful operation five or six times—a feat
which his long-term bills of exchange enabled him to perform—La Valette was
able not only to restitute the original sum in French livres but to realize an
immense net profit for himself, and all without risking a sou of his own. But in
so doing he engaged in commerce not only with goods but with money,
thereby incurring the penalties of both civil and ecclesiastical law, which
forbade commerce to monks.[7]

   The second question—whether or not the entire Jesuit Order could be held
responsible for the commercial debts of the single mission at Martinique—was
not so easily decided and opened a veritable Pandora's box of legal casuistry.
But only subsequently. When in February 1756 Lioncy and Gouffre declared
their bankruptcy, they did not think to negotiate with the entire Jesuit Order,
but only with the Jesuit mission at Martinique. Nor were more than three years
of fruitless attempts on the part of Lioncy and Gouffre to tap the Jesuit coffers
enough to dissuade their creditors' syndic from employing the same tactics
when, in August 1759, he too entered the judicial lists against the Jesuits. He
directed his case only against the père de la Valette as superior general of the
Jesuits in the West Indies and his immediate superior, the père de Sacy, who was
attorney general of missions in South America. Moreover, the sentence which
the syndic obtained on November 12, 1759, condemned only La Valette to pay
the sums in question. The court postponed the case against Sacy until another
day.[8] Then suddenly on January 30, 1760, a certain widow named Grou from
Nantes, the unfortunate endorser of one of La Valette's many worthless bills of
exchange, obtained a sentence from the consular court of Paris, this one not only
against La Valette and Sacy but against the père de Montigny, attorney general

7. *Nouvelles Ecclésiastiques* (July 10, 1761), p. 110; and Charlemagne Lalourcé, *Mémoire à
consulter pour Jean Lioncy, créancier, et syndic de la masse de la rasion de commerce, établie à
Marseilles sous le nom de Lioncy frères, et Gouffre, contre le corps et société des P.P. Jésuites* (Paris,
1761), pp. 4–7. Henceforth cited as *Mémoire à consulter pour Jean Lioncy.*
   8. Lalourcé, *Mémoire à consulter pour Jean Lioncy,* pp. 44–45.

of the Jesuit Order in the province of France, and with him all the Jesuit possessions within the dominions of the king.[9]

The case is not without dramatic interest. Sacy himself represented the province of France and pleaded its case in person. He began by asking Grou's attorney three questions: Who drew the bill of exchange? On whom was it drawn? At whose order was it drawn, and who endorsed it? The attorney, a certain M. Benoît, answered that the père de la Valette had drawn the bill on one Rey, a merchant at Marseilles, at the order of M. Rachon, who had endorsed it to M. Charlery, who had endorsed it to the widow Grou. "Now," replied Sacy, "I am neither the père de la Valette, nor M. Rey nor Rachon nor Charlery, and you have therefore no case against me." Sacy seemed to triumph until the attorney Benoît, in turn, questioned him about the position of La Valette and his relation to his superiors in the Jesuit Order. Sacy replied that La Valette was superior general of missions in the West Indies and that he rendered account for his administration to himself, the attorney general of missions in the West Indies, who in turn rendered account to the attorney general of the province of France, who rendered account, finally, to the superior general of the Jesuit Order in Rome. Benoît then proceeded to demonstrate from the Jesuits' own *Dictionnaire de Trévoux* that the authority of the general of the Jesuit Order over all its members was absolute and lifelong, that the père de la Valette possessed no authority of his own but was only the commercial mandatory of the entire Jesuit Order from the general on down, and that the entire society was therefore responsible for the commercial debts of La Valette and the mission of Martinique.[10]

The attorney Benoît's argument carried the court, whose decision against the Jesuits set off a small landslide of similar decisions in other consular courts in France. Encouraged, the syndic of the creditors of Lioncy and Gouffre returned to the charge in March 1760, and on May 29, 1760, persuaded the consular court of Marseilles to extend its previous sentence against La Valette to the Jesuit Order as a whole. At the same time, he pressed charges against the Jesuit Order for two other unacquitted bills of exchange, one for thirty thousand livres and the other for more than ninety thousand, obtaining favorable judgments from the consular court of Marseilles on April 22 and June 16 respectively. In the face of this sudden and unfavorable turn of events the Jesuits finally

---

9. *Sentence des juge et consuls de Paris, qui condamne tous les Jésuites de France solidairement, à payer la Somme de Trente mille livres dues en vertu d'une lettre de change tirée par le père Lavalette, superieur des missions aux Iles du Vent, avec les profits et intérêts depuis l'échéance de ladite lettre (30 janvier 1760)*, p. 9. Henceforth cited as *Sentence des juge et consuls de Paris (30 janvier 1760)*.

10. Lalourcé, *Mémoire à consulter pour Jean Lioncy*, pp. 50–52.

decided to appeal the decisions of the consular courts. On July 2, 1760, the Jesuits of the province of France served an opposition to the sentence of May 29 to the syndic of the creditors of Lioncy and Gouffre, and the Jesuits of the provinces of Champagne, Guyenne, Toulouse, and Lyons, since they were also affected by the sentence of the consular court, followed suit on July 4.[11] Following the same procedure, the Jesuits continued to oppose the various sentences of the consular courts until, on August 17, 1760, the Jesuits obtained a judgment from the royal council entitling them to appeal all sentences concerning the commercial debts of La Valette to the *grand' chambre* of the parlement of Paris.[12]

This sequence of events suggests several intriguing questions. How did it happen, first of all, that Lioncy's and Gouffre's creditors suddenly came upon the bright idea of proceeding against the Jesuit Order as a whole? Or to re-phrase the question, how did they suddenly discover that the Jesuit Order was distinguished from most other monastic orders in the unquestioning, almost servile obedience that each of its members owed the superior general? And why, secondly, were the Jesuits so foolish as to appeal their case to the parlement of Paris, the notorious stronghold of their most implacable enemies? Why did they not simply pay their debts to Lioncy and Gouffre and have done with the embarrassing affair?

A clue to the answer of the first question is given to us by Robert de Saint-Vincent. Sometime in 1759, and shortly after Sacy had reduced the merchant Lioncy to despair by informing him in a conversation that he was about to go to Mass and had nothing to offer him but prayers, someone, according to Robert de Saint-Vincent, "suggested to [the merchant Lioncy] that he consult M. de Lalourcé, who passed for *à* Jansenist since it sufficed to take sides against the Jesuits to acquire this reputation. The lawyer Lalourcé," Saint-Vincent continued, "after having thoroughly studied all the documents which Lioncy gave to him and after having determined all the circumstances of this novel and singular affair, decided that it was above all necessary to instruct and inform the public and he began by fixing public opinion on the nature of an affair which resembled in no respect the claims which had previously been formed against the Jesuits."[13] Lalourcé's effort "to instruct and inform the public" refers of course to his celebrated *Mémoire à consulter pour Jean Lioncy,* which he published about a month after the affair of the Jesuits reached the floor of the parlement of Paris at the end of March 1761.[14] But what is especially interesting about

11. Ibid., pp. 40–50.
12. Ibid., pp. 55–56.
13. Saint-Vincent, "Mémoires," p. 218.
14. In the *Nouvelles Ecclésiastiques* (September 25, 1761), p. 156, it was asserted that the *Mémoire à consulter pour Jean Lioncy* was "properly" Lalourcé's work, although 15 additional lawyers, among them Le Paige, Maultrot, Pinault, and Mey, had signed the consultation as well.

Robert de Saint-Vincent's observation is that it indicates that Lalourcé began advising Lioncy and Gouffre and their creditors at about the same time that Rey first brought their case against the Jesuits to the consular courts and certainly before the Jesuits appealed the decisions of those courts to the parlement of Paris.

Who was Lalourcé? Our best source of information concerning him is his obituary printed in the *Nouvelles Ecclésiastiques* on June 27, 1768. Indeed, the very fact that he was deemed worthy of such an obituary proves that his Jansenism, like that of Saint-Vincent himself, consisted in something more than mere hostility toward the Jesuits, and that in fact he was accounted as something of a saint within Jansenist circles. The obituary itself gives us reason to believe as much. "His affection for the Truth and for those who defend it, the role he played in the destruction of the Jesuits, the wisdom with which he prepared and we can even say conducted by his counsels that important affair, the rare piety which he manifested above all during his long and very painful illness—here without doubt," according to the *Nouvelles Ecclésiastiques,* "are just incentives to sound his praise." Nor did his behavior lag behind his affection for the "Truth." In his private life he neither neglected to attend regularly the services of his parish nor permitted his numerous professional responsibilities to impinge upon time set aside for prayer and the recitation of the divine service. He gave abundant alms, deprived himself of all entertainment, never dined outside his home, and recited Sexte every day at noon with his family and as many pious neighbors as he was able to invite. In his role of consultant lawyer at the parlement of Paris he opposed Christophe de Beaumont's measures against Jansenists in every way and went considerably beyond most of his colleagues in his opposition to the exaction of *billets de confession*.[15] But it was above all his role in the destruction of the Jesuits that won him renown. "Lalourcé," according to the *Nouvelles Ecclésiastiques,* "was the soul of that entire affair," and the manner in which he conducted the trial "did him infinite honor and won him the most flattering esteem of the magistrates of the parlement of Paris but also of the other sovereign courts of the realm and even at the Court." To have overcome the many legal obstacles in his path, thought the gazeteer, "required nothing less than a genius of his type, full of zeal and light, incapable of being rebuffed and skillful at foreseeing and even profiting from the mistakes of his adversaries while giving them no hold on himself."[16]

Now, as it happened, Lalourcé was also the colleague and good friend of Adrien Le Paige, who at this very moment—the closing months of 1759 or the first months of 1760—was busily at work on the monumental *Histoire générale de la compagnie de Jésus en France*. That the composition of the *Histoire générale*

15. *Nouvelles Ecclésiastiques* (June 27, 1768), p. 101.
16. Ibid., p. 102.

itself had nothing directly to do with the La Valette affair but was part of a more general campaign against the Jesuits seems certain, not only because the *Histoire générale* contains no references whatever to the La Valette affair, but because it was already composed by June 1760, a full month, that is, before the Jesuits had even appealed a single sentence of the consular courts to the parlement of Paris. Le Paige, moreover, communicated the *Histoire générale* section by section as it was being printed to Lalourcé while the latter was engaged in the first stages of work on his *Mémoire à consulter* for Lioncy and Gouffre during the parliamentary recess from September to November—a process which would by no means have been necessary if the *Histoire générale* itself had been written with the La Valette affair in view. But why in that case did Lalourcé find Le Paige's and Coudrette's *Histoire générale* so indispensable to the composition of his own *Mémoire à consulter*? Undoubtedly because the *Histoire générale* was the first anti-Jesuitical pamphlet both to formulate and elaborate the charge of excessive authority or tyranny on the part of the Jesuit Order and most especially its superior general—precisely the charge, as we have just seen, which persuaded the consular courts to sentence the entire Jesuit Order to pay the commercial debts of the père de la Valette.

What we have here, then, is a case of exceptional luck—or providence, as the Jansenists would have it. Le Paige and Coudrette had been quite independently developing the argument that the Jesuit Order was despotic in character when Le Paige's friend Lalourcé was suddenly confronted with an opportunity to employ this argument against the Jesuits in the case of Lioncy and Gouffre. Then, having won the day in the consular courts with this argument and having become in the meantime the chief legal consultant of the Jesuits' creditors, Lalourcé further elaborated the theme of Jesuitical despotism in his *Mémoire à consulter,* which he began writing shortly after the Jesuits successfully appealed their case to the parlement of Paris.[17] To this purpose Lalourcé not only studied Le Paige's and Coudrette's *Histoire générale* as it was being printed, but sent the final draft of his own *Mémoire à consulter* to Le Paige for last-minute corrections before finally dashing it off to the printers in April 1761.[18]

But we have not yet heard the last of divine providence. For what event was more providential from the Jansenists' point of view than the Jesuits' appeal to the parlement of Paris? The Jansenists certainly regarded the appeal in this way, and even more skeptical observers such as Voltaire and D'Alembert marveled that the Jesuits, who otherwise looked after their temporal affairs with such consummate political craftsmanship, could so unwittingly walk into a trap

17. Lalourcé, *Mémoire à consulter pour Jean Lioncy,* pp. 62, 129–235. The term *despotisme* had already been employed in the sentence of the consular court of Paris. See *Sentence des juges et consuls de Paris (30 janvier 1760),* p. 9.

18. B.P.R.: L.P. 582, mss. 44–45, Lalourcé to La Paige, March 11 and 24, 1761.

set by their traditionally more otherworldly adversaries.[19] And what renders the Jesuits' blunder yet more marvelous is that by grant of Louis XIV the Jesuits possessed the right of *committimus*, which entitled them to bring legal cases involving themselves, not to the parlement of Paris, but to the far more trustworthy *grand conseil*.[20] What, then, prompted the Jesuits to appeal their case to the very lair of their most ferocious enemies?

To contemporaries in the know, however, the reasoning behind the Jesuits' choice of the parlement of Paris was not so past finding out as historians have sometimes presented it. To be sure, the parlement of Paris was a citadel of their enemies, but in 1760 the *grand conseil* was hardly less one. For among its members were counselors like Guignac de Villeneuve, "who did not hide his opinions about the Jesuits,"[21] and Claude Guillaume Lambert, the father of Robert de Saint-Vincent's most trusted friend in the parlement of Paris and, if anything, more Jansenist than his son.[22] The *grand conseil* as such was by the mid-eighteenth century a curial anachronism stripped of much of its former jurisdiction and repeatedly caught in the crossfire between the parlement of Paris and the ministry at Versailles.[23] It had just recently emerged none the better from three years of warfare with the parlement of Paris over rival jurisdictional pretensions, and by 1760 was unlikely to court parliamentary displeasure with an unpopular verdict in the affair of the Jesuits. On the other hand, the Jesuits were to be tried not by the assembled chambers of the parlement of Paris but by the *grand' chambre* alone, where they could count upon numerous friends: the *doyen* Jean-Jacques Severt, for example, who belonged to a Jesuit congregation,[24] or Presidents Molé and Maupeou, who at least were not their enemies as well as counselor-clerks ecclesiastically indebted to the order such as the abbés Claude de Tudert and Farjonel d'Hauterive.[25] In contrast, the strength of the *parti janséniste* was concentrated in the lower chambers of inquests, which were not to participate in the trial at all.

A final question remains unanswered. Why did the Jesuits appeal their case at all? Why did they not open their coffers and avoid the scandal of a trial in the parlement of Paris or anywhere else? In fact, the same question seems to have been a cause of controversy among the Jesuits themselves. The Jesuits in Rome wanted to pay the debts and avoid the courts, while the Jesuits in Paris first insisted that La Valette declare bankruptcy and then, after the alarming decisions

19. D'Alembert, *Sur la Destruction des Jésuites en France, par un auteur désintéressé*, p. 94.

20. Crétineau-Joly, *Clément XIV et les Jésuites*, p. 101.

21. Saint-Vincent, "Mémoires," p. 221.

22. *Nouvelles Ecclésiastiques* (April 3, 1780), p. 56.

23. François Bluche, *Les Magistrats du grand conseil au XVIIIe siècle, 1690–1791* (Paris, 1966), pp. 17–21.

24. *Nouvelles Ecclésiastiques* (October 16, 1761), p. 167.

25. Saint-Vincent, "Mémoires," pp. 176–79, 184, 240, 531.

of the consular courts in 1760, insisted with equal vehemence that their case against Lioncy and Gouffre was watertight and could not fail in the parlement of Paris. Unfortunately for the order, the advice from Paris prevailed. Meanwhile the Jesuits in Europe seem to have possessed only the most fragmentary picture of La Valette's activities in Martinique, and their best efforts to set in gear the machinery of ecclesiastical discipline foundered on the reefs of accident and war. As early as 1756 the Jesuit general, Louis Centurioni, appointed two visitors to investigate the conduct of La Valette, but they never left land because of causes—if we may believe a Jesuit historian—which were "independent of the human will." Another visitor appointed in 1759 died en route and his successor, the attorney of missions in Canada, broke his leg at Versailles as he was about to set sail. Yet a third Jesuit took voyage on a neutral ship but was captured by pirates. It was not until the père François de la Marche arrived at Martinique in the spring of 1762 that the order was able to investigate the activities of La Valette at first hand. La Marche found him guilty of engaging in commerce and deprived him of all spiritual and temporal administration, but by this date the damage was done. In little more than three months the society would no longer exist in France.[26]

The Jesuits obtained their appeal to the parlement of Paris on August 17, 1760, but it was not until March 31, 1761, that their case reached the floor of the *grand' chambre.* This gave all the parties concerned more than seven months in which to prepare their cases. Nonetheless, the time seems to have been hardly sufficient for Lioncy and Gouffre and their chief legal consultant, Charlemagne Lalourcé, who as late as March 24 was scribbling panic-filled notes to Le Paige concerning last minute revisions of his monumental *Mémoire à consulter* for Lioncy, Gouffre, and the syndic of their creditors. "I tremble in telling you how much the thing presses," he wrote Le Paige on March 11.[27] And he trembled with good reason, for at that date he had only fifteen more days in which to correct and print his consultation. It was not in fact until late April that the consultation finally appeared.[28]

It was with good reason, too, that Lalourcé required all seven months at his disposal to prepare his case against the Jesuits. To be sure, it was simple enough to formulate a case establishing the Jesuit Order's responsibility for the commercial debt of the mission of Martinique; for that matter, the main lines of such a case had been worked out months before the Jesuits had ever appealed a single sentence of the commercial courts to the parlement of Paris. But in writing his consultation Lalourcé had been aiming his sights far higher than this. For what

26. Crétineau-Joly, *Clément XIV et les Jésuites,* pp. 97–104.
27. B.P.R.: L.P. 582, ms. 44, Lalourcé to Le Paige, March 11, 1761.
28. Barbier, *Journal,* Vol. 7, p. 357.

in reality he had been preparing was nothing less than a full-blown indictment of the Jesuits' very legal existence and behavior in France since their reception in 1561. When it finally appeared in late April, the *Mémoire à consulter* ran more than five hundred pages in length—something of a record, perhaps, among legal consultations of its type. And only a fraction of this total concerned the case of Lioncy and Gouffre and their creditors. At least as much space was employed in proving what Le Paige's and Coudrette's *Histoire générale* had already shown: that the Jesuit Order was despotic in character and therefore unacceptable in a monarchical state like France, that neither in 1561 nor at the time of their reestablishment in 1603 had the Jesuits been legally accepted in France as a religious order, that they had been merely tolerated upon conditions which the Jesuits had never fulfilled, "and that the Parlement," as Barbier expressed it, "would have even a better right to chase them from the realm than in 1594."[29] All this information possessed only the most tangential connection with the Lioncy and Gouffre case, but Lalourcé was only tangentially interested in this case anyway. From the very outset he was far more interested in the possibility of exterminating the Jesuit Order in France.

The Jesuits had also profitably employed the seven months at their disposal, but they had aimed their sights considerably lower than Lalourcé. Their object was simply to avoid paying the debts of their mission at Martinique. Ultimately this limited strategy left the Jesuits totally unprepared for any wider attack, but initially it proved advantageous enough, because Lalourcé, with his sights aimed high, tended to stumble over the legal obstacles with which the Jesuits progressively cluttered his path. And no sooner had the trial begun on the Tuesday after Quasimodo Sunday on March 31 than the Jesuits, with proverbial adroitness, laid down the first such obstacle. The case, the Jesuits' lawyers argued, should be appointed, not pleaded.

For a case to be pleaded meant that it would be publically argued by lawyers representing both parties and publically judged by the counselors present. For a case to be appointed, on the other hand, meant that it would be placed at the very end of the parliamentary role and then privately decided by specially appointed counselors on the basis of purely written testimony.[30] Now the usual justification given for appointment was that of efficiency in the event of extremely complex cases, a justification which seemed to apply to the case of Lioncy and Gouffre. Not only was the Lioncy and Gouffre case for some strange reason to be found in two different locations on the parliamentary role, one which called for pleading but the other for appointment, but the case itself was extremely complicated by reason of the number of parties involved. Besides the

---

29. Ibid. The section in the *Mémoire à consulter* concerning the Jesuits' legal status in France is to be found in pp. 400–500.
30. Shennan, *The Parlement of Paris*, pp. 57–67.

Jesuits of the province of France and Lioncy and Gouffre, there was one additional defendant, the Jesuits of the provinces of Champagne, Guyenne, Toulouse, and Lyons, as well as three additional plaintiffs: one the syndic of the creditors of Lioncy and Gouffre, and the other two, a certain M. Cazotte and one Mlle. Fouque, both unfortunate bearers of La Valette's worthless bills of exchange. The Jesuits' lawyers Claude-François Thevenot d'Essaules and Laget-Bardelin argued with good reason that if the cases of all these parties were to be pleaded separately, the entire affair would be well nigh interminable and justice might never be done.[31]

Whether the Jesuits were really very concerned that justice be done is doubtful. The *Nouvelles Ecclésiastiques* quite rightly identified the Jesuits' preoccupation with the complexity of the case as a pretext for far more real concerns. Among them was the fact that the already printed memoirs on the side of the plaintiffs—the lawyers Rouhette's and Jean-Baptiste Target's *Mémoire sur les demandes formées contre le général et la société des Jésuites*, the lawyer Jean-Baptiste Le Gouvé's *Plaidoyer pour le syndic des créanciers des sieurs Lioncy*, and Lalourcé's enormous *Mémoire à consulter*—not only manifested an alarmingly irreverent interest in the Jesuit Order and its constitutions, but raised the cry of despotism against the Jesuits' general.[32] Already it was becoming apparent that what might have been a routine commercial lawsuit was rapidly developing into an affair which at the very least could dangerously discredit the Jesuits in the eyes of the public. Nor was the public a mere abstraction. From the very first day of the trial and at every subsequent session a varied crowd of Parisians so filled the galleries of the *grand' chambre* "that one could not enter," enthusiastically cheered every utterance from the mouths of the lawyers of the plaintiffs, and systematically hooted down the Jesuits' lawyers' every attempt to make themselves heard.[33] Barbier, little sympathetic to these public theatrics, nonetheless concluded that they "well demonstrate the animosity of the public against these reverend fathers," while the more enthusiastic *Nouvelles Ecclésiastiques* described the boos which greeted the words of the Jesuits' lawyers as "justly merited" although "little appropriate in truth to the majesty of the place."[34] Small wonder, then, that the Jesuits felt they had everything to lose in a pleaded case, and everything to gain from an appointed one.

However disturbing, the public demonstrations initially affected the Jesuits only by providing them with another powerful argument in favor of appointment. How was justice to be obtained, argued the Jesuits' lawyers, if they were

31. *Nouvelles Ecclésiastiques* (September 4, 1761), pp. 141–42.
32. See below, pp. 179–180.
33. Barbier, *Journal*, Vol. 7, p. 352.
34. Ibid., p. 353; *Nouvelles Ecclésiastiques* (September 4, 1761), p. 142.

to be unceremoniously interrupted at every turn?[35] So powerful, in fact, were the Jesuits' arguments in favor of appointment that only a day before the vote, no less a person than President Etienne François d'Aligre assured Robert de Saint-Vincent that the case would be surely appointed because it was "too complicated and too important to be discussed in open court" and because the public was "so impetuous and so little reasonable" that it was necessary "to avoid public scandal."[36] But at this critical moment—on April 6—the Jesuits' opponents executed a dramatic maneuver. "What joy and one might say transports on the part of the Public," cried the *Nouvelles Ecclésiastiques*, "when it heard Messrs. Rouhette and Target, lawyers of the two intervening parties, declare successively in words full of nobility and eloquence the generous resolution their parties had taken to desist from their intervention in order to render the case more susceptible to public hearing and to better enable the magistrates to give the Lioncys the prompt justice their situation demanded!" The auditors were so ravished, according to the gazeteer, "that people forgot themselves to the point of clapping their hands and feet to better express their joy."[37]

The strategic withdrawal of the two intervening parties of Fouque and Cazotte effectively pulled the rug from beneath the Jesuits' stand that the case was too complicated to be pleaded in open court. This left the Jesuits with only a single foot to stand on: that such "transports" of public "joy" as the one which greeted the announcement of the lawyers Rouhette and Target prejudiced the case in advance and rendered the magistrates unfree in their deliberations. To undermine this remaining foothold the lawyer Jean-Baptiste Gerbier, who represented the party of Lioncy and Gouffre, employed all his eloquence on the following day, April 7. "What, sirs," he rhetorically asked the magistrates, "would you permit yourselves to be seduced by the specious pretext upon which my opponents would like to establish the necessity of appointment, namely the indiscretion with which the public might interrupt your deliberations with indecent murmurs and importunate applause? Fear nothing in that regard," he assured them. "I dare to answer for the wisdom of the public and the profound respect with which it will receive your oracles."[38] To his eloquence Gerbier added the discovery that in their own *Dictionnaire de Trévoux* the Jesuits had defined "appointment" as a device to which judges resorted when they wanted to favor an evil cause, and the two factors, eloquence and discovery, barely carried the day on April 7.[39] The vote, sixteen to fifteen against appointment,

35. Saint-Vincent, "Mémoires," pp. 222–23.
36. Ibid., p. 224.
37. *Nouvelles Ecclésiastiques* (September 4, 1761), pp. 142–43.
38. Saint-Vincent, "Mémoires," p. 226.
39. *Nouvelles Ecclésiastiques* (September 4, 1761), p. 142.

again left the *grand' chambre* resounding "with shouts, applause, the clapping of hands and of feet."[40]

So the case was pleaded. During the remaining weeks in April and the first week of May the magistrates of the *grand' chambre* heard the lawyers Le Gouvé and Gerbier present the case of Lioncy and Gouffre and their creditors, and the lawyers Thevenot d'Essaules and Laget-Bardelin, that of the Jesuits of France and the other provinces. As presented to the *grand' chambre* the case of Lioncy and Gouffre against the Jesuits departed little from the lines laid down by Lalourcé in his *Mémoire à consulter* and ran somewhat as follows.[41]

In nearly all religious orders, the plaintiffs argued, the basic unit and civil entity was the individual monastic community or house. Though each monk had by definition died civilly upon taking his vows, he thereupon merged his civic identity into the particular community or house of which he became a member, and this community, in turn, bought from, sold to, and contracted with other parties as if it were a civil being (*être civil*), and all without prejudice to the other monastic communities within the same religious order. This was so because each monastic community in fact governed itself temporally and was therefore solely responsible for the debts contracted in its name. With other communities of the same religious order it shared only the common spiritual rule which it followed. But with the Jesuits—so the argument continued—all was different. The Jesuits' constitutions invested their general with powers so absolute and unrestricted that he could only be regarded as a despot modeled after oriental patterns. This despot in fact "owned" all the property of the Jesuit Order; he alone among Jesuits possessed the authority to buy, sell, transfer, or alienate the order's property and contract with other parties. All other Jesuits were his slaves who possessed no authority of their own. When the père de la Valette of the mission of Martinique contracted debts to the company of Lioncy and Gouffre, he therefore acted only as the Jesuit general's commercial mandatory—more accurately, his slave—and the debts he contracted were therefore the debts of the entire Jesuit Order and more particularly of its general. That this was in fact the case was recognized by the Jesuits until 1759. As La Valette's immediate superior, the père de Sacy, attorney general of missions in South America, once redirected La Valette's shipments from Cadix and Amsterdam to

40. Ibid., p. 143. The vote was reported by Robert de Saint-Vincent, "Mémoires," p. 226.
41. For the case of Lioncy and Gouffre against the Jesuits, see Lalourcé, *Mémoire à consulter pour Jean Lioncy,* especially pp. 59–166, 241–92 and 400–503. See also Rouhette and Guy-Jean-Baptiste Target, *Mémoire sur les demandes formées contre le général et la société des Jésuites, au sujet des engagements qu'elle a contractés par le ministère du père de la Valette* (Paris, 1761); *Second Mémoire pour le sieur Cazotte et la demoiselle Fouque, contre le général et la Société des Jésuites* (n. p., n. d.), by the same lawyers and; Jean-Baptiste Legouvé, *Plaidoyer pour le syndic des créanciers des sieurs Lioncy frères et Gouffre, négociants à Marseille, contre le général et la société des Jésuites* (1761).

Marseilles, spoke of La Valette's debts in his correspondence as "our affair," contracted loans to pay creditors with the authorization of the general, and at one point told Lioncy that he could do nothing without the consent of his general. The general himself, finally, implicitly recognized in some of his letters to creditors that the debts contracted by La Valette were legitimate—in other words, sanctioned by himself.

Formidable though the case of Lioncy and Gouffre might seem, the Jesuits' lawyers were not discountenanced.[42] They immediately launched a strong counterattack at the weakest point in their opponents' formation—namely, the proposition that the Jesuits' general somehow "owned" all the property of the Jesuit Order. According to the Jesuits' constitutions, they argued, neither the general nor any other individual Jesuit owned anything at all but, like all other monks, were bound to perpetual poverty; the general for his part was merely the chief administrator of the property at the order's disposal.[43] Their attack sensibly blunted by this maneuver, the prosecution parried with the argument that if the Jesuits' temporal was not the property of their general, it was then the property of the entire Jesuit Order as a whole and of no individual Jesuit community or house in particular, and that the debts contracted by the père de La Valette of the mission at Martinique were therefore all the same the debts of the entire Jesuit Order.[44] But the defendants swiftly countered with the observation that according to both the Jesuits' constitutions and the laws of the French realm, the Jesuit Order no more than its general owned anything in France but merely administered property destined by its donors to the purposes of education and missions.[45] Now in full retreat, the lawyers of Lioncy and Gouffre first rather unconvincingly argued that if the Jesuit Order possessed no unity of property, it at least possessed a unity of administration vested by its constitutions in the general,[46] and then had recourse to Lalourcé's argument in the *Mémoire à con-*

---

42. For the case for the Jesuits see Gillet, Lherminier, Mallard, et al., *Mémoire à consulter et consultation pour les Jésuites de France* (Paris, 1761); Laget-Bardelin, *Mémoire pour les Jésuites des provinces de Champagne, Guyenne, Toulouse et Lyon, opposants et défendeurs, contre le syndic des créanciers Lioncy et Gouffre, défendeur à l'opposition et demandeur* (Paris, 1761); L. F. Delatour and H. L. Guérin, *Réponse au mémoire intitulé: Mémoire sur les demandes formées contre le général et la société des Jésuites, au sujet des engagements qu'elle a contractés par le ministère du père de la Valette* (Paris, 1761); by the same authors, *Précis pour les Jésuites de France, sur l'appel, par eux interjetté, des sentences des juges et consuls de Paris, qui les condamnent solidairement au payement des lettres de changes tirées par le père de la Valette, procureur de la maison de Saint Pierre de la Martinique* (Paris, 1761), and Claude-François Thevenot d'Essaules, *Plaidoyer pour les Jésuites de France* (Paris, 1761).

43. Gillet, Lherminier, Mallard, et al., *Mémoire à consulter*, pp. 44–52; Delatour and Guérin, *Réponse au mémoire*, pp. 33–34.

44. Rouhette and Target, *Second Mémoire*, pp. 37–38.

45. Laget-Bardelin, *Mémoire pour les Jésuites*, pp. 21–41.

46. Thevenot d'Essaules, *Plaidoyer*, pp. 72–73; *Nouvelles Ecclésiastiques* (September 4, 1761), p. 144.

sulter that the Jesuits had never been legally established in France as a religious order. Since as a monastic order the Jesuits had never been legally accepted but merely tolerated in France, they could not, it was argued, appeal to the laws of the French realm, which protected the temporal of only legally established orders.[47]

But however well taken in themselves, Lalourcé's observations concerning the Jesuits' precarious legal position in France were not really designed to bolster the case of Lioncy and Gouffre but were rather aimed at the Jesuits' very existence in France. To have had dubious recourse to these observations in the context of the Lioncy and Gouffre case was therefore a risky maneuver and handed the Jesuits another opportunity to take advantage of Lalourcé's celestially aimed sights by throwing a stumbling block at his feet.

This the Jesuits lost no time in doing. To the argument, first of all, that the Jesuit Order possessed, if not unity of property, at least unity of administration, the Jesuits' lawyers replied that the order indeed possessed a single supreme administrator—the general—but no unity of administration, since the various Jesuit superiors, once appointed to individual colleges or missions by the general, thereupon became the temporal agents not of the general but of the missions, colleges, or residences they governed. The government of the Jesuit Order therefore differed only in form, not in substance, from that of other religious orders. As in others, each individual establishment was alone responsible for the governance of its temporal and the debts it contracted.[48] And if the Jesuits' opponents insisted upon basing their case solely upon the distinctive nature of the Jesuits' constitutions rather than on the laws of the French realm, which otherwise protected the integrity of monastic establishments, how then, asked the Jesuits' lawyers, could they at the same time insist upon the application of the commercial laws of the realm to the activities of the père de la Valette when the Jesuits' constitutions explicitly forbade commerce to those under its obedience? The Jesuits' prosecutors could not, they argued, have their cake and eat it too.[49]

Outflanked on one side, the prosecution executed a brilliant maneuver on the other by observing that it was really the Jesuits who wanted to have their cake and eat it too. For the Jesuits apparently felt equally free to violate their own laws prohibiting commerce, and then to appeal to those same laws in order to escape the civil consequences of their disobedience, equally free to claim to possess no property and to behave consistently as if they did. Evidently the purpose of the Jesuits' laws prohibiting commercial activities and the possession of property was to permit them to do both at no risk to themselves.[50] Not content with this

47. Lalourcé, *Mémoire à consulter pour Jean Lioncy*, pp. 400–03; Rouhette and Target, *Second Mémoire*, pp. 61–62; 70–71.
48. Thevenot d'Essaules, *Plaidoyer*, pp. 75–80; 111–29.
49. Ibid., p. 87.
50. *Nouvelles Ecclésiastiques* (September 11 and 18, 1761), pp. 147,151.

rejoinder, the prosecution ventured to salvage its other flank as well. If, it argued, the Jesuits were not accorded the protection of French law, which guaranteed the integrity of monastic establishments, while at the same time they were subjected to the laws governing commerce, it was because the existence of the Jesuits in France was tolerated in fact though not by law and as such had to be regulated by laws, just as a foreigner, though not accorded the protection of French law, had nonetheless to bear its penalties if in fact he incurred them.[51] But the Jesuits were quick to observe that if indeed they were "foreigners" in France, it was all the more strange that the property they administered in France could function as surety for a debt contracted on an island across the seas. The island in question of course belonged to France, but could this property, they asked, also serve as surety for a debt contracted by Jesuits in Germany? [52]

Obviously not. Nor was there any good answer to the prosecution's question of why the Jesuits felt entitled to appeal to laws of their own making in order to escape the consequences of disobeying them. The contest therefore ended in something of a draw, with the lawyers of Lioncy and Gouffre victorious on one flank and the Jesuits on the other. It is commonly thought that the Jesuits unequivocally lost their case against Lioncy and Gouffre, but this is not entirely true. The parlement's sentence of May 8, though it condemned the Jesuits to pay 1,552,276 livres to Lioncy and Gouffre, nonetheless recognized the stalemated state of affairs by specifically exempting all property attached to the Jesuits' colleges, missions, and residences in France as surety for the debt. The Jesuits were supposed to pay the debt out of the immense store of liquid capital they were commonly believed to have accumulated by means of their commerce in the four corners of the earth. Had the Jesuits never been expelled from France, they might conceivably have scraped up the sum from somewhere. But when, upon confiscation of the Jesuit property in France, the parlement of Paris assumed responsibility for the Jesuits' debt to Lioncy and Gouffre, it was found that this vast store of liquid capital existed nowhere—at least in France—and that many of the Jesuit colleges were so impossibly crippled with debt as to be insolvent.[53] And if the truth were known, neither the parlement of Paris nor the revolutionary Constituent Assembly, which continued to wrestle with the affair in 1789, ever paid the full debt of 1,552,276 livres to the unfortunate company of Lioncy and Gouffre.[54]

But insofar as the sentence of May 8, 1761, ordered the Jesuits to pay their debt to Lioncy and Gouffre, the latter won their case. And for this, while they

51. Rouhette and Target, *Second Mémoire*, p. 75; *Nouvelles Ecclésiastiques* (September 11 and 18, 1761), pp. 145–46; 150–51.

52. Thevenot d'Essaules, *Plaidoyer*, pp. 7–8; Laget-Bardelin, *Mémoire pour les Jésuites*, p. 44.

53. See B.P.R.: L.P. 585–87; B.N.: Collection Joly de Fleury, fols. 1613–14.

54. Crétineau-Joly, *Clément XIV et les Jésuites*, p. 109.

had above all the eloquence and zeal of the lawyer Gerbier to thank, it was nonetheless one of the parlement of Paris's two solicitors general, Le Pelletier de Saint-Fargeau, who received most of the glory for the sentence of May 8, 1761.[55] Though in no sense a Jansenist, he spoke, to believe one Jansenist pamphlet, "a language truly evangelical," and the pamphleteer openly regretted that the "distinguished magistrate" was not a bishop, because in that case "the clergy of France would have at least one minister of the truth."[56] In what precisely this "evangelical language" consisted is difficult to determine. What is certain is that Saint-Fargeau first made the distinction between free property (*biens libres*) and property donated for a specific purpose (*biens grêvés*), by means of which Lioncy and Gouffre finally obtained their sentence against the Jesuits.[57]

In any case, when Saint-Fargeau had finished his speech, the auditors in the *grand' chambre* waxed so enthusiastic that they seized him as he was leaving the parquet and carried him "in triumph" to his carriage, where "the enthusiasm of joy was such that they embraced his horses as if in homage of admiration and love that they dared not carry to the Master himself."[58] And when a bit later First President Molé pronounced the sentence against the Jesuit Order, "the joy of the Public no longer knew any bounds." The auditors refused to permit

55. By virtue of both family tradition and personal conviction, Pierre-Jean-Baptiste Gerbier, too, must be counted as something of a Jansenist. His father, born in Rennes in 1695, had also been a lawyer and had served for long years in the parlement of Brittany, where, according to the *Nouvelles Ecclésiastiques*, he distinguished himself "by his profound knowledge of Religion, by his zeal for the salvation of Souls, by his love for the Truth, and by his horror of the schism" (Cerveau, *Nécrologe des plus célèbres défenseurs et confesseurs de la vérité du dix-huitième siècle*, Vol. 2, p. 425). An object of hatred on the part of the "enemies of the Truth" because of his determined defense of persecuted appellants, he was in 1738 ordered by *lettre de cachet* to move with his entire family to Paris, where he subsequently practiced law at the parlement of Paris and died in 1759, eulogized by both the *Nouvelles Ecclésiastiques* and René Cerveau's *Nécrologe* as "one of the most illustrious victims of the bull Unigenitus" (Ibid., p. 426; *Nouvelles Ecclésiastiques* [December 13, 1759], p. 197). In the obituary in 1759 the *Nouvelles Ecclésiastiques* noted that Gerbier had "left, among others, a lawyer son who, through his intimate acquaintance with the virtues of his respectable father and by his superior talents which God has given him, would be more than anyone else capable of worthily commending his merits" (*Nouvelles Ecclésiastiques* [December 13, 1759], p. 197). But not all Jansenists were so generous in their estimates of the young Gerbier's fidelity to his father's principles. Robert de Saint-Vincent, who probably knew Gerbier better than the editor of the *Nouvelles Ecclésiastiques,* regretted Gerbier's "weakness for women, his inability to resist the bewitching charms of the young and beautiful women of the court"—in short, his "immorality which formed an incredible contrast to the rigor and austerity of his principles" (Saint-Vincent, "Mémoires," p. 234).

56. *Remontrances au parlement, avec des notes, et ornées de figures* (1761), pp. 5–6, in B.N.: Collection Joly de Fleury, fol. 1616, ms. 220.

57. *Nouvelles Ecclésiastiques* (September 18, 1761), p. 153.

58. Ibid. (September 25, 1761), p. 154.

Molé to enter his hotel by the small door near the Sainte-Chapelle but forced him to traverse the entire length of the court of the Palais de Justice "amid general acclamations and respectful felicitations for having had the courage to condemn the Jesuits and uphold the laws."[59] The festive atmosphere reigned in Paris for the remainder of the day. Even the *Nouvelles Ecclésiastiques* seemed surprised that total strangers "embraced each other as if the State had won some great victory,"[60] and the less enthusiastic Barbier, who described the public joy as "quasi indecent," admitted that the event "constituted that day the conversation and satisfaction of all Paris. . . . If some Jansenism did not enter into it," he added, "it would only be half bad."[61]

59. Ibid., p. 155.
60. Ibid.
61. Barbier, *Journal*, Vol. 7, p. 362.

5. The Jesuits on Trial: April 17–August 6, 1761

DESPITE THE OUTBURST OF POPULAR ENTHUSIASM OCCA-sioned by its passage, the judgment of May 8, 1761, was of comparatively minor importance when it was rendered. For in the meantime, on April 17, 1761, a magistrate of the third chamber of inquests had denounced the Jesuit Order to the parlement of Paris as repulsive to the fundamental laws of France.

There can be no doubt that the lawyers Lalourcé and Le Paige had been from the very outset aiming at such a result. But by prematurely raising the question of the legality of the Jesuits' existence in France, they had employed a very risky tactic, for in the context of the Lioncy and Gouffre case the tenuous nature of the Jesuits' legal position in France constituted a far more potent weapon in the hands of the Jesuits than in their own. Like La Fontaine's dog who had caught a fish, Lalourcé and Le Paige had run the serious risk of losing what they could have surely gained by pursuing what might have been the chimera of much larger game, the destruction of the Jesuit Order as such. As it happened they won their case, but only by making concessions which eventually cost their clients the debt to which they were legally entitled.

On the other hand, by making use of the weapon proffered them—the questionable legality of their existence in France—the Jesuits had employed a yet more dangerous tactic than their enemies. For although a weapon in their battle against their creditors, the question of their legal existence in France was nothing but bait in their as yet undeclared, but no less real, war against those who plotted their destruction. Le Paige and Lalourcé, after all, had only the case of Lioncy and Gouffre to lose and the entire Jesuit Order to gain; whereas the Jesuits had only 1,552,276 livres to gain and their very existence to lose. So thoroughly, moreover, had the Jesuits swallowed the bait offered them that during the course of the trial they had not only hypothetically admitted that their order might not legally exist in France, but in attempting to refute some unwarranted assertions about their constitutions—so much more bait—they had even committed the ultimate indiscretion of citing in one of their legal consultations a 1757 edition of their constitutions, thereby inviting an exposure of these sacrosanct documents before the profane gaze of the magistrates of the parlement of Paris.[1]

1. Lherminier, Gillet, and Mallard, *Mémoire à consulter*, p. 53. In the margin of the same page of Le Paige's copy of this legal consultation Le Paige wrote this note: "M. l'abbé

The Jesuits' enemies were not slow to close the trap. As early as April 13 the lawyer Le Gouvé had reminded the magistrates of the *grand' chambre* that the parlement of Paris had never officially examined or accepted the Jesuits' constitutions and that they might be incompatible with the laws of the realm.[2] But neither Le Gouvé nor anyone else possessed the right to make the Jesuit Order and its constitutions a subject of inquiry for its own sake within the context of a commercial lawsuit against the French Jesuits. Even if he had been able to do so, he would probably not have obtained a very sympathetic hearing from the comparatively aged and cautious magistrates of the *grand' chambre*. Whether the Jesuits had ever been legally accepted in France, whether the constitutions by which they governed themselves were in all respects compatible with the laws of the French realm—these questions fell into the category of *les affaires publiques*, which could be considered only by the assembled chambers of the parlement of Paris, not the *grand' chambre* alone. The problem for Le Paige and Lalourcé, then, was somehow to transform a commercial lawsuit against the Jesuits into an *affaire publique*, somehow to transfer the discussion of the Jesuit Order out of the *grand' chambre* and into the assembled chambers of parlement, where the most influential of their magisterial allies within the *parti janséniste* could make themselves heard.

The problem was easily solved. Throughout the period of the Lioncy and Gouffre trial, as during any other trial, the various chambers of the parlement continued to assemble at irregular intervals for the purpose of dispatching items of state business: the registration, perhaps, of a royal edict or declaration, the drafting of remonstrances, or the examination of a case of a refusal of the sacraments. During any one of these sessions any magistrate whatever had the right to call the attention of his colleagues to a matter he judged to be of public concern and within the competence of the parlement. Cleverly, the parlement's *parti janséniste* chose to strike its blow during one of the more humdrum sessions of the assembled chambers: the reception of a new counselor on April 17.[3] Just as formalities were about to be concluded, the abbé Chauvelin suddenly rose and, with a bulky manuscript in one hand, demanded the "honor to present to the court several observations" which, he said, two memoirs that had been printed on the occasion of the Lioncy and Gouffre affair "furnished naturally and even rendered indispensable."[4] First President Molé tried weakly to inter-

chauvelin a saisi cette citation pour faire demander l'apport au greffe du Parlement de cette Edition des Constitutions, c'est là ce qui a engagé l'affaire" (B.P.R.: L.P. 582, ms. 43).

2. *Nouvelles Ecclésiastiques* (September 4, 1761), p. 144.

3. Barbier, *Journal*, Vol. 7, p. 355.

4. *Discours d'un de messieurs des enquestes au parlement, toutes les chambres assemblées, sur les constitutions des Jésuites*, in *Comptes rendus par un magistrat et par MM. les gens du roi au parlement, toutes les chambres assemblées, les 17 avril, 3, 4, 6, 7 et 8 juillet 1761, au sujet des con-*

rupt Chauvelin, reminding him that the case of Lioncy and Gouffre against the Jesuits had not yet been decided.[5] But the irrepressible Chauvelin assured Molé that what he wished to say had nothing whatever to do with this case and would in no way prejudice its outcome. He then proceeded, "as Christian, as Citizen, as a Frenchman, as a Subject of the King," and "as Magistrate," to present to his colleagues his several reflections on the Jesuits' constitutions and regime, which were "as important," he told them, "as any that could ever merit the entire attention of the Court."[6]

However important, what Chauvelin told his colleagues about the Jesuits that day added little to the already vast store of anti-Jesuitical literature. The Jesuit Order, he said, systematically covered itself with a veil of mystery beneath which one could glimpse no fixed outlines but only a general impression of uncertainty, variability, and instability. The Jesuits' constitutions, first of all, were to be kept secret to all except the professed members of the order and could be altered or even completely changed at the whim of the society's general. The Jesuit Order itself could be defined in four different ways depending on the kinds of Jesuits involved: all those living under the obedience of the general, including novices; only approved students, coadjutors, and professed fathers; only coadjutors and professed fathers; or professed fathers exclusively. Except for the professed fathers, the kinds of vows which the Jesuits swore were of such a nature as to bind themselves to the society but not the society to them. The general of the order could moreover expel any Jesuit from the society and then order him back again, require a professed father who had become a bishop to remain under his orders, arbitrarily fix for every Jesuit a probationary period during which he wore no special habit and resided in no special house, and vary the Jesuits' habit itself according to time and circumstance—all this with the result that a great number of Jesuits could "often not wear a habit" and "be simultaneously scattered and hidden within all conditions, all professions, and perhaps even within all religious orders."[7]

The existence of this Jesuitical fifth column within the realm was all the more dangerous, Chauvelin continued, because "all Jesuits without distinction . . . are subjected and bound to the absolute and arbitrary will of the General alone, by all the fetters which it is possible to imagine." The Jesuits were to regard their general as Jesus Christ himself and obey him as a cadaver; the general was to have every means at his disposal in order to know the precise state of every Jesuit's conscience; all Jesuits were to be of one mind concerning matters theo-

---

stitutions, de la doctrine et la conduite des Jésuites (Paris, 1763), p. 1. Henceforth referred to as *Discours d'un de messieurs sur les constitutions des Jésuites.*

5. "Parlement civil, minutes, conseil secret" (A.N.: X[1B], 8940).

6. *Discours d'un de messieurs sur les constitutions des Jésuites,* p. 2.

7. Ibid., p. 6.

ogical, ethical, and otherwise; and all Jesuits were to look to the general alone for promotion within the society. At this point in his harangue Chauvelin sounded what, since the publication of Le Paige's *Histoire générale,* had become the new *mot d'ordre* against the Jesuits: despotism! Is it possible, he asked, "that there exists, or even to imagine, an authority more extensive, more arbitrary and more despotic?" Yet these same Jesuits, he added, "direct within the Realm the education and the consciences of the Subjects of the King—these men who by their State, by their vows, by their Constitutions, cannot be and are not in reality anything other than the blind and passive instruments of one arbitrary and despotic will or a foreign General *who must reside almost always at Rome.*"[8]

Chauvelin's emphasis on the general's foreign quality and his mandatory residence at Rome introduced a traditionally Gallican element into his harangue: the fear of unwarranted ultramontane papal interference in French affairs. But its setting within the more general emphasis upon purely Jesuitical despotism infused this hoary Gallican theme with new meaning. For it was not so much papal interference in French affairs that Chauvelin feared as "the general independence of all Jesuits from any temporal or spiritual authority, whatever it might be." Not only, he said, had various papal bulls granted the Jesuits complete freedom from the ecclesiastical jurisdiction of the first and second orders of the clergy, but the Jesuits were in fact independent of papal authority itself. Myriad instances of Jesuitical disobedience in the face of papal orders showed, he said, "to what this obedience to the Pope on the part of the Jesuits reduces itself."[9] Worse yet, the Jesuits considered themselves completely independent of any temporal authority, including that of kings themselves, and here Chauvelin introduced a veiled reference to the attempted assassination of Louis XV in 1757, at which "tears flowed from the eyes of the magistrate, his voice weakened, and by a uniform impression within the hearts which shared with him the same sentiments for the King, the same emotion manifested itself in the eyes of the entire parlement."[10] Having concluded, finally, that given "the despotic domination of this foreign General over all those who compose this Society" there existed for the Jesuits "neither Pope, nor Bishop, nor Curé, nor King, nor Magistrate,"[11] Chauvelin suggested that the assembled chambers examine the Jesuits' order and constitutions of which he, for his part, had given only a "slight idea."[12]

Although Robert de Saint-Vincent said of Chauvelin that "he spoke French badly and wrote it even worse," he certainly performed superbly that day,

8. Ibid., pp. 7, 9.
9. Ibid., pp. 11, 13.
10. *Nouvelles Ecclésiastiques* (October 10, 1761), p. 166.
11. *Discours d'un de messieurs sur les constitutions des Jésuites,* p. 14.
12. *Nouvelles Ecclésiastiques* (October 10, 1761), p. 167.

for his discourse had precisely the effect he must have intended.[13] According to the *Nouvelles Ecclésiastiques,* Chauvelin's description of the Jesuit Order "left the magistrates in the greatest stupefaction" and occasioned "a universal murmur, a sort of cry of indignation which arose from all parts."[14] To believe the gazeteer, even Jean-Jacques Severt, who was reputed to be a member of a Jesuit congregation, "entered into the general disposition."[15] In this kind of mood the assembled chambers did not hesitate to deliberate on Chauvelin's suggestion and to decide almost unanimously to decree that the Jesuit Order submit its constitutions to an examination by the *gens du roi* within three days. The Jesuits were quick to obey. On the very next day, April 18, the attorney general of the Jesuits of France brought the 1757 Prague edition of his order's constitutions to the *greffe* of the parlement of Paris, and on April 21 the assembled chambers ordered the *gens du roi* to submit their report of the Jesuits' constitutions on the following June 2.

With the order of April 17 and its prompt execution on the following day, the parlement's *parti janséniste* had effectively sprung its trap on the Jesuits. The Jesuit Order as such was now caught within the parlement of Paris: its very existence, not its responsibility for the commercial debt of one of its members, was now on trial. The next task before the *parti janséniste* was to keep the trap closed long enough to annihilate the victim inside. But this was more easily said than accomplished. Whatever friends the Jesuits possessed within the parlement of Paris had not yet manifested themselves, nor had Versailles yet been heard from. And the crown, the source of all good things the Jesuits had ever received by the "way of authority" in France, could pry the trap open at any moment. Both the dauphin and Chancellor Lamoignon de Malesherbes were known to

13. Saint-Vincent, "Mémoires," p. 230. Chauvelin's performance was of course by no means spontaneous. According to Saint-Vincent, Chauvelin had announced his intentions early the same morning to First President Molé, who, "greatly agitated," had unsuccessfully "employed all possible entreaties and solicitations" in order to persuade Chauvelin to postpone his project until it was known "what they would think and say at Versailles" (ibid.). Chauvelin, moreover, read from a prepared manuscript which was probably not entirely of his own making. Years later, in 1789, the *Nouvelles Ecclésiastiques* let it be known that Chauvelin had composed his speech at the home of Jean Simon, a Jansenist tutor at the College of Beauvais who had regularly opened his doors to certain magistrates of the parlement of Paris "when they had to confer about affairs which demanded secrecy" (*Nouvelles Ecclésiastiques* [May 22, 1789], p. 80). Chauvelin's speech closely followed the abbé Coudrette's *Idée générale des vices principaux de l'institut des Jésuites,* and Chauvelin might very well have had Coudrette's active assistance also. See Christophe Coudrette, *Idée générale des vices principaux de l'institut des Jésuites tireés de leurs constitutions et des autres titres de leur société* (Paris, 1761).
14. *Nouvelles Ecclésiastiques* (October 10, 1761), p. 167.
15. Ibid.

be fanatical devotees of the Jesuits, and Louis XV, by no means their enemy, had only to indicate his *bon plaisir* and his wish would be done.

Or at least in theory. In fact, the parlement of Paris had severely limited Louis XV's authority throughout most of his reign, and since mid-century the Parisian magistrates had been concerting their measures more closely than ever with the other parlements in France. In the face of his recalcitrant parlement, Louis XV could of course always go *jusqu'au bout* and resort to extreme measures such as exiling part of or even the entire parlement of Paris to a particular town or many different towns. Twice previously during the eighteenth century he had done this, once in 1731 and again in 1753. But both times he had done so at the cost of something close to civil anarchy and with only the most dubious results to display for his efforts. Would he hazard another such confrontation for the sake of the Jesuits? And in the midst of a costly European war in which he was more than ever dependent on the parlement of Paris for the registration of his financial edicts? Or would he limit himself to half-measures and token gestures to save the society whose college in Paris bore the name of his illustrious predecessor? Could he perhaps succeed with half-measures? None of these questions could be answered with certainty in April 1761, but at least the lines of battle were more or less already drawn—more or less, because although it was the old confrontation between Paris and Versailles, Paris, as usual, had its agents in Versailles, while Versailles for its part had its henchmen in Paris. The next eleven months or so were to witness the polite, restrained, undeclared, and yet deadly earnest warfare between the parlement of Paris and Versailles which characterizes so much of the political history of eighteenth-century France.

The remainder of April and the month of May passed without notable incident on the side of the parlement of Paris. On May 8, of course, the *grand' chambre* delivered its judgment on the Lioncy and Gouffre affair, but this case was already of only minor interest and somewhat beside the point. As for the now major question of the Jesuits' order and constitutions, the parlement could decide nothing until it had heard the report and conclusions of its *gens du roi,* and they were not scheduled to appear until June 2. Nor, until it had heard these conclusions, could the *parti janséniste* make any important unofficial decisions or knowledgeably plan a general strategy; if it did either of these things, it at least left no trace of its activity behind.

But matters were otherwise at Versailles. Chauvelin's demarche and the parlement's judgment of April 17 had not gone unnoticed there, and as early as May 1 Chancellor Lamoignon de Malesherbes informed the dauphin of a proposal which the *conseil des dépêches* had made to the king. Louis XV was to order his *gens du roi* to deliver to himself the copy of the Jesuits' constitutions deposited at the *greffe* of the parlement of Paris on April 18 and then, since something clearly had to be done, to appoint a special commission to examine these constitutions and report to the *conseil des dépêches*. This commission was to include no magistrates from the parlement of Paris but only members of the King's council and *conseillers d'état,* because, as Lamoignon observed, those magistrates with strong prejudices against the Jesuits "would be concerned . . . only to recall and assert everything which was said and done against them at the time of their establishment in France," while their more unprejudiced colleagues would hesitate to speak their minds for fear of "the malicious gossip and the reproaches and even insults to which they would be exposed in the assemblies of chambers which are very frequent these days."[16] By May 5 Louis XV had already decided to follow the advice of his council; the day set for the deliverance of his orders was Saturday, May 30.[17] They arrived on schedule, and on the same day the *gens du roi* presented the assembled chambers of the parlement of Paris with the King's *lettre de cachet,* which informed his "beloved and faithful counselors" that he wished himself to take cognizance of the Jesuits' constitutions and ordered them to send the first president, two other presidents, and the *gens du roi* with these constitutions in hand to himself at Marly on June 1. "For such is our pleasure," the letter ended. Versailles had finally spoken.[18]

Louis XV seems to have provoked total surprise, for his *lettre de cachet* of May 30 threw his parlement into the greatest consternation. The *lettre de cachet* was also very cleverly conceived, for although it was not a formal evocation of the affair of the Jesuits from the parlement against which the assembled chambers possessed the right to remonstrate, it was nonetheless, as Laverdy observed, an evocation in fact, because without the Jesuits' constitutions, the parlement could decide upon nothing. Murard, Laverdy, and Lambert finally proposed that a commission be appointed to consider the matter and that the chambers be reassembled at five o'clock to hear its report. This proposal the parlement unanimously adopted, and the assembled chambers adjourned for the morning.[19]

Who precisely the members of the special commission were and what was said during its meeting are not known. But when the chambers reassembled at

16. A.N.: A.P., 162 mi. (Archives du marquis de Rosanbo), *carton* 1, *dossier* 6, ms. 3, Chancellor Lamoignon to dauphin, May 1, 1761. I wish to thank M. the marquis de Rosanbo for having granted me the permission to consult his archives conserved in microfilm at the Archives Nationales, and M. Gourmelon, director general of the Archives Nationales, for having obtained this permission in my behalf under the most difficult circumstances.

17. Ibid., ms. 6, Chancellor Lamoignon to dauphin, May 5, 1761.

18. *Procédure contre l'institut et les constitutions des Jésuites suivie au parlement de Paris, sur l'appel comme d'abus interjetté par le procureur général du roi, recueillie par un membre du parlement et publiée par M. Gilbert de Voisins, membre de la chambre des députés* (Paris, 1832), pp. 25–26.

19. Ibid., pp. 27, 26–27.

five o'clock to hear its report, and after the *gens du roi* had reiterated their advice to follow the orders of the king, Clément de Feuillet, one of the commission's members, suddenly interrupted the proceedings with the remarkable news that upon returning from the meeting of the special commission to his own chamber—the second of inquests—he happened to find on his chamber's bureau another copy of the Jesuits' constitutions entirely similar to the one deposited by the Jesuits at the *greffe* of the parlement on April 21. Clément thereupon presented the new copy to the parlement, which immediately decided to appoint a commission of four to compare the new copy with the one delivered by the Jesuits in execution of the judgment of April 17. And when, finally, the collation produced satisfactory results, the assembled chambers voted to send the old copy to the king as he had commanded, but to retain the new one at the *greffe* of the parlement for continued examination.[20]

The *Nouvelles Ecclésiastiques* described the mysterious appearance of the second copy of the Jesuits' constitutions as a "happy . . . circumstance," while another Jansenist pamphleteer, not so reserved, identified it as a "happy event which Providence had prepared in its eternal decrees."[21] But the new copy had hardly dropped like manna from heaven upon the bureau of the second chamber of inquests. If the eternal decrees of providence were in any way responsible, they had not been without a small assist from Le Febvre de Saint-Hilaire, who first informed Adrien Le Paige of the arrival of the *lettre de cachet*,[22] or an even larger assist from Guillaume Lambert, who on May 30 sent Le Paige a panic-stricken note requesting him "for everything in the world" to "discover," "procure," borrow, or buy from someone another copy of the 1757 Prague edition of the Jesuits' constitutions and to send it by five o'clock that afternoon to the *brevetier* of the second chamber of inquests, who would in turn deliver it to Feuillet.[23] But the largest assist of all, of course, was rendered by Le Paige himself, who somewhere managed to find the other copy and deliver the goods in time.

The *Nouvelles Ecclésiastiques* reported that on Sunday morning, June 1, the king's ministers "appeared very surprised to see the Deputies of the Parlement arrive at Marly" and "yet more surprised to learn that the constitutions had been demanded of them and that they were bringing them." Louis XV himself must have found it difficult to suppress a smile of mixed admiration and frustra-

20. Ibid., pp. 29–31.

21. *Nouvelles Ecclésiastiques* (November 13, 1761), p. 183; and *Extrait de ce qui s'est passé au parlement au sujet des constitutions des Jésuites et de leur doctrine* (B.P.R.: L.P. 136, unnumbered ms.).

22. B.P.R.: L.P. 582, ms. 90, Le Febvre de Saint-Hilaire to Le Paige, n.d.

23. Ibid., ms. 91, Lambert to Le Paige, May 30, 1761. This letter is unsigned, but the handwriting is identical to that of two other letters (B.P.R.: L.P. 541, mss. 19–20), which are signed by Guillaume Lambert.

tion at this latest *chef d'œuvre* of parliamentary ingenuity in evading the intent of his orders, and his response to the parlement's deputies, that he assumed that his parlement would enact nothing without knowing his intentions, reportedly left Chancellor Lamoignon considerably less than satisfied. Certainly no one took His Majesty's instructions very seriously, least of all, probably, Louis XV himself. The first skirmish between Versailles and the parlement of Paris therefore ended, with the result that the Jesuits—as the *Nouvelles Ecclésiastiques* expressed it—now saw "their constitutions sustain two examinations instead of one, and the monstrous and intolerable vices of their Institute manifested at the same time to the First Tribunal of the Realm and the Council of the King."[24]

That these "vices" be manifested to the first tribunal of the realm was precisely what Louis XV's *lettre de cachet* of May 30 had been timed to prevent, and the parlement's successful evasion of this *lettre de cachet* meant, of course, that the report of the Jesuits' constitutions by the *gens du roi* would take place on June 2 as originally scheduled. But when the *gens du roi* appeared before the assembled chambers of the parlement on June 2, they declared themselves unprepared to deliver their conclusions. The two-volume 1757 edition of the Jesuits' constitutions was printed in such small type, they argued, that they had only with difficulty been able to arrive at a "first acquaintance" of the contents of the first volume. The parlement therefore reluctantly granted its *gens du roi* a delay of one month, and ordered them to present their report on July 3.[25]

But one may well doubt that this was the only reason that the *gens du roi* had found themselves in need of more time. Another is that they had known long in advance of the coming of Louis XV's *lettre de cachet,* and that they had never really expected to deliver their report of the Jesuits' constitutions until the parlement's ingenious maneuver on May 30 caught them unprepared. For among Versaille's agents in the parlement of Paris none, including the first president himself, were more important than the *gens du roi,* and it is therefore most unlikely that Louis XV would have decided to send his *lettre de cachet* to the parlement without their advice.

The parlement's *gens du roi* included the attorney general and usually two solicitors general. In 1761 these positions were occupied by Guillaume François Joly de Fleury, his younger brother Jean Omer Joly de Fleury, and Michel Etienne Le Pelletier de Saint-Fargeau, respectively. As their title implies, they were the official representatives of the crown's interests in the parlement of Paris. They were the first to receive all royal edicts, declarations, ordinances, letters patent, and *lettres de cachet* from the king; it was they who presented these royal documents to the parlement and were immediately responsible for

24. *Nouvelles Ecclésiastiques* (November 13, 1761), p. 183.
25. *Procédure contre l'institut et les constitutions des Jésuites,* pp. 32–34.

their registration. But the *gens du roi* were often the king's unofficial agents as well. Like the first president, the *gens du roi* were directly indebted to the crown for their appointment, and they were well situated to receive additional favors from that quarter.[26] When, therefore, a matter of public interest arose within the assembled chambers themselves—a case of the refusal of sacraments, for example, or in this instance the constitutions of the Jesuits—the *gens du roi* would usually consult with Versailles before submitting their "conclusions" to the assembled chambers of the parlement and in general would do nothing without Versailles' approval. No more than the first president, of course, could the *gens du roi* afford openly to flaunt the sensibilities of their colleagues. They too had to walk the precariously narrow line between the royal good pleasure and parliamentary recalcitrance. But except for the rarest occasions, they could always be expected to work hand in the gauntlet of Versailles when—an eventuality they consistently dreaded—the parlement of Paris decided to throw down its own.

In the affair of the Jesuits the exigencies of their office and their personal sentiments coincided neatly, for the two most influential of the *gens du roi,* the brothers Joly de Fleury, seem to have been favorably disposed toward the Company of Jesus. To be sure, they were both good Gallicans and as such they were bound to take a generally dim view of the excessive obedience which all Jesuits owed their general and a yet dimmer view of the special vow of obedience which the Jesuits alone swore to the papacy. In a short memoir written about 1760 and seemingly for his own instruction the attorney general, Guillaume Joly de Fleury, expressed concern about both these characteristics of the Jesuit Order.[27] But those typically Gallican sensibilities were inflamed by no religious or theological passions. When in the spring of 1759 a young professor of rhetoric in the Jesuit college at Amiens was accused of teaching irregular maxims to his students, the brothers Joly de Fleury had the attorney general's substitute in Amiens excuse the young Jesuit on grounds of inexperience and in general did all they could to prevent the affair from becoming another Jansenist cause célèbre.[28] A very cordial correspondence occasioned by this affair between the solicitor general and a Jesuit from the order's residence in Paris moreover reveals that the two Joly de Fleurys numbered more than one Jesuit among their friends.[29]

It was the younger of the two brothers, Solicitor General Jean Omer Joly de Fleury, who presented the *Compte rendu* of the Jesuits' constitutions to the

26. Ford, *Robe and Sword,* pp. 48, 97.
27. B.N.: Collection Joly de Fleury, fol. 1609, mss. 8–11.
28. Ibid., mss. 16–40 and 1552; 65–300.
29. This Jesuit's name was Desnoyers. His letters are to be found in B.N.: Collection Joly de Fleury, fol. 1609.

assembled chambers of the parlement on July 3, 4, 6, and 7, and it was he, too, who did most of the research and writing.[30] In preparing the *Compte rendu* Jean Omer relied heavily on Le Paige's and Coudrette's recently published *Histoire générale* and on the abbé Chauvelin's speech of April 17. From Chauvelin's speech he took his principle of organization; from the *Histoire générale* he garnered most of his information, although in this case not without the precaution of demanding from its authors a substantial memoir attesting to its accuracy.[31] But from neither source did he take the animosity and religious passion which informed them both. His *Compte rendu* rather transformed the content of both these polemics into an exercise in studied and moderate Gallicanism.

Like Chauvelin, Omer Joly de Fleury, too, complained about the Jesuit Order's secrecy and variability, but unlike Chauvelin, his only concern was to make its structure stable and open to all. Like Chauvelin, Coudrette, and Le Paige, the solicitor general denounced the Jesuits' nonreciprocal vows and the order's right to expel anyone at any time from the society, but his concern was not to demonstrate the order's systematic perfidy but to eliminate the possible existence of either hidden Jesuits or "vagrant, fugitive and unhappy subjects" expelled from the society without good reason. And like the Jansenist polemicists, again, on whose information he relied, he objected to the papal bulls which granted the Jesuit Order virtual independence from both secular and ecclesiastical authority, yet like any good Gallican, his sole concern was to protect the rights of the Gallican Church and the independence of the secular sovereign and his parlements by placing the Jesuits under the jurisdiction of both. And unlike his Jansenist informants, Joly de Fleury saw nothing reprehensible in admitting that the Jesuit Order had produced some "very skillful controversialists and theologians who have rendered services to the Church as well as men of Letters who have enriched our Literature" and that individually the Jesuits lived "with such edification among the public that in this sense they have no need of reformation."[32] Throughout his *Compte rendu,* in short, the solicitor general assumed that the Jesuit Order was valuable and useful. His only concern, again, was to render it yet more useful by eliminating from its constitutions all those structural characteristics which threatened the Gallican liberties of the French Church and the stability and independence of the secular authority.

Perhaps the most instructive contrast between the *Compte rendu* of the *gens du roi* and the polemics of Chauvelin, Lalourcé, Le Paige, and Coudrette lies in

---

30. *Compte rendu des constitutions des Jésuites, par MM. les gens du roi, M. Omer Joly de Fleury, avocat dudit seigneur roi portant la parole, les 3, 4, 6 et 7 juillet, 1761, en exécution de l'arrêt de la cour du 17 avril précédant, et de son arrêté du deux Juin audit an,* in *Comptes rendu par un magistrat. . . .* Henceforth cited as *Compte rendu des constitutions des Jésuites.*

31. B.N.: Collection Joly de Fleury, fol. 1616, mss. 200–10.

32. *Compte rendu des constitutions des Jésuites,* pp. 52, 57, 100.

their respective treatments of the authority of the Jesuits' general. To be sure, all decried what they considered the general's excessive authority over the order's property and members and the constitutions' prescribed cadaver-like obedience to his every order. But these features of the Jesuit Order the spokesmen of the *parti janséniste* described as despotic, and though they sometimes concealed their charge of despotism under the veil of traditional Gallicanism, the mere use of this pejorative term indicates that it was the very structure of the Jesuit Order as such to which they objected. In contrast, Omer Joly de Fleury's *Compte rendu* carefully avoided the pejorative term *despotism* and instead described the general's authority within the Jesuit Order with the neutral—and, in France, even favorable—adjective *monarchical*.[33] Nor, of course, was it "monarchical" authority as such to which the solicitor general objected, but rather the possible threat which an independent spiritual "monarchy" such as the Jesuit Order might pose to the temporal monarchy of the Bourbon crown within whose borders it thrived. "Suppose within this Society an ambitious General eager to extend the domination of his corps," Joly de Fleury asked his fellow magistrates. "Suppose him also," he continued, "filled with ultramontane sentiments and receptive to the impressions which a Sovereign power might give him to establish his entirely spiritual authority upon the debris of the temporal authority . . . . what a temptation," he intoned, "to abuse his power for a General who can, with the twinkling of an eye, put into movement all the members of an immense Body spread out over the whole surface of the earth and which, given the sentiment of blind obedience, ought always to regard his voice as that of Jesus Christ! How many Agents will he not have within a Realm!"[34] It was this thoroughly Gallican nightmare, not despotism or monarchy as such, which troubled the habitual calm of the solicitor general.

The official conclusions which Omer Joly de Fleury presented in the name of the *gens du roi* to the assembled chambers of the parlement on July 8 followed logically from the content of his *Compte rendu* and in no respect deviated from the premises of orthodox Gallicanism. Using as an historical model the parlement of Paris's reform of the four orders of mendicant friars in the seventeenth century, he suggested that the king be requested to confer with the papacy to the purpose of sending to his parlements new letters patent which would bring the Jesuit Order into complete conformity with the laws and Gallican liberties of the French realm. These letters patent, the solicitor general stipulated, should place the Jesuits thoroughly under the jurisdiction of both the ecclesiastical and temporal authorities in France, ensure that the Jesuits taught

33. Ibid., p. 46. Omer de Joly de Fleury here complains of the Jesuit Order as an "Institut qui ne connoit de loi, d'autorité, que celle d'un Supérieur monarchique, lequel concentre tout à lui."
34. Ibid., p. 55.

their students nothing contrary to the four Gallican articles of 1682, exclude all unauthorized contact between French Jesuits and foreign Jesuits, and render the order's vows reciprocal and indissoluble. But the most important of his suggested provisions were designed to curb the general's authority over the property and members of the order. The general was to have no more authority over his subjects than that in other monastic orders; the property of each Jesuit establishment was to be inalienable and administered solely by the Jesuits who resided there; and all provincial superiors were to be elected by plurality vote in triennial assemblies in each of the five provinces. Thus altered, the Jesuit Order and constitutions, Joly de Fleury hoped, would be definitively accepted and registered by all the parlements in France.[35]

Many responded with admiration to the moderate and strictly Gallican tone of Omer Joly de Fleury's *Compte rendu*. One of his correspondents, a former *doyen* of the parlement of Paris, contrasted the "measured terms" of the *Compte rendu* of the *gens du roi,* who were "animated by no party spirit contrary to the authority of the Church," to Chauvelin's discourse of April 17, which, he said, was "animated by nothing but this spirit."[36] Even the père Balbani, one of the Jesuits' most acrid polemicists, noted the difference between the two discourses. "That of the Solicitor General de Fleury," he wrote, "is full of equity, wisdom, modesty, moderation, humanity and respect for Religion," whereas the other "assumes a moderate tone only to better seduce those whom it might have shocked, parades itself as religious only to undermine religion," and "is cruel while pretending to be humane."[37]

But not all observers reacted with equal enthusiasm to the solicitor general's *Compte rendu,* and among those least enthusiastic were the members of the *parti janséniste* of the parlement of Paris. In a memorandum composed sometime after July 8 and probably sent to the counselors Laverdy, Chauvelin, and others, Adrien Le Paige outlined his objections to the conclusions of the *gens du roi.* The first and most basic of them concerned the first and most basic of the *gens du roi*'s conclusions, that the Jesuits should be forced to accept new rules and constitutions at all. This disposition Le Paige judged "dangerous" because it would be tantamount to legally recognizing and accepting the Jesuits in France as a monastic order, something which the parlement of Paris had never previously done. The Jesuits were monks "in fact," Le Paige conceded, "but the examination of their order demands that they no longer be tolerated as such."[38]

35. Ibid., pp. 99–102. See also B.N.: Collection Joly de Fleury, fol. 1612, mss. 289–91.
36. B.N.: Collection Joly de Fleury, fol. 1612, ms. 291.
37. Balbani, *Appel à la raison des écrits et libelles publiés par la passion contre les Jésuites de France,* p. 170.
38. B.P.R.: L.P. 582, ms. 95.

What did it mean to say that the Jesuits were tolerated as monks "in fact" though not recognized as such by law? Le Paige explained his meaning more clearly—or had his meaning more clearly explained—in a lengthy review of the solicitor general's *Compte rendu* published in the *Nouvelles Ecclésiastiques* some four months later. As both Coudrette and Lalourcé had previously observed, Le Paige insisted that France had never accepted the Jesuits as a monastic order, but only as a college: the College of Clermont in Paris, renamed the College of Louis-Le-Grand under Louis XIV. Hence when the Jesuits were originally admitted into France in 1561, the assembly of the Gallican clergy at Poissy and the parlement of Paris forbade them the denomination "Jesuits" but required instead that they call themselves "priests and students of the College of Clermont." Hence, too, the parlement of Paris had never officially examined or registered the Jesuits' constitutions, because as a monastic rule they could have no legal status in France. The parlement of Paris had expelled the Jesuits in 1594 because of their supposed complicity in Jean Chastel's unsuccessful attempt on the life of Henry IV, but when Henry IV himself readmitted them in 1603, he in no way altered the status of their legal existence in France. To be sure, Henry IV's Edict of Rouen in 1603 finally allowed the Jesuits to call themselves "The Company and Society of Jesus" and freely mentioned their monastic vows. But "it follows," Le Paige argued, "neither that this denomination assures them the title of monastic order . . . or accords them new favors nor that it results in the legal reception in France of their status as monks, as it appears that *messieurs* the *gens du roi* seem inclined to suppose." In taking certain precautions against the Jesuits, the edict of 1603 only recognized the Jesuits' existence as monks in fact, although it did not legally receive them as such, "just as *messieurs* the *gens du roi*," Le Paige continued, "employed their constitutions against them in the affair of Lioncy, although these constitutions had certainly not been legally received."[39] Monks in fact, the Jesuits were not monks by law.

Now once it was admitted that the Jesuits had never been legally accepted in France as a monastic order, the entire framework of reform so painstakingly constructed by the *gens du roi* collapsed like a house of cards. For how could the parlement presume to reform a monastic institute which it had never legally recognized as such in the first instance? Yet as Le Paige observed in the *Nouvelles Ecclésiastiques,* the entire *Compte rendu* supposed "this point of view, according to the personal opinion toward which *messieurs* the *gens du roi* are inclined, that the Jesuits are legally accepted in France as monks and that it is only a question today of having their Institute reformed. But as the supposition is inadmissible," he concluded, "there can be no question of this reform in regard to men who are admitted only 'as College' and not as a 'monastic order newly instituted.'"[40]

39. *Nouvelles Ecclésiastiques* (November 20, 1761), p. 192.
40. *Nouvelles Ecclésiastiques* (November 27, 1761), p. 193. Within the period from 1561 to

However powerful, this argument was of little use to the *parti janséniste* when the solicitor general delivered his conclusions to the assembled chambers of the parlement on July 8. The *gens du roi* could have easily responded that if the Jesuits had not been admitted to France as a monastic order in either 1561 or 1603, it was all the more necessary to accept them as such in 1761, while at the same time reforming their constitutions along the lines laid down in the *Compte rendu*. To prevent the possibility of any such response, the *parti janséniste* had first to confuse the issue of the Jesuits' constitutions by raising yet another: that of the solicitor general's assertion that the Jesuits had produced some "very skillful . . . Theologians who have rendered services to the Church" and that the Jesuits "lived with such edification among the public that in this sense they have no need of reformation." To attack these assertions, however, was to attack the Jesuits' doctrine and morals, and to do this the *parti janséniste* had to abandon the already exhausted ammunition of Gallicanism and to open fire with the heavy artillery of Jansenism. In short, the *parti janséniste* had to show

---

1603 Le Paige was on firm legal ground. The assembly of the Gallican clergy at Poissy and subsequently the parlement of Paris received the Jesuits in 1561 "par forme de Société et de collège, et non de religion nouvellement instituée, à la charge qu'ils seront tenus prendre autre titre de Société de Jésus ou des Jésuites et que, sur icelle Société et Collège, l'évêque diocésain aura toute superintendance et jurisdiction, et correction de chasser et ôter de ladite compagnie les forfaiteurs et malvivans; n'entreprendront les Frères d'icelle Compagnie, et ne feront en spirituel ni en temporel aucunes choses au préjudice des évêques, chapitres, curez, paroisses et universitez, ni autres religions; ains seront tenus de se conformer entièrement à la disposition du droit commun, sans qu'ils ayent droit ne jurisdiction aucune, et renonçant au préable, et par exprès, à tous privilèges portez par leurs bulles aux choses susdites contraires; autrement, à faute de ce faire, ou que par l'avenir ils en obtiennent d'autres, les présentes demeureront et de nul effet et vertu, sauf le droit de ladite assemblée et d'autrui en toutes choses" (A.N.: G⁸, 589p). In claiming, however, that the Edict of Rouen, which reestablished the Jesuits in France in 1603, in no way altered the status of their existence as "Société et de collège, et non de religion nouvellement instituée," Le Paige was on somewhat shakier grounds. The Edict of Rouen simply avoided the subject of the exact status of Jesuits in France, with the consequence that both the Jesuits and their enemies could draw whatever conclusions they wished. The Jesuits understandably appealed to the edict's use of the appelation "Jesuit" as well as its provisions concerning their monastic vows as evidence that the edict had in fact recognized them as a monastic order. On the other hand, Le Paige could with equal cogency appeal to the edict's reticence on this important point as evidence that Henry IV had meant only to reestablish the Jesuits in their original position as "Société et de Collège" alone, and in addition could argue that even if Henry IV had wished to change the Jesuits' status in France, he could not have done so without the authority of the Gallican clergy, which in 1561 had defined the Jesuits' position in the first instance. And of course there remained the fact that the parlement of Paris had never examined or approved the Jesuits' constitutions as such. Taking everything into consideration, therefore, it would seem as if Le Paige had the better argument. (See P. Henri Fouqueray, *Histoire de la Compagnie de Jésus en France des origines à la suppression* (Paris, 1910–25), Vol. 2, pp. 593–690; Lalourcé, *Mémoire à consulter pour Jean Lioncy*, pp. 400–500; B.N.: Collection Joly de Fleury, fol. 1612, mss. 174–79.)

that the Jesuits were corrupted by a moral and doctrinal gangrene so vicious, so pervasive, and so tenacious that their order was immune to reformation of any kind. A delicate task, to be sure, for the clergy, not the parlement, was the lawful judge of doctrine. But with Armageddon at hand, every risk had to be taken.

The *parti janséniste*'s chosen vessel for this task was again the abbé Chauvelin. On July 8, just after the solicitor general had finished pronouncing the conclusions of the *gens du roi,* Chauvelin arose and, with another bulky manuscript in hand, unburdened himself for more than two hours of almost as many centuries of Jansenist polemics against the Jesuit Order. Beginning with one of the most recent Jansenist polemicists, the Bishop of Soissons, whom be quoted as saying that the Jesuits were undermining the Christian religion "even to its foundations," Chauvelin then proceeded to the earliest and most revered of them all, Pascal and Arnauld, and to the original accusations of Molinism, probabilism, and lax moral teachings. The Jesuits, Chauvelin admitted, had from time to time denied that they held any such ethical system, but its existence in their writing was uncovered by "a Work unique and inimitable of its kind as early as 1656"—Pascal's *Les Provinciales*—and subsequently verified by the second order of the clergy "word for word."[41]

Chauvelin conceded that "those whom the Holy Spirit has established the Depositories and Ministers of the power of the Keys are the constituted judges of questions concerning the Faith and Morals" but—assuming throughout that the clergy had already condemned the doctrines in question—he justified his broaching these questions with the fact that the "exterior and public teaching of Morals and even Doctrine is nonetheless under the inspection of the King and his magistrates, not," he added, "to determine, change or alter a deposit entrusted to the Holy Ministry but . . . to protect . . . its immutability, maintain its purity," and "prevent its alteration or corruption." He then further buttressed his position by concentrating on the allegedly Jesuitical doctrine of regicide, a matter obviously within the competence of the parlement. Recalling the assassinations of Henry III, Henry IV, and the reprinting of the Jesuit Busembaum's *Theologia moralis* in the very year that Damiens had attempted to assassinate Louis XV Chauvelin requested the parlement in the name of "the most tender love engraved on the heart of all Frenchmen . . . for the Sacred Person of the King" to deliberate on what he had said in order "to assure . . . one of our dearest and most sacred concerns."[42]

41. *Discours d'un de messieurs des enquestes au parlement, toutes les chambres assemblées, sur la doctrine des Jésuites,* in *Comptes rendus des magistrats* . . . , pp. 3, 5–6, 7–8. Henceforth cited as *Discours d'un des messieurs sur la doctrine des Jésuites.*
42. *Ibid.,* pp. 2, 10. No more than his speech of April 17 was Chauvelin's performance of

Chauvelin's second performance was again a success. To be sure, he had in the process exposed the *parti janséniste* for what it was. He had courted the risk of serious backfire by abandoning the safe but none too powerful weaponry of Gallicanism in favor of the highly explosive but potentially more effective cannonry of Jansenism. But to believe the *Nouvelles Ecclésiastiques,* the parlement of Paris had never witnessed "a greater silence, an attention so sustained," or "so much satisfaction on the part of the listeners" than during Chauvelin's harangue, after which he was "covered" with applause. It was even said that the "celebrated Pucelle" could not have done as well.[43] More important, Chauvelin succeeded in his principal object, that of infinitely complicating the *gens du roi*'s goal of reforming the Jesuits' constitutions by raising the issue of the Jesuits' doctrines and ethical teachings. Rather than deliberate immediately upon the conclusions of the *gens du roi,* the parlement referred these conclusions as well as Chauvelin's two discourses to a special commission which was to report on the whole at an unspecified date, and ordered the *gens du roi* to submit their conclusions on Chauvelin's second discourse on July 17.[44]

It surprised no one when on July 18 (the report of the *gens du roi* had been postponed by one day) Omer Joly de Fleury announced to the assembled chambers of the parlement that the *gens du roi* had examined Chauvelin's discourse of July 8 but that they persisted in their conclusions given to the parle-

---

July 8 either spontaneous or entirely his own. A manuscript draft of Chauvelin's speech of July 8 is in fact to be found among the papers of Adrien Le Paige (B.P.R.: L.P. 136, unnumbered ms.), a circumstance which strongly suggests Le Paige's collaboration in its composition. Although not in the hand of Le Paige himself, a part of the draft is in an unidentifiable hand which I have concluded to be that of a copyist, while yet another part is in the hand of Durey de Mesnières, president of the second chamber of inquests, who, though by no means a Jansenist, often cooperated with the *parti janséniste.* More interesting, however, are marginal additions to the draft which subsequently appeared in the final printed version and which nearly all concern the more theological and distinctively Jansenist portions of the speech. These marginal additions, like part of the main draft, are in the hand of the copyist, but might very probably have been dictated by Le Paige. One example is the following passage: ". . . une moral dont le principe particulier renverse les deux règles des moeurs, scavoir la loi de Dieu, en établissant qu'on peut la violer impunément à la faveur d'une ignorance prétendue invincible [qui puisse excuser de l'infidélité et de l'hérésie même, lorsquil ne se présente aucune raison de la quitter], la conscience en établissant qu'on peut la suivre sans danger, soit qu'elle soit probable, soit qu'elle soit erronée, enfin en substituant à ces deux règles la probabilité, même la moins probable, préférablement non seulement à l'opinion la plus sûre mais encore à une opinion plus probable [en un mot ce sistême si général chez les jésuites du probabilisme] que tant d'évêques de ce Royaume jugeroit en 1658 la maxime la plus impie, l'erreur la plus dangereuse, la venin le plus nouvel de la morale chrétienne." (Ibid., pp. 5–6.) The marginal additions are in brackets.

43. *Nouvelles Ecclésiastiques* (December 4, 1761), pp. 207, 208.

44. *Procédure contre l'institut et les constitutions des Jésuites,* p. 36.

ment on the same date.[45] The parlement simply contented itself with referring these reiterated conclusions to the same commissioners already appointed to examine the *gens du roi*'s previous conclusions, their *Compte rendu,* and Chauvelin's two discourses.[46] Now precisely who these commissioners were is not known. Laverdy was certainly among them. So, probably, were Chauvelin and Clément de Feuillet. But the commission also included the abbé Terray, who, according to Robert de Saint-Vincent, was "no enemy" of the Jesuits, and First President Molé presided over its meetings.[47] In other words, this commission included magistrates both for and against the Jesuits, and it therefore served at most as a kind of sounding board for unofficial but important decisions arrived at elsewhere.

For by July 18 it was elsewhere—the backrooms, corridors, and private apartments of the various magistrates—which had for the moment replaced either the *parquet* of the *grand' chambre* or the meetings of any official commission as the most important scene of developments in the affair of the Jesuits. And in the backrooms, corridors, and private apartments two loosely constituted but no less real forces were already busily mapping their respective strategies in preparation for the impending and inevitable showdown. One side was determined to conserve the Jesuits, even if to do so entailed reforming their constitutions, and among its ranks were some of the highest ranking members of the court and the parlement of Paris: the king—at least officially—the dauphin, Chancellor Lamoignon, First President Molé, President Maupeou, Attorney General Guillaume Joly de Fleury, Solicitor General Omer Joly de Fleury, and the abbé Joseph Marie Terray, counselor-clerk in the *grand' chambre,* habitual

45. *Nouvelles Ecclésiastiques* (December 4, 1761), p. 208. See also B.N.: Collection Joly de Fleury, fol. 1612, ms. 309.

46. *Procédure contre l'institut et les constitutions des Jésuites,* p. 37.

47. At least I have been unable to determine who precisely these commissioners were. That First President Molé presided over this commission was a matter of course and in any case confirmed in a letter to the attorney general. (B.N.: Collection Joly de Fleury, fol. 1612, ms. 332, n.d.). On the other hand, both Laverdy and the abbé Terray are mentioned as members in Gilbert de Voisins, *Procédure contre l'institut et les constitutions des Jésuites,* on pp. 38–39. The cases of Clément de Feuillet and Chauvelin are more conjectural. It would seem that Chauvelin was a member of the commission because he was best in a position to confirm the statements in his speeches of April 17 and July 8, which the commission was supposed to examine. And it was at Clément de Feuillet's home that the high command of the *parti janséniste* met on the eve of the decisive day of August 6, 1761 (Saint-Vincent, "Mémoires," p. 242). What is clear, however, is that those who met with Clément de Feuillet on August 5 —Robert de Saint-Vincent, Chauvelin, Laverdy, and Lambert—were not all on the official commission. Rather, they constituted an unofficial, although on that account no less important, commission much as the same people had done in 1753 when they composed the famous remonstrances of April 9, 1753, (B.N., ms. fr., nouv. acq. 8496 518), pp. 97–99). Robert de Saint-Vincent's description of the abbé Terray as "no enemy" of the Jesuits is to be found in his "Mémoires," p. 254.

reporter of royal edicts, and "no enemy" of the Jesuits. But the other side, the parlement's *parti janséniste,* was no less determined to destroy the Jesuits utterly, and though its ranks included no one as illustrious as the least of its opponents, it possessed the advantages of a more rigorous internal discipline, the conviction of the righteousness of its cause, and the self-confidence which several important tactical successes had already inspired. Led by the lawyers Adrien Le Paige and Charlemagne Lalourcé, the *parti janséniste* could count upon the services of the magistrates Robert de Saint-Vincent, Guillaume Lambert, Le Febvre de Saint-Hilaire, Clément de Feuillet, Laverdy de Nizaret, and last but not least the abbé Chauvelin, who, though most recently recruited and suspect for other reasons, had already proven his worth on several occasions.

The *parti janséniste* lost no time in mapping the strategy for the destruction of the Jesuits. No sooner had the *gens du roi* delivered their conclusions to the parlement of Paris than Adrien Le Paige, the *parti janséniste*'s chief strategist, outlined his plans for the conquest of the Jesuits and submitted them to Laverdy, a member of the parlement's special commission. Le Paige based his entire "sketch of a general plan"—so he entitled it—upon the fundamental premise which he, Lalourcé, and Coudrette had so assiduously endeavored to establish: that France had never accepted or recognized the Jesuits as a monastic order, but only as "priests and students of the College of Clermont." Not even Louis XIV's edict of 1715, Le Paige argued, had altered the Jesuits' legal status in France. This edict, though it seemingly recognized the Jesuits' legal existence as monks by limiting at thirty-three the age before which individual Jesuits who left their order could resume their rights of inheritance, had in reality done no such thing but had only prevented the Jesuits, who were monks "in fact," from abusing the state by enjoying the civil rights to which only secular citizens were legally entitled. The Jesuits, Le Paige repeated, were monks "in fact" (*de fait*) though not "by law" (*de droit*).[48]

The distinction between *fait* and *droit* had already played an illustrious role in the history of Jansenism. When in 1653 Innocent X condemned the five famous propositions from Jansenius's treatise on Saint Augustine, not only Arnauld and Nicole but even Pascal had defended themselves against the charge of heresy on the grounds that, though heretical *de droit,* the propositions in question were not contained *de fait* in Jansenius's book. Now in these latter days Le Paige transformed this originally defensive distinction into a powerful offensive weapon against the Jansenists' age-old persecutors, for once understood, Le Paige argued, the distinction between Jesuits as monks *de fait* and as monks *de*

48. B.P.R.: L.P. 582, ms. 96, "Esquisse d'un plan général," dated July 1761, and sent to the "commissaires." Since the reply came from Laverdy, it is safe to presume that Le Paige sent his plan to Laverdy in particular and not to the "commissaires" in general.

droit rendered everything "clear and luminous." The parlement had, properly speaking, nothing new to decree; it had no need to pronounce on the monastic vows of an order it had never accepted. It had only to implement the various consequences which could be drawn from the terms of the Jesuit Order's original acceptance in France as merely "college": to separate the various Jesuit colleges from each other and from any common ecclesiastical authority and to require each college to govern itself; to separate the Jesuits themselves from the authority of their general, provincials, and immediate superiors; to place them all, like the regents of other colleges, under the jurisdiction of the local bishop; to prohibit the Jesuits from recruiting any more novices; and to replace each Jesuit professor who died with someone chosen by the parlement. All Jesuits who had taken solemn vows would continue to be bound by them, and those Jesuits unemployed in the colleges would receive a sufficient pension from the state. But when the last living Jesuit had rendered up the ghost, the order would be no more and the colleges would be completely secularized. With the lifeline of its novitiates cut off, the Jesuit Order would gradually wither and die like a girdled tree. "Such is the sketch," Le Paige concluded, "of what appears to result from the principle, from which we must never depart, that the Jesuits have not been received in France as monks, but only as colleges."[49]

It was not often that Le Paige's advice was disregarded, but in this instance Laverdy objected strongly to his plan and in the end prevailed. Le Paige had admitted in his memorandum that his plan "would not be the work of one day" and that there were obvious disadvantages in "leaving the education of the youth in the hands of men whose doctrine and morality are as perverse as their constitutions." To avert this danger he had proposed to place each college under the direction of a "reliable man," to change the books used in the Jesuit colleges and forbid the Jesuit professors "to teach this doctrine and that morality," and to inspect regularly the professors' notebooks and expel all "pertinacious Jesuits."[50] But Laverdy did not think Le Paige's precautions sufficient guarantee against the wiles of the Jesuits. "You have left them [the Jesuits] among us, to be sure with precautions," he replied, "but they [the Jesuits] are sufficiently cunning to render our precautions useless. My goal," he said, ". . . is to exterminate them as Jesuits, but since this cannot be the work of a single day I am preparing all my batteries to attain my object."[51]

49. Ibid.
50. Ibid.
51. B.P.R.: L.P., ms. 97, unsigned letter to Le Paige dated July 10, 1761. The handwriting is actually neither that of Laverdy nor that of any other magistrate I have been able to identify. But since the plan outlined in this letter is undoubtedly the one which, according to the testimony of Robert de Saint-Vincent ("Mémoires," p. 242), Laverdy quite independently formulated and finally implemented on August 6, 1761, it is safe to presume his authorship.

The principal battery on which Laverdy proposed to rely was the *appel comme d'abus*, a legal device which since the late fifteenth century had enabled the parlements to review the decisions of the ecclesiastical tribunals when these decisions involved judical irregularities, threatened the jurisdiction of the secular courts, or in some way violated the liberties of the Gallican Church.[52] "After having qualified the constitutions with all the names they merit," and after having given the Jesuits' moral teaching and doctrine "all the colors of which they are susceptible, I go next," Laverdy wrote, "to the vows themselves, and I say that vows conceived and solemnly pronounced in order to execute and observe constitutions, a doctrine and a morality of this quality are not tolerable in any state whatever and . . . can be annulled by means of the *appel comme d'abus*." Laverdy therefore proposed to receive the attorney general *appellant comme d'abus* of the emission of all Jesuit vows and in consequence to prohibit all novices from making these vows and to disengage the rest of the Jesuits, including the professed fathers of the fourth vow, from whatever vows they had already sworn. If some Jesuits thought themselves illegally disengaged from their vows without the judgment of the Church, "well then," Laverdy threatened, "I would in good time do in regard to the Jesuits what was done (unjustly) in relation to the Daughters of the Congregation of the Infancy," a convent in Toulouse associated with Port-Royal and dispersed at the behest of the Jesuits in 1686.[53] "I would send them to the ordinary ecclesiastical authorities of the area to attend to the annulment of their vows or their transformation into vows of any religious order received within the Realm," while the recalcitrants, he added, "would be obliged to leave the Realm and go to execute their vows at Rome or anywhere they would like, but most assuredly not within the Realm of France." At the same time, he would oblige all parents with children attending Jesuit colleges to withdraw them and send them to colleges of the university, and to prohibit all students whatever from studying at any Jesuit college outside France.[54]

Laverdy's plan was to that of Le Paige as decapitation is to slow strangulation. This indeed was its chief advantage. For despite the fact that his proposed judgment would be only provisional (a certain amount of time would necessarily have to elapse between the attorney general's initial *appel comme d'abus* and its definitive judgment), Laverdy's plan was susceptible of far speedier execution than that of Le Paige. Another advantage of Laverdy's plan was that it rested firmly on two legal premises instead of precariously on only one. Like Le Paige's proposal, Laverdy's rested at least in part on the premise that the parlements had never legally accepted the Jesuits as a monastic order. The use

52. Shennan, *The Parlement of Paris*, p. 82.
53. Gazier, *Histoire générale*, Vol. 1, p. 212.
54. B.P.R.: L.P. 582, ms. 97.

of the *appel comme d'abus* would have been impossible in the case of monastic vows legally authorized by the parlements. But the plan rested equally on the premise which Chauvelin had already established on July 8, that the Jesuit Order was by its very nature irreformable and hence no more susceptible of legal acceptance in 1761 than originally in 1561.

At the same time Laverdy's scheme had the disadvantage of having to pronounce on monastic vows and thereby ran the serious risk of trespassing over the thin line which separated secular from ecclesiastical jurisdiction. This danger did not escape Le Paige, but in general he seems to have been convinced by Laverdy's arguments. In a note written shortly after Laverdy's reply and apparently for his personal instruction alone, Le Paige articulated what seemed to him the alternatives facing the *parti janséniste*. "The more one thinks about it," he wrote, "the more it appears necessary either to terminate everything definitively concerning the abuse of the constitutions, vows and colleges and leave nothing provisional to decree except concerning the examination of the revenues and property, persons and the vows . . . or to keep everything in the greatest secrecy and not actually do anything except to nominate the commissioners and bailiffs to draw up an account of the houses and their property, the persons and their vows without including anything which could permit a glimpse of the plan." In the second case Le Paige hoped that Versailles would think that the parlement was only executing the plan of the *gens du roi* until suddenly, after the autumn vacation, the parlement "would decree concerning everything at the same time." As it happened, events were to dictate a third course, but both alternatives envisioned by Le Paige at this time already excluded his own original plan for the slow strangulation of the Jesuit Order.[55]

Meanwhile the opposing forces, intent upon conserving the Jesuits in France, were far from idle. Although he presided over the official commission appointed to examine the Jesuits' constitutions, doctrine, and moral teachings, First President Molé, like his counterpart Laverdy, habitually passed into "his double"—so he expressed it—and participated in the proceedings of an unofficial though far more significant committee, this one composed, besides himself, of the *gens du roi* Guillaume and Omer Joly de Fleury, President Maupeou, the Bishop of Orléans, Choiseul, the abbé Terray, and the comte de Saint-Florentin, secretary of the king's household.[56] At the same time that the inner councils of the *parti janséniste* were deciding whether to decapitate or slowly strangle the Jesuit Order, this committee was equally occupied in contriving means to keep the Jesuits both intact and alive.

55. Ibid., ms. 98, dated July 1761.
56. B.N.: Collection Joly de Fleury, fol. 1612, ms. 332. Molé to Guillaume Joly de Fleury, n.d.

The committee's chief strategist was the solicitor general, Omer Joly de Fleury, who had no sooner delivered his conclusions to the assembled chambers of the parlement on July 8 than he and his brother, the attorney general,began, at the request of the king, to expand these conclusions into a projected royal edict designed to reform but preserve the Jesuit Order in France. Except for a few modifications of detail, the articles of their proposed royal declaration followed the conclusions they had already given to the parlement: indissoluble vows, periodic provincial assemblies, election of the order's superiors, and so on. But the most important of the draft edict's articles, the eleventh,was new. "We confirm," it read, ". . . the said Jesuits in the ownership of all the houses and property of foundations or other which belong to them whether in houses of novitiate, profession or residence or in Colleges and Seminaries and in which we desire that they continue to reside, instruct and teach as they have done until the present, the whole following and conformable to the dispositions of our present Declaration and in conforming themselves . . . to the laws and regulations of the universities."[57]

An explanation of this article which Omer Joly de Fleury sent in a confidential memorandum to Saint-Florentin at Versailles makes it clear that the solicitor general had correctly divined the *parti janséniste*'s strategy of pushing through the parlement a provisional judgment seriously compromising the Jesuits' position in France. Indeed, the special article, described as "the most important of all" and "truly necessary to the Jesuits," was specifically designed "to prevent any provisional judgment by which the Jesuits would be ordered to dismiss their students from their colleges and to cease all courses of study." But the solicitor general's explanations make it equally clear that he had incorrectly guessed the legal argument upon which the *parti janséniste* intended to base its case against the Jesuits. While Laverdy and Le Paige were deducing their entire case from the two premises of the Jesuits' illegal existence as monks by law and their essential general perversity as monks in fact, the solicitor general was preoccupied with yet another shaky block in the foundation of the Jesuits' legal position in France. It seems that not only had the parlements refused to authorize the Jesuits as a monastic order in 1561 and 1603, but they had really never, though accepting them as a college, entitled them to give public instruction. Both in 1609 and 1610 Henry IV had sent letters patent entitling the Jesuits to open their College of Clermont to the parlement of Paris. But the University of Paris, whose right to be heard in the matter was incontestable, had appealed these letters patent to the parlement of Paris, and the case between the university and the Jesuits, appointed by the parlement, had never been judged and was actually still pending in 1761. The Jesuits had finally opened the College of Clermont in 1618 by virtue of a decree of the

57. Ibid., mss. 329–30. The entire "projet de déclaration" is to be found in mss. 318–32.

king's council which evoked the affair from the parlement of Paris and, without hearing the University of Paris, entitled the Jesuits to open classes. But good *parlementaire* that he was, the solicitor general could not avoid observing that the councils' decree was legally irregular and provided only the shakiest foundation to the Jesuits' continued right to give public instruction in France.[58]

Joly de Fleury's plan was therefore to set the Jesuits' legal house in good order by means of a royal declaration which would at once regularize their position as a monastic order and specifically authorize them to offer public instruction to students. The declaration would of course have to be registered by the parlement of Paris, and the solicitor general fully expected the parlement to respond with remonstrances which "will not fail to repeat everything that was ever said against the Jesuits." But he thought it wiser "to sustain the fire of these remonstrances . . . to which the king will persistently respond by persevering in his desire to maintain the Jesuits' Colleges" than "to leave the spirits to the chance of the present deliberations and permit them to render a provisional judgment unfavorable to the Jesuits." What was above all important, he stressed, was to steal a march on the Jesuits' enemies by sending the royal declaration to the parlement before the parlement itself acted against the Jesuits. If the parlement acted first and the king then annulled its provisional judgment, the Jesuits "would always find themselves embarrassed by the irregularity of the titles which in the actual state of affairs have authorized them to open their colleges in Paris, whereas if the King has manifested his will by Letters Patent and the Parlement then renders a provisional judgment . . . this provisional judgment would be infinitely more susceptible of being regularly annulled."[59]

Together, then, with his brother, First President Molé, and the abbé Terray, Omer Joly de Fleury had produced by the end of July a strategy for reforming and saving the Jesuits which was both carefully formulated and realistic. True, the solicitor general had somewhat miscalculated the *parti janséniste's* intended point of attack, but at least he had made careful if slightly misinformed provision for parliamentary opposition to the projected royal declaration. Not so, however, for the confusion which reigned in the king's council. The solicitor general had of course every reason to believe that Louis XV would accept and follow his plan. Not only had he, the attorney general, and Molé been working on the plan at the express orders of his Majesty, but the three of them had consulted with Saint-Florentin at every turn. However, at the last possible moment the *gens du roi* and Molé encountered opposition from the least likely person, Chancellor Lamoignon. Evidently Lamoignon persuaded Louis XV that the special royal commission which had been established on May 29 to examine and

58. Ibid., mss. 330–31. Omer Joly de Fleury's information was quite accurate. See, for example, Fouqueray, *Histoire de la compagnie de Jésus en France*, Vol. 3, chaps. 2 and 8.

59. B.N.: Collection Joly de Fleury, fol. 1612, mss. 330–31.

report on the Jesuits' constitutions should be given more time to reach its own conclusions. And without previous consultation with Molé or the *gens du roi,* without, in fact, even taking the trouble to warn them of what was to come, Louis XV on August 2 sent to his attorney general a royal declaration which ordered the Jesuits to send the titles of all their establishments in France to the *greffe* of the royal council and forbade the parlement to render any provisional or definitive judgment on the Jesuits' society and constitutions for one year. The *gens du roi* were to present the royal delcaration before the parlement the very next day.[60]

The unexpected arrival of this declaration at eleven o'clock on Sunday evening of August 2 threw the *gens du roi* and the first president into the greatest consternation. And with good reason. It was another disguised evocation of the type of May 29; it contained several lines which were bound to insult the parlement; it referred to a *greffe* of the royal council whose existence the parlement would surely deny; and it was altogether certain to draw heavy parliamentary fire at a point where Versailles was least able to return it. The next morning the brothers Joly de Fleury and the abbé Terray hurriedly met at the home of First President Molé, where Molé was persuaded to arrange yet another hurried meeting between themselves and Saint-Florentin. Molé, according to the solicitor general, "wrote immediately to Saint-Florentin and was unable to resist noting . . . how much this plan was removed from the one which we had proposed at the order which the King had given him . . . that the project . . . could occasion on the part of all the parlements . . . remonstrances which would not fail to say some very harsh things against the Jesuits," and "that spirits would thereby be indisposed against the dispositions of the law which his Majesty would issue at the expiration of the delay." But when Saint-Florentin finally arrived from Versailles, he lamely replied that the chancellor had persuaded the king of the merits of the new declaration and that nothing in it could be altered because the king was at Choisy and the chancellor at Versailles. There was no alternative, he insisted, but to bring it to the parlement as it was the next day.[61]

After months of scheming and plotting, events now moved rapidly. The same afternoon—August 3—President Maupeou took the place of the slightly ill Molé in the parlement's special commission in order to discover what was being said. But he found out nothing.[62]

60. Ibid., fol. 1609, ms. 101; and *Procédure contre l'institut et les constitutions des Jésuites,* p. 37.

61. B.N.: Collection Joly de Fleury, fol. 1609, ms. 101. A remarkably personal and revealing document in an otherwise generally impersonal and official set of papers, this manuscript contains Omer Joly de Fleury's recollections of what transpired during the critical days from August 2 to August 6, 1761.

62. Ibid.

The morning of August 4: The *gens du roi* finally presented the new royal declaration to the assembled chambers of the parlement. The parlement contented itself with returning the declaration and *lettre de cachet* to the special commission already appointed to examine the Jesuits' constitutions and—since Chauvelin's discourse of July 8—doctrine.[63]

August 4 and 5: The Jesuits, unable to penetrate the deliberations of the parlement's special commission, spread around and about Paris that the one-year delay ordered by the declaration of August 2 was only a prelude to another royal declaration which, at the end of the one-year period, would tie the parlement's hands for ten more. To demonstrate their confidence "they tranquilly walked about in Paris, even affecting to show themselves in the public promenades as far as the Boulevards in the midst of the *beau monde.*"[64]

The afternoon of August 5: The high command of the magisterial *parti janséniste*—the abbé Chauvelin, Clément de Feuillet, Guillaume Lambert, Robert de Saint-Vincent, and Laverdy—met in utmost secrecy at the home of Feuillet, where Laverdy, to believe Saint-Vincent, "performed for us something like a rehearsal of what he counted upon saying the next day to the assembly of chambers" and "spoke for more than one hour without paper, without books, but from memory, with a grace and talents of which those of us who knew him remained confounded."[65]

That same afternoon: The solicitor general wrote the last of a curious and somewhat acrimonious exchange of notes between himself and Laverdy. Laverdy had asked the solicitor general whether he was certain that his *Compte rendu* of early July had faithfully reported everything contained in the parliamentary registers about the Jesuits. Puzzled as to Laverdy's purposes, the solicitor general wrote his brother that "apparently" they had to do with "the subject of the doctrine of the Jesuits . . . which is to be the object of an assembly of chambers next October 15."[66]

The night of August 5: All the magistrates of the parlement of Paris received notices that they should be at their respective chambers at seven o'clock the next morning.[67]

August 6, at 7 A.M.: Laverdy told his chamber (the first chamber of requests) that he did not think the declaration of August 2 could be rightly discussed except in a session of the assembled chambers, and therefore suggested that his chamber request that all the chambers be assembled. Persuaded by Laverdy, the first chamber of requests sent two of its members to all the other chambers,

63. *Procédure contre l'institut et les constitutions des Jésuites*, p. 37.
64. *Nouvelles Ecclésiastiques* (December 11, 1761), p. 209.
65. Saint-Vincent, "Mémoires," p. 242.
66. B.N.: Collection Joly de Fleury, fol. 1612, ms. 345. The entire exchange of notes is to be found in mss. 341–45.
67. *Procédure contre l'institut et les constitutions des Jésuites*, pp. 37–38.

which, in turn, indicated their approval of the proposition. The first chamber of requests then sent couselors Noblet and Charlet to the eldest of the presidents to demand an assembly of chambers, and he, in turn, informed the first president who finally set the time for the assembly at 8:30.[68]

August 6, at 8:30 A.M.: The chambers finally having been assembled, the question arose whether to discuss only the declaration of August 2 or everything which concerned the Jesuits. The representatives of the inquests and requests insisted that "it was necessary to deliberate on everything."[69]

The abbé Terray, reporter of the declaration of August 2, rose to defend this declaration and argued that the parlement should register it with only minor modifications because, first, the jurisdiction of the parlement of Paris contained only a third of the Jesuits' establishments in France, whereas the king's declaration would enable him to decide about them all; secondly, because the parlement had already waited 150 years to judge the Jesuits' constitutions and could easily wait another; and finally, because the parlement should avoid a conflict of authority with the king.[70]

Laverdy then rose and told the company that it had never judged a more important affair, because the "security of the person of kings, the tranquillity of the state, the preservation of religion and the education of the youth" were all at stake. He then proposed to examine the affair of the Jesuits from two points of view: the Jesuits by themselves and in relation to what specifically had transpired in France. Under the first heading he belabored the premise already established by the abbé Chauvelin on April 17 and July 8, that because of its incompatibility with the laws of France the Jesuit Order was unacceptable as it stood, and because of its "vicious" nature and "anarchical, murderous and parricidal doctrines," it could not be reformed in the future. Proceeding to his second heading, Laverdy next established the premise which Le Paige had so insisted upon, that neither in 1561 nor in 1603 had France accepted the Jesuits as a monastic order. And with his premises well in place, Laverdy finally drew the conclusions he had mapped out to Le Paige nearly a month earlier, that the parlement should receive the attorney general *appelant comme d'abus* of the Jesuits' constitutions, papal bulls, and "formulas of vows," forbid the Jesuits to receive any more novices or pronounce any more vows, and close the Jesuits' colleges, seminaries, associations, and congregations as "the sole means of preserving the subjects of the King, especially young ecclesiastics, from such pernicious instruction." All these measures Laverdy moreover proposed under the guise of provisional (pending the judgment of the *appel comme d'abus*) modifications to the registration of the Declaration of August 2, which forbade

68. Ibid., p. 38.
69. Ibid., p. 39.
70. Ibid., p. 40.

the parlement to judge definitively or provisionally concerning the Jesuits for an entire year.[71]

The parlement regarded Laverdy's proposals as "so beautiful" that it adopted them by a majority of about 130 to 13.[72] It therefore passed two judgments, one which received its attorney general *appelant comme d'abus* of the Jesuits' constitutions, formulas of vows, and all acts which had founded the Jesuit Order since its origin; the other which, under the pretext of provisionally protecting the "most precious patrimony of the realm" from the "pernicious" doctrine of the Jesuits until the definitive judgment of the *appel comme d'abus,* forbade the Jesuits to recruit novices or pronounce further vows, dissolved their congregations and associations, and closed their colleges from the date of October 1, 1761, in towns with colleges other than those of the Jesuits and, on April 1, 1762, in the others. The magistrates also registered the declaration of August 2, but with the reservation that without waiting for the expiration of the one-year delay, they would render all judgments—the two already mentioned—"in regard to which the oath of the court, its fidelity and love for the sacred person of the said Lord the King, and its attention to the public repose would not permit it to employ delay and dilation."[73]

The reaction of ordinary Parisians to the parlement's judgments of August 6, 1761, seems to have been remarkably enthusiastic. Writing on August 8, 1761, a certain Brunet d'Evry, one of the king's *maîtres des requêtes,* reported that "even the lowest sort of public takes the side of the *arrêts*; in the space of a single hour this morning the least individuals carried off everything which the colporteurs possessed in the way of copies, and since ten o'clock this morning until this evening the impatience to have more was so great that the door of the printer had to be locked and guarded; it is rumored that a foreign minister whose name I did not hear ordered the purchase of three of four hundred copies; the fermentation is extreme."[74]

Reactions on the part of the actors in the drama varied as one might expect. At Versailles the dauphin wrote to Chancellor Lamoignon that the dispositions

71. Ibid., pp. 41–51.
72. *Nouvelles Ecclésiastiques* (December 11, 1761), p. 210. The *Nouvelles Ecclésiastiques* reported a vote of 98 to 14, whereas the *Procédure contre l'institut et les constitutions des Jésuites,* p. 54, records a vote of 128 or 129 to 13. Since the latter source consists of notes taken by one of the magistrates, its count should be regarded as more accurate than that of the *Nouvelles Ecclésiastiques.*
73. *Procédure contre l'institut et les constitutions des Jésuites,* pp. 55–70.
74. A.N.: O¹ 604, p. 268. This letter—for whom it was intended I do not know—is dated Paris, August 8, 1761, and was signed simply "Brunet." That the author was Brunet d'Evry, "maître des requestes honoraire," represents speculation on my part, but seems probable because this Brunet was a member of the Bureau pour les Affaires Concernant les Unions de Bénéfices aux Maisons et Collèges des Jésuites. See *Almanach royale* (1761), pp. 149, 156.

of the parlement's measures impressed him as "so monstrous that I can hardly believe them,"[75] while back in Paris the solicitor general, Omer Joly de Fleury, arranging the manuscript proposals and plans upon which he had so recently but vainly lavished his attention, bitterly scrawled at their head the sentence: "Plan of a Declaration for which they had asked us and which would have prevented the judgments of August 6, 1761."[76] Great rejoicing, on the other hand, reigned in the camp of the *parti janséniste*. But there was also among its members a feeling that the victory against the Jesuits was not so much their own as that of previous generations, and that what they had just accomplished was at best the work of dwarfs who sat on the shoulders of giants. Laverdy, the hero of August 6, had even before this date seen his efforts as the revenge of the Daughters of the Congregation of the Infancy, a Jansenist congregation which the Jesuits had dispersed in 1686. But his colleague Robert de Saint-Vincent discovered an even more appropriate connection. "Now the day of August 6, 1761," he wrote, "was the centennial anniversary day of the death of the mère Angélique Arnauld, the celebrated abbess of Port-Royal. One cannot doubt," he continued, "that the mère Angélique, who all her life combatted along with the *messieurs* of Port-Royal the lax doctrine of the Jesuits, had conceived ardent vows for the destruction of the Society. It is on the same centennial anniversary day of the death of the mère Angélique that the Parlement renders a judgment which leads necessarily to this dissolution. *Dignitus Die est hic,*" he concluded. "It is impossible not to recognize it—God is not hurried in the execution of his resolutions. A hundred years are in his eyes as a single day!"[77]

75. A.N.: A.P. 162 mi. (Archives du marquis de Rosanbo), *carton* 1, *dossier* 6, ms. 17, dauphin to Chancellor Lamoignon, August 7, 1761.
76. B.N.: Collection Joly de Fleury, fol. 1612, ms. 318.
77. Saint-Vincent, "Mémoires," pp. 242–43.

6. The Defense of the Order: The Jesuit Polemics against La Chalotais and the Jansenists

THE PARLEMENT OF PARIS HAD CAST ITS JUDGMENTS OF August 6, 1761, in the form of an *appel comme d'abus*, which meant that those judgments were only suspensive and provisional in character. The case of the Jesuits' constitutions and doctrine was not to be definitively judged until a year later. Undoubtedly such parliamentary moderation was motivated in part by a desire not to break overtly with Louis XV, who had ordered his parlement to judge neither definitively nor provisionally concerning the Jesuits' constitutions for an entire year. But partly, too, the parlement acted as it did in order that the Jesuits, as Laverdy expressed it, "might not in any case be able to complain of having been judged without being heard."[1] From August 6, 1761, until the same date on the following year the Jesuits were therefore legally entitled to appear before the parlement of Paris and defend themselves.

Curiously enough, however, they at no time formed legal oppositions either to the parlement of Paris's provisional sentence of August 6, 1761, or to those which the provincial parlements, following the lead of Paris, rendered in subsequent months. Why this unwonted docility on the part of the Jesuits in the face of the parliamentary offensive against them, especially in the wake of the foolhardy courage with which they had brought the La Valette case to the parlement of Paris in the first place? Why such reluctance to defend their very existence in France after having so doggedly defended their claim to 1,552,276 livres? Did the Jesuits suddenly lose their nerve? Did, as some of their enemies suggested, they doubt the justice of their case? Or was their systematic boycott of the parliamentary proceedings part of a well-calculated strategy? As the Jesuits' refusal to appear before the parlements did not prevent them either then or subsequently from asserting (Laverdy's best efforts notwithstanding) that they were condemned without a hearing, these questions merit some consideration.[2]

1. *Procédure contre l'institut et les constitutions des Jésuites*, p. 48.
2. For a contemporary witness who charged that the Jesuits had been condemned without a hearing, see *Mes Doutes sur l'affaire présente des Jésuites*, pp. 41–42.

Explanations of the Jesuits' official silence by contemporary observers differed as one might expect. On the Jansenist side stood someone like Robert de Saint-Vincent, to whom the Jesuits' legal silence was evidence of a dark conspiracy, a sin of calculated omission designed to engender doubts about the legality of a trial conducted in their absence and which they surely would have lost.[3] Among those sympathetic to the Jesuits, on the other hand, the abbé Baston, in 1761 a theology student at the Sorbonne and later Bishop of Séez, explained the Jesuits' "incomprehensible lethargy" with the suggestion that they perceived "from the very first moments that their destruction was resolved, that they would resist in vain, that by supplicating they would be left only with the shame of having supplicated, and that they preferred to these useless humiliations a magnanimous and silent fall."[4]

But happily we are not entirely without the witness of the Jesuits themselves. For in the same breath with which the abbé Baston speculated about the Jesuits' "incomprehensible lethargy" and "silent fall," he also bemoaned the "deluge of writings" which "innundated Paris and the provinces, some in favor of the Jesuits, others against them, others so masked and badly written that one could not divine whether they offered the hand to the unfortunates or worked for their ruin." Among these, moreover, he singled out two works in defense of the Jesuits which he thought especially distinguished, one entitled *Apologie de l'institut des Jésuites*, a "solid work," the other called *Appel à la raison*, which he described as "brilliant in spirit and levity, but whose manner, even the title, was injurious to those whose defense it embraced."[5]

Now as it happens, the writers of both these books were Jesuits. The author of the justly famous *Apologie de l'institut* was a certain Joseph-Antoine Cerutti, then a young professor of rhetoric of Piedmontese origin at the Jesuit college in Lyons who later renounced his order and distinguished himself during the Revolution as the editor of the *Feuille Villageoise*, a journal which attempted to explain the Revolution's legislation to rural France. And it was a certain père André Christophe Balbani who composed the *Appel à raison*, which appeared in 1762.[6] Nor

3. Saint-Vincent, "Mémoires," p. 248.

4. L'abbé Baston, *Mémoires, d'après le manuscrit originel publiés pour la Société d'histoire contemporaine*, eds. Julien Loth and Charles Vergier (Paris, 1897–99), Vol. 1, p. 134.

5. Ibid., pp. 134–35.

6. The *Appel à la raison* has also been attributed to Charles Frey de Neuville, the court preacher, and his brother Pierre Claude Frey de Neuville, but it seems more likely that the author is André Christophe Balbani, since the Neuvilles usually expressed themselves in more measured terms. (See Aloys de Backer and Charles Sommervogel, *Bibliothèque de la compagnie de Jésus* [Paris, 1890–1932], Vol. 1, col. 791.) The young Cerutti, on the other hand, was not solely responsible for the *Apologie de l'institut des Jésuites*, but wrote it under the direction of the pères de Menoux and Griffet (ibid., Vol. 2, col. 1005). Cerutti renounced the Jesuit order in 1767 to the great scandal of his confreres.

does this exhaust the list either of Jesuits who rallied to the defense of their order or of polemical pamphlets they published in its behalf. Besides a considerable number of anonymous pamphlets probably of Jesuitical origin—*Les Pourquoi, ou Questions sur une grande affaire pour ceux qui n'ont que trois minutes à y donner; Tout le Monde a tort, ou Jugement impartial d'une dame philosophique sur l'affaire présente des Jésuites; Mes Doutes sur l'affaire présente des Jésuites*; and so on—the père Balbani returned to the charge with a *App Nouvelleel à la raison*; Charles Frey or his brother Pierre Claude de Neuville entered the lists with some *Observations sur l'institut de la société des Jésuites*; and the redoubtable Henri Griffet, one of the more bellicose of Jesuit polemicists during this period, struck twice with his *Coup d'œil sur l'arrêt du parlement de Paris du 6 août 1761* and his *Remarques sur un écrit intitulé: 'Compte rendu des constitutions des Jésuites'.*[7]

If, then, the parlements condemned the Jesuit Order behind the backs of the Jesuits, the Jesuits themselves were not above defending themselves with unauthorized and, for the most part, anonymous pamphlets behind the backs of the parlements. And if the suggestions of contemporaries provide only imperfect explanations of the Jesuits' refusal to appear before the parlements, perhaps the Jesuits' legal silence is at least in part better explained by the content of their simultaneous, if illegal, verbosity.

Even the briefest perusal of the works which the Jesuits published in their order's defense reveals yet another curious fact, that nearly all the Jesuit polemicists addressed themselves, not to the writings of Chauvelin, Le Paige, Coudrette, or Lalourcé—in short, those who were actually masterminding the destruction of their order—but rather to a single and relatively uninfluential work: The *Compte rendu des constitutions des Jésuites* by Louis-René de Caradeuc de la Chalotais, attorney general of the parlement of Brittany.[8] The same Jesuit polemicists were moreover likewise unanimous in accusing La Chalotais, not of Jansenism, but of an entirely different variety of heresy: encyclopedism, or of being a disciple of Voltaire, D'Alembert, and the philosophes.

The père Henri Griffet was most blunt and vicious in his accusations of encyclopedism. Speculating about La Chalotais's motives for having involved himself in the affair of the Jesuits at all, Griffet noted that many "rare and distinguished talents are in a manner buried in the Provinces," that the judicial

7. On Henri Griffet's work and activities, see ibid., Vol. 3, col. 1819. For the authorship of the *Nouvelle appel à la raison*, ibid., Vol. 1, col. 791; and for the authorship of *Observations sur l'institut de la société des Jésuites*, ibid., Vol. 5, col. 1692.

8. *Compte rendu des constitutions des Jésuites, par M. Louis-René Caradeuc de la Chalotais, procureur-général du roi au parlement de Bretagne, les 1, 3, 4 et 5 décembre 1761, en exécution de l'arrêt de la cour du 17 août précédent* (1762), henceforth cited as La Chalotais, *Compte rendu des constitutions des Jésuites.*

affairs of Normandy and Brittany were for the most part "unknown to the rest of the world," and that La Chalotais had evidently found in the affair of the Jesuits "an entirely natural occasion to make manifest the singularity of his talents." Speculating further on why La Chalotais had chosen to condemn the Jesuits rather than to defend them, Griffet suggested that "the desire to please our great men of Letters, the new Philosophes, the authors and disciples of the *Encyclopédie* whose principles are everywhere insinuated without being overtly adopted" and "the pressing and powerful solicitations arriving from the capital without doubt contributed far more in deciding the suffrage of this Author than"—and here Griffet quoted La Chalotais himself—the desire "to work to the discharge of his conscience" in order that "God might be praised and honored by his good and holy intentions."[9] But Griffet's confreres were hardly less bellicose in their denunciations of La Chalotais's encyclopedic proclivities. The Jesuit Balbani, for one, observed that the magistrates, so vigilant in denouncing the assertion of one's right to kill in self-defense in the Jesuit Busembaum's *Theologia moralis*, had totally ignored the same proposition in the *Encyclopédie*. "Without doubt it escaped their notice, but with what countenance," he asked, "was a Breton Encyclopedist able to reproach the Jesuits for a maxim advanced by his Teachers?"[10]

La Chalotais a disciple of the philosophes? If the reception which he and his *Compte rendu* received from undeniable philosophes is taken as the criterion, then he certainly must be so considered. When in 1763 La Chalotais visited Paris, he arrived, to believe the abbé Georgel, "with all the pomp and circumstance of a conqueror," and was subsequently feted not only by the magistrates of the parlement of Paris but by Buffon, Duclos, Marmontel and D'Alembert, genuine Encyclopedists all of them.[11] D'Alembert characterized La Chalotais as a "philosophe" and an "enlightened magistrate" in his book *Sur la Destruction des Jésuites en France* in 1765, and Voltaire himself christened his *Compte rendu* "the only philosophical work ever to have come from the Bar."[12]

But guilt by association is hardly a legitimate method by which to categorize a thinker. Interestingly enough, the only contemporary philosophe whom Griffet named in particular as La Chalotais's teacher was the author of the *Esprit des lois*, the baron de Montesquieu, whose very name is enough to remind us how difficult it can be to define the "Enlightenment" and how thin the line sometimes is which divides Catholic from unbeliever, conservative from

9. Griffet, *Remarques sur un écrit*, pp. 9–12.

10. Balbani, *Appel à la raison*, pp. 160–61.

11. L'abbé Georgel (ex-Jésuite), *Mémoires pour servir à l'histoire des évènements de la fin du XVIIIe siècle, depuis 1760 jusqu'en 1806–1810, par un contemporain impartial* (Paris, 1817), Vol. 1, pp. 79–80.

12. D'Alembert, *Sur la Destruction des Jésuites en France*, p. 159. For Voltaire's judgment, see B.N.: Collection Joly de Fleury, fol. 1615, ms. 127, undated copy of a letter from Voltaire to La Chalotais.

philosophe, in eighteenth-century France. For to which are we to attach the most importance, the mocking incredulity and rationalistic critique of European customs of the *Lettres persanes* or the *Esprit des lois*'s ponderous vindication of the legislative pretensions of the French parlements, which regularly burned philosophical books, twice condemned the *Encyclopédie*, and finally opposed the vote by head for the estates-general in 1788?[13] And it makes matters no easier that when the père Griffet identified Montesquieu as La Chalotais's mentor, he accused them together of both these crimes: of "annihilating the Sovereign power of monarchs" and of "introducing into France the government of England"—in other words, of bolstering the legislative pretensions of the "unenlightened" parlements, and of "everywhere declaiming against the Religious or Ecclesiastical Celibate," a typically "enlightened" and rationalistic critique of the ecclesiastical institution of monasticism.[14] La Chalotias's *Compte rendu* itself sharply criticized the Jesuits for the despotic nature of their order, their ultramontane loyalty to the papacy, their nonreciprocal vows, and their doctrines of tyrannicide, but in little of this was there anything which was not simply Gallican or which differed essentially from the *Compte rendu* of the brothers Joly de Fleury, who, however, received no praise whatever from philosophical quarters. Nor do any of the antitheses traditionally used to distinguish "enlightened" from conservative thought—reason versus faith, nature versus grace, science versus revelation—or even some of the newer ones—empiricism versus rationalism, pragmatism versus idealism, and most recently, neopaganism versus Christianity—measurably facilitate the task of placing La Chalotais in either one category or the other. La Chalotais nowhere questioned the validity of faith or the reality of grace or revelation, nor was his approach particularly empirical or pragmatic in character or his prose so larded with classical allusions as to justify characterizing him as pagan in outlook.[15]

It is with a profound sense of humility, however, that one realizes that what has become something of an historiographical problem in this century constituted no problem whatever to those in the eighteenth century. Eighteenth-century Jesuits, at least, apparently felt no lack of confidence in their ability to identify philosophes or encyclopedists, and whether or not that showed presumption on their part, it might in any case be instructive to observe how they did so.

Was it perhaps in the style of La Chalotais's *Compte rendu* that his Jesuit

13. For the interpretation of Montesquieu's *Esprit des lois* as a justification of parliamentary pretensions, see Ford, *Robe and Sword*, pp. 233–45, and Peter Gay, "Carl Becker's Heavenly City," in *The Party of Humanity* (New York, 1964), pp. 207–08.

14. Griffet, *Remarques sur un écrit*, pp. 28–29.

15. For empiricism, pragmatism, and neopaganism as criteria by which to distinguish "enlightened" thought, see esp. Peter Gay, *Voltaire's Politics: The Poet as Realist* (Princeton, 1959), and his *The Enlightenment: An Interpretation*, Vol. 1: *The Rise of Modern Paganism* (New York, 1966), passim.

detractors recognized the marks of the philosophical beast? Certainly his *Compte rendu* was well written, which already set it apart from most Jansenist, parliamentary, or even Jesuitical productions of the time. Even the Jesuit Balbani felt obliged to concede that it displayed the "graces of style and a boldness of expressions."[16] But it was not so much the "graces of style" as the "boldness of expressions," a certain flippancy bordering on irreverence in tone best exemplified, perhaps, by La Chalotais's characterization of the Jesuits as an order with "fifty thousand professors of philosophy and no philosopher of reputation, as many professors of belles lettres and so few good books of literature," that most irritated the Jesuits.[17] D'Alembert himself was later to identify this flippant, jaunty method of attacking the Jesuits as properly philosophical and to contrast it favorably to the more serious, often theological approach of the Jansenists. The philosophes did not, like the Jansenists, tell the Jesuits: " 'you are ambitious men, intriguers and rogues'; that accusation," D'Alembert explained, "would not have humiliated the Society: they rather said to them: 'you are ignoramuses; you do not have among yourselves a sole man of letters whose name is celebrated in Europe and is worthy to be so.' "[18]

Yet even more than La Chalotais's "boldness of expressions" in general, it was several such bold expressions in particular that most intensely scandalized the Jesuits. Balbani put his finger on what are probably the two most important of these expressions, or rather terms, in a lengthy declamation against what he called La Chalotais's "politics" or political philosophy. Where, he asked, "are the politics of him who treats our Religion as enthusiasm, who accuses a Religious Order of irreligion, who supposes that an Institute approved by the Holy See and confirmed by a General Council is 'fanticism reduced to principles and rules.' Where," he continued, "are the politics of him who . . . extends his temerity much farther, who says that fanaticism derives from the system of the infallibility of the Pope, from which he lets it be inferred that the same infallibility which he does not dare dispute openly with the Councils can become a source of error and fanaticism by describing the Bishops who are united to the Holy See as rash men. He who . . . calls the wisdom of the Cross a folly and the zeal of Christians a delirium, is he, we do not say Catholic, but *Politique*? Is it a Christian magistrate who speaks, or a Rhetorician of ancient Rome . . . ?" Balbani finally concluded that La Chalotais harbored "evil intentions against Religion" behind "his affected protestations" to the contrary.[19]

Whether and to what extent that was true, whether indeed he regarded the "wisdom of the Cross" a "folly"—these are questions to which neither his

16. Balbani, *Appel à la raison*, p. 172.
17. La Chalotais, *Compte rendu des constitutions des Jésuites*, p. 180.
18. D'Alembert, *Sur la Destruction des Jésuites en France*, p. 136.
19. Balbani, *Appel à la raison*, pp. 122–23.

Compte rendu nor his other published writings furnish certain answers. In all probability La Chalotais, like so many others, sincerely thought that by attacking the Jesuit Order, he was purifying rather than destroying Catholicism in France. But one need not take Balbani's rhetoric at face value to recognize that to any Catholic there was something very disquieting about La Chalotais's use of the terms *fanaticism* and *enthusiasm* in connection with the papacy, church councils, and religious orders. Indeed, La Chalotais employed these terms as well as others equally suspicious—*prejudice, ignorance,* and *barbarous,* for example —in great profusion. The religious wars of the sixteenth century, according to him, were "either the cause or the effect of enthusiasm and fanaticism"; the Jesuits' founder Ignatius Loyola, a product of this century, "brought to his projects a kind of enthusiasm, which came from an imagination which overheated his zeal"; the Jesuits' educational system was likewise the result of the "prejudice and ignorance of the sixteenth century" and had therefore remained "vicious and barbarous"; the strict and unquestioning obedience which individual Jesuits owed their superiors was "the complete fanaticism" and "visibly either fanaticism or folly"; the mutual reproof and correction enjoined upon all Jesuits by their constitutions was the "summit of fanaticism"; and—we have not yet reached the summit—the practice of reading and rereading Ignatius Loyola's *Spiritual Exercises* was "to inspire enthusiasm and prepare the ways to fanaticism" and could not, La Chalotais thought, "be regarded except as the art of having visions and ecstasies reduced to a method."[20]

With all this squandering of the terms *fanaticism* and *enthusiasm,* it is somewhat disconcerting to find that La Chalotais did not deign to provide his readers with a precise definition of either. He came rather close to defining "enthusiasm"— "to have persuasions and convictions without motives," he called it—but as for *fanaticism,* he contented himself with the remark that if the Jesuits' supposedly excessive obedience to their superiors was not its very incarnation, he demanded "that someone give him the definition"—as if all were agreed on precisely what it meant.[21] From his partial definition of "enthusiasm," however, taken together with his judgment of Ignatius Loyola as a saint whose basically right-headed religious zeal, whose "rectitude of heart" and "always pure and disinterested views" were unfortunately overstoked by a meridional "imagination" producing "enthusiasm," we can perhaps conclude that what La Chalotais

20. La Chalotais, *Compte rendu des constitutions des Jésuites.* For his judgment on Loyola as "enthusiastic," see p. 61; on Jesuit obedience as the "complete fanaticism," p. 157; on the reading of *Spiritual Exercises* as fanatical, pp. 174–75; and for remarks on the Jesuits' education, p. 177 and *Second Compte rendu sur l'appel comme d'abus des constitutions des Jésuites, par M. Louis René de Caradeuc de la Chalotais, procureur général du roi au parlement de Bretagne, les 21, 22 et 24 mai, 1762* (1762), p. 122.

21. For his de finition of "enthusiasm," see La Chalotais, *Compte rendu des constitutions des Jésuites,* p. 62; for his remark on "fanaticism," ibid., p. 157.

meant by enthusiasm or fanaticism or both was a misdirected, somehow benighted religious zeal, and that he had no objection whatever to an "enlightened," reasoned, and somewhat lackadaisical zeal.[22] But even if this be hi
meaning, one can yet legitimately wonder with the Jesuits whether the distinction between an "enlightened" and benighted zeal is admissible, and whethe
it was not with all religious ardor whatsoever, not merely misdirected religiou
ardor, that La Chalotais wished to quarrel.

Be that as it may, behind La Chalotais's bold declamations against religiou
enthusiasm and fanaticism, the Jesuit polemicist Griffet detected another, more
fundamental assumption: that religious enthusiasm and fanaticism were in the
last analysis to be despised because their manifestations were at best useless and
at worst harmful to the State and society. And nowhere was this assumption
more clear than in what La Chalotais had to say about the multiplication of
monastic orders. "Here," cried Griffet, "is the great complaint that everyone
has these days against all the Religious Orders, or perhaps more accurately
against every Ecclesiastical Order, the Celibate who perceptibly depopulate
the States."[23]

Now La Chalotais had indeed complained, to use his own words, that a
single act of devotion had often been used to justify the establishment of new
religious orders and that "by force of pious works the States ruin and depopulate
themselves perceptibly."[24] But depopulation resulting from monastic celibacy
was to La Chalotais's mind only one of the many plagues which, like Moses'
rod, the multiplication of monastic orders had visited upon Europe. These
mushrooming religious orders had also "surcharged" the State with mendi-
cants, with "idle people" who, "forgetting their first institution," accomplished
nothing except to institute "bad studies," had prevented the "curés and their
assistants, those who carry the burden of the day, from instructing themselves
and being adequately endowed," and worst of all, had "produced wars and
theological hatreds with which the State has sometimes the benevolence to
encumber itself, as if they were the concern of the State instead of despising
them or prohibiting them."[25] To the question of why, with all these evil
effects, ecclesiastics had ever taken it into their heads to multiply monastic
orders, La Chalotais's answer was prompt: "Zeal heats the imagination about
an establishment to found; enthusiasm takes hold; the ambition of founding
which is bent upon the glory of commanding unites itself to zeal which seems
to justify it."[26] So we come back to enthusiasm and fanaticism, which, operating

22. Ibid., pp. 61–62.
23. Griffet, *Remarques sur un écrit*, p. 25.
24. La Chalotais, *Compte rendu des constitutions des Jésuites*, p. 14.
25. Ibid., pp. 64–65.
26. Ibid., p. 16.

ometimes mediately through monastic orders and sometimes immediately
upon events and people themselves, produced the depopulation of states,
mendicancy, the corruption of the secular clergy, religious wars, and "theo-
ogical hatreds"—all of them useless and even harmful to the State. Perhaps,
hen, what La Chalotais ultimately or at least partly meant by enthusiasm and
fanaticism was a religious zeal which expressed itself in politically useless and
harmful ways.

In none of this, in any case, was there anything directed exclusively against
he Jesuits. La Chalotais's strictures applied logically to all religious groups and
orders, not to the Jesuits alone. Indeed, La Chalotais's *Compte rendu* differed
sharply from all others in its frank recognition that many of the Jesuit Order's
faults were shared by other religious orders and in its simultaneous and belligerent insistence that this fact in no way excused the Jesuits. Should the Jesuits,
hen, not have taken offence at La Chalotais's remarks about enthusiasm,
fanaticism, and monasticism? Hardly. For herein lies precisely what was un-
questionably "enlightened" about at least a portion—by no means all—of La
Chalotais's *Compte rendu*. La Chalotais did not deign to descend into the closed
and heated arena of combat between Jansenists and Molinists, Dominicans and
esuits, or even ultramontanists and Gallicans, but rather, as Voltaire had already
done in his *Essai sur les mœurs, Le Siècle de Louis XIV,* and *Précis du siècle de Louis
XV,* he distributed his anathemas and blessings—mostly anathemas—to all
religious groups and orders indiscriminately, from the paradoxically Olympian
and this-worldly perspective of political and social utility.[27] D'Alembert,
certainly a competent judge of the matter, said precisely the same thing when
later he remarked that among all the magistrates who had written against the
esuits, La Chalotais alone had "envisioned this affair as a statesman, philoso-
her, and an enlightened magistrate devoid of all hatred and party spirit," because instead of trying to prove that other monks were better than the Jesuits,
he had rather insisted that "the monastic spirit is the scourge of all states."[28]

From the perspective of several centuries it is easy to see that to have attempted to prune religious activity to fit the strict exigencies of political and
social utility was to have attacked its very roots, that to have attempted to
defend a religious order in such terms was only to have implicitly sanctioned the
abolition of others, and that from the point of view of Christian apologetics it
would perhaps have been wiser, if not in the short run more successful, to have
taken issue with the criteria of reason and public utility themselves from the
very outset. That this was so, however, was probably not clear to La Chalotais
himself, to say nothing of the Jesuits who foolishly, if courageously, hazarded

27. See esp. Voltaire, *Essai sur les mœurs,* in *Œuvres complètes,* Vol. 21, pp. 306–09.
28. D'Alembert, *Sur la Destruction des Jésuites en France,* pp. 159–60.

battle on terrain of the Enlightenment's own choosing. If anything, the Jesuits outshone La Chalotais in their appeals to reason and public usefulness as justification for their existence in France.

The very title of Balbani's apology, *Appel à la raison des écrits et libelles publiés par la passion contre les Jésuites de France,* set the tone of much of the Jesuits' self-vindication. Were the Jesuits, as La Chalotais had asserted, the harbingers of religious enthusiasm and fanaticism? Not so, insisted the Jesuits, and then proceeded, not to defend religious "enthusiasm" and "fanaticism" themselves—or whatever reality to which these pejorative terms referred—but to show that it was really their opponents, La Chalotais among them, whose natural lights had been obscured by passion and prejudice, who were possessed of "persuasions and convictions without motives" and therefore walked in darkness, and that it was themselves, the Jesuits, who were reasonable, dispassionate, and who had seen a great light.

That their enemies were benighted, that they alone were enlightened, the Jesuits asserted at every possible turn. Was it just, for instance, that eighteenth-century Jesuits should be held responsible for doctrines of regicide formulated by Jesuits during the sixteenth and seventeenth centuries, or should they not rather be judged according to what they believed in 1762? "Reason and equity," answered Balbani, "solicit for them this justice: only blind passion could refuse it to them."[29] Did the Jesuits' vows make it more difficult for some families to divide the inheritance among their sons? Undoubtedly, answered Neuville, but "reason dictates that the larger interest and at the same time the interest of an infinitely more numerous portion of the State should prevail over a smaller interest."[30] Did the law passed at the Jesuits' fifth general congregation, which enjoined them not to teach opinions odious to the nation in which they resided, prove that the Jesuits were inconstant and perfidious? If anything, Neuville replied, it proved that the "French Jesuits, possessing no other rule than that of political expediency, will not change their teaching as long as France does not change her doctrine"— the four Gallican articles, he meant to say, of 1682. "But prejudice," he added, "does not reflect."[31] Growing somewhat pessimistic, however, about the fate of the Jesuits because their adversaries declined "the tribunal of reason" and insisted instead upon "the tribunal of prejudice," the same author yet found hope in the thought that the Jesuits could "follow them there with confidence, provided that reason retains the right to decide between prejudice and prejudice": on the side of the Jesuits, the prejudice of the successive occupants of the Holy See, the Council of Trent, the episcopacy, the

29. Balbani, *Appel à la raison,* p. 94.
30. Charles Frey or Pierre Claude de Neuville, *Observations sur l'institut de la société des Jésuites* (Avignon, 1761), p. 76.
31. Ibid., p. 30.

Catholic kings of Europe, Saint François de Sales, "all the saints of these last centuries," and the "vast majority of Catholic writers," including Bishop Bossuet, the "light and ornament . . . of the Gallican Church"; and on the side of the Jesuits' enemies, "the prejudice founded upon the compilation of writings dragged from the dust, of histories, facts and anecdotes which possess no guarantee of their reality except the presumed sagacity of their narrators in disentangling the truth and their very dubious fidelity in rendering it; of old speeches composed in the heat and animosities of contestations; of old satires applauded during moments of a manipulated vogue and as soon forgotten; of declamations of an infinitely small number of writers discontented about some proceeding or with some member of the Society."[32]

To be sure, there was nothing singularly "enlightened" here about the Jesuits' use of the word *reason*. They used it in a sense more or less equivalent to that of "justice"; it by no means smacked of an exclusively empirical view of knowledge or of any skeptical attitude toward the reality of miracles and the supernatural. That there existed a certain gap in communication between La Chalotais and his long-robed detractors is indicated by the single instance in which a Jesuit—in this case Cerutti—came substantially to grips with La Chalotais's accusation of enthusiasm. In response to La Chalotais's assertion that the *Spiritual Exercises* inspired enthusiasm, Cerutti answered that "enthusiasm, according to the author whom we refute here, 'is to have persuasions without motives, sentiments without ideas,' " that "these exercises tend only to present both greater motives for and more sublime ideas of Religion," and that "they therefore do not tend to inspire enthusiasm."[33] Now obviously whatever La Chalotais meant by the words *motives* and *ideas* and what Cerutti meant by the same terms were two quite different things. La Chalotais most probably, although by no means certainly, used them in the "enlightened" sense of knowledge based firmly upon concrete empirical data, a view which implicitly denied the possibility of spiritual knowledge, whereas Cerutti used them in the baroque sense of spiritual truths, whose reality he of course did not question, made more vivid and sensible by the use of concrete empirical images, a style in which Loyola's *Spiritual Exercises* excelled.[34]

It is nonetheless indicative of the relatively enlightened quality of the Jesuits' apologies that they nowhere chose to defend religious enthusiasm or fanaticism,

---

32.Ibid., pp. 95–97.

33. Cerutti, *Apologie de l'institut des Jésuites*, Vol. 1, p. 179.

34. Unfortunately La Chalotais did not himself employ the word *reason* in his two *Comptes rendus*, an omission which of course excludes the possibility of any comparison between his use of this word and that of the Jesuits. Whether, as I here suggest, he used the words *motives* and *ideas* in a way similar to that in which Enlightenment writers often employed the word *reason* remains therefore a matter of speculation.

that like La Chalotais, they elected to condemn these things in the name of their own variety of reason—in short, that they strained themselves nearly to the breaking point in an effort to express themselves in the terminology of the Enlightenment. Balbani's declamations aside, La Chalotais had not called the "wisdom of the Cross a folly," but even had he done so, Balbani need not necessarily have taken offense at what Saint Paul himself had called "a rock of offense" and "foolishness unto the Greeks."[35] And just as the Jesuits countered the accusations of enthusiasm and fanaticism with an appeal to "reason," so they refuted La Chalotais's charge of uselessness with a concerted attempt to demonstrate their political and social indispensability.

About La Chalotais's assertions concerning the uselessness of monasticism in general the Jesuits hardly bothered at all, except to say—Griffet was here their spokesman—that the abolition of monasticism would be "the source of a great number of very real and very dangerous inconveniences, and that it would not result except in very mediocre and very chimerical advantages," without specifying what either of these would be.[36] And to the extent that the Jesuits persistently and sometimes, one suspects, perversely insisted upon the similarity between what their enemies alleged to be peculiarly Jesuitical manifestations of depravity and those of other monastic orders, they did a real disservice to the cause of monasticism in France.[37] But as for themselves, the Jesuits experienced no difficulty whatever in demonstrating that they were useful, largely because they were not and had never been a contemplative order and had always been dedicated to the performance of functions deemed useful by both Church and State.

Outside Europe the Jesuits were above all a missionary order, and if to convert the heathen to Catholicism could be regarded as a "useful" function (that it was not so regarded by many of the philosophes is well known), the Jesuits were certainly useful in this respect. Within Europe, on the other hand, the most important of the Jesuits' functions was undoubtedly education, and within France alone they were by 1761 operating no less than 111 colleges and 21 seminaries.[38] Yet surprisingly enough, the Jesuits' apologies dwelt upon neither of these activities: their missionary activities—except for several quite just asides about the Jansenists as armchair missionaries—they perhaps did not attempt to defend because the stench of the La Valette affair still lay heavily over

35. Rom. 9:33; I Cor. 1:23.

36. Griffet, *Remarques sur un écrit*, p. 39.

37. See, for example, Balbani's assertion that far more Dominicans, including Thomas Aquinas, had sanctioned homicide and tyrannicide than the Jesuits, in *Appel à la raison*, pp. 41, 83–85.

38. Pierre Delattre, *Les Etablissements des Jésuites depuis quatre siècles* (Enghien, 1948), Vol. 1, p. 3.

he land and that of the old Chinese rites controversy had never entirely lifted; nd their educational activities, probably because their simple utility was so aken for granted that it was never actually challenged. Only to La Chalotais's ssertion that Jesuitical education was "vicious and barbarous" did the Jesuits eign to reply, and then merely to point out, quite rightly, that if the Jesuits' ducation was indeed "vicious and barbarous," it was "only what it must be at east for the largest number of people," whereas La Chalotais's own plan of ducation, the "infant of an idle speculation," was "impracticable" because it id not "suit the multitude." And were the Jesuits expelled from their colleges, vould it be easy, Balbani asked, to find "many people willing to quit Paris to onfine themselves in the mountains of Auvergne, Périgord and the Pyre-ees?"[39]

But in contrast to their relative neglect of their major functions, the Jesuits vere far more bellicose—and also far more utilitarian—in defense of some of heir lesser functions, particularly the operation of special congregations and ssociations for laymen and the conduct of national missions. "Of what does ne finally accuse the congregations?" asked Cerutti, with La Chalotais in nind. "Of being of no perceptible utility to the State. Depositories of the aws," he cried, "it rests entirely with you to convince yourself of the contrary. nterrogate the most worthy pastors you know: they will tell you that they ave no parishioners more submissive, more assiduous than the Congrega-ionists. Interrogate," he continued, "most of the families: they will tell you hat the most docile children, the most united brothers, the most vigilant fathers re Congregationists. Interrogate the villages: they will tell you that the most xemplary and charitable citizens are among the Congregationists. You your-elf," he finally asked, warming to his most telling point—"You yourself xamine with an impartial glance the magistrates seated at your side on the enches of Justice: are there among them ones who render it with more equity nd dignity than those in the ranks of the Congregationists? These certainly re witnesses to be heard in the present case." And "look," he concluded, "for et another proof in your registers: see if among the crowd of condemned riminals, punished libertines, prosecuted debtors and convicted forgers you vill find many Congregationsists."[40]

Cerutti employed precisely the same approach in defending the use of Loyola's piritual Exercises and the Jesuits' national missions. Did, as La Chalotais asserted, he "terrible images" of Satan and hell in Loyola's Spiritual Exercises lead to a

39. Balbani, Appel à la raison, p. 149. Balbani was of course quite right about the anti-opular, unabashedly elitist character of La Chalotais's plan of education. See La Chalotais, ssais d'éducation nationale, ou Plan d'études pour la jeunesse, par Messire Louis-René de Caradeuc e la Chalotais, procureur-général du roi au parlement de Bretagne (1763), esp. pp. 23–29.
40. Cerutti, Apologie de l'institut des Jésuites, Vol. 1, pp. 171–72.

"derangement of the spirit" and a "marked alienation" when presented to laymen? [41] "Experience," replied Cerutti, "proves to us the contrary, by the example of so many persons healed by these exercises, not from a derangement of the spirit but from a derangement of conduct; it proves to us," he continued, "that, struck by these terrible images, some have reconciled themselves with their enemies, others have restituted the exactions of usury."[42] Were the Jesuits' national missions useless or did they inspire enthusiasm? What could be useless or enthusiastic, riposted Cerutti, about "preaching to the People the submission due to the Church and the obedience due to the Sovereign; exhorting them to pay their tithes and taxes, arresting the murmurs raised against authority or Providence," and "scattering everywhere the stumbling blocks."[43] But nothing, perhaps, more perfectly epitomized the tenor of the Jesuits' replies to La Chalotais than Balbani's defense of the peculiar nature of the Jesuits' vows: merely reversible vows until the age of thirty and then, after that, a unique fourth vow to renounce all ecclesiastical dignities and to go at the pope's behest to any mission in the world. One can easily share Balbani's exasperation over the spectacle of complaints arising against the practice of postponing irrevocable vows until an age "of the most perfect maturity" on the part of an order whose founder had designed it in precisely that fashion to counter centuries of complaints about the practice of swearing irrevocable vows "at an age at which they pretend that the reason is not sufficiently strong to triumph over illusion, or the will, they say, is not sufficiently determined to resist alien impressions."[44] But Balbani need neither have countered La Chalotais's image of Ignatius Loyola as a misdirected religious enthusiast with the equally erroneous portrait of the Jesuits' founder as a kind of scheming, calculating, almost Machievellian, and most emphatically unenthusiastic politician, nor have described the order he founded ("if one cannot," Balbani protested, "believe that this holy industry was the product of Ignatius's zeal) as "the masterpiece of his Christian politics."[45]

Yet the curious fact remains that the Jesuits should have trained their heaviest artillery on the single "enlightened" *Compte rendu* to emerge from the entire affair of the Jesuits in France and should have totally ignored the Jansenist magistrates, lawyers, and professional polemicists who, elsewhere, were really masterminding the destruction of their order. Even within the parlement of Brittany the moving force against the Jesuits was the Jansenist counselor,

41. La Chalotais, *Compte rendu des constitutions des Jésuites*, p. 175.
42. Cerutti, *Apologie de l'institut des Jésuites*, Vol. 1, pp. 179–80.
43. Ibid., pp. 186–87.
44. Balbani, *Appel à la raison*, pp. 23–24.
45. Ibid., pp. 30–31.

Charette de la Gaucherie, in correspondence with "all the hotheads of the different parlements," including, probably, Le Paige himself, and to the extent
that La Chalotais's views of the matter were "enlightened," it is unlikely that
he represented anyone there but himself.[46]

Or is it completely true that the Jesuits ignored the Jansenists? Not, certainly,
if we are willing to count some polemical pamphlets whose authors remain
unknown or, among known Jesuit polemicists, certain crabbed asides in the
direction of the Jansenists which occasionally diverted their otherwise forward
thrust against La Chalotais.[47]

Indeed, the Jesuits knew very well that it was the Jansenists who were their
most deadly and determined enemies, and that it was not the writings of Voltaire, D'Alembert, or Diderot, but rather Le Paige's and Coudrette's *Histoire
générale* that was informing the magisterial *Comptes rendus* against them. That
this was so is evident from the fact that when the Jesuits came closest to presenting an official defense of their order, when before the judgments of August
6, 1761, they sent Solicitor General Omer Joly de Fleury and the king's special
commission several memoirs answering some of the objections raised against
them, they wasted no time in addressing themselves exclusively to Le Paige's
and Coudrette's *Histoire générale*, described by the Jesuit La Croix as "a work
. . . full of rancour, malice, false anecdotes, odious imputations, etc.," and
Coudrette's *Idée générale des vices principaux de l'institut des Jésuites*, which
painted the Jesuits "in the blackest colors"—neither of which the Jesuits so
much as mentioned in their public and unofficial defenses of their society. La
Croix's memoir in particular systematically responded to the *Histoire générale's*
every significant accusation, from the charge that Jesuits were unworthy of the
name of "Jesus" to the assertion that Loyola's successor Lainez was guilty of
semi-Pelagian opinions.[48]

46. Barthélemy Pocquet du Haut-Jussé, *Le Pouvoir absolu et l'esprit provincial: Le Duc
d'Aiguillon et La Chalotais* (Paris, 1900–01), Vol. 2, p. 60.
47. Among anonymous pamphlets see, for example, *Tout le Monde a tort, ou Jugement
impartial d'une dame philosophique sur l'affaire présente des Jésuites* (1762), pp. 35–36; among
assuredly Jesuit authors, see Henri Griffet, *Coup d'œil sur l'arrêt du parlement de Paris, du 6
août 1761, concernant l'institut des Jésuites imprimé à Prague en 1757* (Avignon, 1761), Part II,
p. 4. Henceforth cited as *Coup d'œil sur l'arrêt du parlement de Paris*. But all such evidence
together would hardly substantiate the statement made to the solicitor general Joly de
Fleury by one of his correspondents, that the Jesuits "are publishing from all quarters that
the Parlements are Jansenist" (B.N.: Collection Joly de Fleury, fol. 1615, ms. 155).
48. Four such memoirs, a *Précis de l'institut des Jésuites*, a *Mémoire sur l'établissement et l'état
des Jésuites en France*, a *Mémoire contenant des observations générales sur les objections proposées
contre l'institut des Jésuites*, and a *Réponse à quelques objections publiées contre l'institut des Jésuites*,
are to be found in B.N.: Collection Joly de Fleury, fol. 1612. The last of these memoirs
refutes Coudrette's *Histoire générale* in particular and contains on p. 121 the remark quoted
above. Several more such memoirs are to be found in the papers of Gilbert de Voisins

But whether indirectly through La Chalotais in public or more forthrightly
in private, there was a sense in which the Jesuits unanimously responded to the
Jansenists, a sense best defined by the single word *despotism*. For it was the
Jansenists, not the philosophes, who in Le Paige's and Coudrette's *Histoire
générale* had raised the cry of despotism against the Jesuits, and to the extent
that La Chalotais echoed this charge, he was only the sounding board of political Jansenism. Enthusiasm, fanaticism, uselessness, literary and scientific incompetence—none of the characteristically "enlightened" anti-Jesuitical
anathemas were so politically charged or struck a more sensitive Jesuitical nerve
than the Jansenists' accusation of despotism.

We have already observed that for the Jansenists to tax the Jesuits with
despotism was to settle a very old score. Suffice it to add that the charge quickly
enjoyed what must have been an unhoped-for future, and that it soon became
the almost universal battle cry not only of the parlement of Paris but also of
most of the other parlements, which proceeded in their turn against the Jesuit
Order. Even in the remote and obscure *conseil souverain* of Roussillon the
sous-doyen Joseph de Massia de Salelles discoursed on the nature of Jesuitical
despotism for more than twenty-five pages in his *Compte rendu*, and the relatively moderate solicitor general of the parlement of Bordeaux, Pierre-Jules
Dudon, who otherwise, like Omer Joly de Fleury, preferred the more neutral
term of *monarchy* to that of *despotism*, lapsed occasionally and seemingly in
spite of himself into talk about the "despotism of the General."[49]

(A.N.: M. 744, nos. 1–2 and 241, no. 4). Gilbert de Voisins identifies the author of the
Précis de l'institut des Jésuites as the père Berthier, editor of the *Journal de Trévoux* (744, no.
2), and a *Mémoire sur la doctrine des Jésuites* (241, no. 4, pp. 32–33) contains the references to
Coudrette's *Idée générale* quoted above.

49. *Compte rendu de l'institut et constitutions des soi-disans Jésuites par M. de Salelles, sous-
doyen du conseil souverain de Roussillon, en conséquence de l'arrêt de la cour, du 20 mars 1762*
(Perpignan, 1762), pp. 24–54; *Compte rendu des constitutions des Jésuites par M. Pierre-Jules
Dudon, avocat-général du roi, au parlement de Bordeaux, les 13 et 14 mai 1762, avec l'arrêt sur
ledit compte, chambres assemblées, le 26 dudit mai* (1762), p. 45. Some other interesting examples of provincial magistrates' use of the charge of despotism are in the *Compte rendu des
constitutions des Jésuites, par M. Jean-Pierre-François de Ripert de Monclar, procureur général du
roi au parlement de Provence, les 28 mai, 3 et 4 juin 1762, en exécution de l'arrêt de la cour du 15
mars précédent* (1763), pp. 6, 27, 33, 82–84, 90–93; *Compte rendu de l'institut des soi-disans Jésuites, par un de MM. les commissaires, aux chambres assemblées, du 5 juillet 1763*, in *Comptes
rendus des établissements de l'institut et de la doctrine des soi-disans Jésuites, par les conseillers commissaires, au parlement séant à Dijon, chambres assemblées, les 4, 5 et 6 juillet 1763 et arrêt définitif
du 11 juillet 1763* (1763), pp. 15, 27, 38–41, where Montesquieu's *Esprit des lois* is appealed to;
*Comptes rendus du parlement séant à Toulouse, toutes les chambres assemblées, par deux d'entre
MM les commissaires, au sujet des constitutions et de la doctrine des soi-disans Jésuites, les 7, 9, 10
et 11 mai 1762, et déposés au greffe dudit parlement, en conséquence de l'arrêté du 16 juin de la même
année* (1762), pp. 30, 40, 93; and *Compte rendu par un de MM les commissaires nommés par le
parlement de Besançon pour l'examen de l'affaire des Jésuites, sur l'Institut et les constitutions desdites*

On one level the Jesuits defended themselves against that accusation by attempting to demonstrate that their general's powers were less absolute and arbitrary, the obedience they owed him less unquestioning and cadaver-like, than their enemies supposed. Concerning the obedience they owed their general and lesser superiors, the Jesuits pointed out, for example, that the obedience of which their constitutions spoke concerned only spiritual matters and in no way conflicted with the obedience they owed their temporal sovereign, that the metaphors with which their constitutions described the perfect obedience— "blind," "as a cane in the hands of an aged man," "as a cadaver"—were common hyperboles among "the ancient Masters of the spiritual life" which were by no means intended to exclude rational examination of an order given, and that even in the case of some of these expressions their opponents had suppressed some qualifying phrases, such as the clause "when one perceives no sin therein," which followed the constitutions' injunction to "persuade oneself that all which the Superior commands is just." "It is regrettable that those to whom we owe these extracts from the Constitutions stopped precisely at this point," Balbani sarcastically remarked. "It is without doubt the length of the text which discouraged them: for to suppose that they purposely suppressed a corrective so sage and essential would be to suspect them of a horrible and criminal infidelity."[50] As to their general's allegedly absolute and arbitrary authority, Balbani went so far as to suggest that, far from being a "monarch," the Jesuits' general was "a Chief of a Republic."[51]

But his comparison of the Jesuit Order to a republic was exceptional—even for Balbani. For on another level the Jesuits tended rather to take the offensive by comparing their order to a monarchy, denouncing their enemies as "republican," and thereby attempting to drive a wedge between moderate Gallicans like Omer Joly de Fleury, who respectfully labeled their order "monarchical," and more rabid Gallicans or Jansenists, who condemned it as "despotic." In vast unison, therefore, the French Jesuits sang the praises of monarchy and intoned against the evils of republican doctrines. "It is not our task,"

Jésuites, au parlement, toutes les chambres assemblées. Des 17 et 18 août 1762 (1762), pp. 259–61, 274–75.

50. Balbani, *Appel à la raison*, p. 68. For reference to other expressions of "ancient masters of the spiritual life," see ibid., pp. 68–70; for the assertion that Jesuits vowed obedience to their order only in matters spiritual, see Cerutti, *Apologie de l'institut des Jésuites*, Vol. 1, pp. 30–81.

51. Balbani, *Appel à la raison*, p. 88. Balbani's conclusion was based on the facts that the general's alleged right to alter or completely abrogate the order's constitutions was a papal privilege granted to Saint Ignatius Loyola alone, and that these constitutions stipulated that the general be freely elected by the order, that he be given six assistants and an admonisher to observe his conduct, and that in certain cases he be deposed. For other limitations on the general's power, see ibid., pp. 58–66, 91–93, 152.

wrote Neuville, all the while performing it, "to anticipate the reflections which our Readers will not fail to make concerning the bent and furor of so many would be *politiques*, bad subjects, masked behind the name of patriots, who never tire of declaiming against all authority so long as it is the authority of a single person. One hears talk only of precautions to take against the peril of the ultramontane doctrine; they would be far more necessary against the peril of the doctrine of the other side of the channel which people are attempting to render the doctrine of the Nation by writings which the sixteen alone could avow."[52] In France, Griffet added, "better than anywhere else we recognize the advantages of the monarchical power: this monarchy has stood for nearly fourteen hundred years: no Republic has endured as long on the Earth. We felicitate the French Nation for submitting herself neither to the arbitrary empire of a Despot, nor to the capricious whims of an inconstant people, nor to the dangerous intrigues of republican spirits. Why not also," he asked, "felicitate a Religious Order for enjoying the same good fortune under the paternal authority of a Chief who is much less a Monarch than a Father?"[53] The Jesuit Order has a "monarchical government like that of France," admitted the père de Montigny, attorney general of the province of France, in a memoir submitted to Omer Joly de Fleury. "The more it resembles hers, the more it is perfect and the more it ought to be precious to all Frenchmen. Such a government," he continued, "accustoms the Jesuits to love that entire and perfect subordination which alone is able to maintain order and harmony within monarchical States where the will of the Sovereign depository and authority of the Laws ought to be the Rule for everyone, and because they are more inclined and have more reason than other Religious Orders to combat and reject all these English and Republican maxims which incline toward independence and which are only too prevalent these days among all qualities and ranks."[54]

By means of these monarchical effusions the Jesuits obviously hoped to back their opponents against the horns of a dilemma: either the governments of France and the Jesuits were both monarchical and therefore to be praised or they were both despotic and therefore to be blamed. If their enemies chose the former; they would seem to have no substantial quarrel with the Jesuits' form of government; if the latter, they would manifestly be rebellious and seditious subjects of the king. Just as in times past, the Jesuits had often fled to the king for

52. Neuville, *Observations sur l'institut de la société des Jésuites*, p. 44. The "sixteen" refers to the ultra-Catholic committee of sixteen which, in the absence of the assassinated Henry III and the "heretical" Henry IV, governed Paris from 1589–93. During this period the "sixteen" manifested antiregal and even antiaristocratic tendencies and attempted, though with no consistency, to institute a species of municipal democracy.

53. Griffet, *Coup d'œil sur l'arrêt du parlement de Paris,* Part II, p. 49.

54. *Réponse à quelques objections publiées contre l'institut des Jésuites* (a manuscript of uncertain authorship found in B.N.: Collection Joly de Fleury, fol. 1612, ms. 186).

protection against the furor of his magistrates, so now, in their last and purely literary defense, they chose the way of monarchical authority as their last recourse. They would stand or fall with the Bourbon monarchy itself. Balbani— the same Balbani who in an ill-considered moment had called the Jesuits' general the "Chief of a Republic"—drove the point home with an elaborate comparison between the government of the Jesuits and that of France: just as the French had their monarch, so the Jesuits had their general, whose six assistants, attorney general, provincial superiors, and collegiate rectors corresponded respectively to the French government's secretaries of state, controller general of finance, provincial intendants, and village mayors. Not content with these somewhat forced analogies, Balbani went so far as to assert that despite his Spanish "national prejudices," Saint Ignatius himself had consciously modeled the Jesuit Order upon the administration of France, "because it appeared to him the best" and because of his "penchant for French customs" and "the gentleness of our Government." If, therefore, "this disposition of functions makes for Despotism," he concluded, "we must all agree that the French are under a despotic Government. If it does not prevent our Government from being sage and moderate, sometimes even too much so, why attempt to render odious that which resembles it so perfectly? If those who have denounced us respond," he finally challenged, "they will furnish us with an occasion to demonstrate the brilliance of the one by the other, the wisdom of the administration of this Realm as well as that of the Society."[55]

If by this rhetorical flourish the Jesuits had hoped to position their opponents for the *coup de grâce*, they had unwisely chosen to do so by using a debatable conception of the monarchy, which, like a matador's cloak, goaded their opponents into a ferocious and most dangerous charge. For implicit in the Jesuits' denunciation of "republican maxims" was an absolutist, "royal," and blatantly antiparliamentary conception of the monarchy designed to enrage the beast in their Jansenist and parliamentary foes. The author of the memoir to Omer Joly de Fleury made this clear when he asserted that in monarchical states "the will of the Sovereign depository and authority of the Laws ought to be the rule for everyone"; Neuville stated as much when he wrote that "the authority of the King admits of neither inspection nor limitation"; and Balbani repeated the same theme with an even more belligerently antiparliamentary emphasis when he insisted that the King of France was "absolute, independent and Legislator. As absolute," he explained, "there is nobody in his States that ought to resist him, as independent, there is none that could depose him," and "as Legislator he alone makes new Laws and abrogates old ones"—all of them royal prerogatives which, excepting the king's claims as "independent," the parlements of France were then hotly contesting with

55. Balbani, *Appel à la raison*, pp. 100–02.

Louis XV.[56] The response which Balbani so ardently solicited from the Jesuits' denouncers was therefore not long in the making. "The hatred which you have sworn against the Parlements," correctly observed the enraged author of the *Réplique aux apologies des Jésuites*, "has its source in the diversity of opinions about monarchical authority."[57]

Naturally the anonymous author of this pamphlet tried to steer a middle course between the Jesuits' Scylla and Charybdis, between the equally undesirable alternatives of acknowledging the Jesuits' "monarchical" society as good or of denouncing it in the name of "republican maxims." "It is false, my Father," he sarcastically began, "it is false that you have washed your General of the shame attached to the quality of a Despot," and then proceeded carefully to distinguish between his own conceptions of monarchy and despotism. Monarchies, he insisted, were characterized by three conditions and the despotisms "in Turkey, Persia and Mongolia" by the absence of the same: the right of every citizen to administer his own property, the rights of all public servants of the crown to their offices, and the right of all citizens to the formalities of justice. And since the Jesuits possessed none of these rights, since their general could arbitrarily administer the property of the entire order, appoint and discharge his servants without any formalities, and punish or expel any member of the society without trial, "such as a Turk is under the law of his Emperor, such as a Negro is under the domination of his Master, such is a Jesuit," he concluded, "under the scepter of the Sovereign Monk."[58]

Having laid down this theoretical foundation, the author then passed into a paroxysm of anti-Jesuitical rage to which no summary can do full justice. Describing the Jesuits' unhappy general as a "cloistered Sultan," the Jesuits themselves as "the cowardly slaves of an Italian Monk," and their order as a whole as "the masterpiece of pride, ambition and the most unbridled cupidity," he accused the Jesuits of publishing the "atrocious proposition" that the Jesuit Order was "odious to the Parlements only because they themselves are enemies of the Monarchy," of placarding "for a long time principles of conduct contrary to the authority of a true monarchy"—in short, of trying to place a "sceptre of iron" in "the hand of the Bourbons" and of attempting to persuade them of the "horrible project of reducing us to slavery."[59] "Great God! What, my Fathers, if for the misfortune of France, a King were to give you all his confidence, you would then teach him to be a monarch in his States as your General is in your Order?" he asked. "You would then tell him that he could in surety of conscience enjoy all these horrible rights which you attribute to

56. Ibid., p. 88; Neuville, *Observations sur l'institut*, p. 45. For a statement by the author of the memoir to Joly de Fleury, see p. 273.
57. *Réplique aux apologies des Jésuites (1761–1762)*, Part III, p. 52.
58. Ibid., pp. 38–41.
59. Ibid., pp. 52–54.

your Sovereign? . . . Behold, my Father," he concluded after painting a pathetic picture of France in such an eventuality, "Behold the state of the French if ever you are able to persuade a Prince that monarchical authority gives essentially all the rights which Gregory XIV took so much care to assure your General. Look, oh my fellow citizens," he continued, "look at the Serpents which you nourish among yourselves. Look," finally, "oh monarchs full of justice and goodness, who govern as Fathers the children whom you love, look at the abominable maxims which penetrate these imposters who never tire of offering these traps to your confidence."[60]

But just as an absolutist conception of monarchy lay behind the dilemma against which they had hoped to pin their enemies, so an extreme parliamentary conception of the monarchical "constitution"—as the parlements were wont to express it—lurked behind this orgy of pathetic rhetoric. Of the three fundamental rights of monarchies which the author of the *Réplique aux apologies des Jésuites* had enumerated—the rights of private property and the surety of public functions and individual justice—it was undoubtedly the surety of crown functions, the rights, that is, of the magistrates of the parlement of Paris to retain their offices even if they disobeyed the king in whose name they rendered justice—as they had already done in the case of the Jesuits—which most especially occupied his attention. The proverbial cat came out of the bag when, in response to the rhetorical question of why the king sometimes encountered a "firm but respectful suspension of obedience," a "noble resistance always accompanied with the most devoted filial love" to "new laws too little reflected upon, or Orders surprised by treason against the generosity of the Master," he answered that it was because in monarchies "dignities cannot be lost without crime and . . . punishments are not inflicted without Judgment. Take away these two barriers," he explained, "and you would only be left, as in Turkey, with dumb slaves in the place of Magistrates who, when it is necessary, make audible to the best of Princes the voice of reclamation, the prayers and interests of a People whom they love tenderly."[61]

The point did not escape the Jesuits' attention. For Balbani, when shortly he replied in his *Acceptation du défi hazardé par l'auteur d'un libelle intitulé: 'Réplique aux apologies des Jésuites,'* found it "singular that in the midst of the most illustrious and oldest monarchy of the world one dares . . . give reason to believe that monarchy degenerates infallibly into despotism if it is not tempered"—here Balbani anticipated the conclusions of the most recent scholarship—"by a mélange of aristocracy."[62] And though Balbani and his coreligionists undoubtedly exaggerated the institutional similarities between the Jesuit Order and

60. Ibid., pp. 41–42.
61. Ibid., p. 52.
62. André Christophe Balbani, *Acceptation du défi hazardé par l'auteur d'un libelle intitulé: 'Réplique aux apologies des Jésuites'* (Avignon, 1762), pp. 33–34.

the Bourbon monarchy, their conception of that monarchy was certainly closer to legal reality—if not to reality itself—than that of their parliamentary and Jansenist opponents. Balbani's characterization of the Bourbon monarch as "absolute, independent and Legislator" differed little from that of Louis XV himself when, during the famous "session of flagellation" of March 3, 1766, he told "his" parlement of Paris that "it is in my person alone that the sovereign power resides; it is through me alone that my courts hold their existence and authority; it is to me alone that the legislative power belongs, without dependence and without division; the public order entire emanates from me."[63] And though, finally, some of the clerical polemicists of the Restoration undoubtedly exaggerated when they posited a simplistic cause-and-effect relationship between the dissolution of the Society of Jesus and the French Revolution of 1789, it is indeed difficult to avoid the conclusion that the Jesuits succumbed as the staunchest and perhaps the last consistent defenders of royal authority in France, and that monarchical government, at least as both Louis XV and his predecessors had understood it, was solemnly condemned with the Jesuit Order in 1762.

Let us return briefly to La Chalotais. In one part of his *Compte rendu* he appealed to what he called "the Public" as testimony against the Jesuits, not, he specified, the public which "never examines and . . . lets itself be won by flattery or fooled by seduction; not partisan theologians whose opinion is always formed before examining, but well-informed particulars who have deserved well of the human race." This public, he went on, which "does not err and can never err," had formulated "a kind of familiar proverb" concerning the Jesuits, that "when one wishes to give a favorable idea of some Jesuits with whom one has relations, one says that they are not really Jesuits."[64]

Quite naturally the Jesuits took issue with La Chalotais's belief in the infallibility of the public, partly because, as Griffet put it, there were "many sorts" of publics, among them an "ignorant public, an impassioned public, an inconstant public, a biased public, an unjust public; finally almost as many publics as there are different opinions and ideas among men," and partly because "those who make the most noise always say that they represent the *public* and that they never speak except according to *the entire public*."[65] But in attacking La Chalotais's faith in the rectitude of the public, the Jesuits attacked neither Jansenism nor the Enlightenment separately, but rather both simultaneously, because faith in the public was one of the few faiths the two movements shared in common. We have already noted how the *Nouvelles Ecclésiastiques* worshiped the public because it represented a popular movement of political and religious

---

63. Quoted in Rocquain, *L'Esprit révolutionnaire avant la révolution*, p. 256.
64. La Chalotais, *Compte rendu des constitutions des Jésuites*, pp. 190–93.
65. Griffet, *Remarques sur un écrit*, pp. 162–63.

opposition; I shall soon suggest that the Enlightenment to some extent inherited this role from Jansenism. Whether La Chalotais's praise of the public should be regarded as "enlightened" or "Jansenist" is therefore an insoluble problem, for confidence in the public was one of the few points at which around mid-century an expiring Jansenism and a yet adolescent Enlightenment briefly intersected.

Jesuitism—if we may speak of such a thing—had never enjoyed the kind of "public" that Jansenism still possessed and the Enlightenment would soon attain. Too novel and brash even for the spirit of much of the Counter-Reformation of the seventeenth century, already too archaic for the taste of much of "enlightened" France in the eighteenth century, the Jesuits unhappily found themselves caught in a vise between the two in 1761. Yet between Jansenism and the Enlightenment, between the past and the future, the Jesuits—true in this respect to the spirit of their founder—still preferred front-line duty against the most recent heresy. What Robert Palmer has shown to be true in matters purely theological and philosophical—that the Jesuits assigned "religion to a special supernatural sphere" and "marked out large areas of life" for the autonomous "operation of reason, natural law, and free will," the better to communicate with the Enlightenment which itself accepted "nature" and "reason" as its standards—we have seen to be true in questions as specific and concrete as the nature and value of the Jesuit Order as such.[66] The better to combat La Chalotais, the Jesuits argued, not that religious enthusiasm or social uselessness were sometimes to be praised, but that the Jesuit Order was both more reasonable and useful than La Chalotais had ever imagined.

Herein, undoubtedly, lies the answer to one of our questions—namely, why the Jesuits chose to concentrate their heaviest artillery against the *Compte rendu* of La Chalotais, who was doing them little immediate harm, while only obliquely attacking the Jansenists, who were actually masterminding their destruction. The Jesuits simply felt more comfortable doing battle with La Chalotais on the terrain of the Enlightenment. The proposition is impossible to document, but one takes leave of the mid-eighteenth century with the strong impression that by this time the Jesuits were profoundly weary of the theological controversies with the Jansenists. Even before the La Valette affair began to scandalize all Europe, the Jesuits only rarely deigned to respond to the provocations of the *Nouvelles Ecclésiastiques* and Jansenist pamphleteers, and then only in a tone of ill-concealed contempt and boredom. With père Berthier and the *Journal de Trévoux* at their head, the Jesuits were by this time engaged primarily in what they thought the laudable enterprise of arresting the spread of encyclopedist

66. Palmer, *Catholics and Unbelievers in Eighteenth-Century France*, p. 221. See also John N. Pappas, *Berthier's Journal de Trévoux and the Philosophes*, Vol. 3 in Theodore Besterman, ed., *Studies on Voltaire and the Eighteenth Century* (Geneva, 1957), esp. pp. 197–224.

thought; the controversies with the Jansenists over the nature and efficacy of grace they regarded as past battles, battles which, despite Pascal, they had won, and with which they no longer wished to be troubled. Toward their vanquished Jansenist foes the Jesuits were willing enough to show a kind of magnanimity even to the point of admitting that some of their casuists had lost sight of basic evangelical principles and that the père Le Tellier, Louis XIV's last confessor, might have been a bit too zealous in his pursuit of Port-Royal.[67] If only, the Jesuits seemed to ask, the descendants of Port-Royal would return the favor by leaving them undisturbed in the performance of their reasonable and useful functions.

This, however, the Jansenists were unwilling to do. But the fact that the Jesuits seemed equally unwilling to respond to their provocations and reopen the old questions, which they regarded as closed forever, also explains in part the more fundamental question with which we began: Why did the Jesuits refuse to defend themselves formally before the parlement of Paris? For we have observed that the Jesuits knew well enough that it was Jansenism, not La Chalotais or his kind, which was presiding over the judgments of the parlement of Paris, and that to defend themselves before this body entailed the obligation of attempting to communicate to people with whom on no conceivable level they were on speaking terms and who in any case had sworn for them a hatred which no amount of "reason" could dispel. One need not share his sense of indignation to recognize the accuracy of the assumptions behind the series of complex questions posed by the anonymous, perhaps Jesuit author of a pamphlet entitled *Les Pourquoi, ou Questions sur une grande affaire pour ceux qui n'ont que trois minutes à y donner.* "Why," he asked, "hide with such care the passions which discuss and terminate the affair of an individual [La Valette], and why show uncovered those which preside over the ruin of an entire corps?"[68] Again, "why condemn one side to the law of silence [the Jesuits and most of the episcopacy], and favor the other which violates it four times a month [the *Nouvelles Ecclésiastiques*]?"[69] And why, he finally asked, "while declaring themselves the fathers of the people [the magistrates], do they abandon a great number of innocents [the Jesuits] to a dozen fanatics [the *parti janséniste* of the parlement of Paris, which, counting both magistrates and lawyers, consisted of about a dozen people]?"[70]

---

67. On the père Le Tellier, see Cerutti, *Apologie de l'institut des Jésuites*, Vol. 1, pp. 148–49. On admissions of doctrinal sins, see ibid., Vol. 2, pp. 100–01; and esp. the anonymous *Mémoire sur la doctrine des Jésuites* (A.N.: M 241, no. 4).

68. *Les Pourquoi, ou Questions sur une grande affaire pour ceux qui n'ont que trois minutes à y donner* (1762), pp. 5–6.

69. Ibid., p. 17.

70. Ibid., p. 5.

Yet even under these circumstances the Jesuits might have appeared before the parlement of Paris if they had not also realized that by means of a Gallican and sometimes patriotic rhetoric the "dozen fanatics" in question had successfully marshaled not only the majority of the magistrates but a significant and vocal "public" against them. To be sure, an extraordinary assembly of the French bishops met in Paris in December 1761, and in a letter sent to Louis XV on December 31 they nearly unanimously pronounced themselves in favor of the preservation of the Jesuit Order.[71] But this was small consolation to the Jesuits, who knew very well that the first order of the realm was a "public" which the magistrates would, like La Chalotais, cavalierly dismiss as "partisan theologians whose opinion is always formed before examining," that Griffet's "public," the "ignorant," "impassioned," "inconsistent," "biased," and "unjust public," was in this instance also the public that was making the "most noise," and that its noise, finally, had swelled to a deafening roar within the parlement of Paris. As one magistrate was reported to have remarked during the trial of the Jesuits, "there is more silence at *les halles* than in our assembled chambers."[72]

That the Jesuits could have made themselves heard above this din, had they appeared before the parlement of Paris, is most unlikely. For the most summary compilation of some of the accusations leveled against them in the magistrates' *Comptes rendus* and elsewhere reveals that they were variously charged with fomenting heresies and being too faithful to the pope, with dominating the pope and being his henchmen, with dragooning subjects into their order and not dragooning them quickly enough, with failing to adhere to their constitutions and adhering to them too faithfully, with being doctrinally too malleable and enforcing doctrinal uniformity, with having perverse constitutions and not having any at all, with being too monastic and not monastic enough, and with being the assassins of kings and the theoreticians of despotism. How the Jesuits with even the subtlest probabilism could have transformed these sometimes mutually exclusive accusations into a coherent case against them, if only to respond intelligibly, is only dimly apparent. Referring specifically to the fact that the Jesuits had been accused of being at once regicides and the theoreticians of despotism, D'Alembert later spoke truthfully when he admitted that "these two accusations might appear to be a little contradictory, but it was not a question of telling the exact truth, it was a question of saying as much evil about the Jesuits as possible."[73] And Charles Frey de Neuville, for his part, analyzed the situation of his order correctly when, in a letter to a friend, he said that

---

71. *Procès-verbal de l'assemblée extraordinaire des évêques en 1761* (A.N.: fol. 1361, no. 1A).
72. *Mes Doutes sur l'affaire présente des Jésuites*, p. 42.
73. D'Alembert, *Sur la Destruction des Jésuites en France*, pp. 78–79.

"the night of prejudice is too profound, the tempest is too violent; we will not escape shipwreck. I do not know," he added, "whether the State will gain much by the destruction of the Society. I only hope that Religion loses nothing. It is true that the suffrage of the assembled Bishops was highly in our favor, but it will not close the tomb already open and dug to receive us; it will serve us only as an honorable Epitaph."[74]

74. Charles Frey de Neuville to "une dame de Saint Germain en Laye" (B.N.: Collection Joly de Fleury, fol. 1612, ms. 222).

7. Rome, Versailles, and the Provinces: The End of the Jesuits in France

ON APRIL 2, 1763, ADRIEN LE PAIGE, IN A LONG MEMOIR TO THE parlement of Rouen, recalled the "two advantages which were difficult to hope for, and which are now conducting everything toward the total extinction of the society of Jesus, at least for France: the concert of the parlements among themselves: the concert of the ministry with the parlements." Le Paige could not have been more precise. The jurisdiction of the parlement of Paris extended to only a third of the French realm; the cooperation of at least most of the provinces' eleven parlements and two *conseils souverains* was therefore absolutely essential to the complete destruction of the Jesuits in France. Even more essential was the active or at least passive cooperation of Louis XV and his ministry at Versailles; for the work of the parlements would at best remain tenuous without, as Le Paige expressed it, "the solemn acts of the Royal authority."[1]

Yet after the provisional judgments of August 6, 1761, the parlement of Paris enjoyed neither of these advantages. The parlement of Rennes, it is true, ordered the Jesuits within its jurisdiction to deposit their constitutions at the *greffe* of the court as early as August 14, 1761, but for some time Rennes remained alone among provincial parlements, and it was moreover a long way from a decision to examine the constitutions to a judgment of the Parisian type.[2] As for Paris, few if any expected Versailles to acquiesce dumbly in the parlement's perverse "registration" of Louis XV's declaration of August 2, 1761. The magistrates' disobedience to the royal declaration was far too manifest to remain long overlooked. The task confronting Le Paige, the *parti janséniste,* and the parlement of Paris was therefore a difficult one—somehow to set in motion the various provincial parlements against the Jesuits and at the same time persuade a Versailles little disposed against these monks not only to tolerate the parliamentary offensive against them but eventually to lend it its royal sanction. The père de Neuville might have been certain in 1761 of the imminent destruction of his order; his enemies could only have envied his confidence.

1. B.P.R.: L.P. 584, ms. 30, memoir for the parlement of Normandy, April 2, 1763.
2. A. Le Moy, *Le Parlement de Bretagne et le pouvior royal au XVIIIe siècle* (Angers, 1909), p. 234, For Le Moy's account of the whole affair at Rennes, see pp. 229–44.

Certain it is that at Versailles influential members of the royal entourage, especially the dauphin and Chancellor Lamoignon, were convinced that the king should spare no means and face all risks to protect the Jesuits from the parliamentary fury. To the chancellor the dispositions of the parlement's judgments of August 6 constituted clear evidence that "the intention of the parlement is to annihilate the order of the Jesuits," and he concluded in a lengthy memoir to the king that "the greater the evil, the more it is necessary to employ your authority by whatever means available in order to repair it. It is not," he added, "that one wishes to incite the king to harsh measures, but to make him understand that in order not to be obliged to have recourse to them it is imperative to employ the strongest alternative means to destroy parliamentary measures which so flagrantly attack his authority."[3] The existence, among the papers of Gilbert de Voisins, of a projected judgment of annulment of the parlement's suspensive *appel comme d'abus* of August 6, indicates precisely what Lamoignon had in mind. The proposed annulment, probably drafted by the chancellor, described the dispositions of the parlement's judgments as "unusual" and "incompatible with the delay of our said letters," and ordered the parlement to execute the royal letters of August 2 "according to their form and tenor."[4] The chancellor and the dauphin frequently referred to the projected annulment in their private correspondence, and the dauphin, of like mind with Lamoignon, was persuaded that "in regard to the repercussions it appears to me that we can hope that no matter what they are, we will amend ourselves against the humiliating examples of the years 1754 and 1757 and we will hold firm. I think you can count on this," he assured Lamoignon, "if the parlement interrupts the administration of justice."[5]

Whatever the reasons for the dauphin's optimism, his reference to possible "repercussions" and the "humiliating examples" of the years 1754 and 1757, when the parlement of Paris did indeed interrupt the administration of justice in confrontations with royal authority and in both instances ultimately prevailed, reveals clearly enough that Versailles, too, anticipated obstacles. And these obstacles appeared all the more formidable in 1761, when France was floundering to the close of one of her costliest and most disastrous wars which had already entailed an enormous increase in taxation: in 1756 the creation of a second *vingtième,* or revenue tax, which had been first imposed in 1749; the

---

3. A.N.: A.P. 162 mi. (Archives du marquis de Rosanbo), *carton* 1, *dossier* 6, ms. 37, "Réflexions sur l'arrest d'enregistrement de la déclaration du 2 aoust, 1761."

4. A.N.: M241, *dossier* 4, unnumbered ms. with following heading in the hand of Gilbert de Voisins: "aoust 1761. projet dont il a esté parlé mais qui n'a point esté proposé, un autre aiant prévalu."

5. A.N.: A.P. 162 mi. (Archives du marquis de Rosanbo), *carton* 1, *dossier* 6, ms. 23, dauphin to chancellor, August 18, 1761.

suspension of numerous exemptions from the *taille* and a mandatory *don gratuit* from the cities and principal towns in 1759; and in 1760, again, the edict of February, which created a third *vingtième* and doubled—for some taxpayers even tripled—the *capitation,* or poll tax.[6] These fiscal measures had in some instances already encountered alarming parliamentary resistance, particularly from the parlements of Dijon and Besançon. In the latter case Louis XV went to the extremity of exiling thirty magistrates of the parlement to various fortified places in January 1758, only to be faced, in the following years, with repeated remonstrances on the part of the rump parlement and the bellicose intervention of the parlements of Toulouse, Rouen, and Paris. The affair dragged on into the autumn of 1761 and ended only with the triumphal rehabilitation of the thirty exiled magistrates, the complete withdrawal of all disciplinary measures taken against the parlement, the resignation of the very royalist first president, Bourgeois de Boynes—in short, the nearly total capitulation of royal authority.[7] Now if, in the midst of external war, Louis XV was unwilling to face a showdown with his parlements over so vital a matter as taxation, would he do so in defense of a mere religious order, itself accused of foreign allegiance and subversion of monarchical authority?

Blind allegiance to a foreign general, adherence to principles inimical to the temporal independence of the crown—these were potent accusations in France, all the more so because among the commissioners appointed by Louis XV to examine the affair of the Jesuits were Pierre Gilbert de Voisins and Jacques de Flesseles, both of them former magistrates in the parlement of Paris and therefore "nourished," as Voisins forthrightly expressed it to the king, with more than the usual dosage of Gallican "principles."[8] In a decisive combined meeting of the special court commission and the *conseil des dépêches* on August 29, Voisins stressed the gravity of the parlement's accusations. "What is most regrettable for the Jesuits," he observed, "is that in proceeding with this examination [the parlement] has joined to what seems to result from the unity of the entire . . . society under the absolute dependence of the general . . . the

6. Jean Egret, *Louis XV et l'opposition parlementaire, 1715–1774* (Paris, 1970), pp. 93–95.

7. Ibid., pp. 140–44.

8. On the details of the careers of Gilbert de Voisins and Jacques de Flesseles, see Bluche, *Les Magistrats du grand conseil au XVIIIe siècle, 1690–1791,* pp. 78–79, 82. Gilbert de Voisins was a counselor in the parlement of Paris from 1707 to 1711, and its solicitor general during the years 1718–19. Jacques III de Flesseles was a counselor in the parlement from 1752 to 1755; much later, during the turmoil of July 13–14, 1789, he found himself in the unenviable position of *prévot des marchands de Paris.* His manifest lack of zeal, in that capacity, for the project of storming the Bastille made him one of the first victims of the French Revolution. For Gilbert de Voisins's confession of Gallican principles, see A.N.: M241, *dossier* 4, unnumbered ms. entitled "au conseil des dépêches du Vendredi 4 janvier 1702 ou fut raporté et approuvé le plan des commissaires et la rédaction en fut ordonné par le Roi."

chronological catalogue of the pernicious maxims successively published by Jesuit authors not only against the independence of sovereigns but also against the surety of their persons. That," he added, "was to attack the society in France from the most dangerous angle, the most fit to further whatever one should undertake against it."[9] There unfortunately exists no record of what the commission's reporter Flesseles said that day, but the *Nouvelles Ecclésiastiques* assured its readers that he, too, "spoke very eloquently, clearly, and forcefully, that the intolerable vices of the Institute were exposed to broad daylight, and that the Institute . . . was not spared."[10]

What finally emerged from the meeting of the court commission and the *conseil des dépêches* on August 29 were simple royal letters patent which in relatively polite terms ordered the parlement to suspend its provisional judgments of August 6 for one year.[11] This was a far cry, to be sure, from the complete annulment desired by the dauphin and Lamoignon, but "we are persuaded," argued Gilbert de Voisins, "that however little we go beyond what has just been read to your Majesty, things will come to the greatest extremities, and on the contrary if we remain within these bounds we can promise success."[12] Yet the solution of simple letters of suspension was another half-measure which only thinly concealed weaknesses and indecision at Versailles and implicitly recognized the validity of the parlement's provisional judgments of August 6. Worse yet, the letters did not meet with all the success that Voisins had so confidently predicted.

Despite ample indications that something was to be expected from Versailles, the letters patent of August 29 caught the parlement of Paris visibly off balance when the abbé Terray, acting as the court's reporter, presented them to the assembled chambers on August 31. The abbé Chauvelin and the counselors Clément, Lambert, and Laverdy furiously opposed Terray's argument that "after 150 years of existence of the noviciates, congregations, colleges and seminaries there was no great inconvenience in permitting another year to pass"; but Chauvelin himself, convinced that the king's action was evidence that he did not yet fully appreciate the danger of the Jesuits' doctrines to his person, could propose no better course of action than to send First President Molé to the king with a compilation of extracts from the Jesuits' "execrable institutions". How-

9. A.N.: M241, *dossier* 4, unnumbered ms. with only the date "1761" at its head. Internal evidence, however, situates it quite certainly on the occasion of the meeting of the *conseil des dépêches* of August 29, 1761.

10. *Nouvelles Ecclésiastiques* (December 18, 1761), p. 216.

11. The text of these letters patent may be found in *Procédure contre l'institut et les constitutions des Jésuites*, pp. 117–18.

12. A.N.: M241, *dossier* 4, unnumbered ms. with following indication in the hand of Gilbert de Voisins: "réminiscence de ce que j'ai dit au conseil le samedi le 29 aoust 1761."

ever, when, on September 5, Molé reported that this expedient had produced no change in the royal will, the parlement, pressed by the coming of the yearly recess on September 8, endured several more agonizing sessions, until on September 7, at the eleventh hour, Laverdy hit upon the formula for reconciling the magistrates' "desire of obedience" and "sentiment of fidelity" to the king. The parlement, he proposed, should shorten the length of the demanded delay to April 1—the date which the parlement had originally designated for the closing of the Jesuit colleges in towns that had no other colleges—without, however, delaying the provisional execution of the prohibition of the religious vows or the dissolution of the Jesuits' special congregations, associations, and confraternities. Once again, the parlement overwhelmingly accepted his lead.[13]

When Molé reported the registration of the somewhat altered letters patent to the king and his ministry on the afternoon of September 7, Louis XV replied rather lamely that he would "make known his intentions to his parlement after its return."[14] Yet there is little more he could have said. The parliamentary recess was indeed about to begin, and what had probably been a purposely timed maneuver on the part of Versailles the parlement had not untypically turned to its own advantage. Whatever the real feelings of Louis XV, the chancellor and the dauphin expressed themselves more freely in private. "The palliative palliates badly," wrote the dauphin bitterly to Lamoignon, and the chancellor, equally outraged, thought that the "two registrations [of August 6 and September 7] are so similar that it appears that they should have the same fate"— namely, annulment.[15] Still, however painfully, Versailles had won a delay, although a shorter one than it had wished.

But to what purpose was the delay? Surely, to isolate the *parti janséniste* of the parlement of Paris by reforming the Jesuit Order in such a way as to make it palatable for the parlement's Gallican majority. As early as July 1761 Omer Joly de Fleury had suggested such reforms in his *Compte rendu,* and there is every reason to believe that he was acting in concert with the ministry. Moreover, Louis XV's special commissioners, particularly Gilbert de Voisins and Jacques de Flesseles, likewise insisted upon some reforms, not only for the sake of palliating the parlement's Gallican sensibilities but also because of their intrinsic justifiability. "The reclamation which is arising in France against the Jesuits," Voisins assured the king, "finds only too much justification in the

13. The entire parliamentary debate concerning the letters patent of August 29, 1761, including the text of the parlement's *arrêt* of September 7, is to be found in *Procédure contre l'institut et les constitutions des Jésuites,* pp. 81–122.

14. Ibid., p. 123.

15. A.N.: A.P. 162 mi. (Archives du marquis de Rosanbo), *carton* 1, *dossier* 6, mss. 32 and 35, respectively, dauphin to chancellor, n.d., and chancellor to dauphin, September 10, 1761.

characteristics or dependencies of their institute: and at the point at which it is attacked they [the Jesuits] have hardly any other resource than in the remedies which hopefully can be applied without bannishing it or destroying it."[16]

The "characteristics" and "dependencies" in question were of course the Jesuits' excessive subservience to a "foreign" general, the nonreciprocal nature of their religious vows, their somewhat less than total enthusiasm concerning the four Gallican articles of 1682, and their supposed adherence to the doctrine of tyrannicide. The French Jesuits themselves were perfectly aware of the necessity of concessions in at least some of these areas, because already on August 13 and 16 the head of the Jesuits' province of Paris, Etienne de la Croix, had sent letters to the Archbishop of Paris and the king, respectively, in which, on behalf of his province, he disavowed the doctrines of both tyrannicide and the papacy's indirect authority over princes in temporal affairs. The Parisian Jesuits, moreover, went considerably further when, in mid-October, they signed before a notary a document which condemned the doctrine of tyrannicide, proclaimed the complete independence of princes in temporal affairs, asserted that the authority of their general did not extend to the laws and principles of the realm, and renounced the exercise of all papal privileges which usurped the rights of the bishops, priests, universities, and other religious orders.[17]

If by this maneuver the French Jesuits had hoped to forestall the court commission's reformist measures by voluntarily adhering to what was in effect the first of the four Gallican articles—the absolute independence of secular sovereigns in temporal affairs—they were soon sorely disabused. For the court commission had far more substantial measures in mind. On the one hand, it demanded of both the French Jesuits and their general a formal adherence to all four Gallican articles of 1682 and a new decretal against tyrannicide which would remove a notorious ambiguity in the one issued by General Aquaviva in 1610 and condemn in no uncertain terms the hated doctrine.[18] On the other hand—and partly to prevent the French bishops from acting individually and publishing incendiary pastoral instructions in favor of the Jesuits and against the parlements—the court commission, in concert of course with the *conseil des dépêches* and the king, decided to consult the bishops in the vicinity of Paris on the subject of the Jesuits' utility, doctrine, and dependence on their general in an extraordinary assembly to be held in the *hôtel* of the cardinal de Luynes.[19]

16. A.N.: M 241, *dossier* 4, unnumbered and undated ms. The manuscript undoubtedly represents one of Gilbert de Voisins's reports to the *conseil des dépêches*, although precisely which meeting of the *conseil* is not certain.

17. Ludwig Freiherr von Pastor, *The History of the Popes, from the Close of the Middle Ages. Drawn from Secret Archives of the Vatican and Other Original Sources*, Vol. 36, trans. E. F. Peeler (London, 1950), p. 419.

18. See, in general, ibid., pp. 415–31.

19. On the ministry's reasons for this consultation, see A.N.: A.P. 162 mi. (Archives du

Of the fifty-one bishops who met in Paris on November 30, 1761, forty-five resoundingly endorsed the Jesuit Order in a report presented to the king a month later.[20] But unhappily, their endorsement was also Neuville's "honorable Epitaph," because it was in part dependent upon the Jesuits' acceptance of the court commission's demand that they adhere formally to the four Gallican articles of 1682. Now this the French Jesuits were willing enough to do. But their declaration to that effect, which La Croix presented to the commission on December 19, was only a closing episode in a disastrous chain of events which had begun in late September and early October.[21]

At that time the commission's reporter Jacques de Flesseles, according to his own report, communicated to the Jesuit Henri Griffet the declaration and the new interpretative decretal on tyrannicide, which the commission expected the Jesuits and their general to sign. Griffet informed the Paris provincial La Croix, who in turn "presented many difficulties and uncertainties." Indeed, the most the French Jesuits or their general could promise, La Croix maintained, was exterior conformity on these matters. Although the Jesuits' objections enraged Flesseles and confirmed his darkest "suspicion concerning their manner of thinking," the two documents were sent to Rome in amended form.[22] There, however, they encountered even heavier sledding. Rumors circulating in Rome about the important concessions that the French Jesuits were making had thrown both their general, Laurent Ricci, and Pope Clement XIII into the greatest consternation, and when confirmation reached their eyes in the form of the documents, they were thoroughly appalled. The commission's decretal on tyrannicide Ricci refused to sign because it contained, he thought, a subtle condemnation of the doctrine of the papacy's indirect authority over temporal

marquis de Rosanbo), *carton* 1, *dossier* 6, ms. 47, chancellor to dauphin, September 29, 1761.

20. A.N.: K1361, *dossier* 1A, "procès-verbal de l'assemblée extraordinaire des évêques en 1761."

21. This declaration is printed in P. de Ravignan, *Clément XIII et Clément XIV* (Paris 1854), Vol. 1 p. 118; and Vol. 2, p. 190.

22. Archives of the Maison de Saint-Louis at Chantilly, manuscript entitled "Relation exacte de tout ce qui s'est passé relativement au decret interprétif de celuy d'aquaviva de 1610, envoyé à Rome et refusé par le Général, ainsy qu'a la déclaration que le Général a pareillement refusé d'approuver" (pp. 1–3); hereafter referred to as Flesseles manuscript. This manuscript was originally a part of the personal library of President Rolland d'Erceville and still bears the following notation in his hand: "Le manuscrit par lequel celuy cy a été copié m'a été preté par m. de Flesseles en avril 1764." How it came into the possession of the Jesuit Order I do not know, but parts of it have been published by the père de Ravignan, in his *Clément XIII et Clément XIV*, Vol. 1, pp. 517–19, and the whole by August Carayon, ed., *Mémoires du président d'Eguilles sur le parlement d'Aix et les Jésuites, adressés à S.M. Louis XV* (Paris, 1867), pp. 293–303. For the precise text of both the projected decretal and declaration, see Ravignan, *Clément XIII et Clément XIV*, Vol. 2, pp. 204–05, 211–12; and A.N.: M241, *dossier* 4, unnumbered ms. entitled "Texte du projet de decret du général fournis par les jésuites et changemens en marge."

sovereigns, and because the previous decretal, issued by Aquaviva in 1614, he regarded as quite sufficient.[23] Instead, he sent a respectful letter to Louis XV on October 28 in which he condemned the doctrine of tyrannicide as "abominable, as meriting the execration of all centuries and the severity of all the laws both ecclesiastical and civil."[24] With even more indignation, Ricci refused to ratify in any way the Parisian Jesuits' adherence to the four Gallican articles, articles which Rome had always regarded as heretical and Alexander VIII had condemned as such. By their action, the Parisian Jesuits had grievously insulted the Holy See and given the lie to their title of "well-deserving servants of the Church."[25]

Ricci's negative response did not so much create as fully reveal the untenable situation in which the French Jesuits found themselves. The Jesuit Order was by nature a cosmopolitan body in the service of the papacy and dedicated, originally at least, to the restoration of a Catholic "Christendom" which had been rent first by the Reformation and, increasingly thereafter, by the growing autonomy of the various European States. To accede fully to the Gallican demands would therefore have necessarily entailed the disintegration of the society as a whole. The French Jesuits could go so far as to say that opinion concerning the Gallican articles remained "free," by which they meant that they themselves might individually adhere to them and would certainly teach them in their colleges. They could also—and they did—go so far as to brave the anathemas of both their general and the papacy on that account. But they could not possibly hope to engage the general himself by their concessions, since a general of even the most conciliatory dispositions presided over a society with members in states like Rome itself, whose eyes were blinded to the truth of the Gallican liberties and, on the contrary, regarded them as wholly detestable.

This much at least the Paris Jesuits succeeded in making the royal commissioners understand, and in fact wrung from them the concession that the general's ratification not be absolutely insisted upon. But it was otherwise with regard to Ricci's rejection of the commission's proposed decretal against tyrannicide, a rejection which was quite unexpected and singularly crushing for the French Jesuits.[26] According to Le Paige—and his information concerning these goings-on was marvelously accurate—the Paris Jesuits succeeded in convincing the Chancellor Lamoignon that the same reasons which prevented Ricci from ratifying the declaration on the Gallican articles applied with equal force to the decretal against tyrannicide. Lamoignon then met with the cardinal de Luynes,

23. Pastor, *The History of the Popes*, Vol. 36, pp. 420, 429.
24. A.N.: M241, *dossier* 4, unnumbered ms.
25. Pastor, *The History of the Popes*, Vol. 36, pp. 421–25.
26. For the negotiations between the commission and Rome concerning this decretal, see ibid., pp. 429–31.

the Archbishop of Narbonne, and other bishops who also agreed with the Jesuits, and together they decided that they would have to "content themselves with generalities and thereby rescue the Jesuits from the affair." But when the court commissioners found out about "the père" Lamoignon's "venerable council" and its moral "canon," they vigorously remonstrated, threatened to resign, and provoked a ministerial crisis which ended with the defeat of Lamoignon.[27]

Be that as it may, what is quite certain is that the court commissioners themselves reacted to Ricci's rejection of their decretal with the greatest disgust. When the Jesuits La Croix and Routh dolefully announced the news to Flesseles at the end of December, the commissioner's reporter offered them his condolences but insisted that he "owed the king the truth, and that it was bound to be disastrous for them." Indeed, when Flesseles reported all these proceedings to the commission and the *conseil des dépêches*—probably on January 4—he "did not fear to supplicate His Majesty to make known to the Jesuits who have the honor to approach his person his displeasure and even his indignation, and to tell them that if their General has not satisfied that which was demanded of him within a month, the only favor he could grant the Society is to permit the Parlements to decide their fate." All the ministers, according to Flesseles, "appeared deeply struck by the narration of this whole affair, and M. the duc de Choiseul could not restrain himself from crying: 'The Jesuits can become whatever they will wish, they are unworthy of the favors of the King.'"[28]

Not quite, however. The king and his commission had one more "favor" to bestow: that of reducing the French Jesuits' dependence on their ultramontane general by providing them with a special "vicar-general." The idea was far from new in January 1762. As early as September 29 Chancellor Lamoignon had warned the dauphin that the necessity of such a vicar-general was "the nearly unanimous opinion of the commissioners and the ministers."[29] And the danger of such a reform appeared so imminent at Rome and among the Jesuits that the pope's secretary of state, Torrigiani, instructed the French nuncio Pamfili to prevent the French bishops who were to meet in December from entertaining it, and Louis XV's Jesuit confessor, Desmaretz, wrote the king a personal letter supplicating His Majesty not "to detach us from our general, and to change the form of our first vows."[30] The Jesuits also actively opposed

27. B.P.R.: L.P. 582, ms. 11, "du janvier, 1762." See also the *Nouvelles Ecclésiastiques* (October 12, 1762), pp. 161–62, which contains the same story in about the same words. Adrien Le Paige was probably the article's author.

28. Archives de la Maison de Saint-Louis, Flesseles manuscript, pp. 4–7.

29. A.N.: A.P. 162 mi. (Archives du marquis de Rosanbo), *carton* 1, *dossier* 6, ms. 47, chancellor to dauphin, September 29, 1761.

30. On Torrigiani's instructions to Pamfili, see Pastor, *The History of the Popes*, Vol. 36,

the project in their published defenses of the order, and it was perhaps in the face of this nearly unanimous opposition that the court commission seemingly shelved the idea during the negotiations concerning the Gallican articles and the decretal against tyrannicide.[31]

It was in the wake of the failure of these negotiations and in a mood of desperation that the court commission seriously took up the idea of a vicar-general for the French Jesuits and, in a meeting with the *conseil des dépêches* on January 4, unanimously urged it upon the king.[32] After long meetings on January 14 and 15, Louis XV and the *conseil des dépêches* accepted the commissioners' proposal, and on the 17th the comte de Choiseul, the duc de Choiseul's brother and secretary for foreign affairs, dispatched a résumé of the proposal by an extraordinary courier to the cardinal de Rochechouart, France's ambassador to Rome who received the dispatch on January 26 and arranged to meet Ricci at the French embassy the next morning.[33] Ricci's reaction to the cardinal's résumé of the dispatch predictably conformed to his previous stance in the entire affair: he had no intention, he announced, of presiding over any other order than that which Saint Ignatius and his successors had bequeathed him. He predicted that France's request for a vicar-general would be followed by similar demands from other countries, which would result in the separation of the various members of the society from each other and of the whole from its head. The reform would moreover fail to mollify the parlements, which would not stop short of the complete destruction of the Jesuits in particular and all faith and piety in general. In any case, he did not himself possess the power to sanction such a fundamental alteration of the society. After conferring with his six assistants, who encouraged him in his resolution, and with Pope Clement XIII, who also opposed the demanded innovation, Ricci confirmed his rejection of the vicar-general by means of letters to Rochechouart and Louis XV on January 28.[34]

Ricci's response only seemingly ended the matter, for in sheer desperation

p. 416. For Desmaretz's letter to Louis XV, see A.N.: A.P. 162 mi. (Archives du marquis de Rosanbo), *carton* 1, *dossier* 5, ms. 84, Desmaretz to Louis XV, December 5, 1761.

31. See, for example, Neuville, *Observations sur l'institut de la société des Jésuites*, pp. 61–65.

32. On this occasion, Gilbert de Voisins was again one of the commission's chief spokesmen. See A.N.: M241, *dossier* 4, unnumbered ms. entitled "Au Conseil des dépêches du vendredi 4 janvier 1762 ou fut raporté [*sic*] et approuvé le plan des commissaires, et la rédaction en fut ordonné par le Roi. plan particular comme commissaire."

33. The text of this dispatch is located in the Archives des Affairs Etrangères, correspondence politique, Rome, Vol. 832, no. 20, dispatch written "à Versailles, le 16 janvier 1762, envoyé par un courrier extraordinaire," cte de Choiseul to the cardinal de Rochechouart.

34. Pastor, *The History of the Popes*, Vol. 36, pp. 439–42. For the text of Clement XIII's response to Louis XV, dated January 28, 1762, see Ravignan, *Clément XIII et Clément XIV*, Vol. 1, pp. 87–90.

the court commissioners now concocted the expedient of demanding that the general confer plenary authority, not on a vicar-general, but on each of the Jesuits' provincial superiors in France, and that these be elected every three years. Chancellor Lamoignon, one of the very few in the ministry who opposed altering the society in any way, reported bitterly to the dauphin on February 17 that the commissioners had "proposed as a means of conciliation to engage the general to confer upon each of the provincials the power they demand he confer on a vicar-general and they pretend that the Jesuits will not oppose this expedient." Louis XV, in a letter to the chancellor on February 21, indicated his approval of the plan on condition that the "commission content itself with the [Paris] Jesuits themselves, so that after their conference I can determine myself more surely."[35] This the commission duly performed on February 23, when it decided (with or without the consent of the Parisian Jesuits is uncertain) to proceed with the plan.[36]

At last, on the evening of March 8, the long awaited royal edict, the product of months of tortuous and as yet unsuccessful negotiations, reached the hands of the attorney general of the parlement of Paris. The edict attempted at once to preserve and reform the Jesuit Order. On the one hand, it declared the parlement's *appel comme d'abus* and provisional judgments against the Jesuits to be null and void; permitted the Jesuits to hold special congregations, confraternities, and retreats for laymen, with the permission and under the authority of the bishops; and in general guaranteed the Jesuits' right to live according to their Institute in all that was not contrary to the laws of the kingdom. On the other hand, it subjected the order to the laws and usages of the realm and the authority of the bishops; forbade it to contravene the rights of the bishops, chapters, curés, and universities; limited its membership in France to natural-born Frenchmen; and declared all its property to be inviolably attached to its existing houses and colleges. More important, the edict's fourth article required the Jesuits to have their theology students defend the Gallican propositions of 1682 in public theses before the principal personages of the area every year, and—most important—the ninth article required the general to confer all his authority upon the five provincial superiors of the Jesuit Order in France, and to reappoint these every three years. The general was given six months in which to do this; all recruitment of novices in France was suspended until he had complied.[37]

The bulk of the edict's individual articles were noncontroversial enough and had originally been suggested by the *gens du roi* in their conclusions of July 8,

35. A.N.: A.P. 162 mi. (Archives du marquis de Rosanbo), *carton* 1, *dossier* 6, ms. 48, chancellor to dauphin, February 17, 1762; and *dossier* 5, ms. 89. Louis XV to chancellor, February 21, 1762.

36. Pastor, *The History of the Popes,* Vol. 36, p. 445.

37. For text of edict see B.N.: Collection Joly de Fleury, fol. 1609, mss. 178–82.

1761. Since then the French Jesuits had declared their loyalty to the Gallican articles of 1682, and despite certain disapproval at Rome, would probably have raised no fuss about publically defending them every year. But there was no chance that either the general, the pope, or the majority of the French Jesuits would ever accept the abrogation of the general's immediate authority over the order in France, and for this reason the papal nuncio Pamfili had orders from Rome not to solicit the edict's registration.[38] As for the parlement of Paris, the *gens du roi* and the first president were not overly optimistic about the edict's reception there.[39] It was not to its individual articles but to the tenor of the entire document that the parlement would object, because those who had brought the Jesuits to trial were not so interested in reforming the order as in destroying it. The edict, Le Paige predicted, would "displease the entire world; the Jesuits, because it reforms them at several points: the rest of the human race, because it does not reform them as much as the good of the State requires."[40] Why under these circumstances the ministry decided to issue the edict at all remains mysterious. The rumor even circulated that "*Messieurs* the commissioners of the Council disavowed the project, in which they no longer recognized their work," and that "it was M. the chancellor alone who had drafted it." The king, it was said, thought it necessary to let the old warrior charge, that "he would dismount with the disappointment of seeing his work rejected."[41] If in any case there was ever an "edict in air"—as Le Paige expressed it—it was the edict of March 8, 1762.[42]

Meanwhile Adrien Le Paige and the *parti janséniste* were anything but ignorant of developments at Versailles and Rome. How the leakage of information occurred is uncertain, but in a kind of political diary in the form of bogus letters to a fictitious "madame," Le Paige recorded the progress of the three-cornered negotiations between Versailles, the French Jesuits, and Rome with remarkable accuracy. As early as October 15, 1761, he was predicting that the royal commissioners' efforts would resemble the "mountain which gave birth to a mouse," that the "monk monarch" would never consent to see his empire thus lacerated, and that the project of reforming the Jesuit Order would "vanish into smoke." It was of course with exquisite pleasure that he progressively observed his prophecies materialize.[43]

38. Pastor, *The History of the Popes*, Vol. 36, p. 446.

39. B.N.: Collection Joly de Fleury, fol. 1609, ms. 174, attorney general to Saint-Floretin, March 9, 1762.

40. B.P.R.: L.P. 582, ms. 11, "du 20 janvier 1762."

41. *Nouvelles Ecclésiastiques* (October 12, 1762), p. 162.

42. B.P.R.: L.P. 582, ms. 11, "Extraits des letres [sic] d'une dame de Paris à une de ses amis de province, au sujet de l'assemblée des Eveques au mois de Décember 1762 à Paris, et de leur avis sur les jésuites. du 8 février 1762."

43. Ibid., "le 15 octobre 1761."

But Le Paige and his magisterial allies were hardly ones to wait passively upon the workings of providence. In proportion as it became increasingly certain that the royal edict, should it materialize at all, would arrive with no papal support from above, they, for their part, resolved to deprive it in advance of any parliamentary support it might conceivably find from below. By itself the parlement of Paris could do nothing immediately; by its registration of the letters patent of August 29, 1761, its hands were tied until April 1, 1762. But besides Paris there were thirteen provincial parlements or *conseils souverains* which might be prevailed upon to contribute something to the cause. "The metropolitan court and all its colonies," as the parlement of Paris had somewhat pompously proclaimed in its remonstrances of August 22, 1756, "are the divers classes of a sole and unique Parlement, the divers members of a sole and unique body, animated by the same spirit, nourished by the same principles, occupied by the same object."[44] The doctrine of the union of all the French parlements was new to the mid-eighteenth century: Le Paige himself had importantly contributed to its formulation in his *Lettres historiques sur les parlements* in 1755. Le Paige and the *parti janséniste* now busied themselves about the task of transforming this doctrine into political reality.

Though by mid-September 1761 both Rennes and Toulouse had already demanded copies of the Jesuits' constitutions, the two parlements proceeded at a leisurely pace and eventually followed the example of the parlement of Paris by first pronouncing provisionally on the Jesuits' doctrine and constitutions and inviting the order to defend itself.[45] What Le Paige and his friends needed, on the contrary, was a quick and decisive parliamentary blow in advance of the royal edict of reform, which they knew to be imminent. And for this purpose the parlement of Normandy at Rouen was a far more reliable ally, since it had long distinguished itself among parlements by its recalcitrance in the face of the royal will. The "furor of the Normans" was proverbial at Versailles; the great chancellor D'Aguesseau himself, repeatedly frustrated by the parlement of Normandy in his attempt to codify the laws during the first decades of the century, was once moved to remark that "a change in religion would perhaps be easier to introduce into Normandy than a change in jurisprudence." Not so, however. Jansenism had put down substantial roots in parts of Normandy, and many Norman magistrates regarded the bull *Unigenitus* as a change in religion indeed which, especially during the plague of the refusal of sacraments to Jansenists in the 1750s, they resisted more furiously than innovation in the sacrosanct *coutume* itself. Moreover, the leader of the

44. "Remonstrances du 22 août 1756," in *Remonstrances du parlement de Paris au XVIII*e *siècle*, ed. Jules Flammermont, Vol. 2, p. 138.
45. On the parlement of Toulouse, see *Extrait des registres du parlement séant à Toulouse. Du 15 septembre 1761*, in *Journal de ce qui s'est passé dans l'affaire des Jésuites, depuis le 15 septembre 1761 jusqu'au 5 juin 1762*, pp. 1–2.

magisterial *parti janséniste* in the parlement of Normandy, the counselor Thomas du Fossé, was the grand nephew of the seventeenth-century Port-Royalist "solitary" of the same name and an indefatigable correspondent of Le Paige.[46]

The parlement of Normandy was in an ideal position for a decisive maneuver against the Jesuits because, on the advice of its first president, Hué de Miromesnil, Louis XV had not sent to it the royal declaration of August 2, 1761, which forbade any parliamentary initiative against the Jesuits for one year. Louis XV had wanted to send the declaration secretly to Miromesnil so that, in case the parlement seemed disposed to take the initiative against the Jesuits, he could produce it at will. But Miromesnil had persuaded the comte de Saint-Florentin, secretary of the king's household, that the declaration's presence at Rouen would only provoke the parlement into action, just as it had in Paris, and that it was wiser not to send it at all.[47] This would have been sound advice if the parlement of Paris had not already acted, for its example, particularly at Rouen, was bound to be contagious. Suddenly, on November 19, 1761, the parlement of Normandy, led by Du Fossé, demanded the deposition of the Jesuits' constitutions and invited the *gens du roi* to give their conclusions in the shortest possible delay.[48] The attorney general, Le Sens de Folleville, known for his attachment to the bull *Unigenitus* and his friendship with Miromesnil, had conveniently fallen sick, so it was his substitute, Jean-Gaspard-Benoît Charles, who delivered the *Compte rendu* and assured the magistrates that the society was so "injurious to all powers and pernicious even in the Order of the Faith" that they possessed the right to dissolve it definitively then and there, without further formality. Nevertheless, he conformed his conclusions of January 27 "to the plan which several Courts of the Realm have thus far deemed necessary to adopt" by requiring only the provisional *appel comme d'abus* and the notification to the Jesuits' general.[49]

46. Amable Floquet, *Histoire du parlement de Normandie*, Vol. 6 (Rouen, 1842). On the remark of D'Aguesseau, see p. 205; on Du Fossé, see pp. 270–71, 320–24; on the parlement's reaction to *Unigenitus* and refusals of sacraments to Jansenists, see generally pp. 251–324, and for Floquet's account of the destruction of the Jesuits in Normandy, pp. 325–46.

47. B.M.R.: Collection Lebet, Y 67, mss. 4–5, Saint-Florentin to Miromesnil, November 2 and 14, 1761, respectively. Most of Miromesnil's correspondence has been published by P. Le Verdier, ed., *Correspondence politique et administrative de Miromesnil, premier président du parlement de Normandie* (3 vols. Rouen, 1899–1901), and the two letters in question can be found in Vol. 2, pp. 54–55. Since, however, Le Verdier did not actually publish all the Miromesnil correspondence in this collection, I deemed it more prudent to consult the manuscript collection itself.

48. A.D.S.I., "Registre secret du parlement de Normandie, 1761–1762," November 19, 1761.

49. J.-G.-B. Charles, *Comptes des constitutions de la société se disant de Jésus* in *Comptes des constitutions et de la doctrine de la société se disant de Jésus, rendu au parlement de Normandie, toutes les chambres assemblées, les 16, 18, 19, 22, et 23 janvier 1762. Par M. Charles* (1762), pp. 138–45.

Such, certainly, would have been the judicially normal course of action. But this procedure was far too time-consuming to suit the wishes of the *parti jansén-iste* at Rouen, too long also to suit Le Paige and his colleagues in Paris, who were expecting the royal edict of reform on any day. But how to bypass the stage of provisional judgments and notification to the general? In a quandry, Du Fossé turned to Le Paige for advice in an unsigned letter on January 25. The parlement of Normandy, he assured Le Paige, appeared "sufficiently well disposed, but questions of form are causing some division among us. . . . One would like," he explained, "to be able to pronounce *de plano* that [the Jesuits' constitution and doctrine] are abusive without a preliminary inquiry," but a certain "number of gentlemen raise difficulties because it is contrary to usage to pronounce something abusive without an enquiry and to condemn someone without a hearing. Others," he continued, "think that the consideration of the constitutions produced by the society itself can be the equivalent of an instruction," whereas yet "others, finally, think that one could decree both at the same time and by the same judgment on the Constitutions and the doctrine, say nothing about the *appel comme d'abus* of the Attorney General, and pronounce on the basis of the constant and persistent aberrations of the Society in its preaching and teaching and also the default of the execution of the conditions under which it was reestablished in France that the Edict of Expulsion of 1595 should be executed according to its form and tenor. What follows?" he finally asked Le Paige. "I beg of you the greatest secrecy and a prompt response without signature."[50]

Unhappily, we possess neither Le Paige's response to this letter nor any completely certain indication in Rouen that a response was received. In all probability, however, Le Paige sent his response but observed to the letter Du Fossé's plea for the "greatest secrecy." What nonetheless closely follows Du Fossé's letter in Le Paige's papers is a compendium in an unidentifiable hand of judicial precedents for "*appel comme d'abus* lodged by an attorney general and judged immediately without observing any delay or making a preliminary notification."[51] In other words, this list of precedents supported the second option mentioned by Du Fossé, that "the consideration of the constitutions of the society itself can be the equivalent of an instruction." The document is indication enough that Le Paige at least occupied himself with the problem, and if Le Paige sent anything similar to Du Fossé and the parlement of Normandy, it evidently produced the desired effect. The parlement appointed no

---

50. B.P.R.: L.P. 583, ms. 161, Du Fossé to Le Paige, January 25, 1762. Du Fossé therefore wrote this letter only two days after Charles had finished reading his *Compte rendu,* and only one day before its official examination by the assembled chambers was to commence. A.D.S.I., "Registre secret," January 23, 1762.

51. B.P.R.: L.P. 583, ms. 175.

special commission to examine Charles's *Compte rendu;* it delivered no notification to the Jesuits so that they could legally defend themselves. After plenary parliamentary verifications of the *Compte rendu* lasting from January 20 to February 9, the parlement of Normandy, on February 12, 1762, pronounced the first definitive judgment against the Company of Jesus. The judgment declared the Jesuits' monastic vows invalid, ordered all Jesuits living within the parlement's jurisdiction to abandon their residences before July 1, and required those Jesuits wishing to perform any public functions to swear an oath assuring their fidelity to the four Gallican articles and condemning the doctrine and constitutions of their erstwhile society.[52] In the face of the expected royal edict of reform, the parlement of Normandy had presented Versailles with a fait accompli which seriously prejudiced its eventual reception. "That is what one calls going directly to one's target," Le Paige wrote admiringly. "We will see how the court [of Versailles] will take it, and in that way we will judge its attitude toward the projected Edict."[53]

It goes without saying that Versailles was not enamored of the parlement of Normandy's judgment of February 12. When shortly thereafter Miromesnil joined his attorney general, De Folleville, in ill health, Saint-Florentin found it a natural reaction to "a judgment so extraordinary and so irregular and so contrary to the authority of the king."[54] Yet except to rage privately, Versailles did nothing in response to the Normans' fait accompli. To believe the *Nouvelles Ecclésiastiques,* "several Councils were held on the subject," and the "Jesuits even spread the rumor that an annulment had been decided." But—the weekly victoriously added—"the memorable judgment remained nonetheless intact; it was executed without obstacle." Perhaps neither Le Paige nor the *Nouvelles Ecclésiastiques*—in this instance the two were probably the same—were wholly mistaken in judging Versailles' inaction as revelatory of "the intimate thoughts of the Government."[55]

It was with a mixture of disbelief and dismay, then, that Le Paige learned that

52. A.D.S.I., "Registre secret," February 12, 1762. The *arrêt* reads: "La Cour faisant droit sur ledit appel comme d'abus interjetté par le procureur général du Roy des régime, constitutions, institut des pretres et escoliers de la société se disant de *Jésus,* voeu et serments par eux faits de se soumettre et conformer aux règles, dit qu'il y a abus. . . ." The *arrêt* was published as *Arrêt de la cour du parlement de Rouen, qui condamne les deux volumes de l'institut des soi-disans Jésuites, à être lacérés et brulés par l'exécuteur de la haute-justice, en ce qu'ils contiennent les constitutions et règlements de la société, dissout ladite société, et enjoinst à chacun de ses membres de vuider les maisons avant le premier juillet prochain. Extrait des registres du parlement du 12 février 1762* (Rouen, 1762).

53. B.P.R.: L.P. 582, ms. 11, "extrait de letres [*sic*] d'une dame de Paris à une de ses amies de province . . . du 14 février 1762."

54. B.M.R.: Collection Lebet, Y 67, ms. 25, Saint-Florentin to Miromesnil, February 17, 1762

55. *Nouvelles Ecclésiastiques* (October 12, 1762), p. 162.

the *gens du roi* had finally received the edict, which they presented to the assembled chambers of the parlement of Paris on March 12. On the advice of the abbé Terray, the edict's reporter, the parlement unanimously decided to appoint commissioners to examine the edict and thereby bought time to prepare its resistance.[56] It was not, however, the appointed commissioners but rather President François de Murard who, on the part of "several of the *messieurs* of the parlement of Paris"—Counselor Marc Jacques Fermé, and probably Laverdy, Lambert, Clément de Feuillet, and Robert de Saint-Vincent—requested Le Paige to "throw onto paper" a rough first draft of remonstrances against the edict of March 8.[57] Murard was careful to give Le Paige precise instructions for drafting them. "I persist in thinking," he wrote, "that it is not necessary to enlarge in any detail concerning the edict's dispositions and its particular defects. It is its general object which is the conservation of the corps [of the Jesuits] which ought to be principally attacked."[58]

What Murard said in his somewhat antiseptic style Le Paige, in his draft remonstrances, expressed with the warmth of his lifelong convictions. Following a rather grandiose introduction, he turned to the Jesuits' internal doctrine, which, he said, was "designed to pervert morals, to corrupt men, to render them evil, to legitimize their vices, to make them commit crimes without remorse, to extinguish within them every principle of natural rectitude, every vestige of Religion, every fear of the punishments of God; to destroy every principle of obedience and subordination, to transform, finally, cities and realms into retreats for scoundrels."[59] After lingering in some detail over the individual Jesuitical doctrines of probabilism, "that detestable invention," and the philosophical sin, a "dreadful and detestable dogma," Le Paige fastened upon "the doctrine that permits the murder of kings," which, because of the Jesuit general's "despotic authority" and his devotion to the "absolute power of Rome," was "therefore born within the society itself, and as a necessary consequence of its institute."[60] The parlement "punishes these crimes, Sire," but "those who

56. *Procédure contre l'institut et les constitutions des Jésuites,* pp. 159–60.

57. B.P.R.: L.P. 583, ms. 55, which contains the following note by Le Paige: "canevas au sujet de projet d'Edit de Mars 1762 sur les jésuites. Quelques uns de messieurs du parlement de Paris me prierent de le jetter sur le papier à la hate et currente Calamo, le chose pouvant devenir pressé. L'affaire prit une autre tournure." That it was Murard who took it upon himself to represent "quelques uns des messieurs du parlement de Paris" is proven by a letter from him to Le Paige, L.P. 583, ms. 52, unsigned, dated March 16, 1762. The handwriting of this letter is clearly that of Murard, as may be easily confirmed by reference to any number of letters by him in the Le Paige collection which *are* signed, such as L.P. 571, mss. 105, 108, 114, 121, 127, etc.

58. B.P.R.: L.P. 583, unsigned, dated March 16, 1762. On authorship, see above, n. 57.

59. B.P.R.: L.P. 583, ms. 55, p. 8.

60. Ibid. On probabilism, see pp. 8–9; on the doctrine of the philosophical sin, invincible ignorance, and the mistaken conscience, see p. 9; and on regicide, see p. 7.

teach men to commit them, are they not infinitely more culpable?" Le Paige asked rhetorically.[61]

Le Paige's language was in places intemperate. Undoubtedly his magisterial friends would have toned them down somewhat before presenting them as remonstrances to the king. But Le Paige's remonstrances were stillborn. On March 26 the parlement, led again by Laverdy, found a device by which to ignore the royal edict altogether. Fastening on both the fact that the attorney general's *appel comme d'abus* was still outstanding and by law had to be definitively judged, and the edict's fifteenth article, which seemed to contemplate the presentation of new constitutions provided with letters patent and conformable to the maxims and usages of the realm, Laverdy proposed that the parlement not deliberate on the edict at all until both these conditions had been fulfilled. This was in effect to propose the elimination of the Jesuit Order in France because, as Laverdy well knew, the Jesuits would never consent to whatever "new constitutions" the ministry had in mind, and the parlement, on the other hand, would certainly judge the attorney general's *appel comme d'abus* against the society.[62] Persuaded, the parlement judged by a strong majority of eighty votes that "there is no reason, for the present, to deliberate on the verification of the said edict, deeming it nonetheless unnecessary to compose remonstrances . . . to the said lord King concerning the said edict, given the conviction . . . that the extracts which will be presented to the said lord King . . . of the doctrine favorable to all crimes, defended at all times and consistently taught by the said Society, will fix the attention of the said lord King, and will persuade him to close his eyes to all that could give a legal status to the said Society."[63]

The "extracts" of the Jesuits' doctrine mentioned by the parlement's resolution constituted the other half of the parlement's response to the edict of March. The project of compiling these extracts, first ordered by the parlement on September 3, 1761, upon the insistence of the abbé Chauvelin, took on a new urgency when, in response to the king's order, the French bishops met the

---

61. Ibid., p. 10.

62. *Procédure contre l'institut*, pp. 179–82. The somewhat mysterious fifteenth article reads as follows: "N'entendons au surplus innover en ce qui concerne le régime et l'administration de la dite société dans notre province, terres et païs de notre obéissance; voulons que ceux qui la composent continuent d'y vivre suivant leur institut en tout ce qui ne sera pas contraire aux maximes et loix de notre Royaume, à la charge de se conformer aux dites maximes et loix, notamment à l'Edit du mois de 7bre 1603, à la Déclaration du 16 juillet 1715, et au présent Edit; et seront les constitutions de la dite société, ainsi que celles des autres ordres religieux de nos Etats, qui n'auront pas encore obtenu nos lettres sur icelles à nous présentées, pour être, s'il y a lieu, revêtues de nos dites lettres addressés à nos cours et par elles enregistrés en la manière accountumée."

63. *Procédure contre l'institut*, pp. 186–88.

following December to evaluate the utility of the Jesuit Order.[64] In proportion as it became clear that the bishops' report would be favorable to the Jesuits, it became increasingly imperative for the parlement to justify its action in such a way as to retain public opinion on its side. As early as November 30 Le Paige met in utmost secrecy with the prince de Conty, the lawyers Texier and Lalourcé, and the abbés Mey and Maultrot, in all likelihood to consider what could be done to counter the coming episcopal report.[65] And by the time the report appeared at the end of December, they had evidently reached a decision, because President Murard was already writing to Le Paige about the project of having "printed and published a résumé of the doctrine of the Jesuits addressed to all the archbishops and bishops of France."[66]

In sum, the work of the original parliamentary commission, which was conveniently to meet for the first time on December 15, was to be considerably expanded so as to counteract whatever contrary impression might be made by the episcopal opinion. A somewhat reluctant abbé Terray presided over this commission, but the real work was done by Laverdy, the counselor Roussel de la Tour, President Murard, and the abbé Chauvelin, with additional assistance from Le Paige (who compiled the analytical table), Robert de Saint-Vincent (who contributed the section on the Chinese rites), the counselor Lambert (who helped Saint-Vincent), and very probably many others both inside and outside the parlement.[67] When it finally appeared in the spring of 1762, the

64. On the original decision, see ibid., pp. 91–95.

65. B.P.R.: L.P. 582, ms. 137, Texier to Le Paige, November 29, 1761. The letter reads:

"Vous êtes instamment et très instamment prié, Monsieur et cher Confrère, de la part de M. Le. Prieur [the prince de Conty, prieur du Temple], de m. Lalourcé, de m. Maultrot, de m. Mey et de moi de vouloir bien vous rendre demain Lundy fête de S. andré sur les cinq heures du soir rue Christine pour une affaire de la dernière importance à laquelle votre présence est jugée par nous cinq absolument nécessaire. Vous en jugerez de même quand vous serez instruit de ce dont il s'agit.

"Vous aurez le bonté, s'il vous plaît, de prendre une voiture qui sera . . . aux frais des parties.

"Ne vous manquez pas, nous vous en supplions.

"En attendant l'honneur de vous voir, j'ai celui de vous embrasser, Monsieur et cher Confrère avec le plus tendre respect.

Texier

"Il n'y aura qui se soit autre à notre assemblée de demain avec nous que les personnes ci dessus nommées, et il ne pourra y en avoir d'autres."

What seems to suggest that this meeting concerned the publication of extracts of the Jesuits' doctrinal works is that Le Paige himself placed the letter with the documents having to do with this object, particularly ms. 139.

66. Ibid., ms. 138, undated, unsigned ms. written in a formal, unidentifiable hand, very likely that of a copyist.

67. On the roles of the abbé Terray and the counselors Laverdy, Lambert, Chauvelin, and Robert de Saint-Vincent, see Saint-Vincent, "Mémoires," pp. 253–54. On the role of

parlement's famous *Extraits des assertions en tout genre que les soi-disans Jésuites ont, dans tous les temps et persévéramment soutenues, enseignées et publiées dans leurs livres, avec l'approbation de leurs supérieurs et généraux* not only included example of Jesuitical assertions obviously dangerous to public order, such as regicide but also covered the well-trodden ground of the Chinese rites, probabilism invincible ignorance, the philosophical sin, the misguided conscience, and Molinism in general.[68] With considerable justification, the general agents of the clergy could complain to the king in 1762 that the parlement of Paris had arrogated itself into an ecclesiastical tribunal by publishing "a collection of assertions in which it not only stigmatizes propositions contrary to civil order but also includes, in its prescription, objects which can have only to do with dogma and morality of the most spiritual kind, and therefore the most independent of the secular jurisdiction [*police extérieure*]. The little knowledge which magistrates devoted by duty to a study quite other than theology can be expected to have about these questions has exposed them to confounding truths with errors."[69] Indeed, if ever during the eighteenth century the parlement of Paris transgressed the ambiguous line which separated, under the Old Regime, the secular from the ecclesiastical jurisdictions, it was in this instance.

It is in any case most doubtful that the *Extraits des assertions* changed any bishop's mind on the subject of the Jesuits, much less that of the king. What

Roussel de la Tour, see B.P.R.: L.P. 583, ms. 33; and for that of Le Paige and Presiden Murard, see Murard's letters to le Paige on this subject, ibid., mss. 33, 35, 36, and 54. These letters are all unsigned, but Murard's authorship may be ascertained by a comparison of the handwriting in these letters and those by him which are signed; for example, L.P. 571, mss 105, 107, 114, etc. The abbé Picot, in his *Mémoires pour servir à l'histoire écclésiastique pendant le dix-huitème siècle,* (2d ed. 4 vols. Paris, 1815–16), Vol. 2, p. 409, asserts that along with Roussel de la Tour, the abbés Goujet and Minard were "les principaux rédacteurs de ce recueil." I have found no corroborative evidence to support this assertion, although Goujet with his numerous parliamentary contacts, was probably in a position to contribute to the *Assertions* if he had wanted to. On Goujet, see René Cerveau, *Suite du nécrologe des plu célèbres défenseurs et amis de la vérité du dix-huitième siècle depuis 1767 jusqu'en 1806–1810, pa un contemporain impartial* (Paris, 1817), Vol. 1, pp. 78–79. Picot also asserts that La Chalotais Ripert de Monclar, and Joly de Fleury—which Joly de Fleury he does not specify—established at the house of the Blancs-Manteaux of the Benedictine order in Paris "un atelier de jansénistes afin de faire des recherches et les compilations dont ils avoiant besoin pour leu plan d'attaque." The supposition of three attorney generals—one at Rennes, one at Aix-en-Provence, and the other at Paris—in clandestine collaboration on a project for which both Joly de Fleurys were anything but enthusiastic, is too absurd to merit serious consideration and in any case finds no corroborative evidence.

68. *Extrait des assertions en tout genre que les soi-disans Jésuits ont, dans tous les temps et per sévéramment soutenues, enseignées et publiées dans leurs livres, avec l'approbation de leurs supéri eurs et généraux* (Paris, 1762), passim.

69. A.N.: K. 1361, *dossier* 6, "Très humbles et très respectueuses remonstrances des agent généraux du clergé de France."

must have impressed Louis XV far more was the crescendo of provincial parliamentary activity against the Jesuits, particularly in response to his edict of March. From Rouen, for example, where the edict arrived on March 11, Du Fossé wrote to Le Paige on the very same day to request "a good advisor such as youself to lead us and direct our demarches under such delicate circumstances which so essentially concern Religion, the State, and the Sovereign." All "I can think of to justify the ministry," he said, "is that it does not intend that the Parlements register the Edict."[70] What Le Paige's response was is not known, but he was certainly in subsequent correspondence with Rouen because he knew precisely what was to happen there at least a day in advance.[71] Rouen's first president Miromesnil was, however, not so fortunate. Convinced that his company's magistrates "wanted to await what happened at the parlement of Paris," whose "demarches always greatly influence our own," he was caught completely off guard when, on March 27, the parlement of Normandy took a different route by requesting the king to withdraw his edict purely and simply.[72] The edict could have no application in Normandy, the magistrates carefully explained, because since February 12 the Jesuits had ceased to exist in that province.[73]

Nevertheless, in March 1762 the parlements of Paris and Normandy were still among the very few which had to encounter the king's edict head-on, because only they, along with the parlement of Brittany, had yet rendered judgments of any kind against the Jesuits. For many of the other provincial parlements—including some which might otherwise have remained aloof from the affair of the Jesuits—the royal edict itself provided an all too logical occasion to take up the case of the Jesuits in the first place. "Nothing is more natural," Le Paige wrote gleefully. "For speaking as the Edict does about the institute of the Jesuits . . . It is only after an examination and the conclusions which the *gens du roi* will have reached concerning this institute, that one will really be in a position to deliberate about the Edict."[74] Accordingly, the month of March witnessed a small landslide of provincial parliamentary decisions to examine the two volumes of the Jesuit constitutions: the parlements of Bordeaux, Aix,

70. B.P.R.: L.P. 583, ms. 58, Du Fossé to Le Paige, March 11, 1762. Du Fossé was also among the commissioners deputed in the parlement of Normandy to examine the edict (A.D.S.I.: "registre secret," March 11, 1762).

71. B.P.R.: L.P. 583, ms. 64, Le Paige to Deydé, March 26, 1762. "On assure," wrote Le Paige, "que Rouen a renvoyé purement et simplement l'Edit, comme frappant sur un objet qui n'existe plus chez eux: je n'en ai point encore de certitude." Nor could he have had, since Rouen did not act until the following day.

72. B.M.R.: Collection Lebet, Y67, ms. 21, Miromesnil to the duc de Choiseul, March 21, 1762. On the parlement's judgment, see A.D.S.I., "registre secret," March 27, 1762.

73. B.P.R.: L.P. 583, ms. 64; see n. 71.

74. Ibid., ms. 187, memoir of Le Paige for the *conseil souverain* of Roussillon.

Grenoble, Metz, Besançon, and the *conseil souverain* of Roussillon all moved in their turn.[75] Indeed, the Jesuits' enemies themselves could hardly have hit upon a happier device to generalize the order's proscription. "The edict of the king," complained the Jesuits of Grenoble, "which seemed to be bound to restore calm, now hurls us into the tempest."[76]

The edict of March, then, together with indigenous Gallican sentiment, a natural provincial desire to be part of a celebrated national affair, a sense of parliamentary solidarity expressed by the theory of the "union of classes"—all these factors would seem sufficient in themselves to explain the provincial parliamentary offensive against the Jesuits without having recourse to the direct influence of the parlement of Paris and its *parti janséniste*. That such a direct influence at least sometimes existed, however, it is impossible to deny, as is evidenced by Le Paige's correspondence with Du Fossé at Rouen. But perhaps the most interesting case of all is that of the *conseil souverain* of Roussillon at Perpignan.

The plain of Roussillon had been a part of the Spanish province of Catalonia until 1659, when French armies successfully besieged the fortress of Perpignan. Hence the local *conseil souverain*, which Louis XIV created from the remains of the Catalonian judicial apparatus, knew nothing of the parliamentary pretensions of the Fronde, but rather became the docile instrument of the French crown's gallicization of the province. Amid the parliamentary effervescence of the mid-eighteenth century the province of Roussillon was still known as a *pays d'obédience*, where the royal intendent, De Bon, doubled as first president of the *conseil souverain*. Not even the quarrels relating to the bull *Unigenitus* had had any serious repercussions in Roussillon; throughout the fifties, its sovereign court continued to register royal edicts and declarations without difficulty.[77]

At the same time, several among the small court's seventeen magistrates were not insensitive to the parliamentary rhetoric elsewhere in France and became increasingly desirous of placing their *conseil souverain* on the judicial map as

75. *Extrait des registres du parlement séant à Bordeaux. Du 8 mars 1762* and *Du vendredi, 12 mars* in *Compte rendu des constitutions des Jésuites, par M. Pierre-Jules Dudon, avocat général du roi au parlement de Bordeaux*, pp. 6–10: *Arrest du parlement de Provence. Du 6 mars 1762; Extraits des registres des parlements de Metz et de Grenoble*, for Metz, March 1, 4 and 13, 1762, pp. 3–5, and Grenoble, March 20, 1762, pp. 6–7; *Arrest du parlement de Besançon, concernant la société des Jésuites. Du 27 mars 1762;* and *Arrests du conseil souverain de Perpignan, au sujet de l'édit du roi, donné à Versailles au mois de mars 1762, tendant à modifier l'institut des Jésuites, et à fixer leur état, s'il étoit possible. Du 17 mars 1762.*

76. Jean Egret, "Le Procès des Jésuites devant les parlements de France," *Revue Historique,* 204 (July–December 1950), 13.

77. Paul Galibert, *Le Conseil souverain de Roussillon* (Perpignan, 1904), passim; and the abbé Philippe Torreilles, "L'Ultramontanisme et le Gallicanisme en Roussillon sous l'Ancien Régime, *Revue d'Histoire et d'Archéologie du Roussillon,* 5 (1904), 1–16, 33–48, 65–80, 193–210.

indeed one of the "classes" of the "national" parlement. The affair of the Jesuits presented an ideal opportunity to do so. Not only could they count upon the support of other parlements, particularly those of Paris and Rouen, but their own first president and intendant, De Bon, was himself inclined against the order. They could also exploit hoary rancours against the Jesuits dating from 1664, when their College of Saint-Laurent obtained a monopoly of secondary education at the expense of the University of Perpignan. Finally, the arrival of the king's edict of reform in Perpignan on March 14 made it necessary to engage the affair in any case.[78]

But since the *conseil souverain* of Roussillon was hardly accustomed to big affairs of this sort, it is not surprising that the leader of the anti-Jesuitical faction, the *sous-doyen* Joseph de Massia de Salelles, should have looked to Paris for advice. Indeed, as promptly as March 15, the day after the royal edict reached Perpignan, Salelles wrote to his father-in-law, Deydé de Maury, in Paris requesting him to obtain the advice of his parliamentary acquaintances. In the meantime, unfortunately, the father-in-law in question had died, and when Salelles's letters arrived in Paris they were sent to the deceased's brother, the frère Deydé, who seems to have been a member of the notoriously Jansenist order of the Brothers of the Christian Doctrine. Now, as it happened, Deydé knew Le Paige and sent Salelles' letters on to him on March 26. "I know of no one who can better write a memorandum on this subject than you," Deydé wrote Le Paige. "Therefore I send you the whole."[79]

Le Paige's advice, which he quite "willingly" sent to Salelles in Perpignan, somewhat reflected the order of events in Paris: the *conseil souverain* should first use the edict of March as the occasion to demand the Jesuits' constitutions, and then, once the *gens du roi* were busy with these, further assign them the question of the Jesuits' doctrine.[80] But by the time his recommendations reached Perpignan, they were largely irrelevant. For on March 17 the *conseil souverain* had anticipated Le Paige by ordering the Jesuits to deliver the two-volume

78. On the College of Saint-Laurent, see the abbé Philippe Torreilles, *Le Collège de Perpignan depuis ses origines jusqu'à nos jours* (n.p., n.d.), esp. pp. 345–77. On the dispositions of magistrates at the time of the expulsion of the Jesuits, see ibid., pp. 392–96, but more importantly, Philippe Torreilles, ed., *Mémoires de M. Jaume, avocat au conseil souverain, professeur à l'université de Perpignan* (Perpignan, 1884), pp. 106–08.

79. B.P.R.: L.P. 583, ms. 185, Deydé to Le Paige, March 26, 1762. See also biographical information on Joseph-Guillaume-François de Massia de Salelles, in the abbé J. Capeille, *Dictionnaire de biographies Roussillonaises* (Perpignan, 1910), p. 362.

80. B.P.R.: L.P. 583, ms. 187, memoir of Le Paige for the *conseil souverain* of Roussillon. In this instance, at least, the correspondence with Deydé demonstrates conclusively enough that this memoir and those which followed were actually sent to Perpignan, even though no traces of this correspondence are now to be found in the province of Roussillon itself. The absence of such traces is not altogether surprising in view of Le Paige's explicit instructions to Deydé to recopy his memoranda so that his identity would remain unknown and

edition of their constitutions to the court.[81] And the court had moreover done this against the expressed wishes of the acting attorney general, François de Vilar, who in his conclusions on the king's edict had demanded its pure and simple registration.[82] The magistrates hostile to the Jesuits therefore regarded the attorney general as untrustworthy, and on March 20 contrived to persuade the court not to communicate the Jesuits' constitutions to the attorney general at all, but to reserve the all-important task of examining these to Salelles himself.[83] Although Salelles and his allies still hoped "to be able to render a definitive judgment on the institutes and the edict of the month of March," they feared "that it is against the rules to be able to pronounce concerning the institute without a previous *appel comme d'abus* lodged by the attorney general, who will not have been heard except by virtue of his requisition on the edict of the month of March. . . . I pray you," he therefore requested Deydé, "to communicate our doubts to your friend [Le Paige] and to ask him to send me his reflections soon."[84]

Now the attorney general was the king's directly appointed representative in all *affaires publiques,* and as Le Paige well knew, a court could not legally judge a case under this category unless it had at least considered the conclusions of the attorney general. Moreover, the attorney general could not logically deliver his conclusions to the court unless he had taken official cognizance of the evidence, which in this case was the Jesuits' constitutions. Le Paige could therefore only warn Salelles, in his response of May 13, that "it will be rather difficult not to ask the *gens du roi* for their conclusions on the institute." But rather than either communicate the constitutions to the attorney general or attempt to bypass him altogether, "the route one can follow," Le Paige suggested, was to communicate Salelles's *Compte rendu* of the constitutions to the attorney general instead of the constitutions themselves and then request his conclusions on this. If his conclusions "are not good, or not good enough, the parlement will just

his "handwriting not be sent there. It is known," he warned Deydé. "I am sure you understand the consequences." (See ibid., ms. 186, Le Paige to Deydé, March 26, 1762.) The recopied memoranda would have come into the hands of Salelles, but unfortunately no Salelles papers are to be found either in the departmental archives or with the present Massia family.

81. A.D.P.O.: *conseil souverain* of Roussillon, "Arrêts civils enregistrés," 2B 702, March 17, 1762. Most of the *conseil souverain's arrêts* in the affair of the Jesuits were printed, and Le Paige conveniently united them in a single volume (B.P.R.: L.P. 866). But unless, for reasons now inscrutable to me, I did not note them in the *conseil's* archives, I will refer to this source rather than to the printed *arrêts.*

82. A.D.P.O.: *conseil souverain* of Roussillon, "Minutes des arrêts civils," 2 B 548, March 17, 1762.

83. Ibid., "Registre des délibérations," 2 B 88, July 19, 1755–August 17, 1774; March 20, 1762.

84. B.P.R.: L.P. 583, ms. 190, Salelles to Deydé, April 26, 1762.

the same have the right to pronounce whatever it wishes, and even to receive the attorney general *appelant comme d'abus,* though he himself did not request it." Somewhat indiscreetly, it would seem, Le Paige went so far as to cite a precedent of 1719 in the registers of the parlement of Paris to prove that a parlement could dispense with the *appel comme d'abus* altogether and simply pronounce the constitutions abusive. Given these "circumstances and the importance of not wasting time in useless delays," Le Paige strongly urged the Roussillonais "to declare immediately that the Jesuits' constitutions are abusive." It would be too dangerous," he warned, "to permit an affair to drag on which has already lasted nearly a year."[85]

The Roussillonais were hardly in need of Le Paige's thinly veiled invitation to precipitation and illegality. On the contrary, the tempo of the affair in Perpignan was such that his counsels were once again rendered largely pointless by the time they arrived there, probably toward the end of May. For one thing, Salelles had delivered his *Compte rendu* of the Jesuits' constitutions on May 21, and in response the *conseil souverain* had decided on May 26 to deliberate defintively on the entire affair the following June 12.[86] Now this blistering schedule clearly left insufficient time to take up the subject of the Jesuits' doctrine, which, though Le Paige had several times harped upon it, Salelles's *Compte rendu* had hardly touched on at all. In answer to Le Paige's memoir, Salelles therefore proposed "to separate the doctrine from the institute" and dissolve the Jesuit Order in Roussillon on the basis of an examination of the king's edict and the constitutions alone. Later, "when the question arises of examining the [Jesuits'] ethical teachings, we will request [of the parlement of Paris] a copy of the assertions; today," he insisted, "they can only retard and obstruct our progress."[87]

Far more important, however, Salelles had neglected to inform Le Paige that on April 20 he and his allies had succeeded in eliminating as judges in the affair the counselors André Cappot and Michel Serra, both vocally in favor of the Jesuits, on the grounds that neither had been present at the session of March 17, when the attorney general had presented his conclusions on the royal edict. But the two magistrates had consented to their exclusion only with the under-

---

85. Ibid., ms. 192, memoir of Le Paige for the *conseil souverain* of Roussillon. This memoir is undated, but ms. 193, a communication from Salelles to Deydé, contains a "réponse du mémoire du 13 mai" which, in fact, concerns Le Paige's memoir, ms. 192. Hence my conjecture that ms. 192 can be dated May 13, 1762.

86. *Compte rendu de l'institut et constitutions des soi-disans Jésuites par M. de Salelles.* Also, A.D.P.O.: *conseil souverain* of Perpignan, "Registre des délibérations," 2 B 88, July 19, 1755–August 17, 1774; May 26, 1762.

87. B.P.R.: L.P. 583, ms. 193, copy of a letter from Salelles to Deydé, undated; but an accompanying letter by Deydé to Le Paige, ms. 191, dates its reception in Paris at June 7, 1762.

standing "that when following the communication of the constitutions to the attorney general there would be new conclusions whether provisory or definitive these *messieurs* would without doubt have the right to judge."[88] Now in reality Salelles and his allies were far from intending that Cappot and Serra should judge in any part the affair of the Jesuits. In effect, at least eight judges had shown themselves favorable to the Jesuits during the affair, and in a small court of only fifteen active members, that was not an inconsiderable number.[89] It was therefore imperative, from Salelles's point of view, that as many of their votes be eliminated as possible, and even though on May 7 he and his friends successfully eliminated three more, this time on the grounds of personal relations and connections with the accused order, the votes of Cappot and Serra could still be decisive on June 12.[90] For Salelles, then, there could be no question of following Le Paige's advice by communicating either the constitutions or anything else to the attorney general, for this would entail both new conclusions on the part of the attorney general and the right to vote for the two excluded counselors. While Salelles's dubious tactics ensured that the judgment against the Jesuits would be on the borders of legality at best, he was willing enough, as he confided to Deydé, to "sin a little" for the sake of the "good cause."[91]

What now preoccupied Salelles was how to preserve the semblance of legality and, more specifically, how to handle a predictably hostile François de Vilar on June 12, the day of definitive deliberation. Should the *conseil souverain* avoid summoning the attorney general altogether, he asked Le Paige, and instead derive the entire judgment against the Jesuits from a consideration of the edict of March alone? Or—and this was Salelles's preference—should the court rather call in the attorney general, ask him simply if he persisted in his conclusions on the edict of March, and deal with any new conclusions or a request for the constitutions on his part as best it might?[92] Le Paige strongly advised Salelles in favor of the first of these alternatives— "to avoid above all any new conclusions" —but he could not have mailed his reply before June 7, and it is possible that it did not reach Perpignan by June 12.[93] What is certain is that the *conseil souverain* heeded not Le Paige's advice but rather Salelles's, and summoned the attorney general on June 12. Quite possibly Salelles perceived that the counselors Cappot and Serra had not come to the session and that there was no serious danger in

88. A.D.P.O.: *conseil souverain* of Roussillon, "Registre des délibérations," 2 B 88, July 19, 1755–August 17, 1774, April 20, 1762.

89. Torreilles, ed., *Mémoires de M. Jaume,* pp. 106–08. See also his *Collège de Perpignan,* pp. 392–96.

90. A.D.P.O.: *conseil souverain* of Roussillon, "Registre des délibérations," 2 B 88, May 7, 1762.

91. B.P.R.: L.P. 583, ms. 193.

92. Ibid.

93. Ibid., ms. 94, memoir by Le Paige for the *conseil souverain* of Perpignan, n.d.

risking new conclusions. In any case, an understandably outraged Vilar thereupon launched into a systematic condemnation of nearly all procedures which the *conseil souverain* had hitherto employed in the affair, and concluded by demanding that "these constitutions of which we have not taken cognizance ought to be communicated to us before the judgments which will determine their fate."[94]

His were strong words, to be sure, but they did not constitute the "new conclusions" which Le Paige and Salelles had feared. In fact, they were not conclusions at all, or rather they were anticonclusions, since Vilar had only demanded cognizance of the constitutions in order to be able to conclude.[95] But far from acceding to his demand, the ten magistrates present on June 12 did not even receive him *appelant comme d'abus*. Rather, following the model which Le Paige had quite incidentally divulged to Salelles in his memoir of May 14, they summarily and definitively declared the Jesuits' bulls and constitutions "abusive" and so dissolved the order in Roussillon. For the sake of a facade of legality, at the same time, the *conseil souverain* chose to regard Vilar's harangues as "conclusions" and included in its definitive judgment the assertion that the court had "heard the attorney general in his conclusions which he had left on the Bureau, on the date of this day, June 12."[96] To the unhappy Vilar the court, as Le Paige had suggested, left the task of reporting on the Jesuits' doctrine as exemplified in the *Extraits des assertions,* which Salelles had officially requested of the parlement of Paris on June 12.[97] It must be credited to the attorney general that on April 12, 1763, the day scheduled for his report, he maintained that it was incompatible with "the dignity of the Ministry" which he had "the honor to fulfill" that he play the role assigned to him.[98] The judgment of June 12, he pointed out, had already prejudiced the results of the court's investigations, which could not conceivably find the Jesuits' doctrines to be innocent "without destroying your own work and even the foundations upon which it rests."[99]

The expulsion of the Jesuits in Roussillon, then, indicates both the limits and the extent to which the theory of "union" among the various "classes" reflected

94. A.D.P.O.: *conseil souverain* of Roussillon, "Minute des arrêts civils," 2 B 549, June 12, 1762, "Réquisitoire du procureur général."

95. This was in fact de Vilar's intention. He knew very well that the *conseil souverain* was going to render its definitive judgment, no matter what he did, but in order to wash his hands of the whole procedure, he had resolved to force the *conseil* to act illegally by bypassing his conclusions. See Torreilles, ed., *Mémoires de M. Jaume,* pp. 108–09.

96. Ibid., p. 109. Also see *Extrait des registres de la cour du conseil souverain de Roussillon. Du 12 juin 1762 in Compte rendu de l'institut et constitutions des soi-disans Jésuites, par M. de Salelles,* pp. 1–2, 7.

97. *Arrest de conseil souverain de Roussillon. Du 24 août 1762,* in ibid., pp. 10–11.

98. *Compte rendu par M. le procureur général du roi des livres de doctrine et morale des ci-devant soi-disans Jésuites,* in *Comptes, arrests et arrestés, du conseil souverain de Roussillon* (1763), p. 43.

99. Ibid., pp. 40–41. See also *Nouvelles Ecclésiastiques* (December 31, 1763), pp. 214–15.

parliamentary practice in mid-eighteenth century France. Limits, first of all, because as the case of Perpignan clearly demonstrates, the Roussillonais more often than not chose to ignore Le Paige's counsels and to follow their proper inclinations. Preoccupied by the national scene and knowing little about the particular situation in Perpignan, Le Paige constantly urged the Roussillonais to conform to the patterns of Paris and Rouen. But since local circumstances were not susceptible to either of these models, the Roussillonais quite freely used what they could from Le Paige's memoirs and disregarded the rest. Yet for a small, peripherally located, and relatively inexperienced court like Perpignan, the importance of Le Paige's good offices and simple encouragement should not be underestimated. Without this encouragement and the precedent of 1719, which Le Paige quite incidentally revealed to them, it is most doubtful that the Roussillonais would have taken the audacious route they finally did. And if Salelles and his friends had ever suspected that the parlement of Paris might abandon them in an hour of need, it is very probable that they would never have asserted themselves in the affair of the Jesuits at all.

The relatively ample documentation on Le Paige's connections with the *conseil souverain* of Roussillon during the affair of the Jesuits is unhappily unique. Elsewhere, the extent and even the existence of his influence is extremely difficult, if not impossible, to ascertain. It is certain that both Le Paige and his friend Counselor Le Febvre de Saint-Hilaire were in regular correspondence with members of the parlement of Toulouse, where the existence of a strong pro-Jesuitical party led by First President François de Bastard made it impossible to follow Le Paige's urgings to pronounce definitively against the Institute without a suspensive *appel comme d'abus*.[100] Traces also exist of connections with the parlements of Pau and Dijon, and as late as December 1764 we find Le Paige consoling the counselor Renard for the fact that his company, the parlement of Besançon, had chosen to draft remonstrances against the king's edict of November 1764, which finally supressed the Jesuit Order throughout the realm.[101]

100. For Toulouse, see B.P.R.: L.P. 583, ms. 176, a memoir by Le Paige in all probability to Toulouse, because it seems to be a reply to ms. 226, an unsigned letter from a Toulousian magistrate to—again probably—Le Febvre de Saint-Hilaire. "Ne seroit-il pas possible,' this magistrate asks, concerning the possibility of a definitive *arrêt* without *appel comme d'abus,* "de faire dresser en payant, par quelque avocat instruit, une consultation sur ce point, au plutôt? Voudriez vous vous charger de la faire faire? Parmi les avocats qui ont dressé la Consultation de Lionci, et qui certainement connoissent l'institut à fonds, vous en trouverez aisément quelqu'un qui voudra bien s'en charger." My speculation is that Le Febvre de Saint-Hilaire chose Le Paige for this purpose, and that ms. 176 constitutes the requested "consultation," which was sent, in one form or another, to Toulouse. More correspondence with Toulouse is to be found in L.P. 136, but the hopelessly unorganized state of this *receui* makes it difficult to use.

101. For Pau, see ibid., ms. 241; for Dijon, ms. 240; and for Besançon, mss. 148–51 *bis*.

Generally, the letters from these parlements came to Le Febvre de Saint-Hilaire, who passed them on to Le Paige for his erudite responses. But the care which Le Paige usually expended to cover his tracks, the often circumlocutious character of his connections with the provinces, the unsigned communications received from those quarters—in short, the exasperatingly secretive nature of all this evidence—render it fragmentary and inconclusive at best. Even in the case of Roussillon, Salelles never knew that it was Le Paige with whom he was corresponding, and one looks in vain for Le Paige's tracks in the province itself. But the evidence indeed attests to the fact that Le Paige's theory of the "union of classes" was more than a theory alone.

By the late spring of 1762 the Jesuits' situation was desperate indeed. Besides Roussillon and Normandy, the parlements of both Bordeaux and Brittany had pronounced definitively against the Jesuits; the parlements of Paris, Toulouse, Aix-en-Provence, and Metz had rendered provisional judgments against the order; and the parlements of Grenoble, Metz, Besançon, and Pau were already occupied with the Jesuits' constitutions.[102] Only the parlement of Douai and the *conseil souverain* of Colmar had not yet acted at all. More serious, perhaps, were the facts that Versailles not only permitted the parlements to disregard the edict of March but remained totally inactive when, on April 1, the parlement of Paris closed the Jesuit colleges within its jurisdictions. The rumor swiftly got around that Versailles had definitively resigned itself to the destruction of the Jesuits and even secretly desired it.[103] On March 31 Rolland d'Erceville sent Le Paige "first-hand" information to the effect that no *lit de justice* would be held to register the edict of March, "that is to say that they [the ministry] will permit the parlements to continue their course, and consequently that they are not displeased with it."[104] The rumor was far from unfounded. On April 4 Louis XV himself wrote to the chancellor that he believed it "necessary to promulgate

---

102. For Bordeaux, *Arrêt de la cour de parlement, du 20 mai 1762*, in *Compte rendu des constitutions des Jésuites, par M. Pierre-Jules Dudon, avocat-général du roi au parlement de Bordeaux*, pp. 247–48; for Brittany, *Arrêt du parlement de Bretagne, qui juge l'appel comme d'abus interjeté par M. le procureur général du roi, des brefs, bulles, constitutions, etc., concernant les soi-disans Jésuites. Du 27 mai 1762* (Rennes); for Toulouse, *Arrêt du parlement de Toulouse. Extrait des registres du parlement. Du 5 juin 1762*; for Aix, *Arrêt du parlement de Provence. Du 5 juin 1762*; for Metz, *Réquisitoire de M. le procureur général du parlement de Metz, au sujet des soi-disans Jésuites, a MM. du parlement. Arrêt de la cour de parlement, rendu chambres et semestres assemblées. Du 28 mai 1762* (Metz); and for Pau, *Arrestés du parlement de Pau. Des 15 mars, 23 avril et 4 mai 1762, et Arrest du parlement de Rouen. Du 6 mai 1762*.

103. *Nouvelles Ecclésiastiques* (October 19, 1762), p. 166. See also B.P.R.: L.P. 583, ms. 65.

104. B.P.R.: L.P. 583, ms. 64, March 31, 1762. Since the manuscript is Le Paige's copy of a letter to himself, I have been unable to identify the author by an examination of the handwriting.

a declaration whereby I reserve to myself the superiority and nominations of all
the positions of the colleges previously conducted by the Jesuits, but by avoiding
to speak of them"—evidence, seemingly, that Louis XV had resigned himself
to their destruction.[105] In Rouen the harassed first president Miromesnil wrote to
Saint-Florentin: "it appears to me that their [the Jesuits'] fate has been decided;
it would therefore be superfluous to discuss them any further."[106] By April 28 an
ecstatic Le Paige was no longer sure whether he was "awake . . . or dreaming,
at the sight of what is happening."[107]

Yet despite these indications, it was not until nearly two and a half years
later, in November 1764, that Louis XV finally sanctioned his parlements'
actions with a royal declaration dissolving the Jesuit Order in all of France. In
the course of these two and a half years—or at least until 1763—the royal will
remained curiously suspended, equally torn, apparently, in opposite directions,
which seemed now to favor, now to oppose, the parlements' measures. As Le
Paige himself recalled it, "the ministry . . . long contented itself to remain
silent . . . even refused to permit anyone to hope for cooperation on its part
. . . sometimes even appeared tacitly to authorize the demarches and circular
letters of M. the chancellor, which implied views wholly contrary to what the
parlements were doing."[108] How explain, then, these tergiversations on the
king's part? When precisely did he decide to second his parlement's efforts?
Why, finally, did he do so at all?

In mentioning the manuevers of Chancellor Lamoignon, Le Paige accurately
put his finger on at least one of the reasons why Louis XV so long hesitated
before actively cooperating with his parlements. The *Nouvelles Ecclésiastiques*
had long complained about the chancellor's "tender predilection" for the
Jesuits, a predilection which their recent reverses served only to accentuate.[109]
In May 1762—a full month after the parlement of Paris had closed the order's
colleges, and with provincial parlements everywhere entering the lists—the
undaunted Lamoignon undertook the defense of the Jesuits in a long memoir to
the king.[110] His efforts on behalf of the Jesuits were moreover vigorously supported by the dauphin, and together they exercised a far from negligible influence upon Louis XV.

But could they have seriously thought it possible to save the Jesuits after four
parlements had definitively proscribed them, after the parlement of Paris had

105. A.N.: A.P. 162 mi. (Archives du marquis de Rosanbo), *carton* 1, *dossier* 5, ms. 101,
Louis XV to Lamoignon, April 4, 1762.
106. B.M.R.: Collection Lebet, Y67, ms. 17, Miromesnil to Saint-Florentin, April 30, 1762.
107. B.P.R.: L.P. 583, ms. 76, seemingly a note by Le Paige to himself, April 28, 1762.
108. B.P.R.: L.P. 584, ms. 30, memoir for the parlement of Rouen, April 2, 1763.
109. *Nouvelles Ecclésiastiques* (March 21, 1767), p. 49.
110. A.N.: A.P. 162 mi. (Archives du marquis de Rosanbo), *carton* 1, *dossier* 5, ms. 97,
memoir by the chancellor, May 1762.

successfully closed their colleges within its wide jurisdiction, and after seven more parlements had already taken up their case? Probably not within the realm as a whole. Yet there remained the possibility that the Jesuits might be preserved in one or two individual provinces, as in fact was done following their first proscription under Henry IV. From such a base and with the help of a revivified monarchical authority, the Jesuits could aspire eventually to reestablish themselves throughout the realm. In the spring of 1762 they could still lift up their eyes toward the provinces of Alsace and Flanders, which seemed uninclined to take up their case, and to the parlements of Besançon, Toulouse, and Aix, where the partisans of their expulsion had encountered heavy opposition. And of all these, it was soon the parlement of Aix-en-Provence that occupied their particular attention. On June 21 the chancellor Lamoignon received a request from the Jesuits of Provence to annul the parlement's provisional sentence of June 5 on the grounds of illegality.[111]

The affair of the Jesuits began in Aix on March 6, 1762, when the solicitor general, Le Blanc de Castillon, following the examples of Paris, Rouen, Rennes, and Toulouse, demanded the delivery of the Jesuits' constitutions to the *greffe* of the parlement.[112] The parlement ordered accordingly, and the affair of the Jesuits was therefore already under way when the king's edict of reform arrived in Aix a few days later. This edict Le Blanc de Castillon presented to the assembled chambers on March 15. Predictably, instead of presenting his conclusions concerning the edict on the spot, the solicitor general requested that the already delivered Jesuit constitutions be officially communicated to him so that, instructed by his *Compte rendu* of these, the parlement might act more knowledgeably upon the edict.[113] The date originally set by the parlement for this *Compte rendu* was April 27, but the *gens du roi* obtained two successive delays before Jean-Pierre-François Ripert de Monclar, the parlement's attorney general, delivered his celebrated *Compte rendu* during the three sessions of May 28, June 3 and 4. His conclusions of June 4 requested that he be received *appelant comme d'abus* of the Jesuits' constitutions and papal bulls, that the provincial superior of the Jesuit Order be notified to this effect, and that the usual "provisional" measures of precaution—the closing of the Jesuits' colleges, congregations, and novitiates and the prohibition of further vows—be undertaken before the definitive judgment.[114]

111. Ibid., *dossier* 6, ms. 52, chancellor to dauphin, June 21, 1762.

112. *Arrest du parlement de Provence. Du 6 mars 1762.* All the *arrêts* and *arrêtés* of the parlement of Provence concerning the Jesuits, as well as Monclar's *Compte rendu* and the numerous anonymous pamphlets published about the troubles in Aix, were conveniently bound together by Le Paige in two volumes (B.P.R.: L.P. 859–60, *Aix contre les Jésuites*).

113. *Extrait des registres du parlement de Provence. Du lundi 15 mars 1762*, p. 8.

114. *Compte rendu des constitutions des Jésuits, par M. Jean-Pierre-François Ripert de Monclar, procureur général du roi au parlement de Provence* (1763), pp. 261–82.

For the Jesuits' enemies at Aix, so far was so good. It was at this juncture, however, that the plot began seriously to thicken. Monclar's *Compte rendu,* which he finished reading at ten o'clock on the morning of June 4, was immediately followed by a short and favorable report delivered by Joseph François de Gallice, the *doyen* of the parlement. The court had already begun to opine concerning the whole when the counselor Beaurecueil presented a request on the part of the Jesuits of Aix, Toulon, Arles, and Apt to be heard on the subject of the attorney general's accusations against them. This request the parlement sent to the attorney general, who immediately concluded against its admission on the grounds that the judgment to be rendered was only a provisional *appel comme d'abus,* and that the time for such a request was after the *appel comme d'abus* and before the definitive judgment. By a narrow margin the parlement voted in favor of Monclar's conclusions, even though the Jesuits' request opposed not the provisional *appel comme d'abus* itself but rather the provisional precautionary measures which were both legally separable from it and in fact prejudicial to its outcome. On the following day, moreover, the parlement narrowly overruled another counselor, Morel de Mons, when the later demanded that the attorney general deliver his conclusions on the king's edict of March. Monclar and the parlement's majority opposed this demand on the grounds that they could not act upon the king's edict until they had been thoroughly instructed on the subject of the Jesuits' constitutions; yet this lack of instruction, real enough though it undoubtedly was, did not prevent the parlement from receiving the attorney general *appelant comme d'abus* and voting the precautionary measures he had requested, and all this on the very same day. On June 5, in other words, the parlement of Aix had rendered a provisional judgment against the Jesuits with the aid of only the merest shadow of a report on the attorney general's hastily read *Compte rendu,* without any parliamentary examination of either, and without even the ability to perform one, since the attorney general had not deemed it appropriate to deposit his *Compte rendu* at the *greffe* of the parlement. Seeing themselves outmaneuvered, twenty-two magistrates favorable to the Jesuits refused to participate in the discussion which preceded the provisional judgment on the grounds that they were not sufficiently instructed, and on June 7 nineteen of these signed and sent a letter of protestation to Chancellor Lamoignon.[115]

Whether any of the parlement's actions were strictly speaking illegal or not is

115. Ripert de Monclar, *Motifs des arrêts et arrêtés du parlement de Provence, des 5, 19 et 30 juin, 2, 4, 6 et 7 octobre, concernant l'affaire des soi-disans Jésuites,* henceforth referred to as *Motifs des arrêts et arrêtés du parlement de Provence,* pp. 12–46. See also *Relation de ce qui s'est passé au parlement d'Aix, dans l'affaire des Jésuites,* pp. 1–11; *Journal des arrêts et arrêtés du parlement de Provence,* pp. 1–6; and the letter of the 19 magistrates dated June 7 and printed in Carayon, ed., *Mémoires du président d'Eguilles sur le parlement d'Aix et les Jésuites, addressés à S.M. Louis XV,* pp. 6–16.

debatable, and was in fact hotly debated at the time. In defense of the parlement of Aix it might be observed that its sins were merely venial in comparison to those of Perpignan and Rouen. Suffice it to say that if the majority at Aix had been sincerely interested in rendering justice to the Jesuits, they would not have acted so cavalierly as they did. But what made the trial of the Jesuits at Aix into a national affair was not the parlement's judicial irregularities but the existence of a numerically considerable and resolute minority of magistrates who were quite determined to defend the Jesuits, some of them until the bitter end. Yet to call them defenders of the Jesuits is perhaps to unduly prejudice the issue against them. The group's leader, President Boyer d'Eguilles, was not educated by the Jesuits, was certainly not a member of their congregation at Aix, and seems to have had no personal contact with members of the order until 1762.[116] For him, as for at least some of the others, the expulsion of the Jesuits was only one of many manifestations of the French parlement's progressive usurpation of both royal and ecclesiastical authority which had begun in the early 1750s with the quarrel over the refusal of sacraments. As early as 1754, in fact, D'Eguilles and twelve of his colleagues had publically disassociated themselves from their company's remonstrances and judgments, which, according to D'Eguilles, "contained treatises concerning the substance of doctrine," usurped the place of "canonical decisions," and condemned everyone "who had ever preferred his own lights and the decisions of the first pastors to the theology of the bar."[117] Even within the context of the affair of the Jesuits, D'Eguilles did not question a monarch's right "to eliminate within his states a Religious order whose constitutions he believed to be incompatible with the public law of his Realm, or with the actual state of his affairs," but found it impossible to forgive the parlements for having condemned "the intrinsic nature of the Institute itself," for having declared "detestable what the Holy Spirit had declared pious in the last Ecumenical Council," and for having done all this against the expressed wishes of their king.[118]

In any case, the rift which D'Eguilles and his party opened up within the parlement of Aix on June 7 grew alarmingly wider on June 14 and 19, when the parlement's majority declared counselors Thorame, De Mons, and Coriolis—all three adherents to the pro-Jesuitical minority—"suspect" and therefore incompetent as judges in the affair because of their affiliation with the accused order's

116. This was the case, at least, according to D'Eguilles himself. See Carayon, ed., *Mémoires du président d'Eguilles*, pp. 40–43.

117. Ibid., pp. 279–83. See also *Relation de ce qui s'est passé au parlement d'Aix dans l'affaire des Jésuites, depuis le 6 mars 1762 et de ce qui a été statué par le roi, sur cette affaire, le 23 décembre* (1763), p. 3.

118. Boyer d'Eguilles and the abbé de Montvallon, *Mémoires presentés au roi par deux magistrats du parlement d'Aix, contre les arrêts et arrêtés de leur compagnie*, second memoir, pp. 16–18.

local congregation. All three magistrates accepted the judgment at the time, but later, on October 2, both Coriolis and Thorame vainly protested it on the grounds that they had understood their exclusion to apply only to judgments concerning the Jesuit congregations in particular, but not to those concerning the order as a whole.[119] Worse yet, on June 30 the attorney general demanded and obtained the commencement of a disciplinary procedure against the octogenarian counselor, Montvallon, who, during the stormy session of June 5, had indiscreetly accused Monclar of having propounded several inaccuracies in his *Compte rendu*. Whether well-founded or not, Montvallon's accusation had somehow found its way into a pro-Jesuitical pamphlet which was circulating in Aix, and the attorney general's public reputation was at stake.[120] Unfortunately for the company's already precarious internal tranquillity, Montvallon the elder had two sons, both of whom had followed him into the parlement of Aix, and who now jumped to the defense of their father's impugned integrity.[121]

It was amid these embittered circumstances that Boyer d'Eguilles—"that singular man, true phenomenon within the Magistracy, and who has no likeness in history, except perhaps among the ancient heroes of the errant chivalry"— undertook his first journey to Versailles in the company of several of his colleagues during the month of August.[122] Here, according to his *Mémoires*, he was favorably received by the comte de Saint-Florentin and Chancellor Lamoignon, for whom he composed, with the help of his colleague, the abbé de Montvallon, the first of his memoirs to the king.[123] Although D'Eguilles's personal intervention at Versailles did not immediately obtain the desired annulment of the

119. Monclar, *Motifs des arrêts et arrêtés du parlement de Provence*, pp. 46–49, 55–60, 65–73. See also the "Extraits des délibérations" of the parlement on this subject in A.N.: K707, mss. 17 and 20; and *Journal des arrêts et arrêtés du parlement de Provence*, pp. 8–10, 11–51.

120. The pamphlet was entitled *Relation de ce qui s'est passé au parlement d'Aix, dans l'affaire des Jésuites*, which repeated Montvallon *père*'s accusation on p. 5. For the session of June 30, 1762, see A.N.: K707, ms. 18, "Extrait de délibération contenant la plainte de M. le procureur général des imputations à luy faites par m. de Montvallon père, du 30 juin 1762"; and Ripert de Monclar, *Motif des arrêts et arrêtés du parlement de Provence*, pp. 50–55.

121. The counselor, Montvallon *fils*, and the abbé Montvallon, a counselor-clerk. The latter avowed coauthorship, with Boyer d'Eguilles, of the two *Mémoires présentés au roi*. The parlement's disciplinary judgment, of May 17, 1763, deprived him of his functions of magistrate and banished him from the province of Provence for 20 years. The same judgment deprived Montvallon *fils* and *père* of their offices. (See *Arrest de la cour du parlement de Provence, rendu les chambres assemblées, sur la procédure en mercuriale, contre M. le président d'Eguilles, M. l'abbé de Montvallon et autres. Du 17 mai 1763.*)

122. *Nouvelles Ecclésiastiques* (March 14, 1763), p. 45.

123. D'Eguilles and Montvallon, *Mémoires*. The first memoir clearly announced the intention of D'Eguilles and his adherents, "to undertake an act of secession" from their parlement if the king did not himself annul the judgments and rulings in question. See first memoir, pp. 8–10. For D'Eguilles's first trip to Versailles and his reception there, see Carayon, ed., *Mémoires du président d'Eguilles*, pp. 28–31.

parlement's judgments of June 5, 19, and 30, it did result, on September 9, in a
letter to the parlement's first president, Galois de la Tour, from Chancellor
Lamoignon. The chancellor's letter ordered the first president to suspend the
execution of all the parlement's judgments and rulings in the affair of the
Jesuits until he had explained their motivation to the chancellor.[124] Predictably,
however, the chancellor's letter fared no better in Aix than had the edict of
March. Assembled to deliberate concerning the letter in the first session after its
yearly recess, on October 2, the parlement first denied the right of the counselors Thorame and Coriolis to deliberate, then decided that there was no viable
reason to deliberate at all, since the royal will could only be recognized in letters
patent from the king, not in a simple letter from the chancellor to the first
president. No sooner was this decision taken than thirteen magistrates at least
partially executed their resolution to secede from the majority by leaving the
court at once, and by October 7 President D'Eguilles and the abbé de Montvallon, who were among the thirteen, were on their way to Fontainebleau.[125]

There D'Eguilles and Montvallon produced a second memoir for the king
which had more effect than the first—that is, letters patent from the king, dated
October 22, 1762, which ordered the parlement to suspend the execution of all
its judgments and rulings in the affair of the Jesuits until the king decided otherwise, and ordered the attorney general in particular to justify the behavior of the
parlement during the period from June 4 until October 7. Confronted with
such unmistakable evidence of the royal will, the parlement reluctantly registered the letters patent on November 12, while at the same time describing
them as "an imposition without example upon the good faith of the king" and
formally disobeying one of their stipulations by limiting the duration of the
ordered suspension to January 3.[126]

Now it was the majority's turn to send delegations to Versailles. While Ripert
de Monclar prepared his pamphlet-size defense of the parlement of Aix—complete with calumnious and irrelevant asides on the "romance" of President
D'Eguilles's life—the parlement sent Counselor Galiffet to Versailles to plead
its case in person.[127] D'Eguilles, for his part, was also soon back in Versailles, but

124. For a copy of this letter, see *Suite du Journal des arrêts et arrêtés du parlement de Provence
concernant l'affaire des soi-disans Jésuites,* pp. 5–10.

125. Ibid., pp. 1–4. See also A.N.: K707, ms. 17, "Extrait des dires et arrêtés sur l'opposition à l'arrêté du 19 juin 1762 qui déclara les officiers congrégationistes suspects et ne peuvent
opiner dans l'affaire des Jésuites," as well as an account of the session in Monclar, *Motif
des arrêts et arrêtés du parlement de Provence,* ibid., ms. 8, pp. 55–59, 62–64.

126. A.N.: K707, ms. 5, First President La Tour to Gilbert de Voisins, November 12, 1762;
and ms. 21, "Extrait de la réquisition de M. le procureur général. Arrêt et arrêté du parlement de Provence sur les lettres patentes du 22 octobre 1762. Du 12 novembre 1762,"
Ripert de Monclar's *Motifs des arrêts et arrêtés du parlement de Provence,* esp. pp. 3–6, was the
product of these letters patent.

127. *Arrêté du parlement de Provence du 27 novembre 1762 portant députation de M. le conseiller*

unfortunately fell sick shortly after arriving there, which seriously diminished his effectiveness.[128] Worse yet, his presence in Versailles and even his cause now constituted an embarrassment for Louis XV. During the month of November, D'Eguilles's two memoirs to the king had been somehow published—by whom remains a mystery—and all the parlements of France, including of course the parlement of Paris, were fairly stumbling over each other in their zeal to condemn them.[129] The case of Monclar, Galiffet, and the majority at Aix against D'Eguilles was now the case of nearly all the various "classes" of the "sole and unique" parlement of France; for Louis XV, the occasion to attempt a policy of divide and conquer was certainly not the affair of Aix. And to make matters even worse for D'Eguilles and his crew, numbers of its original adherents had abandoned its ship as the storm grew more violent, so that by the month of December, D'Eguilles was left with only nine adherents, most of whom were so interrelated as to make it look like a family affair.[130]

It was now for Louis XV to decide, but by the month of December the affair of Aix was only the most important case he had to decide. On December 1 the none too numerous enemies of the Jesuits at the parlement of Besançon, employing a tactic used successfully at Perpignan, tried to exclude as judges two magistrates favorable to the order, on the grounds that these two had not been present at the previous sessions devoted to the case. When the matter came to a vote, it was discovered that the number of magistrates on either side of the issue was equal—twenty-five against twenty-five—and the parlement was left with no choice except to send the case to the chancellor for his decision.[131] When the matter came before the *conseil des dépêches* on December 10, Louis XV postponed a decision by ordering both sides to send him justificatory memoirs.[132] But a

de Gallifet pour se rendre auprès du roi in *IIIe suite du Journal des arrêts et arrêtés du parlement de Provence concernant l'affaire des Jésuites,* pp. 3–5.

128. Carayon, ed., *Mémoires du président d'Eguilles,* pp. 32–34.

129. Ibid., pp. 116–18. D'Eguilles argues with every appearance of sincerity that neither he nor any of his "party" were responsible for the publication of his two memoirs to the king. He also points out that it was "Simon, imprimeur du parlement de Paris, qui en a vendu les deux premières éditions à toute le ville. Qu'on l'oblige," he demanded, "a dire de qui il a tenu son manuscrit; et en remontant ensuite de l'un à l'autre, rien ne sera si aisé que de découvrir le véritable auteur de cette publication qu'on me reproche" (p. 116). So far as I know, no such investigation was ever undertaken. But the only people who could have received copies—or at least official communication—of the memoirs were the members of the *conseil des dépêches,* and suspicion falls quite naturally upon the duc de Choiseul or Gilbert de Voisins.

130. Boyer d'Eguilles, André de Montvallon, et al., "Le Procès des Jésuites: Letters du président d'Eguilles et des conseillers à André de Montvallon, *Nouvelle Revue Rétrospective,* deuzième serie (January-June, 1901), p. 236.

131. *Arrêsté du parlement de Besançon en partage de voix. Extrait des registres du parlement, à la séance de mercredi matin premier décembre 1762,* pp. 1–2.

132. *Extrait des registres du conseil d'état dur oi. Du 10 décembre 1762,* pp. 5–6.

definitive decision had to be taken before too long. At about the same time—November 23—the chancellor received letters from the first presidents of the parlements of Douai and Toulouse, both of which urgently requested the king to dispense clear advice on what tactics to employ in the affair of the Jesuits.[133] The first president at Douai cleverly succeeded in preventing the Jesuits' case from ever occupying the attention of his parlement, "whose inaction and lack of zeal" were notorious, but the position of the first president of the parlement of Toulouse, François de Bastard, was particularly critical.[134] Newly appointed as first president in November, Bastard took control of a parlement which the affair of the Jesuits had profoundly divided and in which the defenders of the order had succeeded in transforming a projected definitive judgment into a merely provisional one on June 5. Bastard himself was favorably disposed toward the Jesuits and of a mind to prevent the definitive judgment against them if he could. But this definitive judgment was scheduled to begin on January 15, and if he were to block it, Bastard needed all the help that Versailles could give.[135]

By the time he reached Toulouse in November, Bastard seems to have been laboring under the illusion that he was going to get this help, mainly, it appears, on the basis of indications from the chancellor and the dauphin. Certainly that is the way he subsequently behaved. But unfortunately for him, the chancellor and the dauphin did not make policy at Versailles, and the fact that they themselves were perfectly aware that the breezes there were not blowing in their direction is quite evident in their correspondence during the months of November and December. When the letters from Douai and Toulouse arrived at the end of November, the chancellor confided to the dauphin that he expected little good to come as a result of them "if His Majesty does not make up his mind by himself without consultations."[136] By December 5 Lamoignon deemed it "very important to shorten as much as possible the duration of M. Galiffet's stay in this region" and was "angry" that the parlement of Paris, too, wanted to condemn the memoirs of D'Eguilles.[137] As for his own plan for the resolution of the affair of Aix, which unfortunately we do not possess but which evidently

133. A.N.: A.P. 162 mi. (Archives du marquis de Rosanbo), carton 1, dossier 6, ms. 56, chancellor to dauphin, November 23, 1762.

134. On the parlement of Flanders at Douai, see the Nouvelles Ecclésiastiques (September 26, 1763), p. 158.

135. On François de Bastard and the trial of the Jesuits in the parlement of Toulouse, see the vicomte de Bastard d'Estang's Les Parlements de France: Essai sur leurs usages, leur organization et leur autorité (Paris, 1857), Vol. 2, pp. 50–200; but on Bastard, esp. pp. 120–21. See also the Nouvelles Ecclésiastiques (November 21 and December 5 and 12, 1763).

136. A.N.: A.P. 162 mi. (Archives du marquis de Rosanbo), carton 1, dossier 6, ms. 56, chancellor to dauphin, November 27, 1762.

137. Ibid., ms. 57, dauphin to chancellor, December 5, 1762.

already represented a compromise in his eyes, he thought it "the only thing which one can hope to see succeed."[138] And when, on December 8, the split vote at Besançon was occupying his attention, Lamoignon repeated to the dauphin that it was "very important . . . that the King decide this conflict without speaking to any other persons. Monseigneur understands very well what I have the honor to represent to him," he darkly added, "and in which I humbly request that he aid me."[139] By December 10 he ominously announced that he was no longer receiving "any indication of the King's intention concerning the affair of the Parlement of Provence."[140]

Unhappily, no absolutely certain indications exist concerning the identity of the "other persons" to whom the embattled chancellor referred, but among them was probably Gilbert de Voisins, one of the members of Louis XV's special commission appointed to examine the affair of the Jesuits in 1761 and, since that date, a regular member of the *conseil des dépêches*. What is certain is that after the Galiffet mission to Versailles in December, the principal actors on the side of the majority in Aix—Galiffet himself, First President La Tour, the attorney general, Monclar, and the solicitor general, Le Blanc de Castillon—all addressed their most confidential correspondence to Voisins, who merited, in the words of La Tour, "the particular gratitude of the Company."[141] More circumstantial evidence permits the conjecture that the duc de Choiseul, too, was among those to whom Lamoignon referred. Whatever his role in the early stages of the parliamentary attack on the Jesuits, Choiseul later freely admitted that, once the affair had begun, he came to recognize the order's sins and openly advocated its destruction.[142] This advocacy became even more pronounced when, after the definitive liquidation of the order in France, the French government first pressed for the expulsion of the Jesuits in the other Bourbon realms of Spain and Naples—achieved in 1767—and then, in concert with these governments, pushed for the total dissolution of the order by the papacy, which finally and reluctantly complied in 1773.[143]

In any case, and whatever the influences responsible, Louis XV finally decided the case of Aix on December 23. After an extraordinary session of the *conseil des dépêches* which lasted three hours, he ordered the comte de Saint-Florentin to tell the waiting Galiffet that "the two memoirs of M. d'Eguilles had made no impression on his mind, and that in consequence it was pointless to take cogni-

---

138. Ibid., ms. 58, chancellor to dauphin, December 6, 1762.
139. Ibid., ms. 66, chancellor to dauphin, December 8, 1762.
140. Ibid., ms. 62, chancellor to dauphin, December 10, 1762.
141. A.N.: K707, ms. 22, La Tour to Gilbert de Voisins, January 5, 1763. For the confidential nature of this correspondence in general, see esp. mss. 30, 51–53, 56.
142. Calmettes, ed., *Mémoires du duc de Choiseul*, p. 171.
143. For this story, see Pastor, *The History of the Popes*, Vol. 43, (St. Louis, 1952).

zance of them, that His Majesty was very satisfied with the fidelity, the zeal and the conduct of his Parlement of Aix, and that the deputy could return thence."[144] The triumphant Galiffet parted on the spot for Aix, where he arrived on New Year's day and announced the glad tidings to the assembled chambers of the parlement on January 3, 1763.[145]

"Thus it is that Justice and the Laws finally prevailed against the intrigues and calumnies of the Jesuits and those magistrates who were their only too faithful disciples," sententiously announced the *Nouvelles Ecclésiastiques* on March 21, 1763.[146] Le Paige, less solemn but no less gleeful, explained to Du Fossé at Rouen about two weeks later that, viewed in retrospect, the king's decision of December 23 was "a bolt of lightning for the Jesuits, who finally perceived that the government desired their destruction."[147] If by "government" Le Paige understood Louis XV himself, he undoubtedly exaggerated. Louis XV never actively "desired" their destruction; it is much closer to the truth to say that he reluctantly resigned himself to what seemed to be the inevitable. But Le Paige was hardly mistaken in seeing in Louis XV's decision of December 23 the origin of the government's tacit "concert begun three months ago with the parlement for this affair."[148] From that date, Versailles ceased to vacillate between alternative policies; all its decisions went in the general direction of the parlements' actions.

The first such decision came at the beginning of February 1763, when after careful consultation with representatives of both the parlement of Paris and the episcopacy, Louis XV sent to his parlements an edict which regulated the administration of the colleges recently vacated by the Jesuits, as well as letters patent providing for the destination of the revenues of benefices which had been united to these colleges, and a pension for those ex-Jesuits who were over thirty-three years old and had taken solemn vows.[149] For those like himself, who "saw things from nearby and knew the terrain," this "first legal act," Le Paige noted, was "regarded as a decision which said everything to those who wished to listen, and which . . . would become the germ of a multitude of other legal confirmations of what the parlements had done and imperceptibly lead the

144. *Nouvelles Ecclésiastiques* (March 21, 1763), p. 52.
145. A.N.: K707, ms. 27, La Tour to Gilbert de Voisins, January 5, 1763.
146. *Nouvelles Ecclésiastiques* (March 21, 1763), p. 52.
147. B.P.R.: L.P. 584, ms. 30, "Memoir for the parlement of Normandy," April 2, 1763.
148. Ibid.
149. *Edit du roi portant règlement pour les collèges qui ne dépendent pas des universités, donné à Versailles au mois de février 1763* (Paris, 1763); *Lettres patentes du roi, concernant l'administration d'une portion des biens de la compagnie et société des Jésuites. Données à Versailles le 2 février 1763* (Paris, 1763); and *Lettres patentes du roi, pour l'abréviation des procédures et la diminution des frais dans la discussion des biens des Jésuites. Données à Versailles, le 2 février 1763* (Paris, 1763), all in *Actes Royaux*, F21167.

government to issue, finally, some edict which would consummate forever the destruction of the society in France."[150] A bit later, when there was question of suspending the vengeful disciplinary procedure instituted by the victorious majority at Aix against D'Eguilles, the abbé de Montvallon, and eight of their adherents, Louis XV instructed an astounded Lamoignon to inform First President La Tour that "I do not think this is the occasion to suspend the course of justice."[151] Later still, Louis XV finally decided the case of Besançon against the two magistrates favorable to the Jesuits who wished to be judges in their case.

Le Paige also noted that the king's decision of December 23 "determined the parlements of Toulouse, Grenoble and Dijon, which would perhaps not have acted without this circumstance which made them perceive that their [the Jesuits] destruction was decided."[152] In this case Le Paige undoubtedly exaggerated the impact of the king's single decision; the relevant dates suggest that the motivation of these parlements should rather be attributed to the whole series of royal decisions culminating in the edict and letters patent of February 1763. The parlement at Dijon first occupied itself with the affair of the Jesuits on March 8, 1763, when it demanded a copy of the order's constitutions, and brought the trial to a speedy conclusion with a definitive judgment of suppression on July 11 of the same year.[153] At Grenoble the commissioners which the parlement had charged to report on the Jesuits' constitutions were prepared for their performance as early as August 21, 1762, but the rather numerous friends of the order succeeded in holding its enemies at bay until March 1763, when the impatient commissioners finally gave their report. The parlement of Dauphiné pronounced provisionally against the order on March 21, 1763, and definitively the following August 29.[154] And despite the determined resistance of François

150. B.P.R.: L.P. 584, ms. 30, "Memoir for the parlement of Normandy," April 2, 1763.
151. A.N.: A.P. 162 mi. (Archives du marquis de Rosanbo), *carton* 1, *dossier* 5, ms. 104, Louis XV to chancellor, February 15, 1763. For Lamoignon's immediate reaction, see ibid., *dossier* 6, ms. 63, chancellor to dauphin, February 15, 1763.
152. B.P.R.: L.P. 584, ms. 30, "Memoir for the parlement of Normandy," April 2, 1763.
153. *Arrêt du parlement de Bourgogne, qui expulse de son ressort les soi-disans Jésuites, du 11 juillet 1763*, in *Comptes rendus des établissements de l'institut et de la doctrine des soi-disans Jésuites, par les conseillers commissaires au parlement séant à Dijon, chambres assemblées, les 4, 5 et 6 juillet 1763 et arrêt définitif du 11 juillet 1763* (1763), pp. 1–34. The trial of the Jesuits was undertaken at Dijon without a great deal of enthusiasm and in return for the aid it had received from the parlement of Paris in its long and dangerous quarrel with Jacques Varenne, chief secretary of the estates of Bourgogne, supported by the ministry at Versailles. See La Cuisine, *Le Parlement de Bourgogne depuis son origine jusqu'à sa chute* (Dijon and Paris, 1864), Vol. 3, pp. 211–66; and Th. Foisset, *Le Président de Brosses. Histoire des lettres et des parlements au XVIII*e *siècle* (Paris, 1842), pp. 201–42.
154. For the trial of the Jesuits at the parlement of Dauphiné in Grenoble, see Jean Egret, *Le Parlement de Dauphiné et les affaires publiques dans le deuxième moitié du XVIII*e *siècle* (Grenoble, 1942), Vol 1, pp. 122–32.

de Bastard, the leaders of the anti-Jesuitical majority at Toulouse—the attorney general, Bonrepos, the counselor Bojat *père*, and François's father, Dominique de Bastard—finally brought the bitterly contested affair to definitive judgment on February 26, 1763.[155] To complete the list, the parlement of Pau in Navarre, neither last nor least, pronounced definitively against the Jesuits on April 28, 1763.[156] Of France's fourteen sovereign courts—or fourteen "classes" of a single sovereign court—only the *conseil souverain* at Colmar and the parlements of Douai and Besançon remained silent.[157] Or almost. The last of these parlements, that of Besançon, ended by drafting remonstrances against the royal edict of November 1764, which suppressed the Jesuit Order in all of France.

The parlement of Besançon perhaps deserves some special notice, not only because it eventually defended the Jesuits against the king's own edict of suppression, but because the judicially dubious practice, followed at Aix, Perpignan, Toulouse, and elsewhere, of disqualifying in advance probable suffrages in favor of the Jesuits on the grounds of magistrates' associations of one sort or another with the accused order, here backfired in a singularly spectacular fashion. The tie vote of December 1, 1762, which referred to the king the decision of whether two magistrates who had been absent during the first sessions devoted to the Jesuits could be judges in their trial, had rendered the parlement inactive until the royal decision against these magistrates permitted the resumption of the affair on May 7, 1764. Despite this triumph, the parlement's anti-Jesuitical party was apparently not yet sure of a majority, because during the session one of the spokesmen, the counselor Peticuelot, proposed the exclusion of eleven more magistrates, this time on the grounds that the eleven in question were all members of the Jesuits' lay congregation in Besançon. The pro-Jesuitical group, however, proved itself more than prepared for Peticuelot's maneuver. A considerable debate was already under way about the rectitude of such exclusions in

155. *Arrest de la cour du parlement de Toulouse, qui juge l'appel comme d'abus relevé par le procureur général du roi, de l'institut de la société de disant de Jésus. . . . Du février 1763,* in *Plaidoyer de monsieur le procureur général du roi au parlement de Toulouse, dans les audiences des 8, 11 et 17 février 1763, sur l'appel comme d'abus par lui relevé de l'institut et constitutions des soi-disans Jésuites* (Toulouse, 1763), pp. 1–13. See also Bastard d'Estang, *Les Parlements de France,* Vol. 2, pp. 50–200.

156. *Arrêt de la cour du parlement de Navarre. Extrait des registres de la cour, du 28 avril 1763,* in *Compte rendu de l'institut des ci-devant soi-disans Jésuites, des titres de leur établissement à Pau, et de l'édit du mois de mars 1762; par messieurs de Belloc et de Mosqueros le fils, conseillers au parlement, commissaires à ce [sic] députés* (Pau), pp. 66–80. Here, as in Roussillon, the representative of the *gens du roi*—in this case the solicitor general, de Faget-Poms—resolutely opposed the Jesuits' condemnation. See *Lettre à un magistrat, au sujet du compte rendu par M. de Faget-Poms, avocat général au parlement de Navarre aux chambres assemblées les 10, 13, 14 décembre 1762.*

157. On the situation in Colmar, see *Lettre d'Alsace au sujet des Jésuites, le 5 avril 1763,* pp. 1–7.

general when Counselor Arnoulx arose and, after delicately declaring his own "suspicion" as a judge because his brother, a Jesuit, would have to be given part of the family's succession in the case of the order's dissolution, proceeded to divulge the names of no less than twenty-five of his colleagues who were related within the degree of the ordinance governing such matters to living Jesuits within and without the province of Franche-Compté.

Arnoulx's revelation was a veritable bombshell which struck down friends and enemies of the Jesuits alike. Among its more notable victims were Peticuelot himself, as well as First President Grosbois, who had a Jesuit brother in Paris and was also ineligible because he had not, like the two magistrates already excluded, attended the first session of the Jesuits' trial. But the explosion had the desired effect. Counselor Alviset revealed the names of three more magistrates with financial interests in the Jesuits' houses of a sort to be affected by the order's demise; additional individual confessions of consanguinity with members of the order followed; and by the time the dust had fully settled, a total of forty-one magistrates found themselves "suspect" in the affair for one reason or another. This number rose to forty-four when combined with the two counselors previously excluded and the counselor Renard, who was sick, so that out of a working total of fifty magistrates the parlement could produce no more than six who were qualified to judge the Jesuits. Now the required minimum number of judges for the cases of individuals was eight, a regulation which applied with all the more force to the case of an entire religious order, and the trial of the Jesuits thus ground to a miserable halt in Besançon.[158] Renard could rage from his sickbed to Saint-Hilaire and Le Paige in Paris about "all the evil difficulties which the Jesuits have raised through the mouthpiece of their partisans more animated than ever," and about "these *messieurs,*" his colleagues, who had "pushed their researches so far in every genre that the company found itself reduced to six," but it is somehow difficult, in this instance at least, to share his habitual sense of righteous indignation.[159]

Nor did his indignation long lack new objects upon which to fasten. When the royal edict dissolving the entire Jesuit Order arrived in Besançon in December 1764, the pro-Jesuitical group apparently recruited six or seven titular magistrates who did not regularly attend parliamentary sessions and, with their support, achieved a vote of thirty-three against twenty-four in favor of remonstrances against the edict.[160] Nothing could console Renard for this "scandal" of apostasy from the parliamentary orthodoxy of unity amid the diversity

158. *Séance du parlement de Besançon, chambres assemblées, du 7 mai 1764, au sujet de l'affaire des Jésuites,* passim.

159. B.P.R.: L.P. 588, ms. 51, Renard to Saint-Hilaire, May 14, 1764.

160. B.P.R.: L.P. 584, ms. 148, Le Paige's copy of a letter from Renard to Saint-Hilaire, December 14, 1764.

of "classes" (Douai and Colmar had at least held their peace) unless it was the election of his friend and colleague Peticuelot in January as mayor of Besançon, an event interpreted by Renard as a defeat for the Jesuits.[161] Surprisingly enough, however, even the remonstrances, drafted by President Chiflet—the "soul and organ" of the pro-Jesuitical party—paid lip homage to a single "Parlement" and "all the classes which compose it."[162] These classes, the remonstrances explained, "always tend toward the same goal, although they sometimes take different routes to arrive there, according to the diversity and the power of conjunctures."[163] Such language, combined with the detour it was supposed to justify, only imperfectly agreed with Le Paige's doctrine of parliamentary diversity within unity, but Besançon's use of the orthodox phraseology reminds one that its case was perhaps not so much one of outright apostasy as of mere heresy.

The edict against which these remonstrances were drafted was the last of the "solemn acts of royal authority" which in a sense sanctioned the parlements' work, and which the parlements had wrenched from a somewhat reluctant Louis XV by "imperceptible degrees." One rough draft of the edict's preamble in the handwriting of the attorney general, Guillaume Joly de Fleury, and which indicates the cooperation of the *gens du roi* in the edict's composition, expressly places the responsibility for the Jesuits' destruction on the pope's refusal to sanction any reform of the order's constitutions. "But our Holy Father having steadfastly responded that the smallest change in the rules of the said institute would so disfigure the essence and the substance that those who were engaged to the regime would cease to be Jesuits and that it would be preferable for these no longer to exist rather than to exist in a manner different from that under which they had formed their engagements, we cannot differ," the draft reads, and so on.[164] But the draft which the king finally adopted discreetly avoided any mention of the papacy's role in the affair, and after a few royal generalities proceeded to the specific dispositions. The edict unceremoniously ended the existence of the "Society of the Jesuits" in France, but permitted all ex-Jesuits to live "as particulars" within the State "under the spiritual authority of the various

---

161. Ibid., L.P. 584, ms. 151, Renard to Saint-Hilaire, January 2, 1764.

162. For Peticuelot's characterization of Chiflet, see ibid., ms. 148. Bourgeois de Boynes, the unfortunate former first president of the parlement of Besançon, described Chiflet as "fort pieux et fort bon juge," which, coming as it does from De Boynes, more or less confirms Renard's estimate of Chiflet's importance in the Jesuitical party. (See A.N.: A.P. 154, Fonds Lamoignon of Tocqueville collection, *carton* 2, *dossier* 2, De Boynes to Lamoignon, April 1, 1757.)

163. *Très-humbles et très-respectueuses remontrances présentées au roi par le parlement de Franche Compté, au sujet de l'édit du mois de novembre 1764, concernant les Jésuites. Arrêtés dans l'assemblée des chambres, tenue le 12 janvier 1765*, pp. 3–4.

164. B.N.: Collection Joly de Fleury, fol. 1612, ms. 334.

bishops, conforming themselves to the laws of our realm, and in comporting themselves in all things as good and faithful subjects."[165] The edict's generous distinction between the order as such and its individual members was of no small comfort to the French ex-Jesuits, who had seen themselves the objects of physical persecution by several parlements, particularly that of Normandy, which on March 3, 1763, had ordered all the ex-Jesuits within its jurisdiction to sign an oath denouncing their erstwhile order on pain of immediate imprisonment.[166] On that occasion it required all the secret pressure which the parlement of Paris could muster to soften Rouen's excessive zeal in the matter.[167] In contrast, the king's edict required no particular oath of the ex-Jesuits, to whom it nonetheless accorded a minimal pension, although by its silence it left intact the requirement of the various parliamentary oaths in the case of their wishing to exercise an ecclesiastical function of any sort.

In a more personal sense, however, the edict of November was far from representing a royal sanction of the parlements' destruction of the Jesuits. Raised by the cardinal de Fleury to detest everything that vaguely hinted of Jansenism, Louis XV could never have—and in fact never did—approve of what his parlements had done. They had simply forced his hand, and in a way which is hardly obscure. If during the summer and early winter of 1762 Louis XV might have hoped that the approaching close of war with England and Prussia would render the government less dependent on parliamentary registration of fiscal edicts and declarations (this possibility might explain the government's vacillatory movements in the affair of the Jesuits during this period), it soon became clear enough that the government's debts were such that much of the wartime taxation would have to be continued. The Treaty of Paris in 1763 hence brought little relief in the way of taxation, and the edict of April 1763, although it ended the third *vingtième* and the doubled *capitation*, maintained the second *vingtième* and the *don gratuit* from the cities and principal towns until 1770. Moreover, the edict added a sixth sol for every additional livre to the rights of the farmers general, and the declaration of April 24, 1763, taxed *rentes* and venal offices. Against these fiscal measures the resistance of the parlements was so determined that the government was finally forced to a compromise—the declaration of November 21, 1763—negotiated with the edict's principal opponents in the parlement of Paris, who were not themselves able to prevent matters from reaching the boiling point at Grenoble, Rouen, and Toulouse.[168] To gain parlia-

165. *Edit du roi concernant la société des Jésuites, donné à Versailles au mois de novembre 1764* (Paris, 1764), in *Actes royaux*, F21170, p. 2.

166. A.D.S.I.: "Registre secret," March 2, 1763.

167. See the three-cornered correspondence between Laverdy, Le Paige, and Du Fossé on the subject, in B.P.R.: L.P. 584, mss. 17–38.

168. Egret, *Louis XV et l'opposition parlementaire*, pp. 148–56.

mentary cooperation in the long run, Louis XV, prompted by Choiseul, re-placed Bertin with Laverdy himself as controller general of finance in December 1763, even though the latter's expertise on the subject of the Jesuits far outstripped his command of the realm's economy.[169] It goes without saying that any obstinate attempt on Louis XV's part to save the Jesuits would have definitively dashed whatever hopes he entertained to gain parliamentary cooperation in fiscal matters. Madame de Pompadour said precisely as much when, approached by the King of Poland on behalf of the Jesuits, she responded: "I believe the Jesuits to be good men; nonetheless, it is not possible for the King to sacrifice his parlement for their sake, especially at a time when it is so necessary to him."[170]

But whether it was the government's fiscal difficulties, or—and these factors should not in any case be minimized—the papacy's refusal to sanction any changes in the Jesuit Order, or the intense popular passions that the affair of the Jesuits undoubtedly occasioned in France that primarily inclined the royal will, it was a bitter man who in 1766 wrote to Choiseul: "I have no great affection for the Jesuits, but all the heretics have always detested them, which constitutes their glory. I say nothing more. If for the peace of my realm I send them away against my will, at least I do not want anyone to believe that I have personally adhered to everything that the parlements have done and said against them."[171] Neuville himself could not have hoped for a more "honorable Epitaph."

169. Ibid., pp. 98–99. See Laverdy's response to Le Paige's congratulatory note on the occasion of Laverdy's promotion to controller general, in B.P.R.: L.P. 584, ms. 38, Laverdy to Le Paige, December 1763.

170. Archives de la Maison de Saint-Louis, Flesseles manuscript, pp. 3–4. In his allocution to the secret consistory on September 3, 1762, Pope Clement XIII said very much the same thing. The parlements, he said, "gardent à cette société une vieille haine, et saisissent pour le perdre l'occasion de la guerre présente et des embarras qui se prolongent avec elle" (Ravignan, *Clément XIII et Clément XIV*, Vol. 1, p. 438).

171. Quoted in ibid., p. 135. Louis XV's remark does not concern the edict of November 1764, but a draft edict of 1768 which, in response to a parliamentary offensive against the ex-Jesuits still living in the realm—and which in turn was a repercussion of the expulsion of the Jesuits from Spain—would have actually banished all ex-Jesuits from France. Fortunately for these, the edict never saw the light of day. Again, however, Choiseul seems to have been its chief advocate within the ministry. On this subject, see Jean Egret, "Le Procès des Jésuites devant les parlements de France," *Revue Historique*, 204 (July–December 1950), 27.

8. The Jansenists against Philosophy: The Controversy over D'Alembert's Sur la Destruction des Jésuites en France

"IT HAS ALREADY BEEN SEVERAL MONTHS," COMPLAINED THE December 11, 1765, issue of the *Nouvelles Ecclésiastiques*, "that the Public has been infected with a brochure of 235 pages which bears no other title than this: *Sur la Destruction des Jésuites en France, par un auteur désinteressé.*" The ever-vigilant gazeteer assured his public that ordinarily he would not have waited so long as he did to review a book of this stripe. In this instance, however, he had lingered in the hope of being able to announce at the same time some parliamentary decree condemning the book as it deserved to be. "For this libel," he said, "bears everywhere the stamp of irreligion, and the author, by means of the detestable motives he attributes to the magistracy, possesses the rare talent of insulting it even while applauding its decrees."[1]

The author of the libel in question was none other than Jean Le Rond d'Alembert, coeditor, with Denis Diderot, of the already famous *Encyclopédie* and author of its celebrated *Discours préliminaire*. Indeed, it was in part D'Alembert's encyclopedic pretensions, manifest even in a book about the expulsion of the Jesuits from France, that so upset his Jansenist reviewer. "His libel," asserted the reviewer, "is for the rest nothing but a tissue of the most diverse and unrelated observations . . . concerning eloquence, French and Latin poetry, politics, government, the theatre, music—all of them matters entirely foreign to the object which the title *Sur la Destruction des Jésuites* would seem to announce. It is," continued the Jansenist, waxing yet more acrid, "an encyclopedic philosophe who speaks, and who wants it to be known that his mind embraces all the sciences; a new Don Quixote who, thrusting now to the left, now to the right, fells everything in his path." But it was hardly the fact that D'Alembert had used the Jesuits as an excuse to talk of a great number of unrelated matters that most troubled the gazeteer. In using, for that matter, the most disparate subjects as an excuse for talking about the Jesuits, the Jansenists had often enough committed the inverse of the very same sin. What really enraged the Jansenist reviewer was rather D'Alembert's thesis that "it was properly Philosophy . . .

1. *Nouvelles Ecclésiastiques* (December 11, 1765), p. 201.

208

which by the mouths of the magistrates issued the decree against the Jesuits. That phrase alone," added the gazeteer, "indicates not only the entire plan and goal of the book but the stripe of the author as well." It was in developing this thesis, he thought, that D'Alembert had succeeded in insulting the magistracy "even while applauding its decrees."[2]

So it was really "philosophy" which, in D'Alembert's opinion, had condemned the Jesuits.[3] The assertion is significant. For it indicates that, though the ink was barely dry on the royal decree abolishing the Jesuit Order in France, a third party, the "party of philosophy," was claiming not only the credit for the victory but the lion's share of its spoils as well. No less important, however, is the *Nouvelles Ecclésiastiques'* scathing review of D'Alembert's book. After their veritable hundred years' war with the redoubtable Jesuit phalanxes, the Jansenists were not about to share with anyone either the credit or the spoils of what they considered their final victory. With the dust, then, of their last clash with the Jesuits yet settling, the Jansenists, with this issue of the *Nouvelles Ecclésiastiques*, suddenly declared war on the "party of philosophy" and all its adherents.

Not that unbroken peace had previously existed between the Jansenists and this third party. Even before the final campaign against the Jesuits, the Jansenists had, as D'Alembert himself observed, declared against the philosophes "a war almost as violent as that against the Company of Jesus."[4] The *Nouvelles Ecclésiastiques* had neglected to anathematize neither the *Encyclopédie* nor the other major productions of "philosophy" to have appeared before the expulsion of

2. Ibid.

3. The words *philosophy* and *reason,* usually capitalized by D'Alembert, will be used here in the sense in which D'Alembert—and, to a large extent, the Enlightenment in general—understood them. By "reason" D'Alembert meant the exercise of the "systematic spirit" (*esprit systématique*) as opposed to the Cartesian "spirit of system" (*esprit de système*) or, to use his own words, the "thoughtful study of phenomena," "the comparisons we make among them," and "the art of reducing, as much as that may be possible, a large number of phenomena to a single one that can be regarded as their principle" (Jean le Rond d'Alembert, *Preliminary Discourse to the Encyclopedia of Diderot,* trans. Richard N. Schwab [Indianapolis and New York, 1963], pp. 22–23). "Philosophy," on the other hand, D'Alembert understood simply as the "fruit of reason" (ibid., p. 51) or "the principal branches of that part of human knowledge which consists either in the direct ideas which we have received through our senses, or in the combination or comparison of these ideas—a combination which in general we call *Philosophy*" (ibid., p. 36). To D'Alembert's mind, of course, "reason" and "philosophy" stood diametrically opposed to religious "enthusiasm" and "fanaticism."

4. D'Alembert. *Sur la Destruction des Jésuits en France, par un auteur désintéressé,* p. 192. On the relations between the Jansenists and the philosphes, see Jan Christiaan Adolph Havinga, *Les Nouvelles Ecclésiastiques dans leur lutte contre l'esprit philosophique* (Amersfoort, 1925). On the Jesuits and the philosophes, see the excellent study by Pappas, *Berthier's Journal de Trévoux and the Philosophes,* Vol. 3 in Besterman ed., *Studies on Voltaire and the Eighteenth Century.*

the Jesuits. Adrien Le Paige himself had been one of the censors to whom, in 1759, the parlement of Paris had entrusted the examination of the *Encyclopédie*. The Jansenists, in fact, prided themselves on being far more zealous in their attempts to stem the tide of unbelief than the Jesuits had ever been. From the Jansenist point of view, after all, the Jesuits were a group of men who, sharing with the philosophes similar conceptions of God, nature, and ethics, were nothing more than philosophes themselves, cleverly disguised as a religious order. As an anomalous organization clearly representing neither unbelief nor the true Catholic faith, the Jesuit Order, the Jansenists felt, effectively obscured the important issues between the two. Much, then, as the Jansenists of the seventeenth century had regarded their fight with the Jesuits as preliminary to the far more important battle to be fought against the Calvinists, the Jansenists of the late eighteenth century now saw the Jesuits as a force to be eliminated before the real battle, that against the philosophes, could be decisively engaged.

Little wonder, then, that with the Jesuits lying prostrate, the Jansenists now turned with undivided force against the philosophes. It must nonetheless be admitted that, for the duration of their last campaign against the Jesuits, the Jansenists had observed something of a truce in their relations with "philosophy." Symptomatic of this truce is the *Nouvelles Ecclésiastiques'* February 13, 1759 review of the Archbishop of Paris's mandamus against Helvetius's book *De l'Esprit*. To be sure, Helvetius's conception of the soul as sensation, as well as some of his political opinions, were duly condemned, but so also was poor Christophe de Beaumont, behind whose mandamus the gazeteer was certain he detected the hand of the Jesuits. From his discussion of Helvetius's conception of the soul, the gazeteer then proceeded directly to the case of the Jesuits, and ended his review with the hypothesis that, instead of a soul, each Jesuit had been endowed with a devil as his animating principle.[5]

But the Jansenists of this period by no means restricted themselves to using the publications of "philosophy" as excuses, however implausible, to say unkind things about the Jesuits; they also welcomed all attacks against the Jesuits, even if they came from suspiciously philosophic quarters. An obvious case in point is the reception the Jansenists gave to the publication of the celebrated *Compte rendu* against the Jesuit Order by La Chalotais. Not without reason had the Jesuits Griffet, Balbani, and Neuville accused La Chalotais of being a disciple of the encyclopedists. It was to him, in fact, that D'Alembert dedicated his book *Sur la Destruction des Jésuites en France*, and it was he, too, whom Voltaire himself congratulated for the "justly merited success of the only philosophical work ever to have come from the Bar."[6] But neither the anathemas of the

5. *Nouvelles Ecclésiastiques* (February 13, 1759), pp. 29–30.
6. B.N.: Collection Joly de Fleury, fol. 1615, ms. 127, undated copy of a letter from Voltaire to La Chalotais. The dedication in D'Alembert's book is to "M. xxx, conseiller au

Jesuits nor the eulogies of the encyclopedists seemed to embarrass the Jansenists, who, if anything, outdid the philosophes in heaping praise on La Chalotais and his *Compte rendu*. Beginning on May 29, 1761, the *Nouvelles Ecclésiastiques* devoted three entire issues to a summary of this *Compte rendu*. La Chalotais himself was depicted as "wise," "zealous," a magistrate with the interests of true religion at heart.[7] And the Jansenists were hardly less complimentary in private. In a letter expressly ordered to be kept under the greatest secrecy, Jansenism's staunchest representative in the episcopacy, Fitz-James of Soissons, told the lawyer Lalourcé of his "great satisfaction" in seeing La Chalotais treat "a matter of such importance with such solidity and elevation." The Bishop of Soissons described the *Compte rendu* as "a writing which shall pass to posterity and immortalize its author." He felt flattered, he added, "that he [La Chalotais] has a sufficiently high opinion of me to request my approbation. He will most certainly have it and my admiration as well."[8]

The temptation to ascribe Machiavellian motives to the Jansenists is strong at this point, but it must be resisted. The very private character of some of the Jansenist praise of La Chalotais's *Compte rendu* is warning enough. For if privately the Jansenists had suspected La Chalotais of being a dangerous bedfellow, why would they not privately have said so? To assume bad faith on the part of the Jansenists in this instance is to assume that, before 1765, Jansenists were perfectly aware of all the differences which separated themselves from the philosophes. Now despite the fact that the two groups had previously exchanged blows, this was not entirely the case, particularly if the subject under discussion was the Company of Jesus.

Like the Jansenists, and like the other magistrates charged with delivering *Comptes rendus* of the Jesuit Order to their respective parlements, La Chalotais, too, raged against the Jesuits' nonreciprocal vows, their excessive devotion to the papacy, their doctrines of tyrannicide, and, in general, the despotic nature of the order. Indeed, La Chalotais, like any good Jansenist, even went so far as to charge Lainez and his successors with the heresy of semi-Pelagianism.[9] In none of this, of course, could the Jansenists have found anything but cause for rejoicing. But in the same *Compte rendu* La Chalotais also condemned the multiplication of monastic orders as well as religious "enthusiasm" and "fana-

---

parlement de xxx." From D'Alembert's numerous laudatory references to La Chalotais, one can safely conclude that La Chalotais is the mysterious M. "xxx."

7. *Nouvelles Ecclésiastiques* (May 27, 1762), p. 85.

8. B.P.R.: L.P. 583, ms. 153, "lettre de M. l'évêque de Soissons, 25 fevrier, 1762." This manuscript is not original but a copy in the hand of Le Febvre de Saint-Hilaire. At the end of the letter is this note: "cete letre a été éscrite par M. l'évêque de Soissons et addressé a M. Lalourcé avocat du Parlement, qui a bien voulu en donnée une copie, sous le plus grand secret, et a condition que cete letre ne seroit pas rendue publique. . . ."

9. La Chalotais, *Compte rendu des constitutions des Jésuites*, p. 23.

ticism" in such disquietingly general terms that the Jansenists might well have taken pause.[10] For La Chalotais's blanket condemnation of religious "enthusiasm" seemed directed as much against the Jansenists as the Jesuits, and his comments on the evils of monasticism applied as logically, for example, to the Oratorians and Dominicans as to the Company of Jesus. Such, at least, was the interpretation of Voltaire and D'Alembert.

La Chalotais's remarks about monasticism, coupled, probably, with the philosophical "enthusiasm" they aroused, even caused a whisper of consternation beneath the otherwise tumultuous welcome the Jansenists gave his *Compte rendu*. The same issue of the *Nouvelles Ecclésiastiques* which began the long review of the *Compte rendu* observed, though only in passing, that La Chalotais's reflections on religious orders "appeared far too general."[11] Dom Tassin, a Dominican monk, was more emphatic. In a private memoir he sent to Adrien Le Paige, he remarked that La Chalotais had obviously "modeled some of his ideas upon the productions of a few supposed *beaux esprits* of our days. For it is there," he added, "that one finds the sacred austerities of the Christian monks rated below the superstitious and criminal practices of the idolatrous penitents, and it is there that one is inspired with disdain for the exercises of Christian mortification practiced in the cloisters by their being represented as suspiciously prideful, susceptible to illusion and unrelated either to religion or to virtue. Is it not to be feared," asked this agitated monk, "that many readers, finding these ideas in the work of a great magistrate, will persuade themselves that all monks in general perceive no more than the appearances of virtue, without being animated by the interior piety which informs the true Christian?"[12]

Despite their reservations, both the Dominican Tassin and the reviewer for the *Nouvelles Ecclésiastiques* tended to interpret La Chalotais's observations on monasticism as a mere, though regrettable, slip of his pen, and therefore a matter of no real consequence. No mere slip of the pen, on the other hand, could have plausibly accounted for the contents of D'Alembert's book *Sur la Destruction des Jésuites en France*, which, as the reviewer for the *Nouvelles Ecclésiastiques* himself had observed, bore "everywhere the stamp of irreligion." For this reason the publication of D'Alembert's book, together with the literary brawl that event occasioned, was destined not only to reveal D'Alembert's differences with the Jesuits but to clarify those cleavages between Jansenists and philosophes which their common opposition to the Company of Jesus had previously obscured. For the same reason, the Jansenists' December 11, 1765, declaration of war against D'Alembert's book and the "party of philosophy" in general

10. Ibid. On his condemnation of religious enthusiasm, fanaticism, and monasticism, see above, pp. 142–45.
11. *Nouvelles Ecclésiastiques* (May 22, 1762), p. 85.
12. B.P.R.: L.P. 583, ms. 154.

differed qualitatively from the preceding skirmishes between the two camps. This new war's first battle, therefore, promised to reveal much about its nature and probable outcome.

What, then, had D'Alembert written about the Jesuits and their destruction in France?

Though certainly not the most important event of the middle of the century, the fall of the Jesuits in France, thought D'Alembert, was no less surprising than the earthquake in Lisbon, the alliance between Austria and France, or the victory of the King of Prussia over five powers leagued against him. For the Jesuits had been powerful. True, the Jesuits' founder, Ignatius Loyola, was little more than "a Spanish gentleman who, having had his brain heated first by chivalric novels and then by works of devotion, took it into his head to become the Don Quixote of the Virgin and preach to the infidels the Christian religion of which he himself was nearly ignorant." But Ignatius had at least the sense to see that by making a special vow of devotion to the papacy, the new society would always merit its protection as well as that of its "beloved children," the Catholic princes of Europe. Moreover, Ignatius's successors, Lainez and Aquaviva, "much superior" to Ignatius himself, gave their society the direction and form that was to ensure its ultimate hegemony—for it was nothing less than this, thought D'Alembert, to which the society aspired—despite whatever obstacles it might encounter initially.[13]

The Jesuits' founding fathers, continued D'Alembert, endowed their infant society with two unique weapons which, coupled with the special vow of devotion to the pope, later rendered it redoubtable in the face of even earthly powers and principalities. The first of these weapons was the long duration of the order's novitiate. Because the society's subjects were not permitted to take their final vows until the age of thirty-three, the Jesuit superiors, thought D'Alembert, had sufficient time to judge correctly the talents of their subjects and assign them the occupations to which they were best suited, while the subjects, for their part, had enough time to test their own devotion to the monastic life and its rigors. With only useful and well-proven subjects, the Jesuit Order therefore labored under the weight of no excess baggage. The second weapon, in D'Alembert's opinion, was the society's suppression of the common recitation of offices and singing of chants. Because the Jesuits were "not bound, like other monks, to minute exercises of devotion and offices which absorb the better part of the day," they had "the entire time to give themselves to study"—hence the Jesuits' superiority over the other religious orders "in the matter of sciences and lights." Were it not, added D'Alembert, that "hatred makes weapons of everything, one would find it difficult to believe that during their [the

13. D'Alembert, *Sur la Destruction des Jésuites en France*, pp. 14–15, 16, 17.

Jesuits'] trial . . . several Jansenist brochures proclaimed it a crime that, unlike so many other monks, they did not assemble to say matins and complices in common, as if a religious society, whose first obligation is to be useful, had nothing better to do than tediously chant bad Latin several hours a day."[14]

To the weapons of a long novitiate and the elimination of "minute exercises of devotion," the Jesuits, said D'Alembert, added the special tactic of Pelagian ethics. More cunning than Pelagius himself, the Jesuits not only preached the freedom of man's will but, unlike Pelagius, eliminated all that was too difficult in the moral obligations imposed by Christianity. Whereas Pelagius told men, "you can do everything, but you have much to do," the Jesuits told Christians, "you can do everything, and God demands very little of you." Their espousal of Pelagian ethics did not, however, prevent the Jesuits from distinguishing themselves by the purity of their morals. It was indeed precisely the tactic of selling heaven cheaply to others while buying it dearly for themselves that enabled the Jesuits to become the confessors of the Catholic princes of Europe— who were grateful for the permission to keep mistresses—and to impose themselves upon the masses not only in much of Europe but more especially in Paraguay, where the Jesuits ruled an entire people "by persuasion alone and by the sweetness of their government."[15]

In order better to understand the wisdom of these Jesuitical tactics, imagine, asked D'Alembert, how a Jansenist would have preached Christianity to the natives of Paraguay. "My children," the Jansenist would have said, "I announce to you a God whom you cannot serve worthily without a special grace which he has resolved from all eternity either to give you or refuse you." Surely, concluded D'Alembert, the Jansenist would have been "abandoned as a fool or chased away by the people with stones." For the doctrine of the Jansenists, "a singular contradiction of the human mind in the matter of religion," posits a God who, though demanding the fulfillment of the most difficult obligations on the part of men, nonetheless refuses to regard their efforts as anything more than so many new crimes unless he sanctify them with a grace which, in turn, he gives or refuses without consideration of those efforts." Such, exclaimed D'Alembert, "is the God of the Jansenists: such is their theology in its original and primitive purity."[16]

Endowed, then, with Pelagian ethics, a long novitiate, and a dispensation from monastic devotions, the Jesuit Order, thought D'Alembert, was "the masterpiece of human industry in the realm of politics." But despite all the industry and foresight of its builders, the order, like the laboriously drained and cultivated marshes of Holland, was helplessly open to inundation once its

14. Ibid., pp. 42–43.
15. Ibid., pp. 66, 24.
16. Ibid., pp. 59, 60, 63, 65–66.

enemies located the weak spot in its protective dikes. These dikes were severely shaken for the first time when, in *Les Provinciales* and other writings, the celebrated authors of Port-Royal rendered the Jesuits odious to all of Europe even while Louis XIV raised them to the very pinnacle of their power. Unfortunately for themselves, Pascal and Arnauld did not live to see the consummation of the work they had begun. And unfortunately for "reason," the Jansenism with which they had opposed the doctrine of the Jesuits was a cause hardly worthy of their great talents. Ironically, it was not, said D'Alembert, until Jansenism "had no longer for its support any defenders but such as were worthy of such a cause, a few poor and obscure priests unknown even in their quarter," that this "expiring," "despised," and convulsion ridden "sect," this "viper which the Jesuits thought they had crushed," suddenly found "strength enough to turn back its head, bite them in the heel, and kill them."[17]

Whatever the role of the Jansenists in the affair, the Jesuits, D'Alembert maintained, deserved to be destroyed because men were "justly indisposed to see monks bound by their state to humility, solitude and silence, direct the conscience of kings, educate the nobility of the kingdom and engage in intrigue at the court, in the cities and in the provinces. For nothing," he added, "more irritates reasonable men than to see monks who have renounced the world and who attempt to govern it." The crime of the Jesuits was not to have been intrinsically worse than other monks, for other monastic orders, too, taught pernicious maxims and vowed a servile obedience to the pope and their superiors. The Jesuits' crime was rather to have been "more redoubtable" than the others "by their intrigues and by their credit." Of all the magistrates who wrote indictments against the Jesuits, La Chalotais only, insisted D'Alembert, "seems to have envisioned this affair as a statesman, philosopher, and an enlightened magistrate devoid of all hatred and party spirit." For instead of laboriously attempting to prove that other monks were much better than the Jesuits, he rather insisted that "the monastic spirit . . . is the scourge of all states," that "of all those animated by this spirit the Jesuits are the most noxious because they are the most powerful," and that "it is therefore necessarily with them that one must begin shaking off the yoke of this pernicious nation."[18]

It was hence "properly Philosophy," D'Alembert concluded, "which by the mouth of the magistrates issued the decree against the Jesuits; Jansenism was only the solicitor in it." The Jansenists, he asserted, desired the destruction of the Jesuits only because the latter taught versatile grace rather than efficacious grace, but had it not been for this "ridiculous quarrel of schools," the Jesuits might yet have existed. The important thing, thought D'Alembert, was that the intolerance of the "wretched posterity" of Port-Royal did not succeed the

17. Ibid., pp. 17, 107–08.
18. Ibid., pp. 143–44, 143, 159–60.

credit of "Jesuitical intolerance." Given a choice between the two, one would certainly choose the intolerance of the Jesuits, "accommodating people" who permit others to think as they wish provided they not declare themselves their enemy. Were the Jansenists in power, they would surely "exercise over books, minds, discourses, and morals the most violent kind of inquisition." But this eventuality, D'Alembert thought, was not much to be feared. For the Jesuits, he said, were "regular troops, rallied and disciplined under the banner of superstition." With this "Macedonian phalanx" finally crushed, "reason" would easily confound the dispersed and disorganized "Cossacks" and "Pandours" of the Jansenists. Moreover, the French nation, hitherto unable to become impassioned except for *billets de confession* and the bull *Unigenitus*, showed signs of enlightening itself, and would probably enlighten itself more and more. Soon, he felt, religious disputes would be despised and fanaticism regarded with horror.[19]

What precisely, then, was D'Alembert's quarrel with the Jesuits? Was it their intolerance? Though in one place he qualified the Jesuits as "intolerant by system and by state," he had elsewhere described them as accommodating to all who did not declare themselves their enemies—a condition, it would seem, hardly designed to cramp philosophical style.[20] Was it their superstition? D'Alembert had indeed described the Jesuits as regular and disciplined troops rallied under the banner of superstition, but he had elsewhere acknowledged the Jesuit Order as superior to all other monastic orders in the emphatically unsuperstitious profession of "sciences and lights." Nor does the Jesuits' religious "enthusiasm" or "fanaticism" seem to have troubled him, for his description of Jesuit doctrines is that of "reason" itself, sorely harrassed, in turn, by the enthusiastic and fanatical guerilla forces of the Jansenists.

On the other hand, D'Alembert hardly concealed his admiration for precisely those structural and spiritual aspects of the Jesuit Order which both Jansenists and magistrates had singled out as the distinguishing marks of the beast. The order's long and uncertain novitiate, condemned by Jansenists and magistrates as the scourge of families and the State, D'Alembert justified with the argument previously employed by the Jesuits themselves: that the long novitiate left the order with none but the most useful and well-tested subjects. Expressly taking to task those Jansenists who had charged the Jesuits with failure to imitate other monastic orders in saying matins and complices in common, D'Alembert justified the Jesuits' elimination of these "minute exercises of devotion" as precisely the means by which the Jesuit Order, unlike other monastic orders, was able to render itself proficient in "sciences and lights" and thereby useful to society. And the Jesuits' relatively complacent attitude

19. Ibid., pp. 191–92, 193, 202–06.
20. Ibid., pp. 192, 203.

toward "philosophy," as well as their espousal of Pelagian theology, both anathematized by the Jansenists as instances of rank heresy, D'Alembert contrasted favorably to the Jansenists' intolerance and their attachment to what, he said, they "modestly . . . call the doctrine of Saint Augustine and Saint Paul."[21] Even the Jesuits' empire in Paraguay, which the Jansenists saw as the order's despotic proclivities carried to their logical conclusion, D'Alembert extolled as an example of governing a whole people "by persuasion alone." Nor was his general description of the Jesuit Order as "the masterpiece of human industry in the realm of politics" dissimilar to the Jesuit Balbani's own characterization of the order which Saint Ignatius founded as the "masterpiece of his Christian politics."[22]

So the question is worth repeating: What precisely was D'Alembert's quarrel with the Jesuits? The question seemed no less insoluble to the editor of the *Nouvelles Ecclésiastiques* and the other Jansenist polemicists who individually undertook to refute D'Alembert's book. "The Jesuit Order," complained the gazeteer, "so contrary to all laws both human and divine, merits his eulogies; he approves their wisdom in the choice of that morality which is the plague of the Church; he uses every means to extenuate the opprobrium of their proscription; he willingly pardons them the genius of intrigue which had rendered them powerful and redoubtable."[23] The author, grumbled another anonymous Jansenist pamphleteer, "draws profit from everything in his attempt to attenuate the shame of the Jesuits. Despite whatever evil he says of them, he seems to have for them a secret penchant."[24] Most eloquent, however, was Adrien Le Paige himself, who, in a pamphlet entitled *Le Philosophe redressé*, addressed himself directly to the problem of what, in D'Alembert's opinion, "the Jesuits were culpable, and why they deserved to be destroyed." Was it, asked Le Paige, because the Jesuits vowed allegiance to a regime "which frightened the whole world once it was known?" No, he answered, for D'Alembert described this regime as "well conceived" and "very wise." Was it, Le Paige demanded, because of their "frightful moral laxity, which opened the door to every manner of crime?" No, Le Paige again responded, for D'Alembert said that "moral laxity, far from being worthy of censure, renders people happy." After considering and dismissing numerous other alternatives, Le Paige finally decided that "it is not a philosophe who speaks here, but a foul Jesuit." D'Alembert's book, he said, contained "too many palliatives in favor of the Society not to suspect M. D'Alembert . . . of being an honorary Jesuit or, as they say, a

21. Ibid., pp. 59–60.
22. Balbani, *Appel à la raison*, p. 31.
23. *Nouvelles Ecclésiastiques* (December 11, 1705), p. 201.
24. *Le Philosophe redressé, ou Critique impartiale du livre intitulé: 'Sur la Destruction des Jésuites en France'* (Bois-Valon, 1765), p. 52. According to Le Long, the author is P. Mirasson.

Jesuit of the short robe." After all, Le Paige concluded, "what is a true Jesuit if not a disguised philosophe, and what is a philosophe, if not a manifest Jesuit?"[25]

Whether a fifth columnist of the Jesuits or not, D'Alembert had doubtlessly extenuated "the opprobrium of their proscription." But to have been soft on the Jesuits was, in Jansenist eyes, decidedly among his lesser manifestations of original depravity. For in marked contrast to his relatively favorable treatment of the Jesuits, D'Alembert's handling of the Jansenists had been little less than violent. "Cossacks," "Pandours," "wretched posterity" of Port-Royal, ridiculous and convulsion-ridden "sect," "viper"—these are only a few of the terms with which D'Alembert had described the Jansenists. Small wonder, then, that in calling D'Alembert a "Jesuit of the short robe," Le Paige should have responded in kind. Nor had D'Alembert limited his attacks upon the Jansenists to name-calling. In sharp contrast, again, to the rather amorphous marrow of his quarrel with the Jesuits, the bones D'Alembert had to pick with the Jansenists were clear in their outlines. And they were three in number: monasticism, religious fanaticism, and intolerance.

What La Chalotais had only hinted, D'Alembert stated baldly: "the monastic spirit," he said, "is the scourge of all states"; instead of being useful to society, which is every citizen's first obligation to the State, monks spend much of their time tediously chanting bad Latin in their cloisters. The work begun with the destruction of the Jesuits would therefore be consummated with the liquidation of all other orders of the "pernicious nation" of monks; pending that happy day monks should at least be locked up in their cloisters where, without meddling in other affairs, they can pray "entirely at their ease."[26]

The Jansenists' reaction to these antimonastic barbs was unanimous and violent. "God," replied Le Paige, "invites even his inanimate creatures to praise him, while our Philosophe would have even reasonable creatures repudiate this practice. When," he continued, "the head of this Apostate has found a more tranquil posture, I will pray him to tell me how it comes that a Philosophe can render himself useful by his works in going to the Comedy and the Opera rather than by praying to God."[27] Another Jansenist polemicist, the anonymous

---

25. Le Paige, *Le Philosophe redressé, ou Réfutation de l'écrit intitulé: 'Sur la Destruction des Jésuites en France,' par un curé de village*, pp. 22–29. Besides such intangible considerations as style, the most cogent reason for suspecting Le Paige as the author of this pamphlet—which is to be found, to the best of my knowledge, only in Le Paige's personal library—is that it contains marginal corrections in Le Paige's own hand. That Le Paige was not generally in the habit of doing this to books he owned seems to indicate, if not his authorship, at least his collaboration. The pamphlet, moreover, is alone among the refutations of *Sur la Destruction des Jésuites en France*, which mentioned D'Alembert by name, and in general its author speaks not as a scribe but as one having authority. (See B.P.R.: L.P. 1471, no. 6).

26. D'Alembert, *Sur la Destruction des Jésuites en France*, p. 43.

27. Le Paige, *Le Philosophe redressé*, p. 19.

author of a pamphlet entitled *Lettre à M. xxx,* reached the heart of the issue. "Is it really," he asked D'Alembert, "so useless an occupation to celebrate public offices? The Philosophe," he argued, "whose only conception of God is a deaf and dumb idol, indifferent both to the needs of men and everything which happens among us, can envision this holy function in such a contemptible manner. But one acquainted with Religion," he continued, "knows that evil and good are both in God's providence, and that men must therefore ask God that he send them his mercy and spare them his justice. And what is more proper to unite all these duties than public prayer, where a society of men, separated from the world and all its cares and impediments, represent as a body the interests of all other men."[28]

The Jesuits, as we have seen, had been perfectly willing to justify the existence of their own order with a weapon drawn from "philosophy" itself: social utility. The Jesuit Order, they had argued, educated a large portion of the nation's youth, produced outstanding scholars in all disciplines, faithfully combatted heresy wherever it was to be found, and provided valuable assistance to the secular clergy in its sacerdotal and evangelical duties—all of them socially useful functions. Not even D'Alembert was prepared to contest—at least openly—the social utility of any or those functions. He did, in his first reply to his Jansenist detractors, argue that the secular clergy was by itself more than capable of performing its own duties, and that monks, because of their party spirit and rigidly enforced seclusion from the world, were by their nature incapable either of educating the youth or cultivating the "sciences and lights" with success.[29] But by his own admission, the Jesuit Order constituted something of an exception to the general monastic rabble. For by applying themselves to study, the Jesuits, D'Alembert admitted, had rendered themselves largely innocent of the philosophical sin of social uselessness by becoming proficient in the equally philosophical pursuits of "sciences and lights." The Jesuits, therefore, had been somewhat "philosophical" in the defense of their order, and D'Alembert, somewhat "Jesuitical" in his admiration for the order's social utility.

In contrast to the Jesuits' appeal to public utility, the argument which the anonymous Jansenist polemicist employed in defense of monastic orders was unadulterated in its medieval purity. The function of monks, he unashamedly asserted, is to pray. "And the function of nobles," he might very well have added, "is to fight, and that of peasants is to work." The argument, as the Jansenist pamphleteer himself admitted, rested on the premises of the existence

---

28. *Lettre à M. xxx, chevalier de l'ordre de Malte, touchant un écrit 'Sur la Destruction des Jésuites en France'* (France, 1765), p. 39.

29. Jean le Rond d'Alembert, *Lettre à M. xxx conseiller au parlement de xxx pour servir de supplément à l'ouvrage qui est dedié à ce même magistrat, et qui a pour titre: 'Sur la Destruction des Jésuites en France, par un auteur désintéressé'* (1767), pp. 145–50.

of a God personally concerned about the affairs of men and the efficacy of efficacious prayer, and the whole, premises and conclusion, constituted monasticism's pristine and, in the last analysis, ultimate justification. It was therefore with good reason that the Jansenists felt stung by D'Alembert's antimonastic darts. For they had been aimed, not at the Jesuits, but directly at themselves because they, not the Jesuits, were monasticism's most loyal defenders. That this was so D'Alembert himself had made clear when, with feigned disbelief, he remarked that "several Jansenist brochures" had actually proclaimed it a crime that the Jesuits did not, like other monks, regularly assemble to recite matins and complices in common. Not to say matins and complices in common was not to pray in common, and not to pray in common was, to the Jansenists, not to be monastic at all. And in fact—as D'Alembert well knew—the Jansenists had anathematized the Jesuits for precisely this reason, that the Jesuits were not really monks, or at least not monkish enough.[30]

Nor was it in any way accidental that the Jansenists, in this brawl, came forth as monasticism's staunchest champions. For the Jansenist movement was and had always been monastic both in fact and in spirit: in fact, because its strongholds had always been within monastic communities—within the abbey of Port-Royal in the seventeenth century and among the Oratorians, Dominicans, the Benedictines of Saint-Maur and Saint-Vannes, the Brothers of the Christian Doctrine, the Carmelites, the Daughters of Calvary, and still others in the eighteenth century;[31] in spirit, because its conception of the Christian life and doctrine, with its simultaneous emphasis upon both moral perfection and efficacious grace, led almost inevitably to monastic renunciation and condemnation of the *beau monde*. If the Jansenists' fray with D'Alembert had left any doubts in anyone's mind about their position on monasticism, the Jansenists soon dissipated these doubts when, during the same year, the Benedictines of Saint-Germain-des-Prés requested that they no longer be obliged to wear their "degrading" habit and chant matins at night. The Jansenists, led by the Benedictine monk Clémencet and the editor of the *Nouvelles Ecclésiastiques,* launched a publicity campaign against these monks and their request which was at least as vitriolic as that against D'Alembert. Jansenism, they made it clear, regarded any alteration of the monastic rule with a jaundiced eye.[32]

Between D'Alembert and the Jesuits, dialogue was possible. Since both

30. See, for example, Le Paige and Coudrette, *Histoire générale de la Compagnie de Jésus en France,* Vol. 1, pp. 18–19; *Nouvelles Ecclésiastiques* (January 9, 1760), p. 3.

31. Gazier, *Histoire générale du mouvement janséniste,* Vol. 1, pp. 320–39.

32. D'Alembert, *Lettre à M. xxx,* pp. 142–43. For a very complete account of this affair, see the *Nouvelles Ecclésiastiques* (December 20, 1778, and January 9, 1779). This account was published on the occasion of the death of Dom Clémencet.

accepted public utility as a criterion, their quarrel concerned the public utility of the functions which the Jesuit Order in fact performed. Between D'Alembert, and a group of men who persisted in arguing the case of monasticism by society's obligation to pray, dialogue was out of the question. And in fact none took place. In the *Lettre à M. xxx conseiller au parlement de xxx*, his first reply to the Jansenists, D'Alembert contented himself with a more precise statement of his position on monasticism. The only useful functions monks could possibly perform, he thought, were the care of the sick and manual labor. "I mean," he said, "an employment profitable to the public, and which is not limited to nourishing or enriching the Community itself." The essential thing, he concluded, "is to render useful in whatever manner possible so many men absolutely lost to the fatherland . . . to whom their vows deny the right to be useful to anyone except themselves."[33] Or as Voltaire later expressed it in his *L'Homme aux quarante écus*, "what would England do today if, instead of forty thousand sailors, she had forty thousand monks?"[34]

It was again in the name of public utility and again as a flanking movement against the forces of Jansenism that D'Alembert attacked religious fanaticism and its inevitable allies, religious disputes. Humanity, he said, referring to the Jansenists, would have just reason to complain if these disputes had done nothing more than deprive philosophy and letters of the talents of such otherwise great men as the writers of Port-Royal, "who squandered so much energy and time on ridiculous controversies about the good or bad doctrine of Jansenius, on hollow and interminable discussions about free will and grace, and on the all-important question of whether five unintelligible propositions are to be found in a book which no one reads." But what is worse, he added, invoking the welfare of states, these "sacred bagatelles" had also resulted in "seas of blood" and "numberless usurpations by the spiritual power."[35]

Toward Pascal and the other writers of Port-Royal, D'Alembert was able to maintain at least a facade of respect, because they, in his estimation, had made contributions more valuable than the multiplication of "sacred bagatelles." But toward his Jansenist contemporaries, the "wretched posterity" of Port-Royal, D'Alembert had nothing but disdain. For no redeeming qualities offset their religious fanaticism—a fanaticism, he thought, which should not be allowed to succeed the more restrained fanaticism of the Jesuits. "The magistrates," he said, "who proscribed that of the Jesuits are too enlightened, too patriotic, too abreast of their century to suffer yet another fanaticism to take its place. Already," he added, "several of them (among others M. de la Chalotais)

33. D'Alembert, *Lettre à M. xxx*, pp. 49–50.
34. Voltaire, *L'Homme aux quarante écus*, in *Œuvres complètes*, Vol. 57, p. 188.
35. D'Alembert, *Sur la Destruction des Jésuites en France*, pp. 89–95.

have explained themselves clearly enough to displease the Jansenists and to merit the honor of being placed by them among the ranks of the philosophes."[36] D'Alembert, of course, was exaggerating. Although La Chalotais, as we have seen, had made some Jansenists somewhat uncomfortable, they had by no means lost hope in him or dismissed him as a philosophe. But the respect which the Jansenists were eager to display toward the attorney general of the parlement of Brittany they were unwilling to show D'Alembert, who, in Jansenist eyes, was La Chalotais's "wretched posterity."

D'Alembert's remarks about theological quarrels brought the predictable descent of Jansenist fire and brimstone upon his head. "Are these controversies really harmful to the State?" asked the abbé Guidi, author of a pamphlet entitled *Lettre à un ami.* "Are they not," he continued, "even necessary? Do they not necessarily result from the diverse tempers of the human spirit? . . . Since the birth of the true religion, has one seen the Church a single day without dispute? . . . Is it not from the conflict of opinions that come the sparks which lead to the truth? . . . To want to impose silence on all the theologians of the kingdom because they are not in agreement about a point of doctrine is not," he concluded, "the way to reconcile them. It is to place error on the same level with truth."[37] The anonymous author of yet another pamphlet entitled *Le Philosophe redressé* hit D'Alembert with a similar barrage of questions. "Should the cause of these controversies," he asked, "be imputed to the true religion herself or to her enemies? Would she have stirred herself had she not been attacked?"[38] And so on.

As in the case of his attack upon monasticism, D'Alembert's remarks about theological controversies had obviously struck a sensitive Jansenist nerve. For perhaps even more than by monasticism, the Jansenist movement had always been defined by religious controversy. From the days of Antoine Arnauld's *De la Fréquente Communion* and Pascal's *Les Provinciales* to the time of the expulsion of the Jesuits, Jansenism had been a movement *against* the theological, ethical, and, in the eighteenth century, political thought of the Jesuits. To be sure, the Jesuits, too, had taken part in theological quarrels against both the Jansenists and the Protestants, but these quarrels by no means exhausted the order's purpose. For the Jesuit Order existed not only to combat heresy, whether Jansenist or Protestant, but to convert, at the pope's behest, the heathen in the four corners of the world, to educate the youth of the Catholic states of Europe, and to aid the secular clergy in its functions. Opposition to the Jesuits, on the

36. Ibid., p. 205.

37. L'abbé Guidi, *Lettre à un ami sur un écrit intitulé 'Sur la Destruction des Jésuites en France,'* pp. 21–22. The only copy of this work I have been able to locate is in B.P.R.: L.P. 1471, no. 4.

38. *Le Philosophe redressé, ou Critique impartiale du livre intitulé: 'Sur la Destruction des Jésuites en France,'* p. 107.

other hand, had become part of Jansenism's very raison d'être. The Jansenist movement had little else to sustain itself in the event that either religious controversies or, for that matter, the Jesuits themselves were eliminated. And again, just as in the debate about monasticism, the conceptual weapon with which D'Alembert attacked the value of theological disputes, the principle of public utility, shattered against the hard medieval coat of armor of Jansenist extraterrestrial considerations. D'Alembert was certainly right in his contention that religious disputes, most recently those between the Jansenists and the Jesuits, had wreaked much havoc in France and were therefore harmful to the State. But the Jansenists' concern for the welfare of the State was strictly limited by their concern for the integrity of what they regarded as divine truth. D'Alembert was also quite right when he pointed out that the existence of a large number of monks did the State very little good. But again, the Jansenists' concern for the State was limited by what they maintained was society's duty reto pray. Not, of course, that the Jansenists were unconcerned about the welfa of the State. In comparison to what either Voltaire or D'Alembert had to say about the Jesuits, the nature of Jansenist opposition to the Jesuits was extremely political, extremely impregnated with concern for the State indeed. But the Jansenists could not, without ceasing to be themselves, allow their conception of the State's welfare to infringe upon their self-appointed role as the "defenders of the truth."

When the abbé Guidi accused D'Alembert of wanting to silence all contentious theologians, he was wrong. Not the philosophes, for that matter, but the Jansenists had been most enthusiastic about Louis XV's Law of Silence in 1754, a law which, as D'Alembert had quite rightly pointed out, had not prevented the Jansenists from printing "enormous volumes" in its praise.[39] D'Alembert's solution to the problem of theological disputes was rather the separation of religion from the State and a consequent policy of governmental toleration of all religious opinions. "The inconvenient disturbances of the public tranquillity which theological quarrels bring in their train," he argued, "is the fruit of the mistake committed in France as well as practically everywhere else, to bind civil matters to those of religion, to require of a bourgeois of Paris not only that he be a faithful subject, but also that he be a good Catholic, just as exact in rendering his consecrated bread as in paying his taxes. . . . It is not," he concluded, "except through a wise tolerance . . . that these frivolous disputes can be prevented from disturbing the repose of the state and the unity of her citizens. But when," he asked, "will that happy time arrive?"[40]

With his additional observation that the Jansenists, were they in power, would be far more intolerant than the "accommodating" Jesuits, D'Alembert

39. D'Alembert, *Sur la Destruction des Jésuites en France*, p. 124.
40. Ibid., pp. 120–21.

made it plain that these remarks were directed most especially at the former. Quick to perceive this, the Jansenists retorted much as D'Alembert's description of their intolerance would have led one to expect. Typical of their responses was that of the *Nouvelles Ecclésiastiques*. "When will that happy time arrive," cried the gazeteer, "when we will see mosques in one street of Paris, synagogues in another, here some Protestant temples, there some pagodas, when we will make our Capital into a Pantheon where every race will find its temple, and every idol its altar. It is by this confusion of cults," he added, "that religious troubles will be banished; it is from this chaos that peace will be born. Happy Empire of tolerance, when then will you come to free our Bourgeois from the obligation to render his consecrated bread!"[41] Obviously, the Jansenists could no more accept D'Alembert's idea of tolerance than they could that of the elimination of monasticism, the abolition of religious disputes, or the universal application of the principle of public utility upon which all his suggestions were ultimately based.

In the course of censuring his views on tolerance the *Nouvelles Ecclésiastiques* reproached D'Alembert for having contradicted himself. In one place, observed the Jansenist weekly journal, he had described the Jesuits as "intolerant by system and by state" and as the "big grenadiers of fanaticism," while in another, where it was more important to render the Jansenists odious, he had called the Jesuits "accommodating people" who "permit one to think as one wishes."[42] In response, D'Alembert clarified his position in his *Lettre à M. xxx conseiller au parlement de xxx.* The Jansenists, he said, were "tolerant toward no one except their friends, declared or secret," whereas the Jesuits were "tolerant toward all those who did not attack their society." He added that in quoting him, the Jansenists had been careful to delete the phrase "provided that he does not declare himself their enemy," which qualified his assertion that the Jesuits permitted one to think as one wished. Nor would he have bothered, he said, to reveal this "bagatelle" had its example not shown that the Jansenists "know how to employ at need . . . the mental restrictions for which they so reproach the Jesuits."[43]

This venomous little exchange would be no more worth revealing than the "bagatelle" it concerned if its example were not the answer to the question with which we began: What was D'Alembert's quarrel with the Jesuits? In one sense, of course, he did not accuse them of intolerance. On the contrary, he regarded them as not only more tolerant than the Jansenists but perhaps more tolerant than any other Catholic group or organization. But good logician that

41. *Nouvelles Ecclésiastiques* (December 11, 1765), p. 202.
42. Ibid., p. 203.
43. D'Alembert, *Lettre à M. xxx*, pp. 85–86.

he was, D'Alembert would not commit the fallacy of composition. The tolerance he saw as characteristic of Jesuits as individuals he was unwilling to ascribe to the order as such, an order which, dedicated as it was to the conversion of the heathen and the eradication of heresy, could not but remain, as he put it, "intolerant by system and by state." The Jesuits' relative tolerance D'Alembert regarded as a tactic only, a tactic which the order had carried to the farthest possible point, that of tolerating all those who did not in the first instance throw down the gauntlet. But he could not describe as basically tolerant an organization unwilling to tolerate those who, like himself, questioned its authority to be intolerant if, of its sovereign good pleasure, it so chose to be.

Similarly, D'Alembert persisted in viewing the Jesuit Order as substantially monkish—indeed, the aristocrat of the monastic orders—even though the order was in many respects less monkish than the others. Its somewhat less than monastic characteristics did not obscure, in his mind, the fact that Jesuits, too, took the three vows of chastity, poverty, and obedience and a fourth of obedience to the pope as well. Nor did their successful cultivation of the sciences and the arts impede D'Alembert from regarding the Jesuits as the "big grenadiers" of fanaticism or the "regular troops rallied and disciplined under the banner of superstition." Their cultivation of the "sciences and lights" was only, he thought, religious madness with a method. The Jesuit Order, as La Chalotais had earlier pointed out, had been born in the sixteenth century, a century of monkishness, religious fanaticism, and intolerance, and being conceived in monkishness, religious fanaticism, and intolerance, had stained the Jesuit Order with an original sin which, in D'Alembert's judgment, could be effaced neither by the baptism of "sciences and lights" nor by the penance of sacrificing the "minute exercises" of monastic devotion. And far from obscuring its original depravity, the Jesuits' rise to glory and power only rendered it the more despicable, for nothing, said D'Alembert, "more irritates reasonable men than to see monks who have renounced the world and who attempt to govern it." But D'Alembert's sentence of damnation against the Jesuits applied in either case, whether in fact they had renounced the world or attempted to govern it, and nothing, not even their adherence to the doctrine of man's free will, could reverse his decision.

It remains nonetheless true that D'Alembert had written his book as much against the Jansenists as the Jesuits. The "sometime, self-styled" disciples of Jesus, after all, were no more, but the Jansenists, like the poor, he had always with him. And if he saw the Jesuits as unalterably blemished with the original sins of monkishness, religious fanaticism, and intolerance, he regarded Jansenism as a reincarnation of the very "viper"—the word is his—which had brought them into the world in the first place. This viper, he insisted, had to be crushed before "reason" could come into its own.

It becomes the more comprehensible, then, that on December 11, 1765, the

Nouvelles Ecclésiastiques should have declared war on D'Alembert and "philoso-phy," for D'Alembert, not the Jansenists, had fired the first shot. That D'Alem-bert had fired first, however, raises an interesting question: Why should he have thought it worth his trouble to attack those whom he described as a "few poor and obscure priests unknown even in their quarters," the "expiring re-mains of Jansenism," and as "solitary" and "dispersed" Pandours and Cossacks over whom "reason" would soon have a cheap victory? D'Alembert's attitude toward the Jansenist menace was indeed curious. In one breath he assured his readers that after the successful siege of the high and well-fortified fortress of Jesuitism, the already crumbling walls of the Jansenist structure would, like the walls of Jericho, come crashing to the ground at the first resounding blast of the trumpet of "reason." In another breath, however, he darkly hinted that the relatively benevolent despotism of the Jesuits might be replaced by that of the uncompromising Jansenists, and that the Devil might have been cast out only to make straight the highway for Beelzebub.

D'Alembert's ambivalent interpretation of the disaster which had befallen the Jesuits reflected a real tension in his thought. On the one hand, he was con-vinced that his nation was growing ever more enlightened, and that the death of the Jansenists' enemies "would soon bring about their own, not," he added, "with violence, but slowly, by insensible transpiration, and as a necessary con-sequence of the disdain with which this sect inspires all sensible people."[44] On the other hand, he knew very well that it had not been the philosophes, but the Jansenists, who had successfully laid low the high places of the Jesuits, that the Jansenist stronghold which "philosophy's" clarion blast was to topple was none other than the parlement of Paris, and that even within the parlement of Brittany, La Chalotais had probably represented no one but himself. This much D'Alembert himself admitted when he wrote that "the viper which the Jesuits thought they had crushed" suddenly found "strength enough to turn back its head, bite them in the heel, and kill them." And presumably a viper strong enough to smite the Jesuits could at the very least have philosophical books lacerated and burned "at the foot of the great staircase of the Palace."[45]

But D'Alembert need not have worried, for the Jansenists' declaration of war against "philosophy" was stillborn. By 1765 it was far too late for the Jansenists

---

44. D'Alembert, *Sur la Destruction des Jésuites en France,* pp. 207–08.

45. Voltaire had far stronger reservations about the benefit the philosophes could hope to draw from the destruction of the Jesuits. "D'Alembert," says Professor Peter Gay, "wrote excitedly to Ferney that the parlements were executioners serving the philosophes without knowing it. Voltaire, far more politically acute than his brethren, was afraid that the parle-ments were executioners serving no one but themselves, and that the magistrates were right to celebrate the suppression of the Jesuits as a great victory." (Gay, *Voltaire's Politics: The Poet as Realist,* p. 311.) On the relations between Voltaire and D'Alembert in general, see the study by John N. Pappas, *Voltaire and D'Alembert* (Bloomington, Ind., 1962).

to turn their guerilla armies from the easily located and classically defended Jesuit fortresses to face, on another front, forces as elusive and ill-defined as their own. Whatever maneuverability the Jansenists might have possessed they had lost in the course of their more than one hundred years' war against the Jesuits. The Jansenists' response to their new predicament was practically to ignore the menace of "reason" and pretend that the Jesuit Order still existed in France. Not content with their victorious siege of the Jesuit fortresses, the Jansenists now undertook to level them, burn them, and exhume whatever bones they could find therein. It was all very reminiscent of the Jesuits' destruction of Port-Royal in 1709, except that in this case there was no real abbey to destroy, but only phantoms to pursue. First it was the episcopacy, which, to believe the *Nouvelles Ecclésiastiques*, had been brainwashed by the Jesuits and was still controlled by them.[46] Then, in 1767, it was the expulsion of the Jesuits from Spain which occupied both the parlement of Paris and the Jansenist press.[47] In 1769 it was a supposed concentration of ex-Jesuits in the town of Nantes who, it was said, were engaging in seditious activities.[48] In 1771 the Jansenists let it be heard that it was really the Jesuits who had engineered the suppression of the parlement, and that the chancellor, Maupeou, was only their agent.[49] In 1777, three years after the papal dissolution of the society, the Jansenists announced yet another concentration of ex-Jesuits in the town of Lyons who were conspiring, among other things, to infiltrate the Ecole Militaire.[50] Not

46. The Jesuitical nature of the episcopacy was the subject of the *Nouvelles Ecclésiastiques'* New Years' editorials for the remainder of the decade.

47. On April 29, 1767, the abbé Chauvelin again addressed the assembled chambers of the parlement of Paris on the subject of the Jesuits. After assuring parlement that the Jesuits had fomented revolts against the King of Spain in many cities and had therefore been expelled from that country, Chauvelin urged the parlement to expel all the remaining ex-Jesuits in France who had not taken the oaths of August 6, 1762, and February 22, 1764. The parlement issued a decree to that effect on May 9, 1767. (See B.N.: Collection Joly de Fleury, fol. 1611, mss. 111–53). The affair of the Jesuits in Spain, of course, as well as the reaction of the parlement of Paris, occupied the *Nouvelles Ecclésiastiques* for the remainder of 1767.

48. Robert de Saint-Vincent took this rumor seriously enough to write Adrien Le Paige on the subject. (See B.P.R.: L.P. 589, ms. 134.)

49. On January 12, 1771, Robert de Saint-Vincent went so far as to propose that the parlement adopt an *arrêté* accusing Maupeou of being, among other things, an agent of the Jesuit Order. In this instance, however, his colleagues had the good sense to delete the passages concerning the Jesuits. "On insista," he later recalled, "je devais obéir, et je fis dans ce moment-là, comme je l'ai souvent fait depuis, la triste réflexion que les Jésuites avoient plus de protecteurs dans le Parlement en 1771 qu'en 1761 lorsqu'ils ont été détruits" (Saint-Vincent, "Mémoires," p. 504).

50. This supposed plot, too, was a matter of parliamentary concern. On February 21, 1777, M. Angran, president of the third chamber of inquests, addressed the assembled chambers of the parlement of Paris on the subject. For Angran's speech, the parliamentary reaction, and pamphlets published on the occasion, see B.N.: Collection Joly de Fleury, fol. 1611, mss. 300–400.

even the French Revolution could abate their zeal. From his exile in Germany, for example, Robert de Saint-Vincent wrote memoirs to a Spanish minister, Alcudia, advising him never to allow the reestablishment of the Jesuits in that country.[51]

But this anachronistic anti-Jesuitical din only made it clearer that the Jansenists themselves had become anachronistic. They had so defined themselves in terms of their opposition to the Jesuits that by expelling the Jesuits from France they defined themselves out of existence. Like some parasitic creature, they had destroyed the substance upon which they depended for life. It was in vain that the abbé Guidi warned D'Alembert that "having no longer to combat the corrupters of doctrine and morals, it is against their destroyers that we (Christians) will unite our forces," and that the anonymous author of *Lettre à M. xxx* announced that all the "learned men" previously engaged against the Jesuits would now "turn their efforts against unbelief, which will consequently make less progress."[52] This loudly heralded campaign came to little. Though the Jansenists had always insisted that "Jansenism" was an imaginary heresy concocted by the Jesuits, the abbé Guidi spoke more truly than he thought when he asserted that "the Jesuits having ceased to exist, there are no more Jansenists."[53]

51. Saint-Vincent, "Mémoires," pp. 377–78.
52. Guidi, *Lettre à un ami*, p. 36; *Lettre à M. xxx, chevalier de l'ordre de Malte*, p. 26.
53. Guidi, *Lettre à un ami*, p. 33.

Conclusion

FROM ITS ORIGINS IN THE EARLY SEVENTEENTH CENTURY AS A
revival of Catholic Augustinianism, French Jansenism had in part evolved, by
the mid-eighteenth century, into the loudest voice of opposition to both royal
and sacerdotal "despotism." Many circumstances furthered this development—
opposition from the Jesuit Order, the papal condemnations of 1653 and 1656,
persecution on the part of Louis XIV—but most decisive was the promulgation
of the bull *Unigenitus* in 1713. To be sure, the Jansenists objected to this bull in
the first instance because it condemned what they regarded as self-evident
religious truths. Naturally, too, the bull intensified their hatred for the Jesuits,
whom they regarded as its real authors and most ardent enthusiasts. But the bull
also drove them into Gallican opposition to the papacy, its visible author and
protector; into Richerist hostility toward the French episcopacy, which tried to
enforce the bull's acceptance by *billets de confession,* rigged provincial councils,
and the like; into overt war with royal authority itself inasmuch as it protected
the bull, the Jesuits, and the ultramontanist episcopacy; and into the waiting
arms of the parlement of Paris, which had its own quarrels with all of these
institutions.

The alliance between Jansenism and the parlement of Paris, facilitated enor-
mously by *Unigenitus*'s violence to the parlement's Gallican susceptibilities,
resulted in the pooling of their respective grievances and the reinforcement of
both. The Jansenists, for their part, placed themselves in the service of the robe
and its causes, such as its whittling away at the clergy's "spiritual" jurisdiction,
and several among them, especially Adrien Le Paige, significantly developed the
parlements' conception of the French constitution, which pitted them, the
depositaries of the fundamental laws of the realm, against the menace of royal
despotism. And guided as it was by a hard core of Jansenists within its walls,
the parlement of Paris, among others, became the protector of Jansenism and
its causes, a role which sometimes led it perilously beyond its proper tradition,
that of antipapal Gallicanism, and into lands strangely theological in nature. The
result was a political rhetoric that advanced into territory where Jansenism or
parliamentary Gallicanism had separately feared to tread, and that called upon
all "good Frenchmen" to unite against foreign, papal influences which, led by

the Jesuits, were trying to transform the Gallican clergy into its instrument and the French monarchy into a "despotism."

This rhetoric could evidently command the allegiance of a sizable literate—and perhaps even illiterate—"public." Difficult as it is to determine such things, the Jansenist press was at least successful enough in focusing popular discontent upon the bull *Unigenitus,* the *billets de confession,* and the Archbishop of Paris's reorganization of the *hopital général*—in making, that is, its own grievances those of a certain public to the point that in 1752 Barbier could write that "the greater portion of the Parisian people, the bourgeoisie, and even that which is above it, is Jansenist," while in 1757 the quite illiterate domestic servant Damiens could be agitated by Jansenist-parliamentary rhetoric to the extent of attempting to assassinate—or at least wound—the king.[1] Around the same time, the marquis d'Argenson specified, however, that Jansenism was not a "positive heresy" but concerned only "the intrigues of the Jesuits, against whom the entire realm is rising."[2] For it was against the Jesuits, above all, that the *Nouvelles Ecclésiastiques* directed the popular rage, and the journal was successful enough in this to prompt the Jesuit Cerutti to remark, in 1762, that the scandalous activities of the père La Valette on the island of Martinique had occasioned far more public consternation than had the capture of the island itself by the British during the same year.[3]

It is tempting on the basis of this and other evidence to follow Sainte-Beuve and others in concluding that eighteenth-century Jansenism was a purely political phenomenon, wholly devoid of any real religious or theological content. Yet not only did the French Jansenists carry on the old theological campaigns against Molinism and other variants of Pelagianism during this entire period, but the very nature of the controversies which so dominated the public stage—the bull *Unigenitus,* the *billets de confession,* and the Jesuits—were of a sort to maintain the authentically theological aspects of Jansenism in conspicuous view. It was impossible to polemicize against the exaction of *billets de confession* without reference to the bull *Unigenitus,* and it was impossible to argue against this document's status as a law of Church and State without eventually stating what was theologically objectionable about it. And though the Jansenists indeed leveled the highly political charge of "despotism" against the Jesuits in 1761, they just the same harped with undiminished fury upon the highly theological and authentically Jansenist accusations of Pelagianism, probabilism, the philosophical sin, and so on. Despite, therefore, the certain ambiguity in the term *Jansenist* by the 1750s, even the most blatantly political of the Jansenist quarrels of the mid-eighteenth century continued to be recognizably Jansenist—in other

1. Barbier, *Journal,* Vol. 5, p. 225.
2. D'Argenson, *Journal et mémoires,* Vol. 7, p. 270.
3. Cerutti, *Apologie de l'institut des Jésuites,* Vol. 1, pp. 122–23.

words, associated with the theological language in which the movement originally articulated itself.

But Jansenism's very success in finally destroying the Jesuits drastically altered this state of affairs. Not, of course, that Jansenism literally ceased to exist in France; its principal organ, the *Nouvelles Ecclésiastiques,* continued its weekly existence until the end of the French Revolution. With the destruction of the Jesuits, however, the Jansenists played out their most reliable act in their repertory of causes célèbres, and hence ceased—at least recognizably—to play so conspicuous a role in the history of France. The Jansenists' other acts, moreover, soon followed the Jesuits to the backstage. So far as the infamous *billets de confession* are concerned, the clergy for the most part ceased to use them by 1765, and the ultimate source of these *billets,* the bull *Unigenitus,* Pope Pius openly acknowledged to be a dead letter in 1782. Inevitably, the "shadowy theological quarrels" which D'Alembert and Voltaire so deplored but which, well into the 1760s, impressed hard-headed observers such as Marais, Barbier, and D'Argenson as the most important controversies of their century, thereafter gradually lost their hold on the public's attention and gave way to issues of a different, more palpably political sort. Nothing more accurate, then, than D'Alembert's prediction that "disputes concerning religion will be despised and fanaticism will be held in horror." And the decline of these disputes in turn resulted in the Jansenists' own eclipse as leaders or at least as conspicuous participants in the controversies of their century.[4]

This development inevitably affected relations between Jansenism and the parlement of Paris. As perceived at the time, the destruction of the Jesuits represented the penultimate triumph of the parlement no less than that of the Jansenists, and it was not entirely without reason that D'Alembert and Voltaire feared a kind of Jansenist-parliamentary reign of terror against the "party of philosophy" in 1765. The parlement had perhaps never so unequivocally imposed its will upon the sovereign since the Fronde, and its success inaugurated at least an attempt on the monarchy's part to coordinate both its ecclesiastical and fiscal policies with those of the parlement, aptly symbolized by the appointment of Laverdy—a Jansenist—to the post of controller-general of finance.[5] The parlement and Jansenists continued to be of one accord in vilifying the "Acts" of the general assembly of the Gallican clergy in 1765 (in this affair the Jansenists discovered that the French bishops had inherited the "despotism" which they thought they had safely interred with the Jesuit Order) and in trumpeting the victory of "providence" and "Bourbon blood" over an allegedly Jesuit-directed sedition in Spain in 1766.[6] In the minds, at least, of

4. D'Alembert, *Sur la Destruction des Jésuites en France,* p. 205.
5. Egret, *Louis XV et l'opposition parlementaire,* pp. 98–99.
6. See, for example, the pamphlet *Réflexions sur le despotisme des évêques, et les interdits*

pamphleteers and some participants, the complex series of quarrels known as the La Chalotais affair, which led directly to Chancellor Maupeou's suppression of the parlements in 1771, were related in not altogether obvious ways to Jansenism and the defunct Jesuit Order.

Nonetheless, with the disappearance of the Jesuits, Jansenism and the parlement of Paris found themselves of less and less use to each other, and beginning around 1765 their paths tended to diverge. Already in 1771, but "many times thereafter," Robert de Saint-Vincent could make the "sad reflection that the Jesuits had more protectors in the Parlement . . . than in 1761 when they were destroyed," by which he really meant that the parlement as a whole had ceased to concern itself very much with matters that continued to interest Jansenists exclusively.[7] What increasingly preoccupied the parlement, especially after its restoration in 1774, were the monarchy's fiscal measures, and its opposition to these eventually carried it willy-nilly to the very mouth of eighteenth-century political strife, the Revolution of 1789. But Jansenism as such seemed to get caught in the eddies and backwaters. No source more clearly reflects this trend than the *Nouvelles Ecclésiastiques*. Fewer and fewer of its pages, after 1765, concern the proceedings of the parlement of Paris, and its attention, between the years 1789 and 1794, is so exclusively riveted upon ecclesiastical affairs as to leave one not altogether certain that a political revolution took place.

But what of another of D'Alembert's prophecies, that "the nation will probably become more and more enlightened?"[8] Did the Jansenists' victory over the Jesuits in some way contribute to the triumph of the Enlightenment in France? Undoubtedly so. For by destroying the Jesuits and thereby eliminating itself as the most conspicuous "party" of political and ecclesiastical dissent, the *parti janséniste* created a kind of vacuum which, to a certain degree at least, D'Alembert's *parti philosophique* was quick to occupy. It is perhaps not accidental that in 1762, the very year in which the parlement of Paris promulgated its definitive decree abolishing the Jesuit Order, Voltaire himself launched the "party of philosophy" upon its first successful cause célèbre against an instance of the "infamous thing": the fanatically Catholic parlement of Toulouse's condemnation and execution of the Protestant Jean Calas for supposedly having strangled his son. D'Alembert might have falsely attributed the victory over the Jesuits to the "party of philosophy," but there could be no disputing this party's part in the victory when, in 1764, the King's private council annulled

---

arbitraires, which was directed against the "Acts" of the General Assembly of the Gallican Clergy of 1765–66. On the expulsion of the Jesuits from Spain, see the abbé Chauvelin's harangue on this subject of April 29, 1767, in B.N: Collection Joly de Fleury, fol. 1611, mss. 113–14.

7. Saint-Vincent, "Mémoires," p. 504.

8. D'Alembert, *Sur la Destruction des Jésuites,* p. 205.

the verdict of the parlement of Toulouse, and in the following year pronounced the Calas family innocent.[9] Moreover, the years following the end of the Jesuits' affair—the mid- and later 1760s—roughly approximate the beginning of the period which Daniel Mornet, in his monumental attempt to measure the spread of the Enlightenment in France, called the "exploitation of the victory," when the "philosophical spirit" achieved a general "diffusion" of France, became increasingly political, and, within this realm, passed from a consideration of abstract principles to concrete consequences and a demand for "real and practical reforms."[10]

Yet to conclude that Jansenism's only contribution to the remainder of the eighteenth century was to have conveniently gotten out of the way in time for the Enlightenment to lead France to the Revolution is to shortchange considerably the historical significance of both Jansenism and its victory over the Jesuits in 1764. To conclude no more than this would be to contribute only a variation on a theme originally composed by D'Alembert—that "Philosophy" was the ultimate beneficiary in the condemnation of the Jesuits and that "Jansenism was only the solicitor in it"—and to pass on a distortion implicit in a widely held view of eighteenth-century France as a whole, that of a purely passive, receptive entity which a uniquely active "Enlightenment" influenced in sundry ways. Even by itself, the evidence of Jansenism's words and deeds in its campaign against the Jesuits points unmistakably toward the conclusion not only that Jansenism's relation to the rest of the eighteenth century was more than merely negative and circumstantial, but that it was positive and direct as well.

After all, Jansenism's very "disappearance" after the dissolution of the Jesuit Order is something of an optical illusion. What grew less visible, to be precise, is theological Jansenism, or rather the kinds of controversies through which Jansenism could recognizably articulate itself. But in the course of these very controversies Jansenism had developed some deep-seated political attitudes—toward the State, toward the ecclesiastical "establishment" both national and international, and on the proper relations among all these—which not only survived the demise of the Jesuits but became the patrimony of the later eighteenth century, including the Enlightenment.

Jansenism as positive contributor to the Enlightenment in France? The idea would have appalled D'Alembert, and the evidence from the Jansenists' literary brawl with this philosophe mainly buttresses the conclusions of those studies

9. On the Calas affair, see Bien, *The Calas Affair: Persecution, Toleration, and Heresy in Eighteenth-Century Toulouse;* and on Voltaire's part in it, see Gay, *Voltaire's Politics,* pp. 273–308.

10. Daniel Mornet, *Les Origines intellectuelles de la Révolution française* (6th ed. Paris, 1967), Part III ("L'Exploitation de la victoire"), but esp. the conclusion, pp. 473–76.

which have stressed the profound differences in outlook between the two movements.[11] Indeed, in their general views of God, the world, and man, no two groups could be more opposed than were the Jansenists and philosophes in eighteenth-century France. But if by "Enlightenment" we understand, not just the writings and opinions of the major philosophes, but the extreme anticlericalism, the denunciations of "despotism," and the rhetoric of "patriotism"—in a word, the general "climate of opinion" which came to characterize late eighteenth-century and revolutionary France—then not only did Jansenism importantly contribute to the "Enlightenment," but around mid-century was perhaps in specific respects more "enlightened" than some of the philosophes themselves.[12]

The Jansenists might have defended the validity—even the necessity—of religious disputes against D'Alembert in 1765, but as D'Alembert himself observed, they heartily approved of Louis XV's Law of Silence of 1754 by which the State severely limited the clergy's right to carry on religious disputes, at least in certain matters. Again, the Jansenists might have defended the sanctity of monasticism against D'Alembert's irreverent remarks, but they nonetheless justified the State's dissolution of the monastic vows of the Jesuit Order in France, as well as the confiscation of its property. To be sure, the Jansenists balked at the idea of the separation of Church and State when it was hinted at by D'Alembert, but such an arrangement did not soon come to prevail and in any case only imperfectly represents "philosophical" thinking on the matter. The revolutionary settlement of 1790, the Civil Constitution of the Clergy, by democratizing the Church, ending its independence, and subjecting it largely to the State, went far toward implementing what had long been the profound, if sometimes hesitating, direction of Jansenist ecclesiastical thought: a Constantinian subordination of Church to State and the consequent—if largely unintended—secularization of society. Among the Jansenists we have encountered, Le Paige lived to welcome the Civil Constitution, and the abbé Clément went on to become "constitutional" Bishop of Versailles.[13]

---

11. Esp. Palmer, *Catholics and Unbelievers in Eighteenth-Century France,* and Groethuysen, *Die Entstehung der Bürgerlichen Welt-und Lebensanschaung in Frankreich.*

12. For another attempt to relate Jansenism and the Enlightenment in some positive sense, see Robert Shackleton's suggestive article, "Jansenism and the Enlightenment," *Studies on Voltaire and the Eighteenth Century,* 57 (1967), 1387–97.

13. Préclin, *Les Jansénistes du XVIIIᵉ siècle et la constitution civile du clergé,* pp. 502, 509. Moreover, several Jansenists figured importantly in the National Assembly's committee which drafted the articles of the Civil Constitution as well as in the assembly's debates preceeding its adoption: the abbés Grégoire and Saurine, and the lawyers Camus and Lanjuinais (ibid., p. 463). The above comments are not intended to obscure the fact that diverse influences went into the making of the Civil Constitution, some of them "philosophical" or purely Gallican, and that the final product alienated a good many Jansenists whose

It is easy to see that the driving force behind the reluctant "secularization" of Jansenist ecclesiastical thought was an anticlericalism born of the hard experience of episcopal and papal persecution. It is doubtful that Jansenists would have ever thought to justify the State's interference in so "spiritual" a matter as the administration of the sacraments, for example, had they not been so frequently denied them, or that they would occasionally have gone so far as to ridicule religious "zeal"—zeal for the bull *Unigenitus,* of course—had they not so often been its victims. Nevertheless, the consequences of Jansenist anticlericalism were much the same as if they had flowed from an unimpeachably "enlightened" source. It is, after all, the central point of this study that the Jansenists, not the philosophes, first engineered the suppression of a religious order in eighteenth-century France, thereby paving the way for the later suppressions by the *commission des réguliers* and, of course, the Revolution itself.[14] And when directed against the episcopacy, it is arguable that the sheer virulence of Jansenist anticlericalism could at least keep pace with, and perhaps even surpass, anything that a Voltaire or a D'Alembert could muster around mid-century.[15]

In fact, Jansenism contributed to the growing anticlericalism in eighteenth-century France in two ways: directly, by injecting its own, and indirectly, by eliminating the one group of apologists—the Jesuits—who, because of the proximity of their conceptions of man and nature and a common appropriation of the yardsticks of reason and utility, were able to argue with the philosophes with some degree of civility and mutual comprehension. By proudly insisting upon going it alone against "unbelief" and then having it their way, the Jansenists ensured that Catholic Christianity would appear all the more remote and unintelligible to the philosophes, thus unwittingly contributing to the making of an Enlightenment much more vitriolically anticlerical—even anti-Christian—than its considerably tamer counterparts elsewhere in Europe.

It was not in its attitude toward the ecclesiastical "establishment" alone, but in its conception of the State, too, that Jansenism, together with its inevitable Gallican and parliamentary allies, profoundly influenced the later eighteenth century. The combination of antipapal Gallicanism and Jansenist religious "enthusiasm" produced an explosive xenophobia—indeed, a kind of nationalism

---

Richerism had remained relatively uncontaminated by elements of what Préclin specifies as "laïcisme," "césarisme," and "gallicanisme parlementaire" (ibid., pp. 480–89). These elements, however, were by the mid-18th century only theoretically distinguishable from Jansenism.

14. On the work of the *commission des réguliers,* see S. Lemaire, *La Commission des Réguliers, 1760–1780* (Paris, 1926), passim.

15. See, for example, the anonymous pamphlet, obviously of Jansenist inspiration, entitled *Parallel de la conduite du clergé avec celle du parlement à l'égard des Jésuites* (1762), esp. pp. 106–09.

before the letter—which became a constant element in Jansenist and parliamentary hostility toward the Jesuit Order. Unlike the comparatively cosmopolitan philosophes, who could at least derive an aesthetic satisfaction from the contemplation of the Jesuit Order's structure and tactics, the Jansenists could only view the society, in the words of Ripert de Monclar, as a "monster of error" which had diabolically eschewed a "French Regime" (that is, not a despotic one) and a "national spirit," and hence snatched potential "Citizens," whom it carried away from the "fatherland."[16] The evidence from their respective attitudes toward the Jesuits, at least, suggests that Jansenists and extreme Gallicans were well in advance over the philosophes in disseminating the notion of the State as a "nation" and in propagating what Mornet has called the "morality of patriotism," so characteristic of the mentality of pre-Revolutionary France.[17]

With the one hand the Jansenists were reducing the "independence" of the clergy in the name of the king; with the other, however, they were busy limiting the power of the king in the name of the parlements, the "fundamental laws of the realm," and—ultimately—the "nation" itself. And here too (independently of the question of whether or not the parlements were really agents of "feudal" reaction) the Jansenists, in loudly denouncing "despotism," were generally ahead of the philosophes in the 1760s in disseminating a kind of political rhetoric that became commonplace in "enlightened" literature on the eve of the Revolution. It is of course true that despite the less than ecstatic review which the *Esprit des lois* received in the *Nouvelles Ecclésiastiques,* the Jansenists probably borrowed a page or two from Montesquieu in their definition of "despotism."[18] But while Montesquieu safely relegated the phenomenon to hot African climates and vast Oriental expanses, the Jansenists un-

---

16. Monclar, *Compte rendu des constitutions des Jésuites, par M. Jean-Pierre-François Ripert de Monclar, procureur général du roi au parlement de Provence,* p. 260.

17. Mornet, *Les Origines intellectuelles de la Révolution française,* pp. 258–66. See also Bickart, *Les Parlements et la notion de souveraineté nationale;* and R. R. Palmer, "The National Idea in France before the Revolution," *Journal of the History of Ideas,* 1 (January 1940), esp. 103–05. Nothing could be more untrue, in any case, than Hans Kohn's statement that "Jansenism played only a minor part in determining French nationalism" (*The Idea of Nationalism: A Study of Its Origins and Background* [New York, 1944], p. 190.

18. *Nouvelles Ecclésiastiques* (October 9–16, 1749), pp. 161–67. Jansenism, for its adherents, perhaps functioned as a vehicle of political radicalization in much the same way as Mesmerism, according to Robert Darnton, so functioned for people like Brissot and Carra later in the century. Both experiences, Jansenist and Mesmerist, resulted in denunciations of "despotism" against the unlikeliest institutions. Indeed, there may exist more direct connections between Jansenism and Mesmerism. Robert Darnton provocatively suggests in one place that Mesmerism "might even be viewed as a lay revival of Jansenism" (*Mesmerism and the End of the Enlightenment in France* [Cambridge, Mass., 1968], p. 61, but also pp. 36–38 and, in general, pp. 83–125).

covered examples of despotism much closer to home and in the most unlikely places: the king's council, episcopal behavior, and the structure of the Jesuit Order itself.

In most if not all of these matters, however, it is quite true that the philosophes could go much further in principle than the Jansenists. Philosophes could condemn all monastic orders, whereas Jansenists could only condemn the Jesuit Order—and perhaps a few others too closely associated with it. Philosophes could condemn all religious disputes, whereas Jansenists could urge the suppression of only those which involved the bull *Unigenitus* and employed pejorative terms such as *Jansenist*. Philosophes could urge the total subordination of the Church to State and the laicization of the latter, whereas Jansenists could only whittle away at the "independence" of the episcopacy here and there in the name of these and those precedents and by means of the trusty *appel comme d'abus*. What the philosophes could do globally and in principle the Jansenists could do only in particular and by way of exception. Yet within this restricted arena the Jansenists could often be far more intense and serious than the philosophes. Not only did the Jansenists rail at the Jesuit Order—even if only at this order—but they destroyed it. And perhaps more than anything else, it was its very intensity and seriousness, its religious "enthusiasm" which Jansenism bequeathed to the "philosophical" cause of the later eighteenth century. One comes away from the exposure to Jansenist·rhetoric and activity of the mid-eighteenth century with the strong impression that if indeed the "Enlightenment" triumphed in France by the eve of the Revolution, it did not do so without itself becoming, in both concrete and amorphous ways, more Jansenist.[19]

19. The notion that Jansenism might have positively influenced the shape of the French Enlightenment, however foreign to 20th-century views, was not at all uncommon among 19th-century French historians. None of these, however, more succinctly expressed this notion than Théophile Foisset. After marveling, in one place, at how "by a transformation hardly discernible, entirely plebiscitory maxims should have emerged from originally theological clashes," he added: "One is permitted to doubt whether the principles of liberty and the theory of a royalty not merely limited, but even controlled in its movements, would have acquired an authority so general and prompt in France, if these principles and that theory had not been as it were grafted into the old Jansenist trunk, if they had not thereby sent profound roots into consciences, misled no doubt, but austere and strong all the same, by associating themselves with that which is most profound and invincible in the world: the religious sensibility" (*Le Président de Brosses. Histoire des lettres et des parlements au XVIII*e *siècle*, p. 36).

Bibliography

PRIMARY SOURCES

Manuscripts

Archives des Affaires Etrangères
Série Mémoires et Documents
    France: Vols. 1289, 1366, 1371, 1384.
    Rome: Vol. 9: "Mémoires relatifs à l'affaire du P. la Valette (1761–1767), aux griefs qui ont amené la suppression de la compagnie, déclaration du roi et arrêté du parlement contre les Jésuites de France (1761–1762)"; Vol. 86: "Concernant la suppression des Jésuites en Portugal."
Série Correspondance politique
    Rome: Vols. 819–39: "Années 1755–1765."

Archives de la Bastille
    Mss. 11,825; 11,853; 11,882–83: Lettres de l'abbé Bottari, précepteur des princes Corsini, puis garde de la bibliothèque du Vatican, adressés à M. de Caylus, évêque d'Auxerre, et à l'abbé Clément, trésorier de l'église cathédrale à Auxerre; and mss. 11,953; 12,027; 12,228; 12,264–65; 12,295.

Archives de la Maison de Saint Louis (Chantilly)
    Manuscript of Jacques de Flesselles: "Relation exacte de tout ce qui s'est passé relativement au decret interprétif de celuy d'aquaviva de 1610, envoyé à Rome et refusé par le Général, ainsy qu'à la déclaration que le Général a pareillement refusé d'approuver."

Archives Départmentales des Pyrénées Orientales
Série 2B (Greffe du tribunal civil)
    Liasses 88–89: Registre des délibérations du conseil souverain depuis 1756 jusqu'en 1770; 548–49: Minutes des arrêts civils; 702: Arrêts civils enregistrés.

Archives Départmentales de la Seine Inférieure
Archives du parlement de Normandie
    Registre secret des délibérations: années 1761–1764.

Archives Nationales
Série E (Conseil des Dépêches)
    Cartons 1684–87, 1696–1982, 2043–45, 2047–2661b, 2784 (2).
Série G⁸ (Agence générale du Clergé)
    Cartons 617: Etat des Jésuites poursuivis en France; 692–93: Procès-verbaux des

assemblées du clergé de 1760–1762; 694–96: Procès-verbaux de la grande assemblée du clergé de 1765–1766; 2589–91: Correspondance des agents généraux du clergé, 1760–1762; 2628: Correspondance des secrétaires d'état avec les agents généraux du clergé, 1729–1765; 2790–91: Délibérations du Conseil du clergé de France, 1760–1762.

Série K and KK

    Cartons K 682: Recueil de projets, de mémoires et de lettres sur les affaires intéressantes le parlement depuis 1752 jusqu'en 1757; 698, I-VI: Affaires du parlement de Paris; 703–04: Affaires des parlements; 707, I-VI: Suppression des Jésuites au parlement d'Aix; 711, I-II: Parlement de Rouen; 712, I-IX: Parlement de Rennes; 713, I-II: Suppression des Jésuites au parlement de Toulouse; K 1361: Procès-verbal de l'assemblée extraordinaire des évêques en 1761; KK 821: "Journal anecdotique sur la vie du parlement à Bourges" by Pierre-Augustin Robert de Saint-Vincent and Durey de Mesnières.

Série L (Monuments écclésiastiques)

    Carton 20: Notes de Joly de Fleury sur les poursuites exercées, principalement pour refus de sacrements, à la suite de la promulgation de la bulle *Unigénitus*.

Série M and MM

    Cartons M 240(2): Jésuites: mémoires sur l'ordre, extraits des constitutions; 241: Etablissement et bannissement de l'ordre, mémoires historiques; 243: Recueil de pièces et mémoires concernant les Jésuites de France; 244: Lettres patentes et arrêts du parlement concernant les Jésuites; 249–50: Collèges des Jésuites; 250: Jésuites: organisation, doctrines, biens et rentes; 744: Mémoires et pièces diverses sur la doctrine des Jésuites; 746: Mémoires, lettres et pièces diverses sur la bulle *Unigénitus* et le Jansénisme; MM 648: Jésuites: la tradition meutrière, ouvrage manuscrit; 649–53: Jésuites: serments à la Vierge; 654: Jésuites: séquestre; 655: Jésuites: collège d'Aix.

Série X (Parlement de Paris)

    Sous-série X¹ᴬ (Parlement civil, registres)

    Conseil secret: 8503–33; lettres patentes, ordonnances.

    Sous-série X¹ᴮ (Parlement civil, registres)

    Plaidoiries: 8167; conseil secret: 8937–46; procès des Jésuites: 9695–97.

Série AP (Archives privées)

    1 AP 687: Correspondance Fermé; 690: Correspondance Maultrot; 695: Correspondance Texier; 26 AP 36 B: Papiers de Mesnières; 54B: Liquidation des créanciers des Jésuites; 111 AP, 14 d.3: Lettre d'Aubry, avocat; 154 AP II: Chartrier de Tocqueville, fonds Lamoignon Malesherbes, liasses 1–56.

Documents hors série

    Archives du marquis de Rosanbo, fonds Lamoignon de Malesherbes, carton 1, dossier 6.

Archives Privées

    Archives de M. Michel Vinot Préfontaine

    Fonds Robert de Saint-Vincent: "Mémoires de Pierre-Augustin-Robert de Saint-Vincent, 1725–1791."

Bibliothèque Municipale de Rouen
Collection Lebet
    Y 67: Correspondance Miromesnil.

Bibliothèque Nationale (*Cabinet des Manuscrits*)
Fonds français
    5751: Affaires de la bulle *Unigénitus*, 1756–1757; 7563–64: Religion, droit canonique; 7568: L'Hôpital général; 7570: Refus de sacrements; 10908–09: Délibérations et procès-verbaux du parlement.
Fonds français, nouvelles acquisitions
    8496: "Histoire des remontrances du 9 avril 1753 par Rolland d'Erceville"; 12865: Lettres du P. N. Fabre, S.J., au président du parlement de Provence N. de Gueydon (1739–1759), et des PP. Albertin, Dugaiby, Pontevès, Tolomas, suivies de déclarations ou arrêts imprimés concernant les Jésuites (1715–1763).
Collection Joly de Fleury
    Folios 563–608: Avis et mémoires sur les affaires publiques, 1712–1787; 609–920: Conclusions du procureur-général, 1720–1789; 1048–49; Lettres patentes non enregistrées au parlement de Paris, 1714–1763; 1247–48: Hôpital-général; 1337: Conseil d'Artois, affaire des Jésuites en 1762; 1552: Affaire des Jésuites au collège d'Amiens; 1609: Jésuites: suppression de l'ordre, 1759–1763; 1610: Jésuites: suppression de l'ordre, 1763–1765; 1611: Jésuites: suppression de l'ordre, 1765–1777; 1612: Constitutions de l'ordre, critique de ces constitutions, mémoires et réponses des Jésuites et de leurs adversaires, appels comme d'abus, projet de déclaration (1761), correspondance avec les ministres, 1761–1764; 1613–1614: Biens et dettes de l'ordre (1762–1779), documens sur les collèges; 1615: Correspondances diverses; 1616: Actes anciens et pamphlets, 1560–1760 (collection formée par le procureur-général et l'avocat-général); 1617–28: Affaires locales; 1629: Affaires de Paris; 1630: Pays étrangers; 1631: Table des affaires, liste des Jésuites qui se trouvent dans chacun des cas prévus par les différents arrêts du parlement; 1664: Matières écclésiastiques: document se rapportant principalement aux Jésuites et au Jansénisme; 1684–86: Censure de la collection des conciles du P. Hardouin; 1687: Thèses sorbonniques; 1688: Plans d'études proposés au procureur-général par diverses personnes en 1762; après l'expulsion des Jésuites; 1709; Paris: faculté de Théologie (1703–1780), thèses censurées, doctrines hétérodoxes, affaire de la bulle *Unigénitus;* 1825–56: Affaires judicaires, causes célèbres (1757–1764); 2068–77: Procès Damiens; 2103: Parlement: exile à Pontoise (1753), affaires religieuses (1753–1757), intervention du prince de Conti, lettres écrites par lui au procureur-général; 2482–86: Affaires particulières; 2491–92: Bibliographie étendue des ouvrages relatifs aux Jansénisme et aux Jésuites.

Bibliothèque de Port-Royal (169 rue St. Jacques, Paris V[e])
Collection Le Paige
    Recueils 22: Projets pour les remontrances de 1753, Paris sur le schisme, schisme; 136: Supplément aux Jésuites; 457: Religion, Prades, "Encyclopédie" (1734–1750); 468: Jésuites, casuistes, réguliers (1560–1660); 469: Jésuites, casuistes, réguliers (1660–1680); 470: Supplément aux Jésuites et réguliers, 1535–1698; 471:

Supplément aux casuistes, 1660–1680; 472: Auxerre contre les Jésuites, P. Berruyer (1725 et suivante); affaire du P. Berruyer, 1754; 516: Schisme, billets,
hôpital, affaires publiques (1751–1752), 517: Schisme, billets de confession (1752–
1783): 518: Deuxième supplément au schisme, 1749–1760; 519: Supplément au
schisme: Châtelet, Rouen, Orléans, Aix (1752–1755); 520: Supplément au schisme,
1752–1756; 524: Affaire du P. Pichon, 1747–1749; 532: Supplément au parlement;
534: Sur le parlement, origine des troubles (1754–1755); 535: Déclaration de 1754,
suites (1754–1755); 537: Assemblée du clergé, schisme, Auxerre (1755); 541:
Lettres, 1755–1783; 547: Démission du parlement, schisme, mort de Benoît XIV
(1756–1758); 548: Affaire de Damiens, Luçon (1757–1783); 549: Suite du procès;
550: "Voyage d'Italie et d'Espagne" (manuscript of part of the abbé Clément's
*Journal de correspondances et voyages d'Italie et d'Espagne pour la paix de l'église en 1758,
1768 et 1769* [2 vols. Paris, 1802]); 551: Clément XIII, schisme (1758–1759); 554:
Instruction pastorale de M. de Soissons, 1760; 555: Assemblée générale du clergé
(1760–1762), Mesengui, schisme (1760–1765); 556: Parlement de Besançon, 1759–
1760; 562: Assemblée du clergé (1765), schisme, autres (1765–1769); 569–570:
Destruction des parlements, 1771; 577: Schisme, miracle, doctrine, Jésuites (1779–
1785); 581: Jésuites de Portugal, 1757–1761; 582: Paris contre les Jésuites: Lioncy,
institut; 583: Parlement contre les Jésuites (Paris), 1762; 584: Suite des Jésuites:
édit de destruction, 1763–1764; 585: Comptes sur les Jésuites et collèges, 1765–
1768; 586: Lettres patentes sur les Jésuites, créanciers, collèges (1763–1769); 587:
Recueil des délibérations: collège de Louis-Le-Grand, 1763–1782; 588: Suite de
l'assemblée Castillon, supplément aux Jésuites (1765–1768); 589: Bulle apostolique,
Espagne, Parme, abolition des Jésuites (1765–1770); 590: Clément XIV, extinction
des Jésuites, schisme, doctrine (1769–1774); 859–860: Aix contre les Jésuites; 866:
Roussillon contre les Jésuites.

Bibliothèque du Sénat

Founds Boissy d'Anglas (Bibliothèque et Manuscrits du President de Mesnières)
Folios 434: "Mémoire sur la nécessité de laisser au parlement sa juridiction sur
l'hôpital général de Paris, par l'abbé Chauvelin"; 561–571: Registres du parlement
de Paris, première chambre des enquêtes (1758–1766); 732: Registres du parlement
de Paris, deuxième chambre des enquêtes (1717–1756); 800, tome I, fol. I: "Journal
de M. le président de Mesnières"; 800, fol. 101: "Journal de M. Lambert, depuis
le 8 mai 1749 au 8 juin 1758"; 800, fol. 186: "Journal de M. d'Erceville, mai 1751
à septembre"; 802–806: "Journal du parlement de Paris, formé par M. de Brou-
ville (1760–1770)."

Printed or Published Works

*Anonymous**

Abrassevin, le père. *Tout le monde a tort, ou Jugement impartial d'une dame philosophique sur
l'affaire présente des Jésuites.* France, 1762.

---

*All authorship indicated under "anonymous" is to one degree or another conjectural.
In order to avoid the use of brackets, the authors in cases of near or total certainty have
been given in the footnotes, but are usually indicated as officially anonymous in the text
or elsewhere in the notes.

Additions aux Motifs pressants et déterminants d'anéantir la société des Jésuites (1er septembre 1759). N.p., n.d.

Additions aux problèmes historiques: Qui, des Jésuites, ou de Luther et Calvin, ont le plus nui à l'église chrétienne? N.p., n.d.

Additions importantes et nécessaires, pour servir de supplément à la première édition de l'Abrégé de l'histoire de la société de Jésus. N.p., n.d.

Affaire des cent-un tableaux. N.p., n.d.

Alembert, Jean Le Rond d'. *Lettre à M. xxx conseiller au parlement de xxx pour servir de supplément à l'ouvrage qui est dedié à ce même magistrat, et qui a pour titre: 'Sur la Destruction des Jésuites en France, par un auteur désintéressé.'* N.p., 1767.

———. *Second lettre à M. xxx conseiller au parlement de xxx sur l'édit du roi d'Espagne, pour l'expulsion des Jésuites.* N.p., 1767.

———. *Sur la Destruction des Jésuites en France, par un auteur désintéressé.* N.p., 1765.

L'Ami des Jésuites, ou Éloge de la société, avec un précis de sa justification. Par M. Lxxx, ex-jésuite. N.p., 1762.

Analyse des réponses à toutes les apologies des Jésuites, et des principaux griefs contre la société. France, n.d.

Anecdotes écclésiastiques jésuitiques. N.p., 1760.

Anti-ladrérie des Jésuites de France, ou Lettre de M. xxx à M. xxx, sur le silence des Jésuites. N.p., n.d.

L'Apologie des Jésuites, convaincue d'attentats contre les loix divines et humaines. 3 parts in 1 vol. N.p., 1763.

L'Apparition de la comète. Preuve astronomique contre les Jésuites. N.p., 1759.

L'Apparition du cardinal Bellarmin au révérend père Ricci général des Jésuites, la nuit du 5 janvier 1760. Ouvrage traduit de l'italien. N.p., n.d.

Avis aux évêques assemblées à Paris en décembre 1761, au sujet des Jésuites. N.p., n.d.

L'Avocat du diable, ou Les Jésuites condamnés malgré 'l'Appel à la raison.' Tartare (?), 1762.

Balbani, André Christophe. *Acceptation du défi hasardé par l'auteur d'un libelle intitulé: 'Réplique aux apologies des Jésuites.'* Avignon, 1762.

———. *Appel à la raison des écrits et libelles publiés par la passion contre les Jésuites de France.* Brussels, 1762.

———. *Nouvel appel à la raison, des écrits et libelles publiés par la passion contre les Jésuites de France.* Brussels, 1762.

Barral, Pierre. *Manuel des sourverains.* N.p., 1754.

———. *Maximes sur le devoir des rois et le bon usage de leur autorité. Tirées de différents auteurs.* France, 1754.

Cerutti, Jean-Antoine-Joachim. *Apologie de l'institut des Jésuites.* 2d ed. 2 vols. in one. N.p., 1763.

Clémencet, dom. *Authenticité des pièces du procès criminel de religion contre les Jésuites depuis deux cent ans: démontrée contre un libelle intitulé: Additions aux 'Motifs pressants et déterminants qui obligent en conscience les deux puissances, écclésiastiques et séculières, à anéantir la société des Jésuites.* N.p., 1760.

———. *Lettre (-seconde) du doge de la république des Apistes au général des Solipses, pour lui demander du secours dans une guerre qui intéresse les deux nations.* N.p., n.d.

Compte rendu au public des comptes rendus aux divers parlements et autres cours supérieures. 2 vols. Paris, 1765.

Conversation intéressante dénoncée par un espion de la société à l'auteur de la ladrérie prétendue des Jésuites français, où l'on trouve des faits graves, des reproches fondés, des avis salutaires pour et contre les bons pères Jésuites (31 juillet 1759). N.p., n.d.

Coudrette, Christophe. *Idée générale des vices principaux de l'institut des Jésuites tirées de leurs constitutions et des autres titres de leur société.* Paris, 1761.

Déclaration de guerre contre les auteurs du parricide tenté sur la personne du roi (22 mars). N.p., n.d.

De la Destruction des Jésuites, par un ancien magistrat: Dedié aux ministres présents et à venir. Paris, 1826.

Documents historiques, critiques, apologétiques concernant la compagnie de Jésus. 2 vols. Paris, 1827.

Durey de Mesnières, Jean-Baptiste François. *Indication sommaire des principes et des faits qui prouvent la compétence de la puissance seculière pour punir les évêques coupables de crimes publics, et pour les contenir dans l'obéissance qu'ils doivent aux lois, et dans la soumission qu'ils doivent au roi.* France, 1755.

Griffet, Henri. *Coup d'œil sur l'arrêt du parlement de Paris, du 6 août 1761, concernant l'institut des Jésuites imprimé à Prague en 1757.* Avignon, 1761.

———. *Mémoire concernant l'institut, la doctrine et l'établissement des Jésuites en France.* 2d ed. Rennes, 1762.

———. *Remarques sur un écrit intitulé: 'Compte rendu des constitutions des Jésuites, par M. Louis-René de Caradeuc de la Chalotais.'* N.P., n.d.

Grosley. *Mémoires pour servir de supplément aux 'Antiquités écclésiastiques du diocèse de Troyes par M. N. Camuzat.'* N.p., 1750.

Guéret, Louis Gabriel. *Lettre d'un théologien, sur l'exaction des certificats de confession pour administrer le saint viatique.* N.p., January 17, 1751.

Guidi, l'abbé. *Lettre à un ami sur un écrit intitulé: 'Sur la Destruction des Jésuites en France, par un auteur désintéressé.'* N.p., n.d.

L'Histoire de Robert François Damiens. Paris, 1757.

L'Inutilité des Jésuites demontrée aux évêques. France, 1752.

Le Jésuite mal défendu, à M. l'abbé Platel: ou Dispute entre M. Brokter, docteur en théologie, et M. l'abbé Tusselein, prieur de Rxxx, au sujet de la Réponse des R.R. pères Jésuites, à l'ouvrage intitulée: Idée général des vices principaux de l'institut des Jésuites. N.p., n.d.

Les Jésuites assassins, ou Anecdotes pour servir à la continuation des lettres édifiantes du révérend père Patouillet et associés. Leiden, 1762.

Les Jésuites criminels de lèse-majesté, dans la théorie et dans la pratique. The Hague, 1758.

Les Jésuites justifiés par les parlements. N.p., n.d.

Les Jésuites marchands, usuriers, usurpateurs, et leurs cruautés dans l'ancien et nouveau continent. The Hague, 1759.

Jouin, Nicolas. *Procès contre les Jésuites, pour servir de suite aux 'Causes célèbres.'* Brest, 1750.

Journal de ce qui s'est passé dans l'affaire des Jésuites, depuis le 15 septembre 1761 jusqu'au 5 juin 1762. N.p., n.d.

Lambert, le père. *Anecdotes jésuitiques, ou Le Philotanus moderne.* 3 vols. The Hague, 1740.

Le Paige, Louis-Adrien. *Le Philosophe redressé, ou Réfutation de l'écrit intitulé: 'Sur la Destruction des Jésuites en France, par un curé de village.'* N.p., 1765.

———. *Lettres adressés à MM. les commissaires nommés par le roi pour délibérer sur l'affaire* présente du parlement au sujet du refus des sacrements ou Lettres pacifiques au sujet des contestations présentes. N.p., 1752.

———. Lettres sur les fonctions essentielles du parlement, sur le droit des pairs, et sur les lois fondamentales du royaume. 2 vols. Amsterdam, 1753–54.

———. Réflexions de l'auteur des 'Lettres pacifiques' sur les lois que les souverains sont en droit de faire pour rétablir la paix dans leurs états, quand ils sont troublés par les disputes de religion. N.p., n.d.

———, and Christophe Coudrette. Histoire générale de la naissance et des progrès de la compagnie de Jésus en France et analyse de ses constitutions et privilèges. 4 vols. Paris, 1761.

Lettre à l'auteur de l'article 'Jésuite' dans le 'Dictionnaire encyclopédique,' ou Compte rendu de cet article à son auteur. N.p., 1766.

Lettre à un magistrat, au sujet du compte rendu par M. de Faget-Poms, avocat général au parlement de Navarre aux chambres assemblées les 10, 13, 14 décembre 1762. N.p., n.d.

Lettre aux Jésuites. N.p., n.d.

Lettre aux révérends pères Jésuites (1752). N.p., n.d.

Lettre d'Alsace au sujet des Jésuites, le 5 avril 1763. N.p., n.d.

Lettre de M. xx à M. de xxx, où l'on discute ce qui est avancé dans l'Instruction pastorale de M. l'archévêque de Paris au sujet des censures visées dans l'arrêt du 6 août 1762. N.p., n.d.

Lettre d'un avocat à un ami. A Rennes, ce 20 mars 1759. N.p., n.d.

Lettre d'une demoiselle de considération, dévote des Jésuites, à un de ses amis, copiée sur l'original. 22 avril 1754. N.p., n.d.

Lettre d'un évêque à un de ses confrères assemblées à Paris, par ordre du roi, pour donnér leur avis à S.M. sur quatre points concernant l'affaire des Jésuites. N.p., n.d.

Lettre d'un patriote, où l'on rapporte les faits qui prouvent que l'auteur de l'attentat commis sur la vie du roi a des complices, et la manière dont on instruit son procès (11 mars). N.p., n.d.

Lettre écrite de Paris à un ami de province, sur l'éducation des jeunes gens dans les collèges des Jésuites, par un homme de qualité. N.p., n.d.

Lettres d'un ecclésiastique à un magistrat, sur le pouvoir des Jésuites, et sur les effets de ce pouvoir consideré relativement à l'esprit de l'évangile. N.p., n.d.

Lettres sur les opérations du P. de Lavalette, Jésuite, et supérieur général des missions des iles françaises du Vent de l'Amérique, nécessaires aux négociants. Europe, 1760.

Lignac, Joseph-Adrien Le Large de. Avis paternels d'un militaire à son fils, Jésuite, ou Lettres dans lesquelles on développe les vices de la compagnie de Jésus, qui le rendent également pernicieuse à l'église et à l'état, et fournissent les motifs et les moyens de la détruire. N.p., 1760.

Lombard, l'abbé. Réponse à un libelle intitulé : 'Idée générale des vices principaux de l'institut des Jésuites, tirée de leurs constitutions et des autres titres de leur société.' Avignon, 1761.

Maultrot, Gabriel-Nicolas. Mémoire sur le refus des sacrements à la mort, qu'on fait à ceux qui n'acceptent pas la constitution, et une addition concernant les billets de confession. N.p., 1750.

———, and Claude Mey. Apologie de tous les jugements rendus par les tribunaux séculiers en France contre le schisme. 2 vols. N.p., 1752.

Mémoire sur un ouvrage ayant pour titre : 'Ordonnance et instruction pastorale de M. l'évêque de Soissons, au sujet des assertions extraites par le parlement des livres, thèses, cahiers composés, publiés et dictés par les Jésuites . . .' et sur un mandement . . . ayant pour

titre: 'Mandement de M. l'évêque de Soissons, qui ordonne qu'on chantera dans toute.
   les églises de son diocèse une messe solennelle et le Te Deum en action de grâce de la pro-
   tection qu'il à plu à Dieu d'accorder à ce royaume, en préservant le roi du danger qu'
   couru sa personne sacrée.' N.p., 1763.
Mémoire sur un projet au sujet des Jésuites. N.p., n.d.
Mes Doutes sur l'affaire présente des Jésuites. France, 1762.
Mey, Claude. *Dissertation dans laquelle on démontre que la bulle Unigénitus n'est ni loi de*
   l'église ni loi de l'état. 2 parts in 1 vol. N.p., 1752–53.
Mirasson, le père. *Le philosophe redressé, ou Critique impartiale du livre intitulé: Sur la Destruc-*
   tion des Jésuites en France. Bois-Valon, 1765.
Le Molinisme et le matérialisme démasqués. N.p., n.d.
Motifs pressants et déterminants qui obligent en conscience les deux puissances, écclésiastiques et
   séculières, à anéantir la société des Jésuites. N.p., n.d.
Moyens de récusation contre plusieurs des évêques assemblées à Paris au mois de décembre 1761
   au sujet de l'affaire des Jésuites. N.p., n.d.
Neuville, Charles Frey de. *Lettre d'un ami de la vérité à ceux qui ne haissent pas la lumière,*
   ou Réflexions critiques sur les reproches faits à la société de Jésus relativement à la doctrine
   N.p., n.d.
Neuville, Charles or Claude Frey de. *Observations sur l'institut de la société des Jésuites.*
   Avignon, 1761.
Nouvelles Ecclésiastiques, ou Mémoires pour servir à l'histoire de la bulle Unigénitus. 71 vols.
   rebound into 25 vols. Paris, 1728–98.
Oraison funèbre de très-haute, très puissante et très sainte princesse la bulle Unigénitus, prononcée
   dans l'église métropolitaine de Sxxx, par M. l'évêque de Mxxx, le 1er *septembre 1752.*
   La Flèche, 1752.
Paradoxes, sophismes, déguisements, faux principes, principes dangéreux pour la tranquilité de
   l'état, calomnies, fausses citations, qui sont contenues dans une instruction pastorale que
   M. l'archévêque de Paris a signée et adoptée, qu'il a lue publiquement dans l'église de
   Conflans, lieu de son exile, qu'il a fait imprimer à Chartres, et qu'il a distribuée dans
   Paris et au dehors. N.p., n.d.
Parallèle de la conduite du clergé avec celle du parlement à l'égard des Jésuites. N.p., 1762.
Petipied, Nicolas. *Juste idée qu'on doit se former des Jésuites, et leur vrai caractère; avec un*
   recueil de pièces concernant leur bannissement du royaume pour avoir enseigné et fait mettre
   en pratique qu'on peut tuer les rois, etc. Utrecht, 1755.
Plaintes de l'Unigénitus à la société, sa mère, au sujet de son désastre en Portugal. N.p., n.d.
Les Pourquoi, ou Questions sur une grande affaire pour ceux qui n'ont que trois minutes à y
   donner. N.p., 1762.
Précis pour les Jésuites de France, sur l'appel par eux interjeté, des sentences des juge et consuls
   de Paris, qui les condamnent solidairement au payement des lettres de change tirées par le
   père de La Valette, procureur de la maison de Saint-Pierre de la Martinique. Paris, 1761.
Préservatif contre les livres et les sermons des Jésuites. N.p., 1751.
Problème: Qui, de M. de Caulet, évêque de Grenoble, ou de M. de Caulet, son oncle, évêque de
   Pamiers, mérite mieux notre croyance dans les témoignages contradictoires qu'ils ont rendus
   sur le compte des Jésuites. N.p., n.d.

Problèmes historiques, proposés à nosseigneurs les évêques de France en général, et à plusieurs d'entre eux en particulier, sur le respect porté par les Jésuites à l'épiscopat. N.p., 1762.

Procès pour la succession d'Amboise Guys; on y a joint les affaires des Jésuites de Liège, de Fontenay-le-Comte, de Châlons, de Muneau, de Brest, de Bruxelles, avec la phrophétie de Georges Bronsuel. Brest, n.d.

Quesnel, Pasquier. *Histoire des religieux de la compagnie de Jésus, contenant ce qui s'est passé dans cet ordre depuis son établissement jusqu'à présent . . .* N.p., 1740.

Question importante touchant les Jésuites. La société mérite-t-elle les égards qu'on a pour elle à Rome, relativement à l'affaire de Portugal. N.p., n.d.

Questions proposées à l'auteur de 'l'Appel à la raison.' N.p., n.d.

Questions sur lesquelles des évêques assemblées ont à répondre, avec des réflexions. N.p., n.d.

Recueil de lettres sur la doctrine et l'institut des Jésuites. N.p., n.d.

Réflexions d'un Portugais sur le mémorial présenté par ces pères à N.S.P. le pape Clément XIII heureusement régnant: Exposées dans une lettre écrite à un ami à Rome. N.p., 1759.

Réflexions impartiales d'un Français papiste et roialiste sur le réquisitoire de maître Omer Joly de Fleury et l'arrêt du parlement de Paris du 1 juin 1764 qui supprime les Brefs de N.S.P. le Pape Clément XIII au Roi de Pologne Duc de Lorraine et de Bar et à M. l'Archévêque de Paris. Alais, 1764.

Réflexions sur l'attentat commis le 5 janvier contre la vie du roi (5 mars). N.p., n.d.

Réflexions sur l'avis des évêques au roi. N.p., n.d.

Réflexions sur le despotisme des évêques, et les interdits arbitraires. N.p., n.d.

Réflexions sur l'Instruction de M. de Beaumont, archévêque de Paris, du 28 octobre, 1763, N.p., n.d.

Réfutation d'un écrit mal nommé: 'Addition aux Motifs pressants et déterminants d'anéantir la société des Jésuites. N.p., n.d.

Relation de ce qui s'est passé au parlement d'Aix dans l'affaire des Jésuites, depuis le 6 mars 1762. Et de ce qui a été statué par le roi, sur cette affaire, le 23 décembre. N.p., 1763.

Relation de ce qui s'est passé au sujet du refus de sacrements fait, par le chapitre d'Orléans, à M. de Coignou, chanoine de ce même eglise. France, 1754.

Relation de l'affaire de M. l'évêque de Luçon avec les Jésuites, au sujet de son séminaire. N.p., 1758.

Relation d'une conspiration tramée par les nègres dans L'ile de Saint-Dominge; défense que fait le Jésuite confesseur, aux nègres qu'on supplicie, de révéler leurs fauteurs et complices. N.p., n.d.

Réplique aux apologies des Jésuites. 3 parts in 1 vol. N.p., 1761–62.

Réponse au livre intitulé: Extraits des assertions dangéreuses et pernicieuses en tout genre que les soi-disans Jésuites ont, dans tous les tems et persévéramment soutenues, enseignées et publiées dans leurs livres, avec l'approbation de leurs supérieurs et généraux. 2 vols. N.p., 1763.

Réponse de l'auteur de la Ladrérie à l'espion des Jésuites (30 septembre 1759). N.p., 1759.

Réponse des Jésuites à la lettre qui leur a été écrite (24 octobre 1752). China (?), n.d.

Roussel de la Tour, Jacques-Louis-François. *Les Jésuites démasqués, ou Annales historiques de la société.* Cologne, 1759.

———, and the abbés Minard and Gouget. *Maximes de la morale des Jésuites prouvées par les extraits de leurs livres . . . ou Table analytique des assertions dangéreuses . . . présentées au roi . . .* N.p., n.d.

Séance du parlement de Besançon, chambres assemblées, du 7 mai 1764, au sujet de l'affaire des Jésuites. N.p., n.d.

Tailhé, l'abbé Jacques. *Abrégé chronologique de l'histoire de la société de Jésus . . . pour servir d'instruction au procès que le public fait aux Jésuites et à la justification des édits du roi de Portugal contre ces pères.* France, 1760.

Témoignages remarquables dans la cause des Jésuites. N.p., n.d.

Témoins à entendre dans la cause des Jésuites. N.p., n.d.

V. . . . *Lettre à M.xxx, chevalier de l'ordre de Malte, touchant un écrit 'Sur la Destruction des Jésuites en France.'* France, 1765.

*Avowed Authorship**

Alembert, Jean Le Rond d'. *Preliminary Discourse to the Encyclopedia of Diderot.* Trans. Richard N. Schwab and Walter E. Rex. Indianapolis and New York, 1963.

Argenson, le marquis d'. *Journal et mémoires du marquis d'Argenson.* Ed. E.-J.-B. Rathery. 8 vols. Paris, 1859–67.

Arnauld, Antoine. *Œuvres.* 42 vols. Lausanne, 1775–83.

Assemblée générale du clergé. *Avis des prélats consultés sur l'affaire des Jésuites.* N.p., 1762.

Assigny, Louis Troya d'. *Dissertation sur le caractère essentiel à toute loi de l'église en matière de doctrine.* Grenoble, 1755.

———. *Suite de la dissertation sur le caractère essentiel de toute loi de l'église.* Grenoble (?), 175(?).

Barbier, C.-J.-F. *Chronique de la Régence et du règne de Louis XV, 1718–1763.* Ed. Charpentier. 8 vols. Paris, 1866.

Baston, l'abbé. *Mémoires, d'après le manuscrit originel publiés pour la Société d'histoire contemporaine.* Eds. Julien Loth and Charles Vergier. 3 vols. Paris, 1897–99.

Beaumont, Christophe de. *Instruction pastorale de monseigneur l'archévêque de Paris sur les atteintes données à l'autorité des tribunaux séculiers dans l'affaire des Jésuites.* N.p., October 23, 1963.

———. *Mandement et instruction pastorale de monseigneur l'archévêque de Paris, touchant l'autorité de l'église, l'enseignement de la foi, l'administration des sacremens, la soumission due à la constitution Unigénitus, portant défense à lire plusieurs écrits.* Paris, 1756.

Bonnaire, Louis de. *Essai du nouveau conte de ma mère l'Oye, ou, Les Enluminures de jeu de la constitution.* Paris, 1722.

Bouty, Maurice, ed. *Choiseul à Rome, 1754–1757: Lettres et mémoires inédites.* Paris, 1895.

Boyer d'Eguilles, André de Montvallon, et. al. "Le Procès des Jésuites: Lettres du président d'Eguilles et des conseillers à André de Montvallon," *Nouvelle Revue Rétrospective,* deuxième série (January-June 1901), pp. 232–64.

*No parliamentary *arrêts, comptes rendus, réquisitoires, or plaidoyers* have been listed here except those which the text dwells upon at some length. To include all of them, with their interminable titles, would inflate the bibliography needlessly. The essential bibliographical information on these documents can of course be found in the notes that refer to them. So far as the parlement of Paris is concerned, most of the important *arrêts* are contained in Gilbert de Voisins, *Procédure contre l'institut des Jésuites* (Paris, 1823).

Calmettes, F., ed. *Mémoires du duc de Choiseul.* Paris, 1904.

Carayon, le père, ed. *Mémoires du président d'Eguilles sur le parlement d'Aix et les Jésuites, adressés à S.M. Louis XV.* Paris, 1867.

Cerveau, René. *Nécrologie des plus célèbres confesseurs et défenseurs de la vérité au XVIIe siècle.* Paris, 1761.

———. *Nécrologe des plus célèbres défenseurs et confesseurs de la vérite du XVIIIe siècle.* 2 vols. N.p., 1760.

———. *Suite du Nécrologe des plus célèbres défenseurs et amis de la vérité du XVIIIe siècle.* N.p., 1767.

———. *Suite du supplément au Nécrologe des défenseurs de la vérité ou Recueil de pièces importantes sur les affaires de l'église des XVIIe et XVIIIe siècles.* N.p., 1765.

———. *Supplément au Nécrologe des plus célèbres défenseurs et confesseurs de la vérité des XVIIe et XVIIIe siècles.* N.p., 1763.

———. *Supplément au Nécrologe des plus célèbres défenseurs et confesseurs de la vérité du XVIIIe siècle.* N.p., 1778.

Clément, Augustin. *Journal de correspondances et voyages d'Italie et d'Espagne pour la paix de l'église en 1758, 1768, et 1769.* Ed. A. Gazier. Paris, 1802.

Colonia, Dominique de. *Bibliothèque janséniste, ou Catalogue alphabétique des principaux livres jansénistes, ou suspects de Jansénisme, qui ont paru depuis la naissance de cette hérésie . . .* 2d ed. N.p., 1731.

Comptes rendus, par un magistrat et par MM. les gens du roi, au parlement, toutes les chambres assemblées, les 17 avril, 3, 4, 6, 7 et 8 juillet 1761, au sujet des constitutions, de la doctrine et de la conduite des Jésuites. Extrait des assertions soutenues par les auteurs de la société condamnés par l'arrêt du 6 août et autres, présenté au roi, par M. le premier président, en exécution de l'arrêté du 31 août 1761. 4 parts in 1 vol. N.p., n.d.

Delatour, L. F., and H. L. Guérin, *Réponse au mémoire intitulé: 'Mémoire sur les demandes formées contre le général et la société des Jésuites, au sujet des engagements qu'elle a contractés par le ministère du père de La Valette.'* Paris, 1761.

Dettey, l'abbé. *La Vie de M. de Caylus.* 2 vols. Amsterdam, 1765.

Fitz-James, Le duc de, Bishop of Soissons. *Œuvres posthumes de monseigneur le Duc de Fitz-James évêque de Soissons, concernant les Jésuites, les IV articles de l'Assemblée du Clergé de 1682, etc.* Avignon, 1769.

Flammermont, Jules, ed. *Remontrances du parlement de Paris au XVIIIe siècle.* 3 vols. Paris, 1888–98.

Fourquevaux, Pavie de. *Catéchisme historique et dogmatique sur les contestations qui agitent maintenant l'église.* 5 vols. Nancy, 1750–58.

Gaultier, J.-B. *Critique du ballet moral dansé au collège des Jésuites à Rouen au mois d'août 1750 (20 novembre, 1750).* N.p., 1751.

Gazier, Augustin, ed. *Fragment inédit des mémoires du chancelier Daguesseau.* Paris, 1920.

Georgel, l'abbé (ex-Jésuite). *Mémoires pour servir à l'histoire des événements de la fin du XVIIIe siècle, depuis 1760 jusqu'en 1806–1810, par un contemporain impartial.* Vol. 1. Paris, 1817.

Gilbert de Voisins, Pierre-Paul-Alexandre, ed. *Nouvelles pièces pour servir de complément à la Procédure contre les Jésuites.* Paris, 1824.

———. ed. *Procédure contre l'institut et les constitutions des Jésuites, suivie au parlement de*

Paris sur l'appel comme d'abus, interjetté par le procureur général du roi, recueille par un membre du parlement et publiés par M. Gilbert de Voisins, membre de la Chambre des Députes. Paris, 1823.

Gillet, Lherminier, Mallard, et. al. *Mémoire à consulter et consultation pour les Jésuites de France.* Paris, 1761.

Grass, Jacques de, Bishop of Angers. *Ordonnance et instruction pastorale de monseigneur l'évêque d'Angers, portant condamnation de la doctrine contenue dans les 'Extraits des assertions.'* N.p., April 19, 1763.

Grou, Jean Nicolas. *Lettre à M.xxx, conseiller au parlement de Paris, où l'on lui propose quelques doutes de l'édit de banissement des Jésuites, porté par Henry IV en 1595, et rapporté en entier à la page 4 de l'arrêt du 6 août 1762.* Paris, 1763.

Hardy, S.-P. *Mes loisirs.* 2 vols. Paris, 1912.

Journal de Trévoux, ou Mémoires pour l'histoire des sciences et des beaux arts. 265 vols. Trévoux, Lyons, and Paris, 1701–6.

La Chalotais, Louis-René de Caradeuc de. *Compte rendu des constitutions des Jésuites, par M. Louis-Réne de Caradeuc la Chalotais, procureur-général du roi au parlement de Bretagne, les 1, 3, 4 et 5 décembre 1766, en exécution de l'arrêt de la cour du 17 août précédent.* N.p., 1762.

———. *Second Compte rendu sur l'appel comme d'abus, des constitutions des Jésuites, par M. Louis-René de Caradeuc de la Chalotais, procureur-général du roi au parlement de Bretagne, les 21, 22 et 24 mai 1762.* N.p., 1762.

———. *Essais d'éducation nationale, ou Plan d'études pour la jeunesse, par Messire Louis-René de Caradeuc de la Chalotais, Procureur-Général du Roi au Parlement de Bretagne.* N.p., 1763.

La Croix, le père. *Le Progrès du jansénisme, par frère La Croix.* Quilon, 1753.

Laget-Bardelin. *Mémoire pour les Jésuites des provinces de Champagne, Guyenne, Toulouse, et Lyon, opposants et défenseurs, contre le syndic des créanciers Lioncy et Gouffre, défendeur à l'opposition et demandeur. Et encore contre les sieurs Lioncy et Gouffre, intervenants et demandeurs en présence des Jésuites de la province de France.* Paris, 1761.

Lalourcé, Charlemagne. *Mémoire à consulter pour Jean Lioncy, créancier et syndic de la masse de la raison de commerce établie à Marseilles sous le nom de Lioncy frères et Gouffre, contre le corps et société des PP. Jésuites.* Paris, 1961.

Legouvé, Jean-Baptiste. *Plaidoyer pour le syndic des créanciers des sieurs Lioncy frères et Gouffre négociants à Marseilles, contre le général et la société des Jésuites.* N.p., 1761.

Le Verdier, P., ed. *Correspondance politique et administrative de Miromesnil, premier président du parlement de Normandie.* 3 vols. Rouen, 1899–1901.

Luynes, le duc de. *Mémoires du duc de Luynes sur la cour de Louis XV, 1735–1758.* Eds. L. Dussieux and E. Soulié. 17 vols. Paris, 1860–65.

Marais, Mathieu. *Le Journal et les mémoires de Mathieu Marais, 1715–1735.* Ed. Lescure. 4 vols. Paris, 1863.

Monclar, J.-P.-F. Ripert de. *Motif des arrêts et arrêtés du parlement de Provence, des 5, 19 et 30 juin, 2, 4, 6 et 7 octobre, concernant l'affaire des soi-disans Jésuites.* N.p., n.d.

Parlement of Paris. *Extrait des assertions en tout genre que les soi-disans Jésuites ont, dans tous les temps et persévéramment soutenues, enseignées et publiées dans leurs livres, avec l'approbation de leurs supérieurs et généraux.* Paris, 1762.

——. *Pièces originales et procédures du procès fait à Robert-François Damiens, tant en la prévôte de l'hôtel qu'en la cour du parlement.* Paris, 1757.

Pascal, Blaise. *Œuvres complètes.* Ed. Louis Lafuma. Paris, 1963.

Patouillet, le père. *Dictionnaire des livres jansénistes . . .* 4 vols. Antwerp, 1752. A continuation of Colonia's *Bibliothèque janséniste.*

Petitdidier, Mathieu. *Apologie des Lettres provinciales de Louis de Montalte* [Blaise Pascal]; *contre la dernière réponse des PP. Jésuites, intitulée, 'Entrétiens de Cléandre et d'Eudoxe.'* Rouen, 1698.

Picot, l'abbé. *Mémoires pour servir à l'histoire écclésiastique pendant le dix-huitième siècle.* 2d ed. 4 vols. Paris, 1815–16.

Rapin, René. *Histoire du Jansénisme depuis son origine jusqu'en 1644.* Ed. l'abbé Domenach. Paris, 1861.

Rouhette and Target, Guy-Jean-Baptiste. *Mémoire sur les demandes formées contre le général et la société des Jésuites, au sujet des engagements qu'elle a contractés par le ministère du père de La Valette.* Paris, 1761.

——. *Seconde Mémoire pour le sieur Cazotte et la demoiselle Fouque, contre le général et la société des Jésuites.* N.p., n.d.

Sacy, Louis Issac Le Maistre de. *Les Enluminures du fameux Almanach des PP. Jésuites, intitulé, 'La Déroute et la confusion des Jansénistes' ou 'Triomphe de Molina Jésuite sur S. Augustin.'* Paris, 1654.

Thevenot d'Essaules, Claude-François. *Plaidoyer pour les Jésuites de France.* Paris, 1761.

Torreilles, l'abbé Philippe, ed. *Mémoires du M. Jaume, avocat au conseil souverain, professeur à l'université de Perpignan.* Perpignan, 1884.

Voltaire. *Œuvres complètes.* Kehl edition. 92 vols. N.p., 1785–89.

OTHER WORKS CONSULTED

Abercrombie, Nigel. *Origins of Jansenism.* Oxford, 1936.

Adam, Antoine. *Du Mysticisme à la révolte, les Jansénistes du XVIIIe siècle.* Paris, 1968.

Anderson, M. S. *Europe in the Eighteenth Century, 1713–1783.* Norwich, Great Britain, 1961.

Antoine, Michel. *Le Conseil du Roi sous le règne de Louis XV.* Paris and Geneva, 1970.

Appolis, Emile. *Le Jansénisme dans le diocèse de Lodève au XVIIIe siècle.* Albi, 1952.

——. *Le 'Tiers Parti' catholique au XVIIIe siècle.* Paris, 1960.

Ardoin, Paul. *La Bulle Unigénitus dans les diocèses d'Aix, Arles, Marseille, Fréjus, Toulon, 1713–1789.* 2 vols. Marseille, 1936.

Aubertin, Charles. *L'Esprit public au XVIIIe siècle: Etude sur les mémoires et les correspondances politiques des contemporains, 1715–1789.* 3d ed. Paris, 1889.

Bachelier, A. *Les Jansénistes à Nantes.* Paris, 1934.

Backer, Aloys de, and Charles Sommervogel. *Bibliothèque de la compagnie de Jésus.* 12 vols. Paris, 1890–1932.

Barber, Elinor G. *The Bourgeoisie in Eighteenth-Century France.* Princeton, 1955.

Bassieux, L. *Théorie des libertés gallicanes du parlement de Paris au XVIIIe siècle.* Paris, 1906.

Bastard d'Estang, le vicomte de. *Les Parlements de France: Essai sur leurs usages, leur organisation et leur autorité.* 2 vols. Paris, 1857.

Becker, Carl. *The Heavenly City of the Eighteenth-Century Philosophers.* New Haven and London, 1932.

Bénichou, Paul. *Morales du grand siècle.* Paris, 1948.

Bernier, H. "Étude sur le Jansénisme," *Revue de l'Anjou,* Sér. II. Vol. 2 (1857), pp. 101–15, 355–87.

Bickart, Roger. *Les Parlements et la notion de souveraineté nationale au XVIIIe siècle.* Paris, 1932.

Bien, David. *The Calas Affair: Persecution, Toleration and Heresy in Eighteenth-Century Toulouse.* Princeton, 1960.

Blond, Louis. *La Maison professe des Jésuites de la rue Saint-Antoine à Paris, 1580–1762.* Paris, 1957.

Bluche, François. *Les Magistrats du grand conseil au XVIIIe siècle, 1690–1791.* Paris, 1966.

———. *Les Magistrats du parlement de Paris au XVIIIe siècle, 1715–1771.* Paris, 1960.

———. *L'Origine des magistrats du parlement de Paris au XVIIIe siècle.* Paris, 1956.

Bontoux, R. "Paris janséniste au XVIIIe siècle: Les *Nouvelles écclésiastiques,*" *Mémoires de la Fédération des Sociétés Historiques et archéologiques de Paris et de l'Ile de France,* 7 (1956), pp. 205–20.

Bournet, Léon. *La Querelle janséniste.* Paris, 1924.

Brémond, Henri. *Histoire littéraire du sentiment religieux en France depuis la fin des guerres de religion jusqu'à nos jours.* Nouvelle édition. 11 vols, but esp. Vols. 1 and 4. Paris, 1967–68.

Brodrick, James. *The Origin of the Jesuits.* New York, 1960.

Cabasse, Prosper. *Essais historiques sur le parlement de Provence depuis son origine jusqu'à sa suppression, 1501–1790.* 3 vols. Paris, 1826.

Cahen, Léon. *Les Querelles religieuses et parlementaires sous Louis XV.* Paris, 1913.

Campardon, Emile. *Madame de Pampadour et la cour de Louis XV au milieu du XVIIIe siècle.* Paris, 1867.

Canal, Séverin. *La Compagnie de Jésus au diocèse de Nantes sous l'ancien régime, 1663–1762.* Nantes, 1947.

Carré, Henri. *La Fin des parlements, 1788–1790.* Paris, 1912.

———. "Louis XV, 1715–1774." Part II of Vol. 8 in Ernest Lavisse, ed., *Histoire de France illustrée depuis les origines jusqu'à la Révolution.* Paris, 1911.

Carreyre, Jean. *Le Jansénisme durant le Régence.* 3 vols. Louvain, 1929–33.

Cassirer, Ernst. *The Philosophy of the Enlightenment.* Trans. Fritz C. A. Kolln and James P. Pettegrove. Princeton, 1951.

Chastonay, Paul de. *Les Constitutions de l'ordre des Jésuites: Leur Genèse, leur contenu, leur esprit.* Paris, 1941.

Chaunu, Pierre. "Jansénisme et frontière de catholicité (XVIIe et XVIIIe siècles)," *Revue Historique,* 227 (January–March 1962), pp. 115–38.

Chevallier, Pierre. *Lomenie de Brienne et l'ordre monastique, 1766–1789.* 2 vols. Paris, 1959–60.

Cobban, Alfred. "The *Parlements* of France in the Eighteenth Century," *History* (February–June 1950), pp. 16–32.

Cognet, Louis. *Le Jansénisme.* Paris, 1964.

Collombert, F. Z. *Histoire critique et générale de la suppression des Jésuites au XVIIIe siècle.* 2 vols. Lyons, 1846.

Crétineau-Joly, J. *Clément XIV et les Jésuites.* Paris, 1848.

———. *Histoire religieuse, politique et littéraire de la compagnie de Jésus.* 3d ed. Vol. 5. Paris, 1856.

Crocker, Lester G. *An Age of Crisis: Man and World in Eighteenth-Century French Thought.* Baltimore, 1959.

———. *Nature and Culture: Ethical Thought in the French Enlightenment.* Baltimore, 1963.

Crousaz-Crétet, le père de. *L'Eglise et l'état, ou Les Deux Puissances au XVIIIe siècle, principalement en Guyenne.* Paris, 1893.

Darnton, Robert. *Mesmerism and the End of the Enlightenment in France.* Cambridge, Mass., 1968.

Degert, Antoine. "Le Jansénisme au parlement de Toulouse," *Bulletin de Littérature Ecclésiastique,* 25 (1924), pp. 260–84, 338–52.

Delassault, Geveniève. *La Pensée janséniste en dehors de Pascal.* Paris, 1963.

Delattre, Pierre. *Les Etablissements des Jésuites depuis quatre siècles.* 4 vols. Enghien, Belgium, 1948.

Demahis, Étiennette. *La Pensée politique de Pascal.* Saint-Amand, 1931.

Desgranges, Légier. *Madame de Moysan et l'extravagante affaire de l'hôpital général, 1749–1758.* Paris, 1954.

Desnoiresterres, Gustave Le Brisoys. *Voltaire et la société au XVIIIe siècle.* 2d ed. 8 vols. Paris, 1871–76.

Doolin, Paul Rice. *The Fronde.* Cambridge, Mass., 1935.

Dudon, Paul. "De la Suppression de la compagnie de Jésus, 1758–1773," *Revue des Questions Historiques* (May–September 1938), pp. 32–55.

Du Hamel de Breuil, le comte J. "Un Ministre philosophe, Carvalho, marquis de Pombal," *Revue Historique,* 59 (1895), pp. 1–28.

Durand, Valentin. *Le Jansénisme au XVIIIe siècle et Joachim Colbert, évêque de Montpellier, 1696–1738.* Toulouse, 1907.

Egret, Jean. *Louis XV et l'opposition parlementaire, 1715–1774.* Paris, 1970.

———. *Le Parlement de Dauphiné et les affaires publiques dans la deuxième moitié du XVIIIe siècle.* 2 vols. Grenoble, 1942.

———. "Le Procès des Jésuites devant les parlements de France, 1761–1770," *Revue Historique,* 204 (July–December), pp. 1–27.

Ferguson, Wallace K. "The Place of Jansenism in French History," *Journal of Religion,* 7 (January 1927), pp. 16–24.

Flammermont, Jules, *Le Chancelier Maupeou et ses parlements.* Paris, 1883.

———. *Les Jésuites et les parlements au XVIIIe siècle.* Paris, 1885.

Floquet, Amable. *Histoire du parlement de Normandie.* 7 vols., but esp. Vol. 6. Rouen, 1840–42.

Foisset, Joseph-Théophile. *Le Président de Brosses. Histoire des lettres et des parlements au XVIIIe siècle.* Paris, 1842.

Ford, Franklin L. *Robe and Sword: The Regrouping of the French Aristocracy after Louis XIV.* Cambridge, Mass., 1962.

Fouqueray, Henri. *Histoire de la compagnie de Jésus en France des origines à la suppression*. 5 vols. Paris, 1910–25.

Füllop-Miller, René. *The Jesuits, a History of the Society of Jesus*. Trans. F. S. Flint and P. R. Tait. New York, 1963.

Fuzet, Edmond Frédéric. *Les Jansénistes du XVIIIe siècle: Leur Histoire et leur dernier historien M. Sainte-Beuve*. Paris, 1876.

Galibert, Paul. *Le Conseil souverain de Roussillon*. Perpignan, 1904.

Gaxotte, Pierre. *Le Siècle de Louis XV*. Nouvelle édition, revue et augmentée. Paris, 1933.

Gay, Peter. *The Enlightenment: An Interpretation*. 2 vols. New York, 1966–69.

———. *The Party of Humanity*. New York, 1964.

———. *Voltaire's Politics: The Poet as Realist*. Princeton, 1959.

Gazier, Augustin. "L'Expulsion des Jésuites sous Louis XV," *Revue Historique*, 13 (1880), pp. 308–25.

———. *Histoire générale du movement janséniste depuis ses origines jusqu'à nos jours*. 2 vols. Paris, 1923.

Gazier, Cécile. *Histoire de la société de Port-Royal et de la Bibliothèque de Port-Royal*. Paris, 1966.

———. "Notice sur Adrien Le Paige et sa bibliothèque." Unpublished article conserved at the Bibliothèque de Port-Royal.

Glasson, Ernest. *Le Parlement de Paris: Son Rôle politique depuis le règne de Charles VII jusqu'à la Révolution*. 2 vols. Paris, 1901.

Godart, Justin. *Le Jansénisme à Lyon*. Paris, 1934.

Godard, Philippe. *La Querelle des refus de sacrements, 1730–1765*. Paris, 1937.

Goldmann, Lucien. *Correspondance entre Martin de Barcos, abbé de Saint-Cyran, avec les abbesses de Port-Royal et les principaux personnages du groupe janséniste*. Paris, 1956.

———. *Le Dieu caché, étude sur la vision tragique dans les Pensées de Pascal et dans le théâtre de Racine*. Paris, 1955.

Gomes, F. L. *Le Marquis de Pombal*. Lisbon, 1869.

Grellet-Dumazeau, André. *Les Exilés de Bourges, 1753–1754*. Paris, 1892.

Grimsley, Ronald. *Jean d'Alembert, 1717–1783*. Oxford, 1963.

Groethuysen, Bernhard. *Die Entstehung der bürgerlichen Welt-und Lebensanschaung in Frankreich*. 2 vols. Halle/Salle, 1927.

Grosclaude, Pierre. *Malesherbes et son temps*. Paris, 1966.

Guéranger, P. "Le Jansénisme et la compagnie de Jésus," *Revue de l'Anjou*, Sér. II. Vol. 2 (1858), pp. 289–309, and continued in following issues.

Guerard, Albert. *France in the Classical Age: The Life and Death of an Ideal*. New York, 1965.

Hardy, Georges. *Le Cardinal de Fleury et le mouvement janséniste*. Paris, 1925.

Harris, R. W. *Absolutism and Enlightenment, 1660–1789*. New York, 1966.

Havens, George R. *The Age of Ideas: From Reaction to Revolution in Eighteenth-Century France*. New York, 1965.

Havinga, Jan Christiaan Adolph. *Les Nouvelles Ecclésiastiques dans leur lutte contre l'esprit philosophique*. Amersfoort, 1925.

Hayes, Carlton J. H. *Nationalism: A Religion*. New York, 1960.

Hazard, Paul. *The European Mind, 1680–1715.* Trans. J. Lewis May. Cleveland and New York, 1964.

———. *European Thought in the Eighteenth Century from Montesquieu to Lessing.* Trans. J. Lewis May. Cleveland and New York, 1963.

Hollis, Christopher. *A History of the Jesuits.* Liverpool, London, and Prescot, 1968.

Jobez, Alphonse. *La France sous Louis XV, 1715–1774.* 6 vols., but esp. Vol. 4. Paris, 1864–73.

Kohn, Hans. *The Idea of Nationalism: A Study in Its Origins and Background.* New York, 1944.

Kossman, E. H. *La Fronde.* Leiden, 1954.

La Combe, Bernard de. *La Résistance janséniste et parlementaire au temps de Louis XV: L'Abbé Nigon de Berty, 1702–1772.* Paris, 1948.

La Cuisine, E. F. de. *Le Parlement de Bourgogne depuis son origine jusqu'à sa chute.* 3 vols. Dijon and Paris, 1864.

Lamache, Paul. *Histoire de la chute des Jésuites au XVIIIᵉ siècle: Réponse à M. le comte Alexis de Saint-Priest, pair de France, par M. Paul Lamache, docteur en droit.* Paris, 1845.

La Porte, Jean. *La Doctrine de Port-Royal.* 2 vols.: *Les Vérités de la grâce* and *La Morale d'après Arnauld.* Paris, 1923 and 1951.

Latreille, André, et al. *Histoire du Catholicisme en France.* 3 vols. Paris, 1961–64.

Lefebvre, Henri. *Pascal.* 2 vols. Paris, 1949–54.

Lemaire, S. *La Commission des Réguliers, 1760–1780.* Paris, 1826.

Le Moy, Arthur. *Le Parlement de Bretagne et le pouvoir royal au XVIIIᵉ siècle.* Angers, 1909.

Le Roy, Albert. *Le Gallicanisme au XVIIIᵉ siècle. La France et Rome de 1700 à 1715.* Paris, 1952.

Mahieu, L. *Jansénisme et antijansénisme dans les diocèses de Boulogne-sur-mer et de Tournai, spécialement dans la région lilloise.* Lille, 1948.

Mandrou, Robert. *La France aux XVIIᵉ et XVIIIᵉ siècles.* Paris, 1970.

Manuel, Frank E. *The Eighteenth Century Confronts the Gods.* New York, 1967.

———. *The Prophets of Paris.* New York, 1965.

Marchal, M. *Les Jésuites et leurs ennemis.* Paris, 1857.

Marion, Marcel. *Le Bretagne et le duc d'Aiguillon, 1753–1770.* Paris, 1898.

Martin, Kingsley. *French Liberal Thought in the Eighteenth Century: A Study of Political Ideas from Bayle to Condorcet.* Ed. J. P. Mayer. New York, 1963.

Masson, Frédéric. *Le Cardinal de Bernis depuis son ministère, 1758–1794: La Suppression des Jésuites, le schisme constitutionnel.* Paris, 1884.

Maugras, Gaston. *Le Duc et la duchesse de Choiseul: Leur Vie intime, leurs amis et leur temps.* Paris, 1924.

McManners, John. *French Ecclesiastical Society under the Ancien Regime: A Study of Angers in the Eighteenth Century.* Manchester, 1960.

———. *The French Revolution and the Church.* New York and Evanston, 1969.

Mesnard, Jean. *Pascal.* Paris, 1962.

Meyer, Albert de. *Les Premières Controverses jansénistes en France, 1640–1649.* Louvain, 1917.

Michel, Emmanuel. *Histoire du parlement de Metz*. Paris, 1845.

Mörner, Magnus, ed. *The Expulsion of the Jesuits from Latin America*. New York, 1965.

Mornet, Daniel. *Les Origines intellectuelles de la Révolution française*. 6th ed. Paris, 1967.

Namer, G. *L'Abbé Le Roy et ses amis: Essai sur le Jansénisme extrémiste intramondain*. Paris, 1964.

Orcibal, Jean. *Jean Duvergier de Hauranne, abbé de Saint-Cyran et son temps*. Louvain and Paris, 1947.

————. *Louis XIV contre Innocent XI: Les Appels au futur concile de 1688 et l'opinion française*. Paris, 1949.

————. *Louis XIV et les Protestants*. Paris, 1951.

————. "Le Premier Port-Royal, Réforme ou Contre-Réforme," *Nouvelle Clio* (Brussels, May–June 1950), pp. 238–80.

————. *La Spiritualité de Saint-Cyran, avec ses écrits de piété inédits*. Paris, 1962.

Palmer, Robert. *Catholics and Unbelievers in Eighteenth-Century France*. Princeton, 1939.

————. "The National Idea in France before the Revolution," *Journal of the History of Ideas*, 1 (January 1940), pp. 95–111.

Pappas, John Nicholas. *Berthier's Journal de Trévoux and the Philosophes*. Vol. 3 in his *Studies on Voltaire and the Eighteenth Century*. Geneva, 1957.

————. *Voltaire and d'Alembert*. Bloomington, 1962.

Paquier, J. *Qu'est-ce que le Jansénisme?* Paris, 1909.

Parquez, Jacques. *La Bulle Unigénitus et le Jansénisme politique*. Paris, 1936.

Pastor, Ludwig Freiherr von. *The History of the Popes, from the Close of the Middle Ages. Drawn from Secret Archives of the Vatican and Other Original Sources*. Vol. 36. Trans. E. F. Peeler. London, 1950.

Piaget, E. *Histoire de l'établissement des Jésuites en France, 1540–1640*. Leiden, 1893.

Plongéron, Bernard. "Une Image de l'église d'après les 'Nouvelles écclésiastiques,' 1728–1790," *Revue d'Histoire de l'Eglise de France*, no. 16 (1967), pp. 241–68.

Pocquet du Haut-Jussé, Barthélemy. *Le Pouvoir absolu et l'esprit provincial: Le Duc d'Aiguillon et La Chalotais*. Paris, 1900–01.

Préclin, Edmond. *Les Jansénistes du XVIIIᵉ siècle et la Constitution civile du clergé: La Développement du richérisme, sa propagation dans le bas clergé, 1713–1791*. Paris, 1929.

————, and E. Jarry. *Les Luttes doctrinales et politiques aux XVIIᵉ et XVIIIᵉ siècles*. 2 vols. Paris, 1955–56.

————, and Victor L. Tapié. *Le XVIIIᵉ siècle*. 2 vols. Paris, 1952.

Raison, L. M. *Le Mouvement janséniste au diocèse de Dol*. Rennes, 1931.

Ravignan, le père de. *Clément XIII et Clément XIV*. 2 vols. Paris, 1854.

Ravitch, Norman. *Sword and Mitre: Government and Episcopate in France and England in the Age of Aristocracy*. The Hague and Paris, 1966.

Remsberg, Robert Gotwald. *Wisdom and Science at Port-Royal and the Oratory: A Study of Contrasting Augustinianisms*. Yellow Springs, Oreg., 1940.

Rochmontaix, P. C. de. *Le Père Lavalette à la Martinique*. Paris, 1908.

Rocquain, Felix. *L'Esprit révolutionnaire avant la Révolution, 1715–1789*. Paris, 1878.

Rothkrug, Lionel. *Opposition to Louis XIV: The Political and Social Origins of the French Enlightenment*. Princeton, 1965.

Rowbothan, Arnold H. *Missionary and Mandarin: The Jesuits at the Court of China.* New York, 1966.

Sainte-Beuve, Charles-Augustin. *Port-Royal.* Ed. Maxime Leroy. 3 vols. Paris, 1952.

Saint-Priest, Alexis de. *Histoire de la chute des Jésuites au XVIIIe siècle, 1750–1782.* Paris, 1844.

Séché, Léon. *Les Derniers Jansénistes depuis la ruine de Port-Royal jusqu'à nos jours.* vol. 1. Paris, 1891.

Ségur, le marquis de. *Au Couchant de la monarchie: Louis XVI et Necker, 1776–1781.* Paris, 1913.

Shackleton, Robert. "Jansenism and the Enlightenment." *Studies on Voltaire and the Eighteenth Century,* 57 (1967), pp. 1387–97.

Shennan, J. H. *The Parlement of Paris.* Ithaca, New York, 1968.

Sicard, Augustin. *L'Ancien Clergé de France: Les Evêques avant la Révolution.* 5th ed. Paris, 1912.

Stegemüller, F. *Geschichte des Molinismus.* Münster, 1935.

Tans, J.-A.-G. "Les Idées politiques des Jansénistes," *Neophilogus* (January 1956), pp. 1–18.

Taveneaux, René. *Le Jansénisme dans la région ardennaise au début du XVIIIe siècle.* Charleville, 1951.

———. "Le Jansénisme dans le diocèse de Verdun au début du XVIIIe siècle," *Annales de l'Est* (1950), pp. 15–33.

———. *Le Jansénisme en Lorraine, 1640–1789.* Paris, 1960.

———. *Jansénisme et politique.* Paris, 1965.

Thomas, Jacques. *Essai sur la morale de Port-Royal.* Paris, 1942.

———. *La Querelle de l'Unigénitus.* Paris, 1950.

Tocqueville, comte Alexis de. *The Old Régime and the French Revolution.* New York, 1856.

Torreilles, l'abbé Philippe. *Le Collège de Perpignan depuis ces origines jusqu'à nos jours.* N.p., n.d.

———. "L'Ultramontanisme et le Gallicanisme en Roussillon sous l'Ancien Régime," *Revue d'Histoire et d'Archéologie du Roussillon,* 5 (1904), pp. 1–16, 33–48, 65–80, 193–210.

Vassard, Maurice. *Jansénisme et gallicanisme aux origines religieuses du Risorgimento.* Paris, 1959.

Vyverberg, Henri. *Historical Pessimism in the French Enlightenment.* Cambridge, Mass., 1958.

Wedgewood, C. V. *Richelieu and the French Monarchy.* New York, 1962.

Index